Henry Trotter

Account of the survey operations in connection with the mission to

Yarkand and Kashgar in 1873-74

Henry Trotter

Account of the survey operations in connection with the mission to Yarkand and Kashgar in 1873-74

ISBN/EAN: 9783337132194

Printed in Europe, USA, Canada, Australia, Japan

Cover: Foto ©ninafisch / pixelio.de

More available books at **www.hansebooks.com**

ACCOUNT

OF THE

SURVEY OPERATIONS

IN CONNECTION WITH THE

MISSION TO YARKAND AND KASHGHAR

IN

1873-74.

BY

CAPTAIN HENRY TROTTER, R. E.,

DEPUTY-SUPERINTENDENT, GREAT TRIGONOMETRICAL SURVEY OF INDIA.

EXTRACTED FROM THE VOLUME OF REPORTS SUBMITTED TO THE GOVERNMENT OF INDIA BY SIR DOUGLAS FORSYTH, C.B., K.C.S.I., IN CHARGE OF THE MISSION.

CALCUTTA:
PRINTED AT THE FOREIGN DEPARTMENT PRESS.
1875.

CONTENTS.

	PAGE.
INTRODUCTORY	1
ROAD TO YÁRKÁND	3
DESCRIPTION OF ROUTES BETWEEN LADÁKH AND TURKISTÁN	9
EXCURSIONS IN THE NEIGHBOURHOOD OF KASHGAR	17
EXCURSION TO THE PÁMÍR STEPPES AND WAKHÁN	29
THE OXUS BELOW WAKHÁN	44
RETURN TO YÁRKÁND VIA THE GREAT PÁMÍR	49
ON THE CONSTRUCTION OF THE MAP ACCOMPANYING REPORT.	54
METEOROLOGY	59
MAGNETISM	61

GEOGRAPHICAL APPENDIX—

Section	A.—LATITUDES	1
,,	B.—LONGITUDES	33
,,	C.—HEIGHTS	45
,,	D.—ALPHABETICAL LIST OF LATITUDES, LONGITUDES, AND HEIGHTS .	67
,,	E.—MAGNETIC OBSERVATIONS	75
,,	F.—METEOROLOGICAL OBSERVATIONS	79
,,	G.—ROUTES	123

MAP OF EASTERN TURKISTÁN		In cover.
PLAN OF YÁRKÁND	To face page	9
,, KHOTAN	,, ,,	15
,, KASHGHAR	,, ,,	17
METEOROLOGICAL DIAGRAMS	,, ,,	60

CHAPTER VII.

GEOGRAPHICAL REPORT.

WHEN the Government of India had decided to send a diplomatic Mission to the Atálik Ghází of Káshghar it was determined to appoint an officer of the Indian Survey Department to accompany the expedition as Geographer; and Captain Henry Trotter, Royal Engineers, of the Great Trigonometrical Survey of India, was selected for the post.

The preliminary arrangements were left by Mr. (now Sir Douglas) Forsyth entirely in the hands of Captain Trotter, subject to such advice as he might receive from Colonel Walker, R.E., the Superintendent of the Great Trigonometrical Survey. The only restrictions insisted on were that everything was to be arranged for mule carriage, and the survey baggage was to be limited to three mule loads, also that the services of two khalasies (carriers) only could be allowed to assist generally in the work. Abdul Súbhán, a Sub-Surveyor in the Topographical Survey Department, was subsequently permitted to accompany Captain Trotter to act as recorder and general assistant. Two of the Great Trigonometrical Survey "Pundits"* with their assistants were also placed at Captain Trotter's disposal.

It has been found convenient to arrange this Chapter in the shape of a General Report by Captain Trotter, to which is added an appendix shewing in some detail the results of the observations, astronomical, meteorological, hypsometric, and magnetic, taken by that officer and his assistants. The appendix includes some observations by Captain Biddulph on the Ling-zi-thung plains and on the road to Maralbáshi, and also contains detailed accounts descriptive of the various routes followed by members of the Mission, as well as of others compiled from native information, principally by Dr. Bellew.

CAPTAIN TROTTER'S REPORT.

Introductory.

THE first point to be decided was as to the instruments and equipment to be taken, and this was an anxious matter; it was impossible to say what sort of a reception we should meet with in Yárkand, and whether I should be allowed to use openly any survey instruments at all; I had also to bear in mind the, to me, totally new condition, that my instruments would have to be packed and carried on mules, and taken over the highest passes in the world. (In the Indian Survey Department delicate instruments such as theodolites, &c., are always carried by men, and even in the survey party attached to the Abyssinian Expedition this rule, I believe, was never departed from.) This condition imposed the necessity of taking only moderate sized instruments and such as were not likely to be injured by violent shakes and jars. Fortunately among the instruments of the department there was one that had already done good service at Magdála, viz., a 6-inch Transit Theodolite, with micrometer eye-piece, by Troughton and Simms. On Colonel Walker's recommendation I took this as my mainstay for astronomical observations, and I may here add that I have used it constantly throughout my absence from India, and have been very much pleased with its performance. A few slight

---

* The term by which it has been customary to designate natives employed by the Great Trigonometrical Survey Department on Trans-Frontier Explorations.

A

alterations having been made in the fittings, it was carried safely in **one of our** leathern mule trunks for more than 3,000 miles **over** I suppose some of the most **difficult roads** in Asia, without receiving the slightest **injury**, or having at any time been **unserviceable. For** its size it is a most perfect instrument.

I had, however, also to consider what I should use in case of secrecy being necessary, and for this of course there was nothing like a sextant, so I provided myself with a 6-inch sextant by Troughton and Simms, as well as a small pocket sextant by the same maker, taking with them the ordinary mercurial artificial horizons.

I may allude to the fact that Captains Biddulph and Chapman **both spent a short time** at the head-quarters of the Great Trigonometrical Survey for the purpose of practising astronomical observations in anticipation of the probability of our party separating in different directions in Eastern Turkestan. It was arranged that the former should take with him a sextant and the latter a theodolite, a sister instrument to my own. There were, therefore, in camp duplicates in case of any accident happening to my own instruments.

I also provided myself with a very small light theodolite for use on high peaks (where it would be unsafe to attempt to carry the large instrument) and for traversing along roads if opportunity should **occur.** Besides the instruments already named I had a supply of prismatic and pocket compasses (I may mention that owing to breakage and accidents I at one time ran short of pocket compasses, and I was much indebted to Colonel Gordon during the Pámír trip for the loan of a very good little instrument), and a small light plane-table, which I had specially made **to** fit on to my theodolite stand. A good hand telescope was fitted to the same stand which **also** served, when necessary, with a slight adaptation, for a Hodgkinson's Actinometer belonging **to** the Royal Society and lent to me by Mr. Hennessey of the Great Trigonometrical Survey for **the service** of the expedition. Colonel Roberts, the Acting Quarter Master General, kindly **gave me** an old astronomical telescope which had been in use for many years **in** the Quarter **Master** General's Department. This telescope was presented to the Dádkhwáh of Yárkand **on our return** to India.

It was proposed that I should **take a complete set of instruments for observation** of the magnetic elements—intensity, **dip, and declination;** but considering the great bulk and delicacy of these instruments, as well as the time that would have been occupied in making the necessary observations—time which I could not expect to be able to snatch from more important duties—I determined to take the dip circle only, a small instrument and one not occupying very much time to observe with. Observations for declination (variation) I was able to manage with my theodolite, with sufficient accuracy for practical purposes.

With regard to chronometers and watches for astronomical **purposes, it was decided** that I should only take pocket chronometers, and as the Survey **Department could only** provide me with one good one, I had **to order** two from England, a gold one by *Dent*, **and** a silver watch by *Brock*, a maker strongly recommended by the Royal Geographical **Society.** These watches, **I found while crossing** the Himalayas, could not be depended on for very accurate results, as **the sudden** and enormous changes of temperature combined with other causes to make the rates very irregular (although all were professedly compensated for temperature), and for that portion of our journey I consider it better to rely upon the Pundit's pacing, checked by latitude observations, rather than on differential longitudinal observations depending on these watches. During trips in Turkestan, however, where there was considerably less variation in temperature, the results are much more satisfactory, **and in** my excursion towards Ush Turfán the resulting positions in longitude depend entirely upon chronometric differences of time, as also in great measure do those between Káshgbar and Panjah in Wakhán.

For meteorological observations and **for** determinations of height I decided to run **the risk** of taking with me mercurial mountain barometers, feeling that the greater confidence that would be placed in results deduced therefrom would more than compensate for the **risk** of loss by breakage; I procured two from Bombay and one from Calcutta, and on **the whole I** am glad that I did so, as I succeeded in safely transporting all three over the Himalayan ranges, having been able to get **them carried by men on** foot. On the other side of the mountains I was not so fortunate. At Sánjú one of them was blown down in front of my tent by a sudden violent gust of wind, and the very next day another, which I had entrusted to the care of Dr. Bellew, was, on account of the length of the march, given to a horseman to carry: the horse fell in crossing a river and No. 2 was smashed. The third survived, and regular observations were taken with it throughout the winter in **Yárkand**. It too was broken on the return journey, its carrier falling with it in a stream.

I was also provided with **numerous** aneroid barometers, hypsometers and thermometers. The latter I had specially made to **order** in England, as none that I could procure in India were graduated **low** enough to register **the** minimum temperature to be expected in the higher ranges of the Himalayas. As was to be anticipated in a journey like ours, very many of these have been broken; **loose horses getting at night** amongst the tent ropes, and in the extreme cold weather even inside **the tent, have much to** answer for.

While at Dehra Dún * prior to starting I was occupied in making myself familiar with the **instruments** I was about to take with me, and in practising the observations I should probably chiefly **be** dependent on; in drawing up and getting lithographed portable and compact forms for registration and computation of observations, and other miscellaneous preparatory work. I prepared a large number of sheets with all the most northerly points fixed **by the Great** Trigonometrical Survey on the frontier of India projected thereon, **as well as the latest** determinations of the Russian survey; in order that by whichever route we might **go or** return, or wherever we might wander, I might lose nothing for want of previous preparation. These charts were not of so much service to me as I had hoped, **as** wherever there was a chance that they might be utilized, the vicissitudes of the climate, and the rapidity with which we had to travel, invariably interposed to prevent my making full use of them. Colonel Walker also designed, and had prepared and photozincographed, a star chart, projected on a new principle, showing only stars of the first three magnitudes, nautical-almanac stars being distinguished **from** all others. I found this chart **a** very valuable practical **guide** while observing.

On Sir Douglas Forsyth's application **to Colonel Walker** four of the Great Trigonometrical Survey "Pundits," **or rather two of the old Pundits** with two assistants, were attached to the Mission, as it **was** hoped that an opening would occur for the despatch of these **men** from Eastern Turkestan **across** the Gobi Desert and through Thibet to Hindustan. **It was** not deemed advisable however to employ them thus, and when the Mission advanced from Yárkand to Káshghar it was necessary to leave them in Yárkand. Permission **was** given, however, for one of them to follow me to Káshghar, and he **did** useful work, of which more hereafter. The remainder were employed in Yárkand **during the winter** in taking meteorological observations.

Road to Yarkand.

For **a** few marches from Leh, in every direction, the country has been carefully and correctly surveyed and mapped in former years by parties of the Great Trigonometrical Survey under Major Montgomerie, R.E., but between this rigorously executed survey (bounded on the north by the head waters of the Núbra and Shyok, and on the north-east by the Ling-zithung plains) **and** the table-lands of Turkestan, lie vast tracts of mountainous country, parts of which, through the enterprise, zeal, and energy of Messrs. Shaw, Hayward, and Johnson, have been mapped with tolerable accuracy, while other parts have probably never yet been traversed **by** man, certainly not by geographers. **It** was my object **to** weld together as far as possible **the** existing materials into **a** harmonious whole and to **add** whatever I could to existing data.

It had been decided that **the Mission** should proceed to Sháhidúla in **two** parties, **the** head-quarters going by the old Kárákorum route, whilst a detached party, consisting **of** Captain Biddulph (in command), Dr. Stoliczka, and myself, was directed to proceed *viâ* Changchenmo by the route by which the former Mission returned from Yárkand in 1870, **and** as we had

---

* The Head-quarters of the Great Trigonometrical Survey.

several days' start of the main party it was hoped that we might be able to discover some alternative route by which that line of road might be shortened and difficulties avoided. The delay of the Hadjí Turrah Sahib, the Yárkand Envoy, in Constantinople made it necessary for the advanced party to halt at Leh until authentic news should arrive of his departure. Authority to advance was not received until we had been there for more than a fortnight, and we left it finally on the 12th September with orders to join the main party at Sháhidúla on the 20th October.

This unfortunate though unavoidable delay not only deprived us of so much time for prosecuting geographical investigation, but postponed our departure to so late a season that inclement weather proved a serious hindrance to our advance, and a still greater impediment to me in carrying out the programme I had laid down for myself.

As the best arrangement I could make, one Pundit with an assistant was left at Leh to proceed with the head-quarters camp; the other one with a better instructed assistant, capable if necessary of doing independent work, was to accompany our own party, and in the probable event of our separation was to be attached to Captain Biddulph, the assistant being attached to Dr. Stoliczka. Abdul Subhán, the Native Surveyor, or "Múnshi" as he is generally called, was to accompany me as recorder and general assistant, and to be sent out with the plane-table should opportunity occur.

It might have been expected that the presence of such a large party would have facilitated arrangements for carrying on work; but the exact contrary was the case, as the demands on the limited resources of the country were so great that it was found impossible to send out any detached parties, the Native Surveyors were therefore obliged to accompany the main camps, to march when they marched, and halt when they halted; and as the marches are arranged for the convenience of travellers and not of Pundits, some of them were found uncommonly stiff and difficult to get through before dark. As the Pundits were in pairs a great part of the way and thus able to divide the work, the ground was got over with a fair amount of accuracy: and checked and corrected by the latitude observations taken both by themselves and myself on the outward and return journeys, the routes are certainly laid down with an amount of accuracy not hitherto attained.

I should explain that in making my plans I was guided by the peculiar nature of the survey work generally done by these natives. This consists of a traverse survey, the angles of which are measured with a prismatic compass and the distances determined by the number of Pundits' paces. These paces have a slightly different unit of length, which is generally determined at the close of operations by comparing the total amount of northing or southing as shewn by the traverse, with the true corresponding distance as determined by the difference of latitude between the starting and closing points. The Pundits are all able to take latitude observations with a sextant and are instructed to do so wherever opportunity occurs. It is obvious that the accuracy of the survey depends upon their being able to keep up a continuous measure of the road; any break in it would ruin the work. Hence the necessity, if possible, of their working in couples, so that they may relieve each other in the pacing, especially where, as in the present case, they were obliged to accompany the large camps and could not select their own halting places. The days were getting short, and if darkness once overtook a man before he had concluded his work, there was every probability of his whole survey being spoiled.

Having thus arranged for the two main lines of road to be laid down with considerable accuracy, I was free to devote myself to what I considered a very important matter, viz., the fixing accurately the correct positions of certain points on the line of march. I wished to do this either by triangulation in continuation of the Great Trigonometrical Survey system of triangles, or by running with the small theodolite a very careful traverse of the road. With the Munshi's help I trusted to be able to carry this traverse up to Sháhidúla, a point whose position it was very important to determine with accuracy I also hoped occasionally to place myself in position on the plane-table by means of certain trigonometrical points which were fixed years ago by the Survey Department in advance of the accurate detailed survey. Many of these points are in the main Kárákorum and Kuen Luen ranges; some of them in the heart of the *terra incognita* before alluded to; and had I had more time at my disposal, and had the weather been more favourable, I might have done very valuable work. As it was, owing to the antagonism of the elements my diary shows one almost continuous succession of disappointments, most disheartening under the circumstances that it was the beginning of the journey, and that I did not know but that circumstances might prevent any work being done after entering Yárkand territory. Climbing hills at the great elevation we were then at was very hard work, and of course occupied considerably more time and labour than similar ascents at a lower level; and in nine cases out of ten when one did arrive at the top of a high hill, snow and clouds entirely obscured both distant and neighbouring peaks. This cloudy weather combined with the necessity of regulating halts and marches according to the places where supplies had been laid out, soon made it evident that it was useless to attempt a continuation of the triangulation. The length of some of the marches and the shortness of the days made the execution of a careful traverse, as impossible as the triangulation, and after some very hard work, I reluctantly came to the conclusion that nothing could be done by myself (i.e., in addition to astronomical work), but to make what use I could of the plane-table. Even with this but little was done owing to the extremely unfavourable state of the weather; but I fortunately succeeded in fixing my position satisfactorily at two or three places on the road to Sháhidúla, the most northerly point where I did so was at Chíbra, south of the Sugét Pass. Throughout the journey the cold was so intense that even the Bhots* who were with me used, on arrival at the top of a hill, to lie down in hollows or crouch behind stones in order to avoid the bitter blast. Under these circumstances, satisfactory work could not be expected, and although I kept my own health in a wonderful manner, I had the misfortune to knock up more or less nearly every man who accompanied me.

From the 24th September, the day on which we reached Gogra, until the 17th October on arrival at Sugét, I was never at a lower level than 15,500 feet, and during the whole of that period the thermometer seldom rose as high as freezing point (32° F.), whereas at night the minimum would vary from zero to 26° below zero.† From 26th September to 8th October I was never below 16,300 feet, my highest camp being at Dehra Kompás‡ 17,900 feet above the level of the sea.§ Snow was frequently falling throughout the whole of this period, and for three days was the only substitute for water, for both man and beast. Captain Biddulph, who travelled by a more easterly route than Dr. Stoliczka and myself, was living at even a greater elevation.

On the 13th of October Dr. Stoliczka and myself reached Áktágh, where we joined the head-quarters camp. It had originally been arranged that Captain Biddulph, accompanied by a Pundit, was to cross the Kárákorum line of road and explore the country to the west of Áktágh towards Kufelong. Dr. Stoliczka, accompanied by the other Pundit, was to have crossed from the Kárátágh Lake by a new route to the Kárákásh River, but his illness, as well as the weak state to which the camp followers were reduced from lengthened exposure to cold and hard work, made it necessary to alter these arrangements.

I was now directed to go up the Kárákásh River, and endeavour to find the road which was believed to exist between some point up the river and the Kárátágh Lake, and which it was supposed might turn out a good alternative route. I returned from this expedition, the details of which are given in another place, on the 20th October, and left the following day with a party under the orders of Colonel Gordon for Sanjú with instructions to await Sir Douglas Forsyth's arrival at that place.

As Sháhidúla was the first point where we struck the Atálik's dominions and met his people, I briefly give the result of survey operations up to that point.

---

* *Bhots* are inhabitants of Ladakh.

† *i.e.*, 58° below freezing point.

‡ So called from having been used as a camping ground by a former Survey Officer or Kompas (compass) wala, the native designation for all surveyors.

§ It was the hardships encountered while traversing this elevated region that brought on the illness which subsequently cost Dr Stoliczka his life.

B

(6)

One Pundit and his assistant accompanied the head-quarters camp and were kindly looked after by Captain Chapman, who himself took some astronomical observations along the road. They ran a route survey from Leh, viâ the Khárdung Pass, up the Nubra Valley to Changlung, thence by the Sáser Pass to Sáser, from which place the Pundit proceeded by the winter route up the Shyok River and by the Remo glacier to Daulat Beguldi, while his assistant took the summer route by Murghí and the Dipsang plains to the same spot. Thence they proceeded by the regular road over the Kárákorum Pass to Aktágh, from which place they carried their traverse down the Yárkand River for three marches to Kirghiz Jangal, returning thence to Sháhidúla by the Kirghiz Pass.

Kishen Sing, the Pundit, accompanying the advanced party commenced his route survey at Chimray, two marches east of Leh. At Zingrál, the next halting place, his assistant diverged from the main road, going over the Kay La (Pass) and joined us again at Tankse. The Pundit went with the main camp over the Chang-la.* From Tankse we all proceeded to Gogra, whence the Pundit was detached to accompany Captain Biddulph, who went over "Cayley's† Pass" and the Ling-zi-thung plains, considerably to the east of the road by which the former Mission returned from Yárkand in 1870, which road, however, he rejoined at Kizil-Jilga, thence following the Kárákásh in all its bends down to Sháhidúla. Captain Biddulph took numerous observations for height on his line of march, generally using one of the mercurial barometers for that purpose. The Pundit kept up a continuous route survey the whole way and took frequent astronomical observations for latitude. Both Captain Biddulph's and Pundit Kishen Sing's observations will be found in the Appendix to this Chapter.

This Pundit's assistant, aided by the Múnshi (as soon as I became convinced that a theodolite traverse was impracticable), carried a route survey along the road I myself followed, i.e., the one by which the former Mission returned from Yárkand, by the Changlung-Pangtung Pass. This road skirts the west edge of the Ling-zi-thung plains and striking the Kárákásh River near its head, follows the course of that river until it turns off suddenly to the north-west, a point a little beyond Khush Maidán; thence the road passes viâ the Kárátágh Pass and Lake to Aktágh. From Aktágh it goes over the Sugét Pass from which place I sent the Route Surveyors up in a north-west direction to cross the hills in front and stike the path passing from the Khirghiz Pass to Sháhidúla. My object in detaching them by that road was to enable the Múnshi to fix himself in position by some of the survey peaks on the Kárákorum away to the west. He had one fine day and succeeded in doing so, but at the cost of frost-bitten fingers, from which it took him a considerable time to recover.

Throughout the march I made astronomical observations with my theodolite which have been reduced (in duplicate) in the head-quarters office of the Great Trigonometrical Survey since my return to India. They, together with my fixings by the plane-table, as well as my astronomical work on the return journey, and the Pundit's own observations, form the basis on which the whole of the Pundit's traverses have been built up. To this frame I have added such material as is available from the maps of the Trigonometrical Survey and of Messrs. Johnson, Shaw, and Hayward. The whole combined form a map more accurate and complete than anything yet published, and should, for geographical purposes, as far as the actual lines of road are concerned, leave but little more to be desired.

Descriptions of the routes traversed by various members of the Mission will be found in the Appendix, Section, *Routes*.

As regards this early portion of our journey the only new contributions I can give to science and geography are the results of a boating expedition on the Pangong Lake, and an account of the excursion, already referred to, which I made from the neighbourhood of Sháhidúla to try and discover an alternative road on to the Karatagh plain.

The Pangong Lake district has been described at considerable length by Captain Godwin Austen in the *Royal Geographical Society's Journal* for 1867, and the additional

---

* 17,590 feet. | † 19,280 feet.

(7)

information I can now supply refers to the depth of the lake, an interesting subject of enquiry, and one which has, I believe, never been investigated with reference to this or any other of the Himalayan Lakes. A portable India rubber boat, which I had procured from England in the hope of ultimately floating it on Lake Lob, was the means which enabled Captain Biddulph and myself to make a section across the bottom of the lake. We arranged to halt a day for the purpose at Lukong.

The soundings were taken by Captain Biddulph with a fishing line, which I had carefully measured and marked before starting. We fortunately had a quiet day, and owing to the entire absence of wind and current there was not the slightest difficulty in getting these soundings most accurately.

Starting from the sandy shore at the west end of the lake we made for the island, lying about two miles off and situate nearly equidistant from the two sides of the lake. At 100 yards from the shore (N.B.—The horizontal distances are only rough estimations) the depth was 55 feet, the bank sinking gradually; 150 yards further on, the depth was 93 feet, and 200 yards further 112 feet; at 550 yards more, depth 130 feet, the maximum depth reached between shore and island. As we approached the latter the water grew rapidly shallow. At a distance of 400 yards from it, there was only 50 feet of water, and at 250 yards only 14 feet, from this point a shelving sandy bottom stretched up to the island, which consisted of a mass of rocks, about 150 yards in length and considerably less in breadth, of irregular shape, and extending in a direction parallel to that of the lake, viz., from north-west to south-east. It was composed mostly of calcareous tubfa, and in no place rose to more than four feet above the surface of the lake. The rock was very brittle and jagged, and in many places was covered with masses of shells, of which I brought away specimens: these shells appeared to me to have become only recently untenanted, but they were pronounced by Dr. Stoliczka to be many centuries old and to be fresh-water specimens. The island or rather islands (a short distance from the main rock in a south-east direction is a long sandbank rising only a few inches above the water) are submerged during heavy storms, for we found many fragments of wood, weeds, and even cattle dung, which had evidently been washed ashore from the mainland. Although the water was beautifully clear we looked in vain for fish, and with the exception of a species of bug, of which myriads were swimming about, we failed to see any animal or signs of life of any description. This is the more curious, as in a small stream which flows into the lake near Lukong there is an abundance of fish. The temperature of the water, which was decidedly brackish, was 55° F.; its color, a very pure blue where deep, and green where shallow.

From the island I pulled to the north shore of the lake, which lying under precipitous cliffs I expected to find much deeper. The water deepened out gradually to 107 feet at 300 yards from the island, and at about half way across, say half a mile from shore, there was a depth of 136 feet; at 250 yards from the mainshore we found 142 feet; at 100 yards, 114 feet; at 50 yards, 95 feet; at 30 yards, 80 feet; at 20 yards, 50 feet; at 10 yards, 12 feet. The boat, 12 feet long, was very well adapted for work of the kind, and in the absence of wind I was, without violent exertion, able to pull it along, carrying one passenger, at the rate of nearly, if not quite, four miles an hour, and this at an elevation of 14,000 feet above the sea. In fact the exertion required was considerably less than would be needed for walking at the same pace. The banks of the lake, which is about forty miles in length, showed evident signs of the water having formerly stood at a much higher level than it does at present: and there can be little doubt but that the valley along which the road passes from Tánkse up to the lake, was, at no very distant period, its main outlet; for although there is now a low pass, about two miles from the head of the lake, yet it is not much more than 100 feet above the present level of the water, and is moreover chiefly formed by detritus washed down from two side ravines, and of very recent formation.

With reference to my short excursion up the Kárákásh in search of a new road, I left Sugét on the morning of the 17th October, and was accompanied as far as Balakchi (9 miles) by Drs. Bellew and Stoliczka, who were paying a visit to the *jade* mines. After leaving them I marched on for two and a half hours to Gulbáshem, where I met Captain Biddulph on his way down the Kárákásh to Sháhidúla. My syce (groom) and guide, the only man in our united camps at Sugét, who professed to know of the existence of the road I was now searching for, had led me to believe that at about one *kos* (2 miles) from Gulbáshem, by turning up a lateral ravine on the south, a journey of 3 *kos* would bring me to a very low and easy pass, with an almost imperceptible ascent, from the top of which we were to look down upon the Kárátágh plains; and the evening we were at Gulbáshem he pointed out a neighbouring spur, beyond which, he said, the road turned off. What then was my annoyance when the next day we did not reach the turning until after a long and difficult march of 13 miles up the Kárákásh River, and even then, according to his account, the pass was further off than he had stated it to be the day before. I was extremely vexed at thus partially losing a day, for my camp was so far behind (I having arranged for a short march hoping to get up to the pass and back before night) that there was no time to move it much further on that day, and I had to halt at the entrance of the valley leading to the pass. I had now only two days left in which to visit the pass and return to Sháhidúla, as it had been arranged that I should have to be there on the 20th so as to be ready to leave with Colonel Gordon on the 21st.

Starting early in the morning of the following day and quitting the Kárákásh River (at a point 12,500 feet above the sea), we went up a broad open ravine, running south for 2½ miles, to a point where it divides into two branches of which we followed the eastern for about half a mile up a steepish ascent to a point where this also divides into two smaller ravines with a steep spur running down between them. These two ravines were bounded externally by precipitous banks several hundreds of feet in almost perpendicular height. There was apparently no practicable path along the lower portion of these defiles, but the road zigzags up the spur running down between them, and then follows the left hand one. The top of this first ascent was about 2,500 higher than our camp on the Kárákásh River.

From the top of the zigzag, the road up which, though steep, was good and practicable for laden ponies, we reached a more open country and the road now followed a broad grassy ravine with a gentle but steady rise. I followed this for seven or eight miles rising to about 16,800 feet, and there was still a stretch apparently of several miles, of gently undulating ground in front. As it was getting late in the day, and there was no time for me to go further, I climbed up a hill from which I obtained a view of the water-shed. I sent on the Pundit (the one who had been accompanying Captain Biddulph, and whom I had brought back from Gulbáshem) with instructions to follow the ravine to the water-shed, and to go beyond and fix by intersection either the Kárátágh Lake or the hill at Támba camping ground between Kárátágh and Áktágh, and, if possible, to return by Áktágh and rejoin the Head-Quarters camp at Sháhidúla. He succeeded the following day in passing the crest which turned out to be not more than a couple of miles from where I had left him, and in fixing by intersections from a distance the position of the hill before alluded to; but the guide having become seriously ill and no one else knowing the country, and the whole of the Kárátágh plain being several inches deep in snow, the Pundit was obliged to return *viâ* Gulbáshem rejoining the camp after I had left with Colonel Gordon. I returned myself that same evening to my camp at Fotásh in the Kárákásh River, not reaching it, however, till late at night and getting two or three falls on the road, which, although tolerably good by daylight, was in certain places, especially at the foot of the steep zigzag, by no means easy in the dark.

I do not think that this route is likely ever to come into general use, for although it is perhaps a better road than that between Sháhidúla and Kárákorum Brangsa (*viâ* the Sugét Pass), yet it is much longer. From Sháhidúla to Brangsa the road *viâ* the Kárákásh is at least 15 miles longer than the one by the Sugét Pass. Should, however, the road *viâ* Kizil-jilga and Kárátágh come into frequent use, I believe the Fotásh route might be employed with advantage, as there is very little difference in length of road, and grass and fire-wood are to be found in abundance all the way from Sháhidúla up the Kárákásh River, and for *two* miles up the (Fotásh) ravine, after which there is plenty of grass all the way to the pass as well as any amount of *Boortsee.** There were numerous tracks, on the higher

---

* Boortsee is a small plant with large woody roots which grows wild in large quantities, and is in many places the only fuel obtainable by travellers.

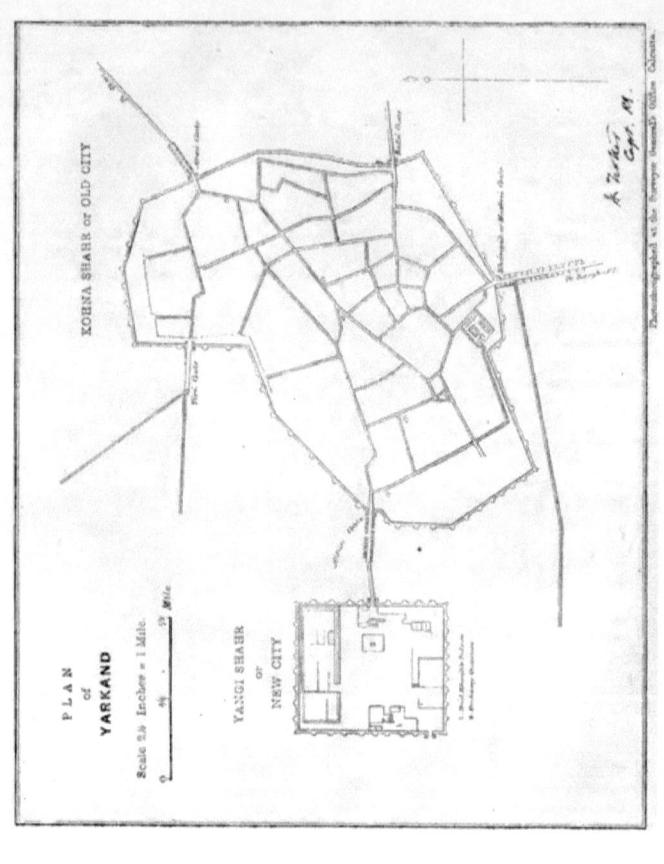

ground, of both *kiang* (wild horse) and wild yák,* a good evidence of the excellence of the grass. The road has evidently been occasionally in use, as it is marked in places where it might easily be lost in the snow by small stones placed in an upright position here and there on large rocks. My guide told me that he had only once travelled by it, when accompanying a very small caravan of not more than five or six ponies, on which occasion, there being a great deal of snow on the Sugét Pass, through which they feared they would be unable to force their way, they had resort to this alternative route to the Kárákorum. I have never met another man who was acquainted with this road, and its existence appears generally unknown to the Bhots of Ladákh.

I returned the following day to Sháhidúla (33 miles) visiting *en route* the jade mines between Gulbáshem and Balákchi. These have been described at length by the late Dr. Stoliczka.

It was deemed advisable, that from Sháhidúla onwards all open survey or display of instruments on the road was to cease. Permission was given, however, for one of the most experienced and wary of the Pundits to take observations quietly with a small pocket compass, with which he carried his route survey up to Yárkand. I also made occasional observations at night for latitude, so that a rough but tolerably correct survey of the road was obtained. On our return to India these restrictions were found to be unnecessary, and one of the Pundits proceeded from Yárkand *viá* Sanjú and Sháhidúla, and without any attempt at concealment paced and re-surveyed the road carefully.

When we left Yárkand for Káshghar the Pundits were directed to remain behind, but one of them was permitted to follow a few days after, and made a very fairly accurate route survey up to Káshghar, the others had to stay in Yárkand until we left the country and returned (with the exception before mentioned of the man who went by Sanjú and Sháhidúla) with the advanced baggage party under Tárá Sing,† *viá* the Kugiár and Kárákorum route. They carried a route survey from Yárkand up to Leh. The ground between Karghálik and Kúlunaldi (on the Yárkand River below Kufelong) had never before been surveyed. The Pundit who followed us to Káshghar did some good work; besides making an excursion with Tárá Sing to some of the neighbouring bazaars, whose position he was enabled to fix, he accompanied a party of the Mission on an excursion to the north of Káshghar in the Altyn Artysh Districts, making a traverse survey of the road. He also went with Colonel Gordon's party to Sirikol (Táshkurghan), and returned to Yárkand by himself, diverging from the route by which he had come at Chehil Gombáz, whence he proceeded by the direct road to Yárkand, a distance of upwards of 100 miles, over ground that has never previously been surveyed. It was arranged for him to return to India *viá* Khotan, a journey he accomplished most successfully. Prior to leaving the country he paid a visit to the Sorghák Gold Fields in latitude north 36°39′51″ longitude 82°42′ east of Greenwich, about 160 miles (by road) to the east of Khotan.‡ Returning thence to Kiria he found his way back to India by Polu, Noh, and the Pangong Lake, a route running from one and a half to two degrees to the east of the most easterly route we have hitherto possessed, *viz.*, that traversed in 1865 by Mr. W. H. Johnson in his journey to Khotan. Details of the route followed by the Pundit are given in the Appendix, as are also his observations for latitude and height.

Description of routes between Ládakh and Turkestan.

It is not proposed to give here a detailed description of the lines of route followed by the members of the Mission on their travels between Ladakh and Eastern Turkestan,‡ but a brief comparison of the various lines of road between the two countries may not be uninteresting.

---

* A yak is a species of mountain ox which only lives at great altitudes, and is much used for the carriage of merchandize over snow and ice. On ice they are far more sure-footed than any other beasts of burden.

† Treasurer to the Mission.

‡ Details of the roads traversed by the members of the Mission will be found in Section G. of the Appendix to this Chapter.

For practical purposes these routes may be divided into three, viz.—
  The Kàràkorum route with variations (leading to Yárkand).
  The Changchenmo route with variations (leading to Yárkand and Khotan).
  The Rudokh (or Changthang)* route (leading to Khotan).

The Karakorum route may be subdivided into two, **the** Zamistání or **winter and the** Tabistání or **summer road,** and although **these** have a few marches and camping **grounds** in common, **and cross the** great water-shed between India and Central Asia at the same point, **the Káràkorum Pass,** yet they diverge from **each** other throughout the greater part of their courses. As a rule it may be laid down that **the winter** road passes wherever possible along and **over the beds of** rivers, which in the **cold** season contain but little water, and are generally **frozen over:** these streams, which form **no** obstacle in winter, are often impassable torrents **in summer. It** is therefore no matter **of surprise that** in spite of the intense cold and hardships **of a** winter journey the merchant **often selects** that season for his travels. The first **great obstacle** to be encountered after leaving Leh, **both** in summer and winter, is the well known Kailás range, which **is** said to run in one unbroken **line** from the sources of the Indus **to the** junction of that river with the Shyok. To the **north of** Leh this range divides the drainage of these two rivers, **and** is one of the most formidable **obstacles to be** encountered by **the** traveller to Turkestan. In winter it is crossed by **the Digar La†** (17,930 feet above sea level), a very difficult pass, in crossing which it is necessary to **employ either yáks** or men for the carriage **of** goods. **A party** of the Mission went over it in **June, and even** then there was snow lying **on the top while ice and** snow combined to render **the passage difficult** along a distance of some miles.

The summer road crosses the Khardung or Leh Pass,‡ almost north of Leh, and is 17,900 feet in height. This Pass also is impracticable for laden ponies, and is so difficult that late in June on **our return journey** from Yárkand, after descending the Nubra river, it was deemed advisable **to go a long detour** vid the Digar Pass in order to avoid the still more formidable obstacles on **the** Khardung. This made the journey from Sati to Leh 42 miles instead of 29. After crossing the Kailás range and entering the Shyok valley the traveller has now before him the great Muz-tagh§ or Káràkorum Range. In the winter by following the narrow, winding, and difficult valley of the Shyok river he reaches the Káràkorum Pass, a distance of 114 miles ; in the course of this portion of **the** journey the frozen surface of the stream has **to** be crossed no less than 36 times. In winter this can easily be done, **as** it is generally **bridged** by snow and ice, but in summer owing to the floods caused by the melting glaciers an **entirely** different route has to be adopted, and instead of ascending the Shyok the traveller **descends** that river to a short distance below Sati and then ascends the Nubra river, a large **tributary** fed from glaciers in the same mountain mass that supplies the Shyok.

The Shyok is crossed in boats near Sati, where in the summer it is a very large and rapid **river. Passengers** and goods are carried over in boats, while the baggage animals are made to swim across. **Many** of the latter are drowned in crossing.

Ascending the Nubra valley, one of the most fertile and richly cultivated in Ladakh, **the traveller goes** as far as Changlung (10,760 feet), almost the highest village in the **valley, and situated** about 40 miles above Sati. The merchant **generally** takes this bit very **easily,** advancing by short marches of ten miles each, **in** order to **make the** most of the supplies **of** grain **and** excellent **lucerne** grass, both of which are here **obtained** in abundance. The caravans from **Yárkand often** halt a week **at Panamik** (a large and flourishing village a few miles below **Changlung)** to feed and rest the baggage animals after the hard work and scant fare that they **have had on the** journey. It is here that on the outward journey the real difficulties of **the march** commence. Instead of following one stream right up **to its** source in the Káràkorum **Pass, as is** done in the winter route, the traveller has first of **all to** cross a

---

* Changthang, in the Thibetan language means ' **northern plain."**
† " La " is the Thibetan **word for** " Pass."
‡ Sometimes also called " Laoche La."
§ **In Turki "Muz-tagh" means "** Ice Mountain " and **"Karakorum"** is the equivalent of " Black gravel."

very high and precipitous hill just above Changlung **village**. **The** road ascends by a zigzag and **rises** rather more than 4,000 feet in a length of about **five** miles, the stiffest bit of ascent **on the** whole journey to Yárkand. After reaching the top of the *Karawal* Pass (so called from **a** karawal or outpost erected many years go at this spot to enable the Ladakhis to defend their country from invasion from the north) the road descends into the Sásér stream and then **passes** up it to the Sásér La, a pass over a mighty ridge covered with snow and glaciers which runs down from the great mountain mass forming the eastern extremity of the so-called Kárákorum Range and separates the waters of the Nubra* from those **of** the Shyok. This pass (17,820 feet) is one of the most difficult on the whole road, and is rarely, if ever, free from snow, while the road passes through, over, and alongside of glaciers **for** many miles.† The road from the top of the pass follows the bank of a stream which enters the Shyok River at Saser Polu, a halting place on the winter road. The Shyok is here crossed with difficulty, as is proved by the fact that two Ladakhis were drowned there when **returning** from laying out supplies for our return journey.

The road now ascends a tributary stream on the **left bank of the Shyok crosses a low pass,** and at Murghi Camp joins another stream which **flows from the Dipsang plains into the** Shyok River. It was at this point, at a height **of 15,200 feet, that the late Dr. Stoliczka** breathed his last, after having traversed the Kárákorum Pass and the perhaps **still more** trying Dipsang plains which rise to **an** elevation of about 18,000 feet above the sea. **The** intense cold of this bleak and dreary waste prevents this route from being adopted in winter, during which season the caravans follow the Shyok River from Saser Polu up to Daulat Beguldi (Turki for "Daulat Beg died," an appropriate name for so desolate a spot). This camp, which is situated in the north-west corner of the Dipsang plain, marks the junction of the winter and summer routes, which unite here, and cross the Kárákorum Pass 11 miles **above the** camp, continuing together a distance of 40 miles further to Ak-tágh. The Kárákorum **Pass,** though 18,550 feet above the sea, is by no means so formidable an obstacle as is generally supposed. It is always free from glaciers, and in summer from snow. The ascent on both **sides** is gentle, and the road good, so that, although it forms the water-shed between Hindústán and Central Asia, it is less of an obstacle to the merchant than the Digar, the Khardung, the Saser or the Sanju Passes. From it the road passes along the Kárákorum stream (one of the head-waters of the Yárkand River) to Ak-tágh, traversing the comparatively open ground **on** the west of the Karatágh‡ plain. At Ak-tágh the roads again diverge, the winter route continues down the Yárkand river, which is crossed 18 times between Ak-tágh and Kúlánaldi,§ a distance of 74 miles. At the latter place this road ascends the range that was called by Hayward the western "Kuen Luen," and crosses it by the Yangi-Diwan (or "New Pass," 16,000 feet) into the Tiznáf River, which it follows for 41 miles to Chiklik. The road is here taken over **one of** the northern spurs of the Kuen Luen by the "Tupa"|| or Ak-Korum Pass (10,470 feet), whence it descends along the banks of a gently sloping stream to Kugiar, a considerable village (containing 400 or 500 houses) on the borders of the plains of Eastern Turkestan, and 41 miles distant from Karghalik, a large town situated at the junction of the Zamistáni (*viâ* Kugiar), and the Tabistáni (*viâ* Sánjú) routes. It was by the Kugiar road that the Mission returned to India. The road had been closed for several years previously by order of the Yárkand authorities owing to the risk to which travellers were exposed of being plundered and sold into slavery by the wild Kanjud robbers (of Hanza and Nagar), who coming down from their fastnesses to the north of Búnji and Gilgit used to render the whole valley of the Yárkand

---

* At the head of the Nubra valley a road passes over the main Kárákorum chain by the Chorbut Pass and descends into the Yárkand river at Khufélong. It was formerly much used by the Baltistan merchants, but **is** now rarely employed. It is probably not less than 19,000 feet high, and **is** always closed for at least nine months in the year, and is at no times practicable for laden animals.

† On the return journey **of the** Mission **several** hundreds **of coolies were employed for some weeks** in preparing the road over this pass.

‡ "Karatagh"="Black Mountain."

§ "Kulunaldi"="the **wild horse died.**"

|| In Turki Tupa means "hill," and Ak-Korum "white gravel."

(12)

River from Kúlúnaldi up to Ak-tágh, utterly unsafe for travellers or merchants unless in large parties and well armed.*

It was in the month of June that the Pámír party returned by the Kugiar route somewhat too late in the season to traverse it with safety, and considerable danger was incurred from the daily increasing floods of the Tiznaf River, which after noon used to come down with such force as frequently to close the road. At this season also the southern slopes of the Yangi-Diwán (Pass) are very difficult to traverse and somewhat dangerous, as the recently dead bodies of numerous baggage animals seen by us on the return journey too surely testified. The floods of the Tiznaf are probably worse in June and July than at any other time of the year, as after that period the snow on the lower mountains has nearly all been melted. The Yárkand River, on the other hand, above Kúlúnaldi, being fed more generously by glacier streams is more difficult later on in the hot weather. We found that although there was a much larger body of water in the Yárkand than in the Tiznaf River, yet in the former the bed was broad and level, and was crossed without difficulty; whereas in the Tiznaf the bottom is narrow and generally composed of large stones and boulders which render its passage very difficult.† The road crossed it nearly 20 times in one march, or about once in every linear mile of its course. A month earlier in the season (May) the river was frozen and was ascended by an advanced party of natives without difficulty.

42. Returning to Ak-tágh, the point of divergence of the two routes, the summer road passes thence over a spur of the Kuen Luen by the Sugét, a tolerably easy pass (17,610 feet), from which the road descends along a winding stream to the Kárákásh river which it strikes a few miles above Sháhidúla.‡

At Sháhidúla the Kárákásh river winds through the Kuen Luen Range.§ The road follows along it for some 20 miles, and occasionally crosses it. In summer its passage is effected by merchants with considerable difficulty. The Kárákásh flows in the direction of Khotan, and between the river and Yárkand lies a formidable spur from the Kuen Luen, which has to be crossed. The traveller, if he be here unfettered by political obligations, has the choice of three roads before him, viz., by the Kilik, the Kilian, and the Sánjú passes. Traders are seldom or never allowed to use the former which is said to be the easiest and

---

* *Note.*—These robbers, apparently from fear of the Káshghar Amír, have of recent years ceased to infest this road, but it is reported that since the return of the Mission from Yárkand, the Kunjadis have attacked a nomadic tribe called Phakpos, who inhabit numerous valleys on the west bank of the Tiznaf river. The road by which these robbers advance must pass over numerous glaciers, and crosses the Kárákorum range by the Shingshal Pass, a short distance to the west of the Shigar or Muztagh Pass. The road from Shingshal descends the Kum stream and joins the road from the Muztagh Pass at a distance of one and a half marches to the north of the latter. After three short marches more the Yárkand River is reached at Dahn-i-Bazar Darah, three short marches below Kulunaldi (on the same river), a frequently used halting place on the road between Kárákorum Pass and Kugiar. The Shingshal Pass is said to be easier than either the Chhorbut or the Shigar Passes, and is at times passable by laden horses. The Muztagh Pass (which was estimated by Godwin Austen at 18,400 feet, and by the
¹ Or natives of Baltistan, a mountainous district inhabited by Shiah Musulmans, and lying to the north-west of Ladakh.
Schlagentweits at 19,000 feet) road lies for a great distance over glaciers, and is difficult and dangerous. It is occasionally used by the Baltis,¹ who have a colony in Yárkand, and who traverse this pass when returning thence to their own country.

† On one occasion during the return journey, when I had gone on a couple of days ahead of Colonel Gordon's party so as to have more time for survey, I had, in order to insure security from water, placed my chronometers in my pockets instead of in the mule trunks where they were usually carried. It was the first time that I had done so, and as ill-luck would have it, I twice got parted from my horse in deep water while searching for a ford, and had to swim for my life with my chronometers in my pocket. On the same occasion my horses and baggage animals were cut off from all supplies by the floods, and were for more than 36 hours without tasting food.

‡ *Note.*—At Shahidúla is a small fort which during the time of the disturbances in Eastern Turkestan (which resulted in the accession of the present King) was occupied by a detachment of the Maharaja's troops from Kashmir. These were subsequently withdrawn and the place is now generally recognized as belonging to the Kashghar ruler. The Kirghiz of Sanju have of late years constantly occupied the Karakash valley up as far as the great bend above Sora, and occasionally ascend some of the valleys to the south, leading up to the Karatagh plain; in many of these valleys there is abundance of grass and wood.

§ Dividing it according to Hayward's nomenclature into Eastern and Western Kuen Luen.

shortest; it follows the course of the Toghra, a considerable stream which enters the Kárákásh nine miles below Sháhidúla. The floods of this stream in hot weather often detain travellers a considerable time on its banks. The Kilik Diwan (Pass) is crossed in the 3rd or 4th march from Sháhidúla, and after going over another low pass the road joins the Kugiar route at Beshterek, one day's march to the south of Karghálik; little is known of this road, but it is said that grass and wood are to be found at every stage. It was once much used by the Baltistan merchants who are settled in Yárkand.

Nearly three miles below where the Togra-su enters the Kárákásh River is the fort of Ali Nazar, where the Kilian road leaves the Karakash valley and passes up an open ravine in a north-west direction. This road is sometimes used in the summer as an alternative to that over the Sánjú Pass; it is somewhat higher than the Sánjú Pass, but, although impracticable for laden horses, is not so difficult to traverse. The Kilian pass is crossed in the second day after leaving the Kárákásh. The road follows the stream from the pass for four marches when it debouches into the Turkestan plain at the village of Kilian, two marches to the south of Bora on the road between Sanju and Karghálik.*

The third and most frequented road from Sháhidúla is *viâ* Sánjú. It leaves the Kárákásh 20 miles below Sháhidúla at Mazár Abú Bakar, from which place the road ascends to the summit of the Sánjú (also happily named "Grim") pass which, although not more than 16,700 feet above sea level, was decidedly the most difficult obstacle encountered by the mission on the road to Yárkand.† Its summit is never free from snow and ice, and is impassable by laden ponies. Yaks have always to be used and are collected from all quarters for the passage of a large caravan. From the pass the road descends to the Sánjú or Sarikia River, which it follows to the large and scattered village of Sánjú, on the borders of the Great Turkestan Plain. Occasionally in the hot season the Sánjú River is so flooded in its lower course as to become impassable, in which case a detour is made by a road which crosses a small spur by the Chuchu Pass (11,800 feet), after which it follows the Arpalek stream to near Sánjú. Thence a good and level road leads to Yárkand, a distance of 122 miles, and meets the Kilian route at Bora, and the Kilik and Kugiar routes at Karghálik.

Returning now to the Changchenmo route from Leh to Turkestan, on this also the Kailás range has to be crossed, but further to the east than on the Karakorum route. The road ascends the Indus for 20 miles, and then goes up a tributary stream for 13 miles to Zingrál, from which place the range may be crossed either by the Chang La (17,600 feet), or the Kay La (17,900 feet). By the former and easier road of the two it is 23 miles from Zingrál to the large village of Tankse, situated on one of the tributaries of the Shyok River. By the Kay La foot passengers shorten the road by some six miles. The roads over both passes, although free from glaciers, are very difficult; and it is usual, although not absolutely necessary, to employ yaks in carrying goods across.

Tánkse is the last place on this road where supplies are procurable, and is, by the shortest route, 350 miles from Sánjú, the first large village encountered in Turkestan. For the whole of this distance supplies of grain, both for men and horses, have to be carried, and at a great many halting places neither grass nor fire-wood is procurable. From Tankse after passing Lukong at the head of the Pangong Lake, the road crosses a lofty mass of mountains, by the Lankar or Marsemik La (18,400 feet), a very high but in summer by no means a difficult pass. It is free from glaciers, and generally clear of snow during the summer and early autumn. Descending into the Changchenmo valley and crossing the stream, a tributary of the Shyok, the road ascends a minor stream to a point eight miles beyond Gogra, from which there is a choice of three different roads all leading on to the Ling-zi-thung‡ Plains. The most westerly path ascends the Changlung Pangtung Pass (18,900 feet), crosses the corner of the plateau and descends into a deep ravine running along the stony and very difficult bed of a stream§ (which ultimately finds its way into the Shyok River), ascends again, and skirts the

---

* In former years the Kilian would appear to have been the most frequented route, but it is now little used.
† Several mules were lost here, although their loads had all been transferred to yaks.
‡ or Ak-sai Chin.
§ The march down this ravine was one of the most trying encountered during the outward journey.

(14)

western border of the gently undulating Ling-zi-thung Plain), in traversing which the traveller crosses, almost without knowing it, the water-shed between India and Central Asia. After passing the water-shed the road crosses a small stream, one of the head waters of the Kárákásh, and then goes over a spur (Kompás La) 18,160 feet in height and descends into the bed of Kárákásh River, which it strikes, at an elevation of 17,400 feet above the sea and follows to Kizil Jilga.

The portion of the road between the Changlung Pass and Kizil Jilga is perhaps the most trying part of this route. The great elevation and consequent bitter cold is much aggravated by frequent snow and a piercing wind which blows from morning to night; the long dreary marches cause one to arrive, after dark, at camps where there are scant supplies of fuel and no grass; occasional ice beds block up the whole road, one of these extends for three miles down the Kárákásh River; all combine to try most severely both man and beast.

At Kizil Jilga the road just described joins an alternative road (taken by Captain Biddulph on the outward journey), which, leaving the usual route a few miles north of Gogra, crosses the Changlung Barma Pass (19,300 feet) on to the Ling-zi-thung plains, along which it passes at a still higher elevation than the western road. It descends into the Kárákásh River at Kizil Jilga; the greater elevation makes this road perhaps even more trying than the western route.

The third route from Gogra before alluded to leaves the Changlung valley 8 miles above Gogra and the Ling-zi-thung plain may be reached by either the Changlung Barma or the Changlung Yokma Pass a little further to the east, and of about the same elevation. This is the pass taken by Mr. (now Sir Douglas) Forsyth in his first mission to Yárkand. By it, the road followed by Captain Biddulph (striking the Kárákásh River at Kizil Jilga) may be joined, but a more northerly route passing over a succession of elevated plains was taken by the former mission, and the Kárákásh River was met a few miles above Sora at the sudden bend that the river takes when its course is turned towards the west (in north lat. 35° 55') by the Kuen Luen Range. From this point the road followed the River to Shahidúla.

In addition to the intense cold the principal objection to all three routes skirting or passing over the Ling-zi-thung (also called Aksai Chin) is the extreme elevation at which the traveller has to remain for so many marches: the cattle are exhausted by this, and too frequently suffer in addition from the pangs of hunger and thirst. These difficulties nearly brought the first mission to Yárkand to a disastrous end, and the same causes have proved, and will probably continue to prove, sufficient to deter the experienced merchant from following this road. The older, shorter, and better known route by the Kárákorum is likely always to be preferred by the merchant even in summer, whereas in winter an attempt to traverse the Ling-zi-thung plains must almost always result in disaster.

From Kizil Jilga the road follows the Kárákásh River to Chong Tash (or " Great Stone"). From this point the eastern variation, taken by Captain Biddulph, follows the Kárákásh River right down to Shahidúla, a distance of 166 miles, while the western or more direct road is only 113 miles in length, and although in the latter there are two high passes viz., the Kárátágh (17,700) and the Sugét (17,600) to be crossed en route, yet they are neither of them difficult ones. The Sugét Pass may be avoided by going over the lower and still easier pass of Fotash by which the Kárákásh River is struck one march above Gulbashem. In the circuitous line from Chong-tash down the Kárákásh, the road is bad, but there is the advantage of plentiful supplies of grass and fuel which are almost altogether wanting on the Kárátágh line. The Ling-zi-thang routes meet the Kárákorum summer route at Aktágh or at Shahidúla according as the western or eastern variation is adopted.

At the angle formed by the Kárákásh River above Sora, when turned by the Kuen Luen range, the traveller can proceed to Khotan direct (a distance of 160 miles or 11 marches) by crossing the Kuen Luen Range by the Yangi or Elchi Diwan (crossed by Mr. Johnson in his journey to Khotan in 1865), and estimated by him at 19,500 feet in height; after passing this there is another formidable glacier pass, the Naia Khan (height 18,659 according to Johnson) which has to be crossed before reaching the plains. The Elchi Diwan is said to be open for only three months in the year.

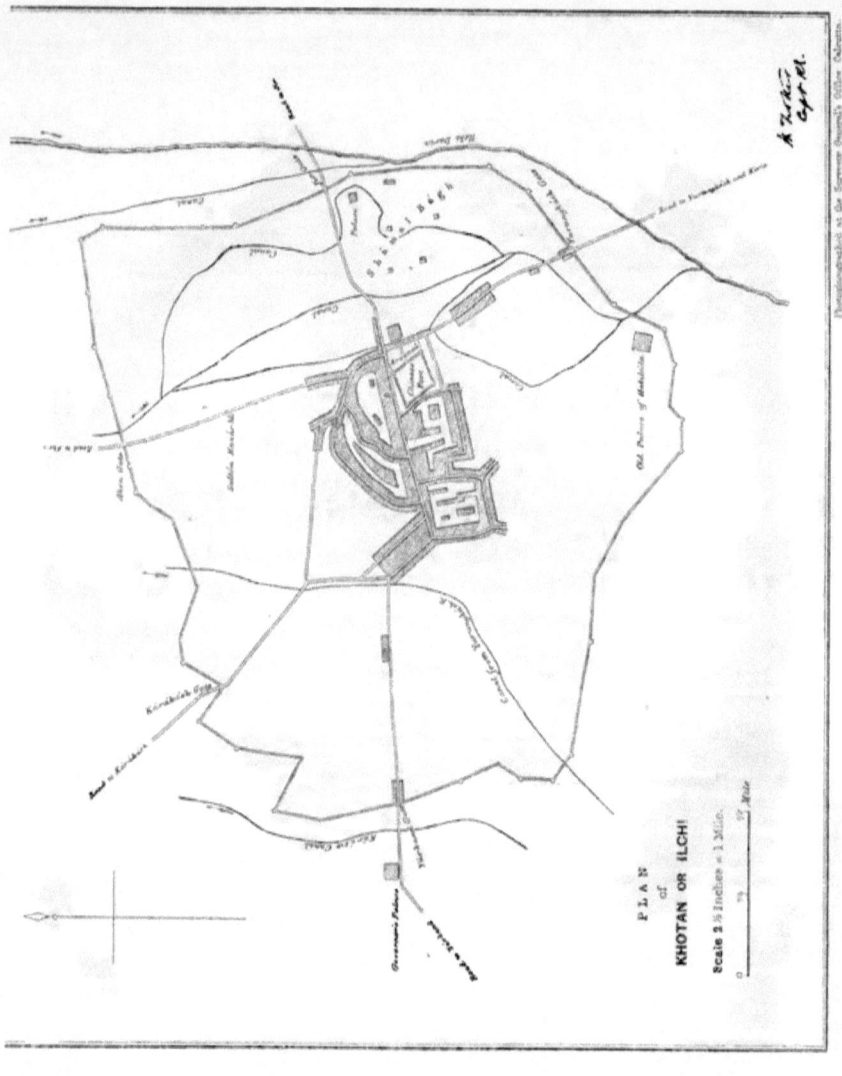

(15)

On the Kárákásh River above Fotash is a camping ground called Sumgal, from which Robert Schlagintweit crossed the Kuen Luen range by the Hindu-tásh Pass, estimated by him at 17,379 feet high. At the top of this Pass is a glacier much *crevassed* and extremely steep. It is a long and difficult march from its foot, to the village of Bushia, where are numerous tents and caves occupied by Kirghiz, and where supplies can be obtained in large quantities. It is eight marches thence to Khotan and the road is described as bad. The road by the Hindu-tásh Pass can only be used by foot passengers.

From all accounts the ordinary trade route between Khotan and Ládakh in former years was, as at present, *viá* the Sánjú and Karakorum Passes. The road from Khotan follows that to Yárkand as far as Zanguia, whence a road goes to Sánjú village direct. Another road from Sháhidúla to Khotan lies down the Kárákásh River, and, going over an easy pass, emerges at Dúba,* a large village said to lie about 20 miles to the south-west of Piálma (on the Khotan and Yárkand road.) The road down the Kárákásh can only be used in mid winter.

We now come to consider the extreme eastern route, *viá* the Chang-thang or "Northern plain." Of this road we have a survey by Kishen Sing Pundit, one of the most important geographical results secured by the mission.† Details will be found in Appendix, Section G., and the road itself is shown on the map accompanying this report.

A traveller from Leh to Khotan might follow the route by the Pangong Lake, along which the Pundit travelled, but he would more probably take a short cut from Lukong to the Mangtza Lake, following the ordinary Changchenmo route to Yárkand as far as the point where that road leaves the Changchenmo valley. Passing up the latter, he would make his way eastward to its head, where an easy pass is known to exist leading on to the high table land beyond. By adopting this road he would save forty miles over the more circuitous road by Noh. From Mangtza the road lies over a series of high plateaux varying from 16 to 17,000 feet in height, crossed here and there by low ridges which rise somewhat irregularly from the surface of the plain which contains numerous lakes, most of them brackish. In latitude 35° 7′ north the Pundit crossed at a height of but little more than 17,000 feet the water-shed of a snowy range, which may perhaps be the true eastern continuation of the Kuen Luen. From the north of the pass the Kiria stream takes its rise; the road follows down it as far as Arash (16,000 feet), but again ascends to the Ghubolik plain, which (17,000 feet above the sea) connects the snowy range just alluded to with another somewhat lower range to the north. This last ridge is a buttress of the vast Thibetan plateau, and in descending the Polu stream from the Ghubolik. At Diwan ‡ (17,500 feet) to Polu, a distance of 28 miles (including windings), there is a fall of about 9,000 feet. Polu is a small village in the Khotan district and from it Khotan (or Ilchi) city may be reached either by the direct road (by Chihar Imám) which skirts the feet of spurs from the elevated plateau above, or the traveller may proceed down the stream to Kiria by the route followed by the Pundit.

Throughout the whole of the road from Khotan to Leh traversed by the Pundit fuel was abundant everywhere, and there was only one stage where there was not a good supply of grass. These facts would indicate the line as one well adapted for the native merchant, to whom time is of no great value. As far as I can learn however from enquiry it never has been used as a trade route on a large scale, the chief reason I believe being fear of the Chang-pas§ or Tagh-lik, wandering tribes of Tartars, nominally subject to the Chinese officials at Gartokh and Rudokh, but probably practically only so far subject to them that they would abstain from committing violent aggression on parties travelling under the protection of those authorities.

---

* Duba is shown on Klaproth's map as a large place about half way between Záwá and Sáajú.

† The only previous account we have of this road is one derived from native information supplied by Mr. R. B. Shaw, and which was published in the proceedings of the R. G. S., No. III. of 1872. This account agrees remarkably well with that given by the Pundit, and every march can be followed on the large scale map I have before me as I write.

‡ Or "Sulphur Horse Pass" so called from its being used by the Polu people when bringing sulphur to Khotan. Sulphur is excavated in large quantities from the ground near the lake in the Ghubolik plain.

§ Chang-pa in Thibetan means *Nord-man* while the Turki name for the same people is *Taghlik*, i.e. *Mountaineer*.

(16)

Habibúla, who was elected King of Khotan when the Chinese were turned out of the country, sent messengers to try and open up this route in 1864. They were seized by the Chang-pa and compelled to return to Khotan with the threat that any subsequent explorers would be put to death. The inhabitants of Keria and Polu go as far south as Ghubolik to procure sulphur. They also go west of this towards the head of the Yurung-Kash (or Ilchi) River where they search for gold and jade, but it would appear that although the Khotanese claim the country up to Lake Yeshil Kul, the head of the Kiria River, as their boundary, yet practically from fear of the Chang-pas they never go quite so far to the south. On the other hand the Chang-pas who probably have equal reason to fear the Turks from the plains, would appear not to wander further north than Rikong Chumik, the ridge to the north of which separates their grazing grounds from plains on the north, through which flows a considerable stream, passed by the Pundit, asserted by his guide to be the head of the Yurung-Kash River.* It would thus appear that owing to the mutual hostility of the two races there is a large tract of neutral ground which is never occupied by one or the other, extending from Rikong Chumik to Ghubolik; here the Pundit saw large herds of yák, antelope, and jungle sheep (*oves ammon*), which had apparently never been scared by the sight of man. Near Rikong Chumik were the remains of numerous huts; others were frequently seen along the road, but fortunately for the Pundit, he did not meet or see a single human being between Ghubolik and Noh, a distance of 244 miles, a circumstance which enabled him to complete his route survey up to Noh† without interruption.

The newly acquired knowledge of this road may perhaps lead to important practical results, but not until our relations with the Chinese Empire, and their too independent subordinates in Thibet, are placed on a more satisfactory footing than they are at present. It is apparent by combining the results of this survey with other information collected by the Survey Pundits during the past few years, that a road exists between the plains of Hindustan and Turkestan which entirely avoids the territories of the Maharaja of Cashmere, and which in the summer months may be traversed without once crossing snow, or without encountering one really difficult pass, such as we know to exist on the Karakorum and Changchenmo routes. Leaving the plains of India at the ancient city of Najibabad (between Hurdwar and Moradabad), the starting point of the old Royal Road stated by Moorcroft to have crossed these same mountain systems, a good road about 210 miles in length, and only crossing one low pass,‡ leads to the Niti Pass (16,676 feet high) over the main Himalayan range. Descending from the Niti Pass, due north into the Sutlej valley, and crossing that river at Totling (12,200 feet) by the iron suspension bridge still existing (said according to local tradition to have been constructed by Alexander the Great), and crossing by the Bogo La (19,210 feet) into the Indus valley at Gartokh (14,240 feet), the road would then follow that river to Demchok.§ Thence it would go over the Jara Pass due north to Rudokh and Noh, and by the newly surveyed route to Polu and Khotan.

Estimating the distance from Najibabad to the Niti Pass at 210 miles, thence to Noh at 275, and from Noh to Khotan (*vid* Keria) 446 miles, we have a total distance of 931 miles

---

* In the map which has been prepared for submission with this report I have not shown this stream as flowing into Yurung-Kash, but I think it not at all improbable that it may find its way through a gap which I have left in the Kuen Luen (just between the letters E. and N. of Luen). I would have inserted it, but it hardly appears consistent with Mr. Johnson's statements as to what he saw when ascending these Kuen Luen peaks in 1865, although, on the other hand, the fact that the river he crossed at Karangolak was a very large and rapid stream would indicate that it probably came from a considerable distance; knowing also as a fact how the Kárakásh cuts through the same range at Shahidula and how extremely difficult it is to form an accurate idea of any mountain range when viewed from a single point, I am inclined to regret that I did not show this stream in my map as the head waters of the Yurung-Kash or River of Khotan.

† From Noh he tried to get to Rudokh, but was not permitted to do so; in fact the inhabitants tried to compel him to return by the way he had come, and it was with great difficulty that he at last got permission to go to Leh direct. Anticipating a search by the first people he should encounter, he had, when nearing the village of Noh, concealed his instruments and papers in a bush. He was duly searched, but of course nothing was found, and he afterwards succeeded in again getting possession of his valuables. In Thibet the great difficulty encountered by persons entering in disguise is always on the frontier, where the examination is very strict. When once allowed to pass into the interior of the country there is little to fear.

‡ The Langar Pass 6,500 feet high which is on the 3rd day's march from the plains.

§ A more direct route exists from Totling *vid* Dankhar to Demchok.

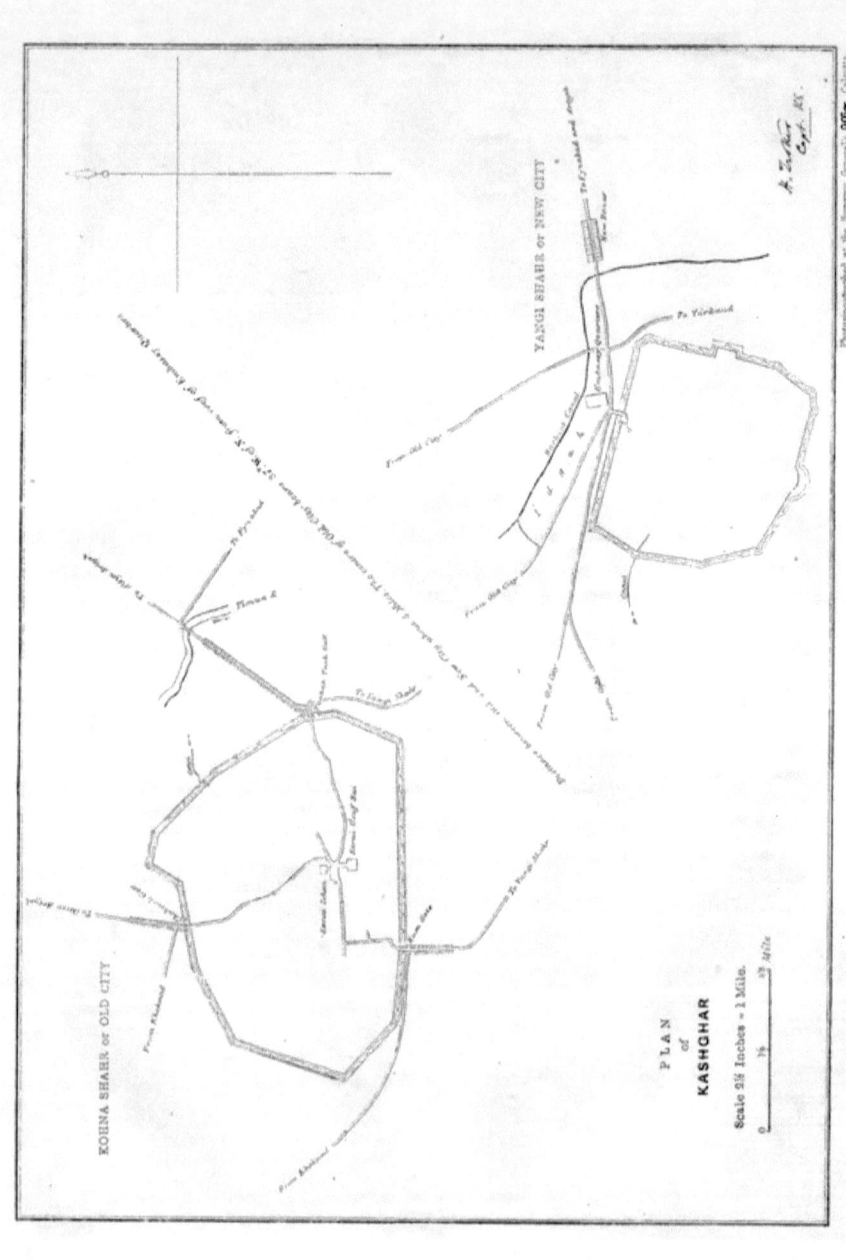

between Najibabad and Khotan, and this even might be considerably shortened by taking the direct road from Polu to Khotan.

[The ancient Royal road probably followed the above to the suspension bridge at Totling, and thence to Rudokh and Noh, whence a road now exists which passes *viâ* the head of the Changchenmo valley and Nischo into the Ling-zi-thung plains, down the Kárákásh river and over the Sánjú Pass to Sánjú (or Sarikia)* which is half way between Yárkand and Khotan.]

Summarizing our knowledge of the lengths of the various physically practicable routes from Hindustan to Turkestan we find that the distances are:—

			Miles.
From Amritsir to Leh *viâ* Rawul Pindi and Srinagar			635
„ „ to „ *viâ* Kangra			522
„ „ to „ *viâ* Sealkote and Cashmere			575
From Leh to Yarkand *viâ* Ling-zi-thung and Karakash River			584
„ „ „ *viâ* Changcheumo and Karatagh			527
„ „ „ *viâ* Karakorum Pass and Sanju (summer route)			445
„ „ „ *viâ* Karakorum and Kugiar (winter route)			472½
„ „ „ *viâ* Noh, Polu, and Khotan			839
„ „ Khotan *viâ* Karakorum and Sanju			415
„ „ „ *viâ* Ling-zi-thung and Elchi Pass (Mr. Johnson's route)			437
„ „ „ *viâ* Noh, Polu, and Kiria			637
„ Amritsar to Yarkand by the road followed by the Mission, *i.e.*, *viâ* Rawul Pindi, Srinagar, Leh and the summer Karakorum route			1,080
„ Najibabad to Khotan *viâ* the Niti Pass and Western Thibet			931

At some distant day it is not impossible that the last named road may form the highway to Turkestan, but as long as Europeans are rigorously excluded from Western Thibet we cannot hope that this consummation will be realized.

Excursions in the neighbourhood of Káshghar.

During the winter at Káshghar I was permitted to make two excursions in the neighbourhood, both of which have enabled me to add something to our geographical knowledge. The second trip was over ground, which, as far as I am aware, has never hitherto been explored, and is very incorrectly represented on existing maps.

During the first of these trips, which occupied us from the 31st December to 10th January, Dr. Stoliczka and myself, under the orders of Colonel Gordon, visited the Russian frontier at Lake Chadyr Kúl, about 110 miles north-west by north of Káshghar. We had hoped, from the extreme point reached by us, to have struck off to the Terekty Pass on the east, and to have returned by the Terekty Forts to Káshghar. Unfortunately difficulties were placed in the way of our doing this, and we had to return to Káshghar by the same road that we went.

Prior to starting, permission was given by the Ámír for me to use my instruments on the road, and I may here mention that from this time forward during the whole of my stay in Káshghar territory I was at liberty to use openly what instruments I chose. Of course a certain amount of caution was necessary. Many of the officials with whom I came in contact were doubtless very suspicious as to what it all meant, yet in no case did any one attempt to hinder my taking observations or notes, although in many cases they endeavoured to neutralize the value of my work by giving me false information on geographical subjects. I allude to this

---

* The three points that have indicated this as the line of Royal Road are:—

1st.—Moorcroft's statement that the road started from Najibabad and emerged in the Turkestan plains at Sarikia (which I identify with Sanju) half way between Yárkand and Khotan.

2nd.—The existence of an iron suspension bridge at Totling said to have been constructed by Alexander the Great (*vide* Major Montgomerie's Report on Trans-Himalayan explorations made during 1867).

3rd.—The statement made by Muhammed Amin, "Punjab Trade Report, Appendix IVA." that—"the old route taken by Moghul conquerors from Tashkend towards China passed through the Aksai Chin. Traces of it are still seen."

E

matter, once for all, as one which gave me much trouble and annoyance during the whole of my stay and travels in Eastern Turkestan.*

It must not be supposed, however, that because I was given permission to use instruments I have been able to turn out very accurate surveys of the countries traversed. The rapidity with which we have always travelled has made it impossible for me to do more than carry on a continuous route survey, checked by frequent astronomical observations taken at night; and even this is sometimes meagre and incomplete owing to the intense cold which we experienced throughout almost the whole of our travels, which made even the handling of a prismatic compass at times an impossibility; this, coupled with the shortness of the winter days, the occasional excessive length of the marches, many of them through snow, and the necessity on these trips of always cutting down both the baggage and the limited establishment of camp servants with which I originally started, must be held to excuse any incompleteness in the maps that I furnish.

During our first excursion the marches we made were as follows:—

		Miles.
From Yangi-Hissár (Káshghar) to—		
1. Besák (Upper Artysh District)		26
2. Chung Terek		20
3. Chakmák Forts		20
4. Balghun Báshi		10
5. Turgat Bela	... ...	15
6. To Turgat Pass and hill above Chadyr Kul and back to (5)		32
7. Back to Chakmak	... ...	25

and back to Káshghar by the same road. I succeeded, with no little difficulty, in keeping up a continuous route survey, and took observations for latitude at four points on the line of march, the most northerly being at Turgat Bela (north lat. 40° 23′ 53″) on which occasion, while observing, the thermometer stood at 10° below zero (Fahrenheit), and an intensely bitter wind was blowing. Later on the same night the thermometer fell to 26°, while inside the *akoee*, (Kirghiz tent) where we slept, it was as low as 8½°, a temperature hardly adapted for carrying on an elaborate Survey.†

We left Yangi-shahr (the new city of Káshghar) and, going northwards, crossed the River Kizil by a good wooden bridge. At a distance of 5½ miles we passed on our left the old city of Káshghar, beyond which we crossed the River Taman by another bridge. This stream passes immediately to the north of the town, and joins the Kizil at a short distance to the east, the two forming the Káshghar Darya. At the time we passed there was but little water in either stream, that little being frozen, so that it was impossible to form any idea of the size of the vast mass of water that must come down in the summer time. The left bank of the Taman is covered by tanneries and cemeteries; the road runs nearly north and enters a narrow lane between two mud walls, on either side of which are enclosed gardens, fields, and hovels. These continue for some four miles, when the road emerges on to an open stony plain forming a very gently rising slope up to a small spur from a low range of hills running nearly due east and west, through a gap in which, formed by the river Artysh, the road passes. On the north side of the range is the wide and fertile valley of the Artysh, a name given to

---

* I may mention that in Kashghar I had been questioning a sepoy, who professed to know all about the Alai and adjacent country, on the subject of the supposed double issue from Lake Karakul. He positively assured me that the waters from it flowed west into the Oxus. A few days subsequently, when talking on the same subject, he assured me with equal confidence that he had seen the place, and that its waters flowed east to Kashghar. He subsequently admitted that he had never been within 50 miles of the lake!

† It may be imagined that taking observations in the open, to stars, with the thermometer standing below Zero, is not a very pleasant occupation. After handling the instrument for a short time, sensation, so far as one's fingers are concerned, ceases, and during a set of observations it is necessary to rush frequently into the adjacent tent to restore circulation over a fire. The recorder, on such occasions nurses the hand lantern with great care, and although the ink is placed inside the lantern, yet it would freeze on the pen between the lantern and the paper. I was eventually obliged to allow a pencil to be used on such occasions. My faithful Madras servant "Francis" also experienced no little difficulty in getting the lamps to burn properly. The oil becomes very thick from the cold. The air holes had to be carefully enlarged for high altitudes, so that while admitting more air, they might still be small enough to prevent the high winds which were frequently blowing, from extinguishing the light.

the whole district, which consists of several small townships scattered over the valley, in one of which, Besák, some five miles beyond where we crossed the river, we put up for the night.

From Besák our road lay for a few miles over fields lying in the broad Artysh valley, but we soon entered that of the Toyanda River, which flows from the Turgat Pass. This stream divides into two branches at the place where it debouches into the Artysh plain— the upper one flows nearly due east, and is extensively used in irrigating the fertile valley; the south or main branch flows into the River Artysh,* which passes along the south side of the valley, and after being joined by the Toyanda stream, cuts through the hills to the south at the gap alluded to in the preceding paragraph. On entering the Toyanda valley, here about two miles wide, we may be said to have fairly entered the Thien Shán mountains, the hills we had traversed on our previous day's journey being an isolated ridge. In marching up this open valley we had in view on our left the sharp serrated edges of the Ming-yol Hill, a prominent object in the panoramic view from the roof of the Embassy buildings in Káshghar; in front of us lay a range of snow-covered peaks also visible from Káshghar; these formed part of a small range running parallel to the main chain (east to west). We passed the old Chinese outpost of Teshek Tásh, or Khitai Karáwal, and a little beyond it the village of Tupa, (or Tapú) near which place through a large ravine on the left, is a road said to come from Kizil-boya, a fort near the head of the Káshngar River. A little further on through a broad open valley we reached the picturesque camping ground of Chung Terek, a Kirghiz village, where were a number of akoees pitched for our reception. From this place the scenery gets much bolder and the road passes between precipitious hills rising to a height of some 3,000 feet above the valley, through which a march of 20 miles brought us to the Chakmák Forts; the road goes steadily up hill, a gentle and regular ascent which continues all the way up to the Turgat Pass, and is passable by laden camels even in "mid-winter." Eight miles short of Chakmák we came across the "Mirza Terek," "Past Kurghán," or "lower fort," a carefully constructed work, which would prove a serious obstacle to an advancing foe. Here as is the case at Chakmák, the overhanging heights are so precipitous and inaccessible that it would be almost impossible for an enemy to effect a lodgment.

The road across the Russian frontier by the Turgat Pass is good, and the slope easy. The road right up to the crest of the Pass was entirely free from snow.† On the slopes near the Pass is an almost inexhaustible supply of grass.

There are two roads over this range of hills converging on a point a few miles north of the Chakmák forts—one from the Suyok Pass, two days' journey in a north-west direction, is little more than a path, and cannot be traversed by horsemen; but the other from the Turgat Pass, about 30 miles to the north of the junction (Suyok Karáwal), is now the main caravan road between Kashghar and the Russian settlement of Almáti (Fort Vernoye), and may be said to be practicable all the year round, although somewhat more difficult perhaps in summer, when there is much more water in the River Toyanda, which has to be crossed some forty times in the course of the journey.

The Suyok Pass is stated on Russian authority to be 12,800 feet above sea level. A fort called Yagachak, covers some road in the direction of the Pass, west of Chakmák, but the accounts of its position were so vague and discordant, that I was unable to fix its position even approximately. A road along a ravine about half-way between Chakmák and the Past Kúrghán was said to lead to it.

Along a ravine lying to the south of the Chakmák forts a road runs across the hills, connecting them with the Terekty Fort, nearly due north of Kashghar. It lies on the shortest road between the Náryn Fort (Russian) and Káshghar viâ the Bogushta and the Terekty Passes.

For 25 miles above Chakmák, the road took us along the course of the frozen stream, passing through volcanic rocks, to Turgat Bela, a little short of which the nature of the country alters, and the precipitous hills are replaced by gently undulating grassy slopes abounding

---
* The Artysh River is said to rise near the Terek Diwan, on the road between Kashghar and Khokand.
† In January.

with the "Ovis Poli" (Ovis Argali of the Russians).* The weather was now intensely cold; one of our party got his fingers frost-bitten from the cold contact of his rifle, and when I stopped for a few seconds on the top of a ridge to get a view of the country, and to record the reading of my aneroid, my hands and feet became entirely numbed.

From Turgat Bela (at an elevation of 11,030 feet above the sea), we rode to the Chadyr Kul Lake, and back to camp the same evening (about 32 miles). Starting early in the morning with the thermometer several degrees below zero, we rode 13 miles to the Pass up a gentle ascent through the broad and open valley, until within a mile of the crest, where the slope though still very easy, is somewhat steeper, there being a rise of about 400 feet in the last mile. On the left of our road was a range of lofty, bold, precipitous peaks, running while near the pass from north-east to south-west, but subsequently in a more westerly direction. The height of these peaks varied from 13,000 to 15,000 feet. On our right were low undulating hills extending away eastward as far as we could see. On reaching the pass (12,760 feet) we did not immediately see the lake, but had to advance for about three miles in a northerly direction, when we came suddenly into full view of the whole lake and the range of mountains beyond, a magnificent panorama. There are two nearly parallel ranges of mountains, the Turgat (sometimes called Koktaw—in Russian maps " Káshghar Daban ") on which we stood, and the Táshrobát to the north, both portions of the Thien Shán range, which westward, like the Kárákorum eastwards, seems to lose its identity and merges into several comparatively unimportant chains of which it is impossible to say which is the main one. The Chadyr Kul lies between these two ridges, and, as far as one can learn from Russian sources, there is no drainage out of it, but several small streams run into it. Their maps include the lake within their boundary, which they place on the crest of the southern or Turgat range, the peaks and passes of which are of about the same average height as of the northern range. The Káshgharees (in Káshghar) claim the lake, and maintain that the Táshrobát range forms the true boundary, but their officials on the spot appeared to take a different view, and maintained that the lake was the boundary. The Ak-sai River, which rises a few miles east of the lake and between the Táshrobát and Kok-tan ranges, flows into East Turkestan, while the Arpa, which flows from a corresponding position near the west end, finds its way into the Syr Darya. This would indicate the lake itself as a good natural boundary, although it must be remembered that the Ak-sai plains to the east, the head waters of the Ak-sai River, which afterwards becomes the Kokshál, are undoubtedly occupied by Kirghiz subject to Russia.

The lake is about fifteen hundred feet below the pass, which would give the former an elevation of 11,300 feet, a result agreeing very nearly with that arrived at by the Russians. From the undulating nature of the low hills to the east of the pass, it was impossible to judge of the direction of the range.

Of course from a single view of the lake and the mountains beyond it, it was impossible to form any accurate idea as to their size, but according to the Russian maps the lake is of oblong shape, about 14 miles in length, and 5 or 6 in breadth at its widest part; its greatest length being from west by south to east by north. From where we stood about three miles north of the pass, the east extremity of the lake bore a little to west of north, while the Táshrobát Pass as pointed out by our guides lay about 17° further to the west. The lake was covered with ice, and the sleet which lay on the surface made it difficult to distinguish the edge of the lake from the nearly level plain by which it is surrounded, and which was covered with a white saline efflorescence. A single horseman near the edge was the only living object visible, a curious contrast to the other side of the pass, where within a few miles of the crest, we had seen a herd of several hundred Cossack ponies grazing at the foot of the precipitous hills before alluded to.

---

* These extensive grassy slopes, somewhat resembling the English downs, are a very curious feature of the country, and not only attract the Kirghiz as grazing grounds for their cattle, but are equally sought after by the large herds of Guljar, in one of which Dr. Stoliczka counted no less than eighty-five.

The caravan road which we **had followed from** Kashghar lay across the plain in front of us. Beyond it is the Táshrobát Pass about the same height as the Turgat, but somewhat more difficult. A traveller who had crossed it in March told me that the road was then **very** bad, and difficult for equestrians, but I think his account must be somewhat exaggerated, as the camel caravans from Almáti traverse it without much difficulty, and the Russians do not write of it as a difficult pass. Between the Náryn Fort and Káshghar, a distance of 180 miles, there are only these two passes—both about 13,000 feet in height. There is a third pass, the Ák Cheta, between the At-báshi River and the Náryn Fort on the Náryn River, but this is, I believe, sometimes avoided by following the Náryn to its junction with the At-báshi, and then proceeding up the latter river to Táshrobát.. When we visited the country early in January there was no snow on the ground, but we were singularly fortunate, for **a** traveller two months later in the year complained of a good deal of snow, while Baron Osten **Sacken** wrote on a former occasion that his party suffered much from cold and snow in July.

A shorter and more direct road between Náryn and Káshghar **is that** over the Ák Cheta, the Bogushta, and Terekty Passes, stated by Captain Reinthal to be **not more** than 134 miles in length, or eight days' journey. The passes, though all about the same height, *i.e.*, between 12,000 and 13,000 feet, are more difficult than on the ordinary caravan road *viá* Táshrobát and Turgat Bela. The Bogashta Pass is sometimes closed in winter. It is covered on the Káshghar side by the Terekty Fort. We never had **an** opportunity of visiting this fort, which lies, as far as I could make out, nearly due east of Chákmak and due north of Káshghar, and although we must have passed within a few miles of it during a subsequent trip in the Artysh districts, my guides studiously avoided pointing it out, and actually, on one occasion even denied its existence. The distance between Fort Náryn and Vernoe (Almati), a military district centre, with large garrison and supplies, is 180 miles by the shortest road, which goes over three passes, all between 12,000 and 13,000 feet in height.

I had hoped that we should have been able to return to Kashghar, over the undulating **plateau to the east of the Turgat** Pass, and by the Terekty Fort, but we had now to retrace **our steps to Kashghar by the road** we had come. A notice of the return journey is therefore unnecessary.

Whilst our party under Colonel Gordon was visiting the Chakmák Forts, another member of the Embassy, Captain Biddulph, paid a visit to *Maralbashi* on the direct road to Aksu. A description of his journey will be found elsewhere. During my **absence Kishen** Sing Pundit, was despatched in company with Sirdar Tara Sing (Treasurer **to the Mission**), on a visit to Khanarik and Kizil-boia, large villages lying to the south-east **of Káshghar**. The Pundit carried **on a** traverse survey wherever he went, which has thrown **some light on** the intricate maze of rivers and canals which irrigate the villages that are thickly **scattered** over the whole of the ground visited by **him**.

My second excursion was **to** the north-east of Káshghar. **The Amír** having granted permission **for a** visit to the Artysh districts, I was enabled to accompany Sir Douglas Forsyth and party **during** their stay there, and on their return to Káshghar, I made a rapid journey in company **with** the late Dr. Stoliczka towards Ush Turfán. Unfortunately on this **trip,** after leaving **the** head-quarters party the weather **was** much against us. Bitter cold was accompanied **by** snow and clouds, which combined to conceal **the** rocks and hills from both Dr. Stoliczka **and** myself, still, as the ground traversed is, *as far as* **I am** aware, entirely **new to** geographical science, a short account ought not to be uninteresting.

We left Yangí-hissár (Káshgar) on the 14th February for Bu Miriam Khána, a village about 11 miles north-east of the old city of Káshghar. The first three miles of one road lay across **a** cultivated and well irrigated plain, and brought us to the banks of the Kizil or Káshghar River, at a place where it was easily fordable; after another four miles we reached the large village of Awát, near which large quantities of salt are collected and taken to the Káshghar market. **Four** miles of level plain brought us **to** Bu Miriam, where we learned that our baggage animals had, by mistake, taken the road to Ostyn (Upper) Artysh, and that we had no chance of seeing them that day. We accordingly pushed on to Altyn (Lower) Artysh, where we found comfortable quarters and a good dinner, provided by our host, the Hakim of the district. Both were welcome, as our own things did not come in till next morning, much to my special annoyance, as the chronometers had all run down in the night, a great misfortune, as I had been very anxious to determine a good *travelling rate* for them, and with that end in view, had taken very careful time observations before departure from Káshghar.

About a mile from Bu Miriam, we crossed the small river coming from Ostyn Artysh, the upper part of whose course I have traced in an earlier portion of this narrative. It (or rather what small portion remains after irrigating the large and fertile village of Beshkerim, which we passed on our left) falls into the Káshghár river near Khush Toghrák, about 25 miles to the east of where we crossed the stream. Five miles further on the road traverses the same low range of hills which, south of Ostyn Artysh, is pierced by the Artysh stream. This ridge, composed of clay and shales, is several hundred feet in height at Ostyn Artysh, but gradually gets lower and lower as it runs eastward, until it dwindles into nothing, and gets lost in the level plain a very short distance to the east of where we now crossed it; a few miles further on, after crossing a small stream supplied from springs on the west, we reached the village of Altyn Artysh, a march of 22 miles.

This village partakes of much the same character as Ostyn Artysh, and, indeed, nearly all the villages I have seen in East Turkestan, consisting of a number of small hamlets, scattered about the plain, at intervals from each other varying from a quarter of a mile to a mile. Each hamlet consists of a number of scattered farm-houses, each farm having its separate irrigation canal, its trees, its fields, and out-houses, and forming the residence of a family containing generally from four to a dozen souls. In a central position is the bazar, with long rows of stalls on both sides of the road, somewhat resembling that of an Indian village, but absolutely untenanted except on the weekly market day. In its neighbourhood the Hakim, who generally owns a somewhat better house than his neighbours, administers justice. Sepoys, if the village be important enough to contain any, are generally quartered near the residence of the Hakim.

The valley in which the two Artyshes are situated runs from west to east, and is throughout about eight miles in breadth; bounded on the south by the low ridge of hills before mentioned which comes to an end south-east of Lower Artysh, it is confined on the north by another and somewhat higher range, which extends eastwards from Teshek Tash on the Chakmák road, to nearly opposite the termination of the southern range, when bending towards the north-east it runs away towards Kalti Ailák, another large group of villages about 22 miles east by north of Altyn Artysh. The valley opens, where loosened from its bounds on the south, into the large desert plain which forms part of the one vast plateau of Eastern Turkestan. The one difficulty, in all this country, is want of water, and one cannot help admiring the ingenuity with which the inhabitants have made the best use of the scanty supply of this precious fluid. Where there is a sufficiency the country is one close net-work of irrigation channels, and in the spring, in these places, one unbroken mass of trees and verdure testifies to the excellence of the system. In the Artysh valley there is water in moderation, and, as far as I could learn, nearly every drop, in the spring and summer, is used in irrigation. In the winter, one sometimes comes across tracts of marshy land, but these are generally caused either by springs which rise in the neighbourhood, or by leakage from canals in autumn, at which time the water is no longer required for irrigation, and the saline nature of the soil causes breaks down and consequent leakage, which it is not considered worth while to repair until the following spring.

In Altyn Artysh, I was informed that there were in all about 3,000 houses forming the following hamlets:— 1, Meshak; 2, Sborchí; 3, Takyun; 4, Langar; 5, Kichingiz; 6, Mai or Táter; 7, Kijja; 8, Bayámát; and 9, Kukíla. It is more thickly inhabited than other parts of the surrounding country, as it forms the seat of the District Government (which includes under it Kalti Ailák and other villages). It is well watered, but the population being large, it barely produces grain sufficient for its own consumption. This deficiency is, however, made up from the neighbouring village of Kalti Ailák, where there is plenty of good rich soil, and a smaller proportionate population, due to an occasional want of water the supply of which is often insufficient to irrigate the whole of the lands. The headman of Kalti Ailák bitterly complained to me, that where there was plenty of water good land was deficient,

(23)

and where little water was met it was often the reverse. This village contains about 1,000 houses, divided into the following petty districts:—Kurghán (the chief centre), Golok, Khush Togbrák, Kuyok, and Jainak.

There are two streams which enter the Artysh valley, the Toyanda before described, and the Bogoz River; a branch of the former irrigates the villages of Beshkerim and Bu Miriam, where the greater part of the water is absorbed; a small remnant however flows eastward, and in favorable seasons finds its way to Khush Togbrák, a southern hamlet of Kaltı Ailák, where it mingles with the canals from the Kashghár River, employed to irrigate that village. The north branch of the Toyanda River is probably almost all expended in irrigating the fields of Upper Artysh, but it is possible that a small quantity may find its way down to Lower Artysh, or at all events may help to form the supply for certain springs which issue from the ground west of that village. The main water-supply, however, for the latter village is derived from the Bogoz River, which rises in the Chakmák range of hills, about 30 miles to the north, but derives a large portion of its water from hot springs a few miles north of the village.

On the 17th of February we started for Tangitár, making a march of about 20 miles in a northerly direction. Following the banks of the River Bogoz, a narrow but somewhat rapid stream, easily fordable, we reached after three miles the range of hills forming the north boundary of the valley. Here on a small isolated mound stand the ruins of an old Chinese fort; a mile beyond this the stream divides, the left (west) branch is the main one and comes from the snows; the temperature of its water was 42°, while that of the right hand one coming from the warm springs before mentioned was 57°. Our road followed the east branch; a path along the other goes to Chung Terek in the Toyanda valley, distant about 32 miles. Continuing our road along a ravine passing through the range of hills (which here have a breadth of about three miles from north to south), we at last emerge on another extensive plain extending like that of Artysh from west to east, and about six miles in breadth from north to south. On the west it was bounded by the hills above Chung Terek, and extended along eastward, as far as one could see, for several miles, merging into the open plain, where the ridge to the south comes to an end. On our right, near where we entered the valley, is the village of Argu, said to contain 800 houses, but from its appearance I should not have judged it to hold half that number. Its water-supply is derived partly from springs, partly by irrigation from the Bogoz River. The road crosses in a north-west direction over a perfectly bare, stony plain, which continues away on the left as far as the eye can reach; one or two houses only near the bank of the river break the monotony and barrenness of the landscape, neither grass nor wood being elsewhere visible. After six miles we enter a gap through which the Bogoz River issues from another range of hills, also running from west to east. Here is another Chinese Karáwul* in good preservation. The road passes to the north along the Bogoz valley through the hills for about nine miles, to Tangitár, 5,800 feet above sea level. The valley was in places of considerable width, and contained much wood and grass, as a natural consequence of which numerous Kirghiz encampments were scattered over it. We passed successively those of Buábi, Bulák, Kuktam, and Jai Ergiz. On our right were some very precipitous hills, forming the ends of spurs running generally from west-north-west to east-south-east.

Our camp at Tangitár, after a march of 20 miles, was at the entrance of a defile, where two small fortifications are perched up on rocks commanding the south entrance. If larger, they might possibly be of considerable use for purposes of defence, but as they cannot hold a garrison of more than 20 men, they could only be useful in keeping in check badly armed Kirghiz or bands of robbers. They are built on the limestone formation which here commences, the hills through which we had hitherto been marching having been composed of clay and gravel.

The situation of such forts, both here and in other parts of the country, are, I think, convincing proofs of the fact that the Chinese in their dealings with the Kirghiz and other robber tribes, nearly always acted on the defensive, and did not attempt to hold the hilly tracts, or claim sovereignty over them. They apparently used to content themselves with posting strong

---

* Karawul is a Turki word signifying "outpost."

guards on their frontier *inside* the lines of hills, which they appear generally to have given over entirely to the wandering tribes. The same facts apply to the hills on the west of the great Turkestan plain, where the line of fortified posts along their base was considered the boundary. This forms a striking contrast to the policy of the present Ruler, who keeps all these tribes in subjection, has disarmed them, and has replaced the former anarchy by peace and quiet.

On the 19th February we continued our way up the stream, here called Tangitár,* through a very narrow defile somewhat difficult to traverse on account of its being filled with ice. After marching a mile or so along this due north, the valley opens, and through a stony ravine on the right comes the main stream from the north-east, while opposite to it, on the left, is an open ravine along which a road is said to go to the Terekty Fort, which *I believe* lay about 10 miles off in a north-west direction. Our own road continued due north for a while, when it edged round to the east over a spur, on rounding which we discovered that we were on the borders of another large open valley, the third we had entered since leaving Káshghar. The view from this spur was very fine; in front of us lay a vast open valley bounded on the north by the snow covered Chakmák range of hills, which, visible about 40 miles off on our left, above the forts of the same name ran in a bold irregular outline from west-south-west to east-north-east, the crest of the range passing about 16 miles to our north, and running away eastward as far as we could see, apparently getting lower and lower as it did so. The broad grass covered valley before us was about 6,000 feet above the sea, and ran parallel to the crest of the hills. Along the middle of it is a low broken ridge running in the same direction dividing the valley into two parts. Small, bare, bold isolated hills also dotted the plain, which was nearly level, draining slightly towards the south. We halted, after a short march of only 10 miles, at Túghamatí, a camping ground situated in the plain, along which we continued the following day in a direction east by north for about 15 miles to another Kirghiz camping ground, called Básh Sogón (head of the Sogón). The road was so level that it was almost impossible to say where we crossed the water-shed which divides the Bogoz basin from that of the Sogón River. The latter has, at this time of the year, its chief source in springs near our camp, but as well as the Bogoz, it must in the hot season get a good supply of water from the snowy range to the north. From a high hill to the south of our camp, I obtained a fine view of the low ranges to the south, but to the north I could not see over the snowy range. The general run of the hills to the south, was from west by south to east by north. It was formed by a succession of nearly parallel ridges starting abruptly from the plain in front, and dying out gradually as they approached the east. A few miles north-west of Básh Sogón, is a largish village called Arkála, near which large numbers of ponies, sheep, and cattle were grazing. We also saw signs of cultivation, which is occasionally carried out in years when there is sufficient water-supply from the melting snow. Throughout the plain there is a good deal of grass and low jungle, and near the camp I saw some small deer (kík), whilst others of the party had good sport in hawking partridges and hares. The nights we spent on this plain were very cold; at Túghamatí the thermometer outside the akoee fell 20° below zero and stood at 16° below zero when I rose in the morning. This great cold was, I think, in great measure attributable to the presence of saline matter in the soil, for our elevation was not much over 1,200 feet above that of Káshghar, where the corresponding minimum was very much higher.

The drainage of the east portion of this large valley runs into the Sogón River, but the supply of water from the hills is apparently very small, owing I presume to the very moderate snow fall. The river, after it emerges into the plains north of Kalti Ailak, wastes away and leaks through crevices in the stony ground, and the Hakim of the latter place assured me that wells had been sunk, but had proved to be of no use, so that the whole of the water from the Sogón runs to waste, if at least we except the small quantity used by the Kirghiz higher up. This diminution in the size of rivers as they descend, is one of the chief characteristics of the country, and occurs in all minor streams that have come under my notice. Of course much of this is due to irrigation, which necessarily carries off large quantities of water, but the stony soil has also much to answer for; on the other hand the frequent appearance of large springs, giving

---

* Tangitár signifies "narrow defile."

considerable supplies of water, and often issuing from the open plains at long distances from the mountains, may account in great measure, if not fully, for the water thus lost in its early infancy.

On the 20th, our march lay in a south-east direction, following the circuitous course of the Sogón through some low hills, for about 15 miles, to Áyok Sogón (foot of the Sogón), a Kirghiz encampment situate at the east of another small plain, covered with grass and jungle and the abode of numerous Kirghiz. This camp is near the direct road from Káshgar to Úsh Túrfán, and it was here arranged that Dr. Stoliczka and myself should leave the main party, and push on in the direction of Úsh Túrfán; as far as the limited time and commissariat at our disposal would permit. It was stipulated however that we were not to go beyond the limits of the Artysh district.

The marches from Káshgar to Úsh are as follows:—

	Miles.	
Káshgar	...	...
Áltyn Artysh	...	22
Kalti Ailak	...	22
Kyr Bulak	...	33
Jai Túpa	...	20
Ui Bulak	...	27
Tigarek	...	17
Ákchi	...	19 — Cross the Belowti Pass between Tigarek and Ákchi.
Kuyok Tokai	...	22
Safr Bai	...	22 — Road from Safr Bai to Bedul Pass across the head of
Karáwul	...	22 the Naryn River to the Zauku Pass, and thence by
Úsh Túrfán	...	16 Karákul to Issighkul.
Total	...	242

From Jai Tupa to Úsh there is said to be an alternative road—

Jai Túpa.
Pichan.
Piklik, over Pass to Guljár Báshi.
Káshgar Tokai.
Kotan Serik.
Úsh Túrfán

This road is somewhat longer than the other, and strikes the Kokshal River a few miles east of Ákchi.

Leaving Áyok Sogón after an early breakfast on the 21st, we passed for a mile over the plain in a south-east direction, and struck the main road; then, turning east went up a ravine, through some hills across a low pass (5,670 feet), and found ourselves on the western edge of another of these large characteristic level plains, 15 miles across from north to south, where we entered it, and extending away eastward further than we could see. It was bounded on the north by our old acquaintance, the Chakmák range, and is probably a continuation of the Túghamatí valley, which apparently narrowed considerably to the east of our camp at Básh Sogón. The main range was here following a more northerly direction than when we had last seen it, but the peaks were involved in snow and clouds, from which they never emerged during the whole of our trip. On the north, at a distance of about 15 miles, was the Kirghiz village of Karghíl, the only habitation visible. Shortly after entering the plain we passed through what proved to be the commencement of a very large forest, composed almost exclusively of poplar trees (toghrak), and a small shrub called " balghun." The poplars were stunted in growth, and although evidently in a natural state, they bore the appearance of having been pollarded. As timber I should not think the wood would be of much value, but it would furnish Káshgar with a plentiful supply of firewood, when the more convenient stocks in its neighbourhood have been exhausted.

Passing along in a north-east direction, a low range of hills at a distance of about three miles bounded the plain on the south. At about 12 miles from our last camp, still traversing forest, we passed on our left the camping ground of Kyr Bulak—inhabited in the summer by Kirghiz, but now untenanted—onwards we pushed our way over a most monotonous flat, and through the bare bleak stems of trees, until after six miles, we came to a slightly rising ground

(26)

called *Dung Jigda Bulák*,* where a little water was oozing from the ground indicating a spring which, with the presence of a "jigda" or wild olive tree, gave the place its name. On over the plain, which in summer would have been pretty enough, but now was dried up and desolate. The forest ceased within about two miles of our camp at Jai Tupa, which was marked by a clump of trees standing conspicuously on an eminence above the plain. We reached it about dusk, after a march of fully 32 miles, through a very heavy sandy road which so delayed the mules carrying our baggage, that they did not arrive till eight o'clock the next morning, having stopped over night, exhausted in the jungle, about five miles short of our camp. Fortunately, we found an old Kirghiz Musjid, in which we went dinnerless to bed, protected, however, from the wind, and from the snow which fell during the night. The officials at the head-quarters' camp had assured us that we should find Kirghiz and supplies at this place, but there were neither one nor the other, and the Diwan Begi,† who accompanied us, spent his whole night (after his day's ride) in going over to the village of Karghíl beforementioned, and hunting up Kirghiz, with whom he returned about daybreak, bringing supplies for man and beast, both of whom had fasted for at least 24 hours. It snowed all the morning, but about noon we pushed on about five miles in a north-east direction to a Kirghiz camp called Jigda, where we obtained further supplies. Snow and clouds prevented our seeing any of the hills around. The forest recommenced about half way between Jai Túpa and Jigda.

The following day (23rd) we pushed on for 22 miles to Ui Bulák, having obtained from the Kirghiz two or three camel loads of grain and other supplies for our future consumption, as we were told we should not come across any more habitations. Just before starting we felt a slight shock of an earthquake, the only one I have noticed during our stay in Turkestan. Our general direction was now north-east. About two inches of snow lay on the ground, and more was constantly falling. After five miles, we saw a low ridge on our right, running parallel to the road, at a distance of about six miles. At its base in what was apparently the lowest part of the valley, was a strip of forest, a portion of the large one that extends right away to beyond Kyr Bulák, a distance of at least 32 miles. Although long, this forest is comparatively narrow, varying, as far as I could judge, from half mile to two or three miles in breadth. The southerly ridge beforementioned is said to extend easterly to Kálpin (about 15 tash)‡ a village between Úsh Túrfán and Marsílbáshi, and to be about five tash from the latter place. At Kálpin, like other ranges that I have traced, it gets lost in the level plain.

Our road now lay through low jungle (balgún) with little or no grass, and at about 12 miles from camp, we reached the limit of the plain and ascended a low spur running from the main range; ground bare and stony. Following this spur in a north-east direction we crossed into an open ravine, about half a mile broad. Ascending it for a short distance we arrived at our camp, near which there was a good deal of grass and plenty of fire-wood. Thermometer at night down to zero.

The next day was fortunately very fine, for we had a hard though interesting journey before us. Leaving our servants and baggage ponies behind at Ui Bulák, Dr. Stoliczka and myself continued our journey in a north-east direction, ascending the ravine, for about eight miles the road way very stony, and some inches deep in snow. Near the head of the ravine we crossed a low pass on a spur from the main range. Descending on the other side we crossed the lower slopes of the main range, passing along which for two or three miles, we came upon another large plain about six miles broad lying between two long spurs. On the further side of this plain, at Tigarek, we had the good luck to come unexpectedly across a Kirghiz encampment, belonging to Úsh Túrfán. Leaving the "Dah-báshi,"§ who accompanied us as escort, to make preparations for our dinner, we procured a Kirghiz guide and started to try and reach before dark the Belowti Pass, which is on the main range that separates the drainage of the ground we had been traversing from that of the Aksai or Kokshál river, which, rising east of Chadyr-kul, flows nearly due east to Úsh Túrfán and Áksú. A march of nine

---

* In Turki *Bulák* is the equivalent for *spring*.
† The designation of the official who was deputed to make arrangements for our party.
‡ A tash here is taken at five miles, but in many parts it scarcely exceeds four miles. See note to Route XII of Section G. of Geographical Appendix.—T. D. F.
§ Or "Commander of ten (soldiers)."

miles, *i.e.*, three miles in a north-east direction across several low projections of a spur running south, then four miles of steady ascent up a ravine to the north, followed by a sharp pull of two miles in a direction 35° east of north, brought us to the Belowti Pass, the goal for which we had been striving. From the pass itself, which is about 11,500 feet above the sea, no view was to be had, but by ascending a hill to the west, some 300 feet above it, I got a very fine view of a portion of the snowy range on the opposite side of the Kokshál river; one peak, nearly due north, stood out conspicuously, of no very great height however, its elevation being only 2½° from where I stood. The range appeared to run nearly due east. Parallel to it at its base lay the deep valley of the Kokshál, apparently about eight miles to the north of where I stood. The road from the pass leads down a steep ravine, at first nearly north-east, and then with a north-westerly course to the river. The position of the next camp, Ák-chi, on the big river, was pointed out to me, bearing 10° east of north, but the man who was with me could not give me a good idea of the direction of Úsh Túrfán or Áksú.

Ak-chi, the first halting-place to the north of the pass, is a Kirghiz camp close to the point where the road from the pass strikes the river. About five miles below it is Kokshál, a large Kirghiz village, between which and Úsh Túrfán, a distance of about 90 miles as far as I could learn, are numerous Kirghiz encampments, all under the orders of the Hakim of Úsh Túrfán. It was a party of these Kirghiz whom we had had the good fortune to encounter on the south of the Belowti Pass.* Near Kokshál, the alternative road from Jai Túpa, before alluded to, joins the river which takes its name from the village. The road is said to be shorter and easier than the one we had followed, but for two days there is no fire-wood. One march above Kokshál (or three marches according to another account) is the fort of Kárá Bulák, above which the Kirghiz subjects of the Amír are not allowed to pass, the ground above being held by the Russian Kirghiz, who in their turn are not allowed to cross the frontier eastward. All these Kirghiz are, I believe, of the same tribe, but being under different rulers are to a certain extent hostile; at all events they are not allowed to communicate with each other.

From Safr Bai, about 38 miles to the west of Úsh, is a road leading to Issigh-kul, by the Bedal and Zaikí Passes. The former of these is on the boundary between Russia and Káshgharia.

There are said to be about 500 Kirghiz families in the Kokshál valley, and about 350 in the valleys north and north-east of Artysh. The Kokshál valley is exceedingly rich in pasture. Its upper waters (the Aksai) were first occupied by the Russians about 10 years ago.

On the range on which I stood there were no high peaks visible, probably none more than 1,000 feet above the pass; the ground on both sides was undulating and grassy, very much resembling that to the east of the Turgat Bela Pass in the same range. It was evident that this range had, as it advanced eastward, become considerably lower, both with regard to its peaks and its water-shed. Like the smaller ranges at its base and parallel to it, I believe it to get lower still, as it goes further east, and at last to be lost in the plains near Áksú.

The sun set while I was at the top of the pass; the thermometer stood at 5° F. with a cold wind blowing, so I was glad to go back to the Kirghiz camp at Tigarek, which we reached at 9 P.M., having made good use of the only fine day we had during our trip. As it was, snow began to fall immediately after we reached the camp. The next day we returned to our standing camp at Ui Bulák; the road was three inches deep in snow, and more falling, accompanied by a bitterly cold wind; next day back to Jigda, 22 miles; weather much the same; next day 25 miles to Kyr Bulák, to which place akoees and supplies had been brought for us from the village of Karghíl, 15 miles off. The following day we marched 29 miles to the village of Kalti Ailák.

The ground we had been traversing is marked on our maps "the Syrt," and is represented as a high table-land. I took some pains to ascertain the limits of the district bearing this name, but could not arrive at very satisfactory conclusions. "Syrt" in Turki means "the back," and is therefore necessarily applied to somewhat elevated lands. The Hakim (Governor) of Artysh included under this designation the whole of the highland districts about Sonkul and

---

* From them we obtained both food and shelter.

Chadyrkul; another authority referred the name more particularly to the plains at the head of the Aksai River. The Kirghiz living in the districts we had passed through seemed to be entirely ignorant of the name, and did not recognize it; but after my return, on asking the Hákim of Kalti Ailák the whereabouts of the Syrt, he immediately replied that I had just come from it, and that the name was applicable to the whole district between Artysh and Ush Túrfán; on his evidence I think the name may remain on our maps where it is. The country can, however, by no means be considered as a high table-land rising immediately above the plains of Turkestan; it should rather be represented as a series of parallel mountain ranges, running, as a rule, from west to east, each one decreasing gradually in height, from the main ridge on the north to the lowest on the south; each subsidiary range also decreasing in height as it goes eastward. Between these ranges and running parallel to them, are extensive level plains, very little higher than the plateau of Eastern Turkestan, but gradually rising towards the north and sloping down towards the east. Thus the Túghamatí Plain, about 45 miles north of Kashghár, is about 2,000 feet higher; while the Jai Túpa plain, the same distance east of Túghamatí, is only 1,000 feet higher than Káshghar. The combined effect is to give a general slope to the south-east.

These large plains have in most cases much grass and fuel, though but little water. From the Sogón eastward we came across no flowing stream. What water is derived from the very moderate annual snowfall seems to percolate into the earth, moistening it generally, and issuing in various places in the form of springs, near which are usually to be found Kirghiz encampments. In the Tigarek plain, at the foot of the Belowti Pass, there are, I believe, no springs; and although there is good grass, the only time of the year in which the plain can be tenanted by the Kirghiz, is that at which we happened to visit it, the sole substitute for water for themselves and flocks being the actual snow, which was then lying on the ground. In the Jai Túpa valley there are water-courses running from north and east, but the supply of water is so precarious that the Kirghiz told me that it was only after years in which there was a more than average snowfall, that they attempted any cultivation at all, and under the most favorable circumstances the extent is extremely limited. There appeared to be no outlet through the hills surrounding this valley, in the lower portion of which lies the forest before alluded to. The moisture in the soil would seem to be sufficient to nourish these stunted trees. Much of the ground in the plain is covered with saline efflorescence, and from near Jai Túpa itself large quantities of crystallized salt are collected and despatched to Káshghar.

The Kirghiz who inhabited the country in the time of the Chinese appear to have led a more jovial life than at present. Under no master, they used regularly to levy black-mail from passing travellers and merchants at every camping ground; and as prompt payment always ensured a safe passage, there was seldom much difficulty in collecting their dues. Under the strict rule of the Amír they are now disarmed, and are comparatively poor, as they dare not venture on any of their old tricks. A single sepoy of the King's, selected from among themselves, is stationed in each encampment, and is responsible for the good conduct of its members; an annual present of a choga, a certain amount of grain, and remission of taxes is the remuneration he receives from the State. The Kirghiz pay as taxes annually one sheep in 40, one sheep for every two camels, and one-tenth of the agricultural produce (when there is any). In these parts horses or ponies are scarce. Nature aids the inhabitants in their poverty by a plentiful supply of a plant called locally kuruk or teric, a kind of millet which grows wild and from which they make a preparation called "talkan" corresponding to the Ladákhi suttoo, which they eat uncooked moistened with a little water. I tried some, and found it to be not unlike Scotch oatmeal, and, as it may be had for the picking it may be looked upon as a bountiful gift of Providence to these otherwise poverty stricken people.

Our march from Kyr Bulák to Kalti Ailák was for a great part of the way down the Sogón River. A kárawul, garrisoned by a few sepoys is situated where the river enters the hills south of the Ayok Sogón plain. The valley occasionally widens out into small grassy flats. After a time, the river is left (it goes off in a south-east direction and is, as before explained, soon swallowed up by the thirsty gravelly soil) and the road traverses some very bleak and desolate broken ground without a scrap of vegetation or sign of life. After passing through these hills and then over a few miles of flat stony desert we reached Kalti Ailák.

(29)

We spent a night there in the residence of the Hákim and went the following day to Khush Tográk, its southern township, about eight miles to the south-east. After arrival there we pushed on two or three miles to the Káshghar River, which we tried to cross in order to shoot in some jungle at the other side; but the ice was now breaking up and was so dangerous that our conductors would not venture to take us over, although the head-quarters party had crossed over a few days before on the ice without the slightest difficulty. Next day we continued our return journey, and forded the river several miles higher than where we had attempted its passage the day before. It took us nearly an hour to cross the river, the combined water, ice, and mud making the passage so difficult that our Turkestani attendants had to strip off their four or five superfluous suits of clothing and go to the assistance of our baggage animals, who, after a good deal of plunging and floundering, at last got across without accident.

Between Khush Tográk and the river there are, at this time of the year, extensive swamps, caused in the manner I have before described. Near this place the waters of the Artysh and Káshghar River mingle together; but in the hot and irrigating season the whole of the water from the Artysh River is said to be expended before reaching the junction, and the Khush Tográk village is then exclusively watered from the Káshghar River.

In the early winter when the ice first begins to form, it partially blocks up the streams and the mass of ice growing larger and larger, great frozen lakes are often formed where in summer there is merely a rapid stream of water. This makes it impossible in winter (the season of our travels) to form any accurate idea of the real size of the streams. After passing the river and crossing a few miles of salt waste we came to Faizabad, a large village on the road between Marálbáshi and Aksu. On this march I saw, for the first and only time in Turkestan, large numbers of geese and duck, all flying eastward.

It was market day in Faizabad, and the crowd attending the bazar was about as large and dense as that I had previously seen at Altyn Artysh, from which circumstance I should infer that the population of the surrounding district is about the same. On the following day (3rd of March) we returned to Káshghar, a march of 37 miles over a perfectly flat country, the road winding almost the whole way through a populous and well cultivated district. We passed successively the scattered villages of Sheaptal, Saug, and Yanduma, every village as usual composed of several hamlets, each with its separate name. At Sheaptal it was market day, but it was too early in the day to be able to form any estimate of the population attending, though on the march we met crowds of people thronging to it. The road crosses several large canals which leave the southern branch of the Káshghar River several miles above Káshghar and irrigate the whole of the ground south, south-east, and east of the city. One of them bears the name of Yamunyar, and possibly a portion of its waters comes from the river of the same name, which, rising in the Little Karakul Lake flows past Opal and Tashbalig, where it divides into numerous branches and canals, some of which probably intermingle their waters with canals from the Káshghar river. The two together form a net-work of rivers and canals which it is nearly impossible to unravel, and which is moreover constantly changing almost from day to day.

From the time of leaving the head-quarters camp at Bash Sogon, the weather was most unfavourable: snow and clouds prevented my seeing the hill tops by day or the stars by night. This lasted until our return to Ui Bulák, 26 miles west of the Belowti Pass. At Ui Bulák, Faizabad and intermediate stations I was more fortunate and was able to secure good star observations, both for latitude and time. These, combined with a rough compass survey which I made of the whole road, have enabled me to map it with a fair amount of accuracy, although the distance traversed during our absence from Káshghar, viz., 340 miles, was accomplished in little more than a fortnight.

Excursion to the Pámír Steppes and Wakhán.

Shortly after our return to Káshghar from the Artysh Districts a party, under the orders of Colonel Gordon, consisting of Captain Biddulph, the late Dr. Stoliczka, and myself, was sent viá Sarikol (Táshkurghán) to Wakhán, and I was instructed to take what advantage

H

(30)

I could of such opportunities as might offer for the increase of our geographical knowledge. The primary object with which the Mission was despatched necessitated a very rapid outward march, and the difficulty of arranging about supplies compelled our return with nearly equal rapidity, giving no time or opportunity for making detours or excursions off the road: with the exception of halts at Panjáh in Wakhán, the furthest point westward reached by the Mission, and at Táshkurghán, where we were compelled to halt for the purpose of resting our cattle, and one day at Ak-tásh for the same purpose, our journey was merely a rapid continuous march from beginning to end. I am induced to make these remarks at the outset, as I have seen paragraphs in the newspapers, and notably in the telegraphic reports of the London Times to the effect that "the Pámír has been completely surveyed," and other similar statements which are apt to mislead the public and induce them to expect a great deal more than has been, or could possibly have been, accomplished under the circumstances.

What I have been able to perform in the way of actual survey chiefly consists of fairly complete sets of astronomical observations, which have enabled me to fix with considerable accuracy the positions of the more important places along our line of march. These places have all been connected by a route survey, executed as carefully as circumstances would permit. I also succeeded in getting good observations with boiling point thermometers and aneroids on all the passes and at all our camps, which, combined with simultaneous barometric readings at Leh should furnish very trustworthy determinations of height. Observations for magnetic dip and declination were made at Sarikol, and for declination only at Panjah. Owing to the necessity for cutting down baggage, servants, and camp followers to the lowest possible limit, I left both my survey khlassies behind in Yárkand, as also all photographic apparatus.

From Yangi-Hissár as far as Táshkurghán I had the advantage of the Pundit's assistance, and he with the Munshi paced the whole road up to that point. The Pundit being a Hindu was not taken beyond Sirikol, but Colonel Gordon obtained permission (from Hussan Sháh, the Governor of Sirikol,) for him to return to Yárkand viâ Chehil Gombáz and the Chárling River. From Panjah the Múnshi was despatched on a special exploration, to be hereafter described. Up to that point I had the advantage of his services as a recorder for astronomical work. On the return journey to India the late Dr. Stoliczka kindly took his place, and recorded for me on several occasions, the last being only a few days before his death.

Before going into the details of my own reconnaissance I may, perhaps with advantage, notice the mistaken ideas * which most geographers have held, at all events until very recently, of the nature of the mass of mountains and high table-lands which separate the provinces of Eastern and Western Turkestan. The labours of the Russian Venuikof, who taking the writings of the illustrious Humboldt for his basis, and working on to them the cleverly constructed but mischievous forgeries of Klaproth, have thrown back the geography of this region into almost inextricable confusion, from which even the recondite researches of Colonel Yule and Sir Henry Rawlinson have hardly yet rescued us. The vague statements of ancient travellers such as Huen Tsán and Marco Polo, who scarcely imagined when they penned their writings, the keen interest with which they would centuries later be studied and criticized, have added to the difficulties of forming a clear and correct idea of the country. The ideas I had myself formed before my visit were vague in the extreme, but perhaps not very much more so than those of others who knew a great deal more about it. Such different descriptions as the following are difficult to reconcile:—

"The Pámír plain extends 1,000 li† from east to west and 100 li from south to north."— *Huen Tsán.*

"The centre of the plateau is "Saryk-kul" out of which there should issue, according to all accounts, the Jaxartes, Oxus, and a branch of the Indus. This plateau, which affords excellent pasturage, extends round the lake for a distance of six days' journey in circumference, and it is said that from this elevation all the adjacent hills appear below the observer."— *Burnes.*

---

* Derived from incomplete and discordant information.
† A *li* is about one-fifth of a mile.

" **For** twelve days the course is along this elevated plain, which is called **Pámír.**"—*Marco Polo.*

"The hills and mountains that encircle Lake Sirikól * give rise to some of the principal **rivers** in Asia. From a ridge at its east end flows a branch of the Yárkand river, one of the largest streams that water China, while from its low hills on the northern side rises the Sirr or river of Khokand, and from the snowy chain opposite both forks of the Oxus as well as a branch of the River Kúnúr are supplied."—*Wood.*

In the last extract, I see how an excellent, careful, and reliable observer like Wood falls into error directly he trusts to what he *hears*; and I must say that from my own experience I have little confidence in geographical information extracted from the inhabitants of Central Asia, **unless from** trained and educated men who are accustomed to take notes of what they see. **I feel** it incumbent on **me** therefore to discriminate clearly between what I have *seen*, **and what I have** *heard*, **and** with **that** end in view I propose first briefly describing that portion **of the country which** has actually come under my notice. **I may** then perhaps hazard a few **remarks on what I have heard.**

We started from Káshghar on our journey to Panjah on the 17th March, reaching Yangí-Hissár (36 miles to the south) on the following day. Halting a couple of days to make preparations for **our** journey, we left on the 21st, starting by the same route by which the "Mirza" **went** to Káshghar from Cabul in 1868-69. Our first march was to Ighiz-yár, eighteen miles; crossing the low broken sand hills that ran down **to** Yangí-Hissár from the mountains on the west, we followed for about three miles the direct road to Yárkand; then crossing the Yangí-Hissár stream at Karabash village we passed in a southerly direction for five miles, over a flat salt waste, to the large but scattered village of Sugat, which it took us nearly half an hour to traverse. On the sandy tract a number of people were digging and collecting a very inferior kind of fire-wood, which is carried off on donkeys to Yangí-Hissár, where fuel is very scarce and dear. From Sugat none of the large mountains on the west were visible on account of the haze; the ridges before mentioned, and another low sandy ridge running parallel to, and on the other side of the Yárkand road, were all that could be seen. Sugat is situated **on a** slope, and our road lay on the bed of a water-course, one of many coming from the Kinkol stream, whose banks we were about to follow for several days' journey. When we passed there was but little water in the stream, and what little came was eagerly swallowed up by **the** thirsty soil. The villagers, on the approach of spring, were commencing to plough **their** lands. As the summer advances the heat increases, and with it the water-supply from the melting snow, which comes at the time when most wanted by the husbandmen **for** their early crops. I was informed that in summer a very small quantity of water trickles from the irrigation canals through a large ravine (which, surrounded by much broken ground, is formed at the foot of the Sugat village) and joins the Yangí-Hissár river. The chief source of supply **of the** river is from a number of springs situated about six miles west by south of the town **from** which it derives its name. I visited them the day we halted at Yangí-Hissár on our journey **to** Káshghar; they are surrounded by several villages, Kargoi, Kona† and Yangi Sálip, and others. At Kona Sálip the bed of the river is dry, and is formed by numerous short **ravines** meeting there. A little lower down, at Kargoi, the banks are fifty feet deep, and a considerable quantity of water bubbles out of the ground; fresh springs issue for a considerable **way** down the river, so that by the time it passes south of Yangí-Hissár there is a considerable **body of** water in the stream, whose bulk is also augmented by drainage from canals supplied from **the** River Kusán which is said to rise in the Kizil Art mountains in the neighbourhood of Tagharma Peak. The temperature of the canals from this stream **was 42°,** while that of the river (from the springs) was 47°. The Yangí-Hissár river, after **receiving** accession to its waters from the Kusán, flows eastward, and is said to lose itself in **the desert** near the villages of Keltarim and Chakar. The river shortly after its issue from **the** mountains **divides** into four artificial branches or canals, the Pasín, the Párách (or Kusán river), **the** Sailik,

---

* Wood's "Victoria Lake."
† In Turki *Kona* means *old*, and *Yangi* means *new*.

and the Tíbiz, the last and southern of these it is whose waters surround the head of, and afterwards mingle with, the river of Yangí-Hissár. There is also no doubt that the waters of the northern branches mingle with, if indeed they are not identical with, the Yámunyár river (also called Tasgún, Khánárik, Oi Kubok, and a host of other names). The latter river issues from or near the smaller of the two Lakes Kárákúl (of which more hereafter) and passes from the hills near the villages of Tash-bálig and Opal. The whole of the country south of Káshghar is cut up by one net-work of canals mingled in such confusion that nothing but a careful survey can lead to a clear comprehension of them* and moreover day by day they alter, and I have often seen one canal (in appearance more like a large river than anything else) eating its way rapidly through the soft soil into another one. These changes are constantly going on, and a map constructed now would be of but little value fifty years hence.

After leaving the village of Sugat the road follows for nine miles, along the edge of a water-course through a stony plain, a narrow border of green showing signs of a scant cultivation. This brings us to our first halting-place, the good-sized village of Ighiz-yar, two miles short of which we pass on the left a conspicuous isolated conical hill with a zyarat (tomb) at top. Before reaching the village a few low hills come in sight on the west, being the ends of the low spurs coming down from the Kizil Art mountains, the first portion of these mountains that we had seen since leaving Káshghar. With our usual ill luck, from the day of our departure, the characteristic Eastern Turkestan haze entirely obscured all view of the lofty mountains on the west, preventing the possibility of forming any opinion as to the shape and direction of the spurs from the main ridge. From Káshghar on a clear day we have often seen the outlines of these hills standing out against the sky, but the distance, to the crest of the range, 70 miles, was much too great to permit of the intervening ranges or spurs being visible. I often longed to make a nearer acquaintance with them, but no opportunity ever occurred for doing so. Fortunately on the upward journey to Káshghar, the Pundit, who followed some days behind us, had some clear days, and was able to fix very satisfactorily the positions of several of the peaks of the main range.

On the second day we marched in a south-west direction, for 18 miles, to Aktala (white plain). The first four miles were up a gently rising stony plain, almost entirely destitute of vegetation, and extending to the entrance of the Kinkol valley, which runs between two spurs of which we had caught a glimpse the previous day. At a distance of two miles up the valley the road passes the foot of an old extensive fortification called " Khatt (lower) Karáwul" constructed by the Chinese on the left bank of the river, to defend themselves against incursions from the Kirghiz marauders from the Pámirs and the Alai. It is built on a commanding position running along a spur which nearly closes up the entrance of the valley. A garrison consisting of only a few sepoys, attests the fact that the Amír's rule has reduced these tribes to order and obedience. Two miles further up is Kichik (small) Karáwul, where a road along an open ravine on the left bank leads direct viá Opal to Káshghar, and a Kirghiz footpath along a ravine on the opposite side leads to Yárkand.

---

* A great source of difficulty in investigating the courses of rivers in Eastern Turkestan is their nomenclature, every portion of a stream having a different name, derived from the nearest village, by which alone is it known to the neighbouring inhabitants. In addition to these purely local designations travellers generally name the rivers after the different large towns situated on their banks, while cosmopolitans have occasionally general names which they apply to a river throughout its whole course, but which are perhaps unknown to the inhabitants of the country. Most rivers are also occasionally known by names expressive their color as Kara-Su, Kizil-Su, or Kok-Su, or Ak-Su (Turki, for black, red, blue, and white rivers), terms which may be seen broadcast in almost any map of Central Asia. No river of Eastern Turkestan carries the same name from its cradle to its grave in the big Tarim Gol or Ergol, which swallows up all the rivers of Eastern Turkestan except those that lose themselves in the desert before they reach it. The final end of the Tarim still remains, and I fear must remain, a matter of mystery. It is generally supposed to flow into Lake Lope (Lob, or Luf); but I have recently heard, on what I considered fairly trustworthy evidence, that at about 25 miles south of its junction with the Karashahr River, i.e., about 65 miles south of Kola (Koila or Kurla), it disappears in the sand near the village of Lop (Lop being I believe a Sanskrit word signifying disappearance). It is further said to reappear in the shape of a large navigable stream at the Chinese city of Saju (? Suchau). I should myself think that it more probably reappears in the marshes and lakes which are believed to exist to the eastward and south-eastward of the still somewhat mythical Lake of Lop. Perhaps Mr. Prjevalski will some day enlighten us on this matter from the east.

Two miles higher is the **Ghijak ravine, along** which a road runs to the Alai and Khokand by the Kárátásh **and Kizil Art Passes***. Another seven miles up the stream brought us to our halting-place **at Aktala. As we** ascended, the increasing bulk of water was very appreciable, partly **owing** to the snow melting under the increased temperature, but also doubtless in some **measure** due to a large quantity being lost in the gravelly soil, which, as I have before had occasion to mention, frequently absorbs much water, that would otherwise profitably be employed in irrigation. We had crossed the river shortly before it enters the plains, and although its banks are there several feet in height, the natural bed immediately afterwards opens out on the stony plain and much water must be lost. The river divides into two main branches, the Odelang to the north, and the Ghalchak to the south. These irrigate the villages on the Grand Trunk Road between Kudok and Yangi-Hissár.

Above Ghijak the road closes in and we get several very picturesque views as we advance. The scenery is very bold, hills several hundreds of feet in almost perpendicular height enclosing the narrow valley. Fuel, water, and grass are in abundance. At Aktala the valley opens and the river branches into two streams of nearly equal size. Some miles up the western branch is the Kirghiz village of Chumbáz, by which a path is said to lead to the Kaskasú Pass. Our third day's march was to Sásak Taka, 13½ miles up stream, by a bad stony road through a very bold defile: there was plenty of wood and grass, which also appeared to be very abundant in some of the lateral valleys. About 2½ miles short of camp, a deep ravine comes in from the east, and the main stream turns to the south-west, retaining that general direction until arrival at the Kaskasú Pass, which we crossed on the 25th March. At five miles above Sásak Taka a stream joins from the south-east called Kinkol, and gives its name to the river lower down. On this day's march (fourth from Yangí-Hissár) we passed numerous Kirghiz camps containing altogether as many as 30 or 40 tents or Akoees; amongst their tenants I encountered some who came originally from the neighbourhood of Almáti. Although passing along a valley bounded on both sides by spurs from lofty hills which rose some thousands of feet above us, the scenery was not so bold as where we had passed through on the previous day; the slopes were more gentle, and numerous grassy valleys entered on both sides, up which we saw many camels, yaks and sheep.

On the fifth day (25th March), we left camp with the thermometer at **7° F.** starting early in order to avoid the slush and water to be expected later on in the day from the melting snow. At first we had a bitterly cold west wind, which however moderated after an hour or so, and we had a very fine day for crossing the Kaskasú Pass. The ridge which we had to cross is a spur from the Kizil Art mountains, and separates the drainage of the Kinkol River flowing towards Yangi-Hissár, from that of the Chárling River, which goes to Yárkand. For two miles after starting our direction was a little north of west, and then for nearly three miles up to the pass nearly south of west. The road leaves the ravine (which is steep and inaccessible) and winds up the side of the valley, passsing round the head of the ravine, and over a flat ridge, at the end of which commences a steep descent of about five miles. The height of the pass is 12,930 feet, and although the length of march was only 10 miles, the baggage ponies did not arrive in camp until late in the afternoon, owing to the slippery descent on the south side, where our loads had to be transferred to yaks. There was a great deal of snow on the pass, as well as on the grassy slopes on

---

* This road is said to cross two passes before it reaches the Kizilart Diwan, and to pass, **by Kichik (little)** Karakul, a small lake probably not more than four or five miles in circumference, from **which a road leads** to Chong (great) Karakul five marches off and probably four or five days' journey in circumference. **This road** is said not to cross any large river but to pass mostly over high table land; abundant supplies of grass **and fuel** exist throughout, and I was told that camels can traverse it the whole year round. It was formerly **used by** merchants going from Yarkand to Khokand but is now closed. A direct road from Yangi Hissar joins it at one day's march from Ghijak at a place called Karatash. Another road leads from Opal (about 30 miles south-west from Kashghar) to the Kizilart Pass and Alai. This road was recently used by an Envoy sent from Karatigin to Kashghar one of whose suite **was** wounded in an encounter with the Alai Kirghiz, **who are** subject to Khokand. The portion nearest to Kashghar is often used as an alternative road to Khokand **when the** Terek **Pass is** closed.

I

either side. The view was very limited, and the deep snow prevented my leaving the road. On our return journey, about five weeks later, the snow was all melted, and there was no necessity for employing yaks.

The camp at Chehil Gombáz was at the junction of the streams coming from the Kaskasú and Torat* Passes, the two forming the Chárling River, along which a direct road goes to Yárkand, now closed against traffic "by order." On the spur between the two streams is an old Chinese building called Khitai Sháhr (Chinese city), a sort of square redoubt built on the steep slope of the hill, presenting a very curious appearance, and reminding one of the perspective pictures of Cæsar's camp, in ancient editions of that author's Commentaries. It was said to have been formerly held by a detachment of Chinese, posted to watch the Chárling passage to Yárkand.

The direct road from Chehil Gombáz to Yárkand† is 132 miles in length. The first march is to Tashkerim, a camping ground 19 miles down the Charling stream. From this place a path crosses the hills to the north, joining at Kinkol, the road we had ourselves followed. The Yárkand road continues down stream for 15 miles to Khaizak passing the villages of Bagh (30 houses), Kiok-tash (8 houses), Mirgul (25 houses), and Joya (15 houses). Between Chehil Gombaz and Bagh (the highest village in the valley) are numerous Kirghiz tents, the grassy valley affording an abundant pasturage to large herds of sheep and cattle, which remain in the valley in the cold weather, but are driven up to higher grazing grounds in the summer. Leaving the Charling stream at Khaizak, the road crosses two low spurs by the Kara Diwan and Kizil Diwan (on which there was no snow in April), and then descending to the bed of the Kizil stream‡ passes over plain and through desert § to Yakirak Kurghan, from which place to Yárkand 23½ miles further on, is a rich, thickly populated, and fertile plain. The Charling and Tashkurghán Rivers unite at Khusherab, five or six miles below Khaizak; the united stream then flows nearly due east, and is said to be met by a still larger river the Raskam (from the Karakorum Pass), at Kosherap, about 20 miles south-south-west of Yakirak.

On the sixth day (26th), we made a short march of only eight miles to Pas Robát, crossing the Pas Robát or Torat (horse's sweat) Pass, which divides the drainage of the Chárling River from that of the Tangitár, which also flows into the Yárkand river. The ascent was steep, and the descent still more so, the slope of the valley being 16° for a distance of about two miles. The height of the pass is 13,130 feet, the rise from Chehil Gombáz being about 3,000 feet, and the fall to Pas Robát about 4,000. While we were on the top the sky was cloudy and a fall of snow obscured the peaks to the north. On the return journey, however, I ascended a hill north of the pass and had a good though limited view in every direction. The ground rapidly rises towards the north and north-west, peaks rising to a height of as much as 4,000 feet above the pass, *i.e.*, to over 17,000 feet. The mountains eastward visibly decreased in height as they approached Yárkand. On my 2nd visit the hills near the pass were covered with fresh, low, short, grass.

About half way down to camp we came upon a number of willow trees (Túrkí, Sugét), which continued in greater or less quantities down to the foot of the hill. In descending the stream we came upon some very thick river deposits having in places a thickness of 300 feet, and containing large boulders of syenite. The rock *in situ* was composed of the same materials, as that through which we had been passing for several days, *viz*: shales and slates.

A stream coming from the north-west had a temperature of 42°, while the temperature of the air was only 24°.

On the seventh day we continued our march up the Tangitár (Pas Robát) River; after five miles we passed on the left bank the Yámbulák stream leading to the pass of the same name, 14 miles off, situate in a direction a little north of west. Our own path lay along the main

---

* Torat or "horse's sweat."
† This road was traversed by Kishen Sing Pandit from whom the information contained in this paragraph is derived.
‡ Nearly dry in winter, but a large torrent when the snow is melting on the hills above.
§ Called "Shaitán Kum" or "Devil's sands."

stream for about five miles more to Tárbáshi, passing through a narrow and dangerous defile. The road was execrable, and we experienced great difficulty and delay in getting our baggage through. This defile would be quite impassable for field guns, and a few determined men might in places defend it against an army. The road often runs along the bed of the stream, which contains large boulders and deep holes of water. In the winter it is probably easier to traverse, but at the time of our passage we had the double difficulties of ice and water to contend with. As far as I could learn the river is never entirely frozen over, on account of the numerous hot springs which issue from the limestone rocks forming its side walls. One of these had a temperature of 125°, and the vegetation in its immediate neighbourhood was much in advance of that lower down the stream, and showed signs of approaching spring. In the summer this road is said to be rendered quite impassable by the floods from melting snow; the alternative route lies up the Yámbulák River.

On the eighth day our road lay alongside the Tangitár stream, which, from Tárbáshi, ascends a gentle slope, bounded on both sides by undulating snow covered hills. The valley rises very gradually for about nine miles, up to an almost imperceptible water-shed (14,480 feet high), by which we reached the Chichiklik plateau, a broad elevated valley whose drainage passes south, through a somewhat narrow defile, to the Táshkurghán river. On the plateau close to the water-shed were two small frozen lakes. The summer road before alluded to which goes up the Yambulak stream enters the Chichiklik plain by the Yámbulák Pass about four miles to the north of where we crossed the water-shed. On the opposite side of the valley, which was between four and five miles wide, in a south-west direction from where we entered it, is the Pass of Kok Maináк, on high spur running down from the Kizilart mountains. By this pass is the shortest road to Táshkurghán, but on our outward journey it was so deep in snow that we were obliged to take the alternative route down the Shindí valley. It is the Kok Mainák Pass that is called "Chichiklik" by the "Mirza," "Fyz Bux," and other travellers, but the correct name as given by the Kirghiz who lived in the neighbourhood is, I believe, as I have given it. Our road lay down the stream. After the first two or three miles, where the slope was very easy, the valley narrowed, and the road became exceedingly steep and difficult, passing for several miles through a succession of rocks and boulders At 10 miles below below the lakes we came to our camp at Balghun, shortly before reaching which the valley had opened considerably although surrounded on both sides by lofty mountains.

The following day (29th), we descended four miles to the junction of the Shindí with the Táshkurghán (or Sarikol or Taghdumbash) River,* just above the Sarikoli village of Shindi, inhabited by Tajiks, and containing about 15 houses, situated in a small well cultivated valley, about two miles long by one broad. Our road now lay up the Sarikol river, but I descended it for about four miles to fix the direction in which it flowed away (south-east by east)†; returning to the junction I crossed the main stream with some difficulty owing to the rapidity of the current, and continued along its right bank, where the road passes through a very wild defile of crystalline rocks, forming almost perpendicular banks about 2,000 feet in height, through which the river winds its way with a most tortuous course. At about 10 miles above the junction we emerged on the north-east corner of the Táshkurghán or Sarikol plain. The road by which we travelled is only open in winter, as in summer the large mass of water in the Sarikol River makes it impassable. The route by the Yámbulák and Kok Mainák Passes is then used.

On entering the Sarikol valley we strike the junction of the Tagharma stream with the main river. The former comes from the plain of the same name on the north-west, and has been incorrectly described by a former traveller as the main source of the Sarikol River. When we saw it there was but little water coming down (temperature 38°), although in summer there is considerably more, but the small size of the water-course, and the evidence of

---

* Sometimes also called Yárkand River.
† From Shindi a path goes down the river, but is only practicable during two or three months in winter.

the inhabitants of the district, all tended to show that the river which flows down the Sarikol valley from the Kanjúd mountains, and through the Taghdumbash Pámír, is undoubtedly the main stream. At the point I crossed, just above the junction with the Tagharma stream, it the river was 15 yards in width, with an average depth of 1½ feet, and a velocity of four miles an hour. Two miles beyond in a southern direction brought us to the village of Chushmán, leaving only five miles for our next day's march (the 10th from Yangí-Hissár) into Táshkurghán, the chief town or rather village of the Sarikol valley. Between Chushmán and Táshkurghán (both on the left bank of the Taghdumbash River) we passed the large village of Tiznáf. It is this village that has caused much confusion to geographers by giving its name to the river, which is frequently called the Tiznáf in its lower course, and is often confounded with another river of the same name which rises on the north side of the Yangí-Díwán Pass and flows past Karghálik.

On approaching Táshkurghán (where we halted two days to rest our cattle), while passing up the valley I saw at its upper end some high peaks occasionally emerging from the clouds, but before I could get to camp they had disappeared, never to be seen again during our stay in the valley, or on our return journey, a great disappointment to me, as it is possible they were peaks in the Muz-tagh range, fixed by the Great Trigonometrical Survey. During our halt at Sarikol I took a set of magnetic as well as the usual astronomical observations, and some careful azimuthal bearings with theodolite to a large mass of snowy peaks called Muz-tagh, situated to the north of Táshkurghán. These are identical with Hayward's Taghalma mountains, which are visible from Káshghar, the highest peak of which I determined by accordant trigonometrical measurements from Káshghar and Yapchan, to be 25,350 feet above the sea.

The general outline of the Tashkúrghan valley towards its head, was fixed by bearings taken from different points on a line across it. On the return journey I was able, by ascending the ridge that separates this plain from that of Tagharma on its north (and by making a detour through the latter on the way to our camp at the foot of the Kok Mainák Pass) to lay down the borders of the northern plain with considerable accuracy. Practically the two form one large plateau divided in the middle by a low range of hills through which flows the Tagharma River. The Táshkurghán plain extends southwards from the dividing ridge before mentioned, right up to the foot of the Kanjúd passes in the Muz-tagh range, constituting in its southern portion, the Taghdumbash Pámír. The Sarikol valley may be said to have an average width of about four miles; it is bounded on the east by the snowy range of Kandár or Kandahar;* on the south-west and south are the Taghdumbash mountains; on the west the Shindí mountains; north-west the Bir-dásh, which also forms the western boundary of the Tagharma plain, to the east of which lie the Muz-tagh (or Tagharma) and the Chichiklik mountains. The Tagharma plain extends from the dividing ridge for about 12 miles in a north-north-west direction; it is only two miles in width immediately north of the ridge, but soon increases in an easterly direction to as much as 10 miles; it then narrows, being nearly closed up by spurs running down from the Bir-dásh mountains on the west and the Muz-tagh on the east. About 10 miles west of this point is the Bir-dásh Pass, over a range which divides this plain from another similar one running nearly parallel to it, viz., the Ak-tash or Ák-su. Opposite the Bir-dásh Pass the Sarikol plain again widens and extends, gently undulating, for some eight or ten miles further in the same direction.† According to statements of the Kirghiz it continues right up to the Kizil Art Pass, which separates it from the Alai, and the valley of the Surkhab River, the most northerly tributary of the Oxus. The height of the valley above sea level may be taken at Tagharma at about 10,500 feet, and I doubt whether it is very much higher in any part of its course. The drainage of the southern portion passes through the Tagharma plain into the Sarikol River;

---

* Over these mountains is a road to Yarkand, which descends into the Tung valley and after passing down it for a march or two, crosses the Arpatalek Mountains, and enters the Turkestan plain near Kosherap.

† Thus far I myself saw, from the ridge dividing the Tagharma from the Tashkurghan Plain.

and in a somewhat central position on its east edge, I would place the lake of Kichik Karakul,* about three short days' march north of Táshkurghán. Further north again, south of the Kizil, Art Pass, is the larger Lake **Karakul,** from which a stream is said to flow westward **into the** M**á**ghábi river. I have shown **in my map,** what I consider the approximate **positions of** the various lakes and mountain ranges in **those** regions, but I of course cannot **guarantee** the accuracy of anything off our own line **of march.**

The Tagharma plain presented a very lively spectacle : **fully** 100 Kirghiz akoees were within view, scattered about in different parts of the valley ; **their** tenants, of the Sark or Syok tribe, **being** subjects of the Amír of Káshghar. Open, grassy, well watered, and speckled **all over** with camels, yaks, horses, sheep, and goats it formed a pleasant sight after the **wilds** through which we had been wandering, **and was a** striking contrast to the Táshkurghán valley, which looked by comparison a picture of desolation, owing to the **numerous** uninhabited villages and tumble down houses with which it is covered. The water **from the warm** springs which issue in numerous places from the earth, causes **the young green** grass **to rise (in** April) in great profusion.

Formerly in the south-east portion of the Tagharma valley, at Kila-i-Tagharma **or Besh Kurghan (the** five forts) there were about 50 houses inhabited by Tájiks, under Sarikól. **Their history has** been a sad one. I got into conversation there with an old man, who told **me that nearly each** fort had its **history. In the principal one, some** thirty years ago, resided **Mahomed Alum, the** Hakim **of Sarikól. He was attacked by a** number of Andijánís from **the** north, himself and many of his **followers** killed, and **the** remainder carried into slavery ; my informant with only one or two others escaping into the neighbouring hills. At the fort where **I was** standing, fifteen **years later, the** Kanjudis had made a raid from the south, and had killed or carried into slavery **the whole of** the inhabitants. Two young men standing by **me** had been carried off **in** this **very raid as** children, and sold as slaves in Yárkand, where they had been released shortly after **the accession** of the Atálik to power, but they had only within the last month been allowed to return **to** their homes, where four Tajik families now represent the fifty that had formerly lived there. They were doing their best, with the help of some of the neighbouring Kirghiz, to put their fields into order, and I there **saw,** for the first time in my travels, the yák yoked to the plough. There is much culturable **ground,** and it is to be hoped that this recommencement of cultivation on **a** small scale is **only** the prelude to a larger.

In the time of the Chinese rule, such was the insecurity in these parts, that the inhabitants of Sarikol dared not wander far from their villages, for fear of being seized and carried off either by the Kirghiz from the Alai, or by their neighbours of Kanjud ; *now* they tell me that if a man drops his *whip* in the middle of the plain, he will find it there if he looks for it a year afterwards. This is a favourite saying amongst the people of Eastern Turkestan, which I have heard more than once employed to describe the sense of security **enjoyed** under the present *régime.*

On our return to Yárkand we passed along the south edge **of the** Tagharma plain. The direct distance from Táshkurghán to the foot of the Darschatt ravine leading to the Kok Mainák Pass is about twelve miles ; thence to the pass itself (15,800 feet) is six miles, by a very difficult and stony road. The pass is four miles from the small lakes on the Chichiklik plain.

The fort of Táshkurghán, said to be of very ancient date, and to have been founded by Afrasiab, the King of Turan, has been described by former travellers who had a better opportunity for inspecting it than we had. The "Takhsobai," **or** Governor, evinced so great a disinclination to receive our visit there, that we had to content ourselves with inspecting it from a distance. The part at present inhabited is apparently of modern construction, and built of

---

* The waters from this lake are said to form the Yamunyar River, which flowing through the Chakar Ághíl defile eastward, under the name of Gez River, enters the plains under the name of Yamunyar, and, as before mentioned, divides into several branches near the villages of Tashballig and Opal and irrigates a great portion of the country south of Kashghar.

stones and mud, but there were in places remains of "roughed" stone facings on the sides of the rock on which the fort is built. In its neighbourhood are numerous **fragments of** broken wall, but I could not recognize any continuous line marking out its former **limits**. Taking a hint from Sir Henry Rawlinson's writings, I kept on the look-out for **Buddhist** remains, but could see **nothing**. The Pandit (who accompanied us as far as Sarikól), seemed to think that the **custom** which prevails throughout the whole country between Turkestan and Wakhán **of heaping** up skulls and horns of sheep and wild animals at the different ziárats or tombs, was a relic of ancient Buddhism. I believe that the custom is common **throughout the whole of** Central Asia. It certainly is so in Ladákh and Eastern Turkestan.

From Tashkúrghán to Panjah there **are two** roads commonly used by merchants; the **first, over the little** Pámir, was followed **by us on the** outward journey, is generally used **in winter;** the second is over the great Pámir **and is** used in summer. The latter is the easier **road**, but passes over much higher ground **than the former** and is impassable for caravans in winter, on account of the deep snow lying on it. **A third** alternative road is by the Tághdumbásh Pámir* at the head of **the Sarikol** valley. **It lies** high, and in midwinter is deep **in snow** in former years it was much used by **the Bajaori** † merchants, who used to go from Bádákhshán to Yárkand by the Taghdumbash and Tung valley roads, thus keeping at the greatest possible distance from the Alai Kirghiz, whom they seem to have feared more than **they** did the Kunjúdis.

On the **Great and Little Pámir** routes the first two marches, *i.e.*, **to the west foot** of the **Neza Tash or Shindi Pass, are common to both lines of road, which meet again** opposite the village **of Zang at the junction of the two large streams which form the Panjah** River, the most southerly **branch of the Oxus**.

Leaving Táshkurghán on the 2nd April, our road lay nearly due west for **four** miles, up a stream which issues from the Shindi mountains through a narrow and difficult defile.‡ The water, which even thus early in the season flows in considerable quantity, combines with the rocky nature of the bed of the river, which has to be crossed and recrossed in numerous places, to make the road exceedingly difficult for laden horses. After passing four miles up the defile we reached **a** camping ground called Jangalik situated in a well wooded open valley, about two miles long by half a mile broad. It is often used as a halting-place by travellers, but we continued up the valley **to Kanshubar, a** march altogether of 16 miles. Shortly before reaching camp we passed **numerous hot springs.** We pushed on the next day in a south-west direction until **we reached the foot of the Neza** Tash Diwan, where we turned westward, and passing over a low spur **continued our** way up the valley, entering a large basin with lofty mountains towering above us on both sides, very bold and precipitous, and of a very peculiar and striking ferruginous colour.§ A stiff pull through the snow to the top of the pass (14,915 **feet** above the sea level) and we were standing on the water-shed between Eastern and Western **Turkestan**.

I had **been given to understand that we should here come in view of** the "**Pámírs**" and was **somewhat** surprised at seeing **in** front of me nothing but a long range of low red colored hills about ten miles distant, a portion of which to the right was pointed out to me as the Great Pámir, **and** another on the left as the little Pámir. Nothing was visible but an irregular mass of **hills whose** serrated tips did not appear to rise more than 1,000 feet above the Pass on which **I was standing**. In front lay a large valley running in a northerly direction which subsequently **turned** out to be that of the **Aksu** River, the principal source, as now appears of the Oxus‖. **The** apparent continuity of the range in front of us was, as we shall hereafter see, a delusion; **the** hills really form the ends of broad transverse ranges, running in a westerly

---

* It is said that Alif Beg fled from Sarikol by this route.
† The district of Bajaor or Bajaur lies to the west **of** Swat, and its inhabitants are well **known** as enterprising traders.
‡ The rocks forming this defile were composed of gneiss.
§ These mountains, Dr. Stoliczka informed me, were composed of triassic limestone.
‖ Which name is perhaps derived, as Venoikof suggests, from Ak-sú.

direction, and separating the various Pamir valleys, which were concealed from our view by the low hills in front.

Descending from the Neza Tash Pass a march of a few miles in a westerly direction, through heavy snow, brought us to our camp at Kogachak, which is about three miles above the junction of the stream from the pass, with the Ak-su River. On the following day (3rd from Táshkurghán) crossing the spur between the two streams we descended into the valley of the Ak-sú, a little north of Ak-tash,* at an elevation of 12,600 feet above the sea. We continued south for six miles up the valley, which was here about two miles broad, and deep in snow. In front of us was a fine range of snow covered peaks, running in a direction a little south of west, forming the southern boundary of the little Pámir, which is really the upper portion of the Aksu valley. The latter as we advanced, gradually turns round south-west by south which direction it retains up to and beyond the lake of little Pamir.

The Little Pámir is generally considered to commence near where we entered the Ak-su stream, and consists of a long, nearly level, grassy valley, varying from two to four miles in breadth and enclosed on either side by ranges of snow covered hills sloping down rather gently towards it. Its length from east to west is about 68 miles. The Great Pámir, and all other Pámirs are as far as I could learn, of precisely similar character. The ground intervening between the Great and Little Pámirs is filled up with lofty mountains of tolerably uniform height and without any very conspicuous peaks, the hills to the west near the junction of the two main branches of the Panjah River being perhaps the highest. Our first halt in the Little Pámir was at Onkul, after a march of 25 miles for a great part of the way over snow, and with such a very bitter wind blowing in our faces, that it was almost impossible to hold an instrument in one's hand. After entering the long straight reach above the turning, near Ak-tash, several large open valleys are passed on the north, where the hills are comparatively low and undulating, those on the south side being generally much higher.

Our second day's march (4th from Táshkurghán) through this Pámir took us along an almost level road for 24 miles. As on the previous day, snow covered mountains lay on both sides as we advanced, and there was a great deal of snow in the valley itself which varied in breadth from 2 to 3½ miles. There was often a good deal of saline matter in the soil, and where this was the case the snow generally melted long before it did so elsewhere. Our camp was on the north edge of the Little Pámir Lake, which has been given by recent travellers the very different names of Barkut Yassin, Chalap, and Gez Kul or Goose Lake (Turki, Oi-kul). I made repeated enquiries as to its proper name, and found that the Wakhis generally call it the Kul-i-Pamir Khurd, or lake of Little Pamir, while the Sarikólis and Yárkandis give it the name of Oi-kul.

As some doubts had been expressed, as to the supposed double exit from this lake, I was naturally very anxious to determine the point, and in ascending the valley on this day's march I took at some twenty different points, observations with aneroid barometers to determine, if possible, the exact water-shed, which from previous accounts I had fully expected to find at the east end of the lake. The ground, however, was so level for several miles there being a rise of only 230 feet in the 24 miles between Onkul and the lake, that the aneroid was not sufficiently delicate for the purpose, and although I walked for a considerable distance on the frozen stream to enable me to satisfy myself on the subject, I arrived in camp on the banks of the lake re-infectâ. The following morning I walked over the lake to its east end, which from a little distance off appeared entirely closed, but on walking round the head to make certain, I was soon undeceived by coming across a very narrow outlet, about nine paces across, and only a few inches deep, all ice of course. I then walked several miles down the stream (east) until I became fully convinced that its bed did slope to the east and drain into the Ak-su. This result being contrary to what I had anticipated, I then rode to the west end of the lake to see whether (as has always been supposed) a stream issued from that end also. I left my horse and started on foot to go round its head; the ice at this

---

* Three miles distant from Kogachak.

end, instead of being firm and strong, as at the other, was very brittle and would not bear my weight, so I had to wade through the heavy snow and slush on its banks. I soon came across a warm spring, from which water was decidedly flowing due east. A little further on I encountered a frozen stream, on going along which westward the barometer showed that I was walking up hill. I advanced still further, hoping to get completely round the head of the lake, so as to be *quite certain* that there was no outlet draining westward, but the walking in the deep snow at so great an elevation had completely exhausted both myself and the man who was with me, and it was with some difficulty that I got back to my horse, and hurrying on with no guide but the tracks in the snow left by the rest of the party, it was with great difficulty that I reached camp, 20 miles from the lake, shortly after dark. On the return journey, the Ressaldar came back by this road, and, according to a promise he had made me, rode completely round the head of the west end of the lake up to the foot of the steep mountain rising on the south side. The snow was then all melted, and water was flowing *into* the lake from the two sources I have just described, and nothing was flowing out. He then went to the east end, whence a stream was flowing towards Ak tásh, so this problem has been solved in a-somewhat unexpected manner. The lake has only one outlet, and that eastward, and its waters flow into the Ak-sú, afterwards the Murghábi, which joins the Oxus near Wámar, *and is in all probability the longest branch of the Oxus.*

I have tried hard to discover the true onward course of this Ak-su River. On our return journey we struck it some 14 miles north-north-west of Ak-tash. It flows thence in a northerly direction for 12 miles and then turns off out of sight north-north-west. It is said to flow in a northerly direction for two marches (say 40 miles) from Ak-tash, after which it either joins, or becomes, the Murghábi River changing its course westward and flowing through the Sariz Pámir to Shighnán. It passes through Bartang, a district of Roshán and joins the river Oxus just above Kila Wámar, the chief town of Roshán.

The Little Pámir Lake is 13,200 feet above the sea level. It lies from south-west by west to north-east by east, and for a length of 3½ miles is from 1 to 1½ miles in width; it narrows considerably eastward, where, for about 1½ miles it is nowhere more than a few hundred yards in breadth. Nearly opposite the south-east corner, in a side ravine is a large glacier which drains into the Aksú stream shortly after the latter emerges from the lake.

The road passes along the north side of the lake and crosses the watershed two miles beyond the west end at a height of not more than 150 feet above the margin of the lake. Other parts of the watershed, which is nowhere well defined, are probably still lower. The descent beyond is somewhat rapid; we passed on our left a small stream which rises near the watershed, and takes the drainage of the hills to the south-west of the lake. We went for about seven miles down an open valley, (crossing several small streams flowing down large open ravines on the north), and reached some deserted Kirghiz huts and tombs called Gombaz-i-Bozai, close to where a large stream, the principal affluent of the Sarhadd branch of the Oxus, comes in from the south-east. This river has it source in the Kanjúd mountains on the west side of the Kárichunkar Pass[*] which crosses the Shíndi or Pámir Range, south of the Neza Tásh Pass, and separates the Taghdumbásh drainage from the head waters of the Oxus.

After passing Gombáz our path lay on the right bank of the Sarhadd stream, where we met with a constant succession of steep ascents and descents. The regular path had often to be quitted in order to avoid drifts of snow, which in places lay very deep. In the winter, when the stream is completely frozen over, its hard surface makes a capital road, which is always used by travellers. We passed at a bad season of the year, too late to be able to keep to the ice with safety as it was now breaking up, and yet before the snow on the upper road was melted. Later on in the hot weather, the lower road becomes altogether impracticable, as it is impossible

---

[*] The road before mentioned which was once much frequented by Bajaori merchants crosses the Karachunkar Pass. It is now but little used.

to cross the then swollen river.* After a while our road left the main valley which makes a detour to the left and ascends a gentle slope to a low pass, crossing which the path returns along another broad valley to our camp at Langar. This point has been considered the end of the Pamír, but I should rather be inclined to consider Gombaz-i-Bozai as the true ending. This would reduce its length from Aktash to about 56 miles.

Our next day's march (6th from Táshkurghán) was to Daráz Diwan, a distance of 15 miles; the road soon struck the main valley and continued along its northern side over a constant succession of ascents and descents, passing occasionally through snow in deep patches. We saw on the hill side a large number of juniper trees, and in some of the side ravines were birch trees and wild roses. In fact, wherever water trickled down there were signs of vegetation, but everywhere else the hills were bare. In one or two places the road descended to the river bank; in places the stream was entirely frozen over, the water flowing underneath, elsewhere it was altogether clear of ice. At two or three such places I estimated the breadth to be about 40 feet, depth 2 feet, and velocity 2½ miles per hour, temperature of water 35°. Before reaching camp was a very steep descent, having a fall of over 1,000 feet, which it only took a quarter of an hour to walk down. The river is here called by various names, Kanjúd, Sarhadd, Panjáb, and *Hamun*. The last name I have heard more than once, and it is of course the same as "Amú." Wakhán seems to be but little better off than Turkestan in the numerous names borne by the same stream. Our seventh day's march (8th April) was at first, as hitherto, on the right bank of the stream, the road crossing high spurs by very steep ascents and descents (which lead me to suppose that this was the road followed by Marco Polo). There are three roads used at different times of the year, one (in midwinter) on the surface of the frozen stream, a second which we followed, occasionally along the stream, but which generally passed over spurs, and a third, much higher up, and avoiding the stream altogether. We passed several small tributary streams and between the fifth and seventh miles we had to cross the main stream many times where it passed through very steep hills. We crossed generally over ice and snow bridges. At last we emerged into a large open gravelly plain watered by several streams and soon arrived at the village of Sarhadd (head of the boundary), the highest inhabited village of the Wakhán valley, and situated about 11,000 feet above the sea. The march was only 11 miles, but difficult. We were here met by Ali Murdan Shah, the eldest son of the Mír of Wakhán, who had marched out from Panjah to meet us. On the 8th day (from Táshkurghán) we took a very short march of only four miles to the large village of Patuch or Patur. From this day forward, in order to avoid all cause of suspicion, I took no observations on the road, but accompanied the rest of the party on the march. We were now a large detachment, as we were always escorted by the Mír Bachcha and his somewhat ragged following. This march was, while it lasted, the most trying I have ever experienced, owing to the intense bitterness of the cold wind and drifting snow which blew in our faces the whole way.

From Patuch to Kila Panjah, the residence of the Chief of Wakhán, there is not much of geographical interest to notice. At Yúr, 15 miles west of Patuch, a very difficult pathway crosses the mountains to Chitral, and at Vost, about seven miles short of the junction of the two Pámír streams, there is a small fort which covers the entrance of a valley up which another footpath leads to Chitral. The road from Patuch to Panjah, about fifty miles in length, lay along the valley of the Sarhadd stream, sometimes on one side of it, sometimes on the other. The valley was bounded on both sides by lofty and generally precipitous mountains, of whose height it was impossible to form any idea, as their tops and the greater part of their sides were always wrapped in clouds and mists. It was perhaps fortunate for me that I was unable to use my instruments, as I know nothing more disheartening to a surveyor than proceeding for days down a valley under such circumstances. Villages were scattered all along the road on both sides of the stream. In the whole distance from Sarhadd to Panjah there are probably about 400 houses, and their corner turrets, like those in the Sarikól valley, are evidence that the inhabitants have not fallen upon much easier times than their neighbours of Sarikól. The houses are not so good as those of Turkestan, and are apparently especially designed to keep out the wind, which seems always to be blowing violently either up or down the valley, generally speaking from west in the

---

* The road by the great Pamir is then adopted.

L

morning, and from east in the afternoon. On entering a house one generally passes through the stables, containing two or three horses or cows, after which one traverses a long winding narrow passage, which leads to the centre of the house which is generally very small and dirty. In the centre is a fire-place, a kind of globe-shaped stove, about $2\frac{1}{2}$ feet in diameter, made of mud, and open in front for the passage of air and fire-wood. Above, is a hole in the timber roof for ventilation. The roof is dome-shaped, supported on cross-beams resting on timber uprights which surround the central fire-place, and help to support the side apartments which all open inwards towards the fire and to one another. Here the different members of the family reside. The larger portion of the house is given up to the females, who, somewhat bashful but good humoured, appear to have a very good idea of keeping the men of the household in decent subjection. The males all wear brown woollen *chogas* or cloaks of country make; *pubboes* or boots of the same kind as are worn by the Ladákhis; loose trowsers of the same material as the coat; and a generally scanty cotton turban, the almost universal colour of which is blue and white. The women, who are not over good-looking, but are pleasant and matron-like, dress very much like the men, and have long plaits of hair falling down the side of their heads. There is no artificial modesty or attempt to conceal their faces. In a cottage where we took refuge the females remained present the whole time we were there, and made some most excellent barley bread for us, kneading the flour into a cake which they plastered into the inner wall of the oven; after frequent turning a capital result was secured. Their physiognomies are very divergent, most of them have Jewish noses, but one boy I saw with a most perfect Greek profile. They all age very early, and attribute their grey hairs to the poverty of the country. The men seem affectionately disposed towards the females, always handing them fruits, sweetmeats, or any little trifles we might happen to give them. They are all poor; money and ornaments seem almost unknown, and hardly anything is seen in their houses that is not the produce of the country.

At Sarhadd the temperature of the water was 32°. At Yúr I found it to be 40° while the stream was about 60 feet in width, one and a half feet in depth, with a velocity of two and a half miles an hour. Near Yúr we passed a large stream on the right, and another on the left bank. Throughout the valley there was much jungle wood, and some old coarse grass, but up to date (April 10th) we saw no signs of spring, neither trees budding, nor grass sprouting. The road throughout is very stony, but not otherwise bad. In many places the tributary streams have brought down immense quantities of stones and *débris*, which threaten to block up the main stream. This *débris* generally spreads in a fan-like shape, from where the tributary stream opens into the main valley, and causes the river to flow round the base of the fan. At Bábátangi, the valley, which from Sarhadd had varied from three miles to one mile in width, is confined by precipitous mountains to a breadth of about one-third of a mile. It soon opens again however, and shortly after leaving Sas (about 13 miles above Panjah) it enlarges considerably, and gradually opens into a considerable plain, being joined a few miles above Panjah by the valley containing the stream from Upper Pámír. Before the junction the Sarhadd stream passes for several miles through rather dense jungle composed of red and white willows.

On our march into Zang (near the junction of the streams) we crossed the river of the Great Pámír here about 30 feet wide, one foot deep, with a velocity of about three miles per hour. It was very considerably smaller than the river we had followed from Sarhadd. Where the streams meet the valley is about three and a half miles wide and almost entirely covered with jungle. It narrows gradually towards Panjah, where it has a breadth of two miles. The height of Panjah above the sea I found to be but little more than 9,000 feet. The vegetation in the valley was very backward, much thrown back doubtless by the violent winds which tear up and down with a bitterness difficult to imagine unless it has been felt. The grass was beginning to show signs of sprouting in the middle of April, and the cultivators were then commencing to turn up the soil preparatory to sowing. The Oxus River flows on the north side of the valley, and on its left bank is Panjah, between which and the mountain range to the south, a distance of nearly two miles, the ground is almost completely covered by fields, irrigated by a stream which issues from a large ravine on the south, and is derived from a large glacier which entirely blocks up the valley in which it is situated, and whose foot merging into a snow bed, is not more than 1,000 feet higher than the Oxus valley.

At the head of the ravine containing this glacier are some snowy peaks, about six miles to the south,* which I estimated to be between 17,000 and 18,000 feet in height, they appeared to be on spurs of the Hindoo Koosh Range. It was most annoying being shut up at the bottom of a deep valley, and unable to get a nearer view of these peaks, but there was no help for it, the ravines entering the main valley from north and south were generally inaccessible, the one on the south being, as I before mentioned, blocked up by an enormous glacier, which was quite impassable, while those on the north are almost vertical chasms which looked as if the mountain had been split up by an earthquake. During our stay at Punjah, I ascended the mountains to the north to a height of about 3,000 feet above the valley only to find that I was on the lower portion of a much higher range behind, which obscured all view further north, while the hills to the south of the Oxus were so high that they intercepted the view of any peaks on the main range of the Hindoo Koosh that might otherwise have been seen beyond; in fact I could see very little more than from the ground below. On the only other fine day that we had during our stay at Panjah I went down the valley for about 12 miles, but saw little more than one or two peaks of the range to north.

Panjah itself is, or rather was, built on five small hillocks, hence perhaps its name,† and I have no doubt in my own mind that the river takes its name from the place, and not the place from the river. These five hillocks are situated near each other on the left bank of the stream, the largest is covered by a fort, the residence of the Mír Fateh Ali Sháh, and most of his followers, the other is of nearly equal size, covered by houses, and surrounded by a strong wall; on two others are small fortified buildings, while on the fifth there are nothing but ruins and graves. These fortified buildings (in one of which resides Alif Beg, ex-ruler of Sarikól) from their near proximity to each other, and commanding situation, form a position of considerable strength, and might hold out against an attacking force for some time if artillery were not brought against them. The Mírs of Wakhán have more than once held out in this stronghold against the forces of the Ruler of Badákhshán to which country they are subject. The whole population of Paujah perhaps does not exceed a hundred and fifty souls.

The district of Wakhan has been described by former travellers. It comprises the valleys containing the two heads of the Panjah branch of the Oxus, and the valley of the Panjah itself, from the junction at Zuug down to Ishkashím. The northern branch of the Panjah has its principal source in the Lake Victoria in the Great Pamir, which, as well as the Little Pámir belongs to Wakhán, the Ak-tash River forming the well recognized boundary between Kashgharia and Wakhán. Both of the Pámirs were thickly inhabited by Kirghiz in former years, subject to Wákhan, but they are now unoccupied, the constant feuds

---

* Their exact distance I was unable to determine, as they could only be seen up the ravine, which has too narrow to permit of a base being measured across it of sufficient length to enable an accurate estimate to be made of the distance of the peaks.

† "Panj" is the Persian for "five." One possible derivation of the word Panjah is given above. Some authorities would derive the word from the five rivers which are supposed to form the head waters of the river on which Kila Panjah stands. There are two objections to this theory:—

1st.— It is contrary to the custom of Turkestan to name a place after a river, and to a hundred cases that I know of where the converse holds good, i.e., a river is named after a place on its banks, I do not know a single instance of a place being named after a river.

2nd.—The word is usually pronounced Panjah, which is nearer in sound to the Persian word "Pinjah" or fifty. The true origin of the word I believe to be from the Panjah or palm (of the hand) of Hazrat Ali (the son-in-law of Muhammad). In a building on a small hill about 2 miles to the south of Kila Panjah is a stone bearing the impress of a hand. Local tradition says that when this country was in the hands of the Zar-dushtis, or atash-parast (fire worshippers) the people were converted to the religion of Muhammad by a visit (in the spirit) from Hazrat Ali, who left his mark on the stone as thus described, which is an object of religious veneration in the neighbourhood. At Bar Panjah in Shighnan is a similar mark over which the Fort "Bar Panjah," "over the Panjah," has been built. Possibly this tradition has something in common with that which attributes the derivation of the word Pámir to "Pa-e-Mír," i.e., the foot of the Mír Hazrat Ali. I would myself be inclined to derive the word from "Pam," the Kirghiz word for roof, and "yer," which is both Turki and Kirghiz, for "earth" corresponding to the Persian word "Zamin." Bam-i-dunya or "roof of the world" is a name by which the Pamir is well known.

between the Shighnis, the Wakhis, the Kirghiz of the Alai, and the Kanjudis, having rendered the country quite unsafe. The highest inhabited village in the northern valley is Langar Kisht, only a few miles above the junction, and on the right bank of the stream. The Sarhadd valley (the southern branch) is inhabited from Sarhadd downwards, and there are villages scattered along both banks of the Panjah river down to Ishkashím. Wákhán formerly contained three "sads" or hundreds, *i.e.*, districts, containing 100 houses each—

1*st.*—Sad-i-Kila Vost or Sarhadd extending from Langar to Hissar.
2*nd.*—Sad Sipanj* from Hissar to Khandut.
3*rd.*—Sad Khandut from Khandut to Sad Ishtragh.

To these three Sads has recently been added that of Sad Ishtragh, which I believe only became a portion of Wakhan in recent times. It lies between Khandut and the State of Ishkashim.† Abdúl Subhán estimates the number of houses in Sad Ishtragh at 250, and allowing 100 for each of the other districts this gives a total of 550 houses, with a population of about 3,000 souls.

The Oxus below Wakhán.

I have now to deal with one of the most interesting geographical problems of the day, *viz.*, the probable course of the Oxus or Panjah from the point where it leaves Wakhán to where it emerges in the plains north of Said village on the frontiers of Koláb, where it has been seen and described by our countryman, Lieutenant Wood. My assistant, Abdúl Subhán, left us at Kila Panjah (the most westerly point reached by the European members of the Mission), and followed the course of the Oxus through Wakhán for 63 miles to Ishkashim, thence turning northwards he followed the same river for nearly a hundred miles, passing successively through the districts of Ghárau, Shighnán, and Roshán, countries which have hitherto been known to us hardly even by name. From his report I have obtained the information following.

The small State of Ishkashim forms, together with Zebák, one of the numerous petty feudal States tributary to Badakhshán. The present ruler of both these small districts is Sháh Abdul Rahim, a Syud of Khorassan, who was placed in power by Muhammad Alum Khan, the present Governor of Balkh. It is said that the hereditary Chief of the country, Mír Hak Nazar, was ejected in order to make room for Abdul Rahim. The present territory of Ishkashim extends for about 16 miles to the north of the village of the same name, which now contains about forty houses, and consists, as is generally the case in those parts, of numerous scattered farm houses. There are small villages throughout this district on both banks of the Oxus; Sumchún and two others on the right bank, and Yákh-duru and Sar-i-Shakh on the left. These belonged to Sad Ishtragh, which was once a separate principality, but is now a district of Wakhán.

The road from Ishkashim runs along the left bank of the river up to six miles beyond Sar-i-Shakh, where the river is crossed by an easy ford. In the month of May the water flowed in a single stream, which was 3½ feet deep and about 200 yards in width. In summer it is impossible to cross the river at this point, and a very difficult path leading along the left bank is followed. Down to this point the valley is open, four or five miles in breadth and richly cultivated. The ford marks the boundary between Ishkashim and the district of *Kucheh Gharau* or "narrow caves," which has been for centuries famous for its ruby mines.

The Ghárau country extends along both banks of the Oxus for about twenty-four miles, and was once upon a time rich, flourishing, and populous. Remains of large villages exist on both banks, and bear witness to the oppression that has been exercised by successive Governors of Badakhshán. The fields near these deserted villages are now cultivated by the inhabitants of the neighbouring districts of Rágh (the chief town of which is Kila Masnúj) and Sar Gholám‡ which are at a distance of a long day's journey on the further side of a range of hills, running parallel to and on the left bank of the river. *Barshár*

---
* Sad-i-Panjah.
† Written in the vernacular Shikashem.
‡ Subordinate to Badakhshán.

or "above the river," situated four miles below the ford, is the first of these large deserted villages. A little beyond it a large stream enters the Oxus from the east deriving its name, the Boguz, from a village of some 30 houses situate ten miles up the stream. From this village a road goes to the Shákhdarah district of Shighnan. Near the junction of the Boguz with the Panjah the road crosses to the left bank of the river. Nearly opposite to Barshár is a ravine by which a road goes over the Aghirda Pass to Faizabad, the chief town of Badakhshán. It is said to be open all the year round. Throughout the remainder of the Gháran district numerous ruins are passed on both sides of the stream, the largest of which, Shekh Beg, on the right bank, must formerly have contained about 200 houses. On the same side of the river some sixteen miles below Barshar are the celebrated ruby mines, once the source of considerable wealth to the Rulers of Badakhshán, but now apparently nearly exhausted. These mines have until lately always been worked for the immediate benefit of the Governors of Badakhshán. At the present time some 30 men are employed there under the orders of a few sepoys belonging to Muhammad Alum Khan, the Governor of Turkestan, who sends the produce to the Amír of Cabul. It was said that during the past year one large ruby about the size of a pigeon's egg was found and sundry smaller ones, the whole of which were sent to the Amír.

The rubies are found in one very large cavern to which there are three entrances, situated about 1,000 feet above the river, and about a mile up the hill side; the task of excavating appears to be not unattended with risks, as three workmen were recently killed, having fallen from the rocks while searching for the precious stones. There is a peculiar kind of soft white stone which is found imbedded in the harder rock and in this the rubies are found. In former years the inhabitants of Gháran who worked these mines paid no taxes and held their lands rent-free. The twenty men who are now employed at the mines have to furnish their own food as well as that of the guard, and also to provide lights, torches, and implements for working. The numerous deserted villages prove the possession of the mines to have been a curse rather than a blessing to the inhabitants of the valley, who have from time immemorial been under the direct rule of the Chief of Badakhshán.

Above the mines is a small village called Koh-i-Lal or "Ruby Mountain," and about one mile below them on the opposite bank of the river is the large deserted village of Shekhbeg whose ruined houses are built with stone and lime.* A small river enters at Shekhbeg on the left bank, and four miles up it lies the village of Gháran Bálá said to contain about 100 houses, invisible from the river. A few miles below Shekhbeg on the right bank of the Panjah is the village of "Garm Chashma" (hot springs) where a large stream of warm water joins the main river. On the banks of this stream the Munshi saw 20 or 30 men employed in washing the sand for gold. They were Badakhshis, and farmed the washings of the Gháran district for Rupees 200† per annum paid to the Ruler of Badakhshán. It is only within the last two years that gold has been found in this district.

Three miles beyond this is the Kuguz Parin,‡ the boundary between Gháran and Shighnán. The road throughout the Gháran district lies along the banks of the Panjah, and is in places very difficult to traverse. The valley near Barshar contracts to about one mile in width, and the road runs over large boulders alongside the river, which flows between nearly perpendicular banks; the stream is narrow and swift being not more than 200 feet across, and is almost a continuous succession of rapids. Throughout the district the Panjab valley is nowhere much more than a mile in width, and is confined by very precipitous mountains; the river is everywhere deep. In Gháran apricots of very large size and fine flavour are produced; these are held in great repute in Badakhshán. Apples and pears are met with in abundance; and but little grain is grown. There is abundance of grass and fuel to be found at the various camping grounds throughout the valley. The water of the Panjab is rarely or never used for

---

* The villages in these countries are usually built of stone and mud.

† About twenty pounds sterling.

‡ Kuguz Parin in Shighai dialect means "holes in the rock." The Persian equivalent is "Rafak-i-Somakh."

irrigation or for water mills. In the hot weather, oxen, horses, and sheep (for which the country is famous) are driven up side valleys to the tops of the mountains for grazing, returning to the valley in October in splendid condition.

Kuguz Parin consists of a tunnel passing through a mountain. On the south side, the road rises by a winding stone staircase, for a height of about 200 feet, to the mouth of the tunnel, which is excavated through solid rock, and is about 100 paces in length, and so narrow and low that it is impossible for a loaded horse to traverse it. The tunnel is said to have been constructed some three hundred years ago. Where the road emerges on the north side the path is so narrow that a projecting mass of rock often precipitates animals into the foaming torrent beneath. The river is here about 150 yards in width, and flows some 500 feet below the mouth of the tunnel.* The Shighnis boast of this place as the natural safeguard of their country, and call it their "father."

From Kuguz Parin the Oxus flows through the country of Shighnán, which extends for a distance of sixty miles down to the Darband Tower on the frontier of Roshán. This tower is situated on a high rock standing over the river, towards which it presents a perpendicular scarp of about 150 feet. The water beneath is very deep. The roadway winds round the tower,† and the ascent on both sides is very steep and difficult. The Shighnis call this place their "mother." It is a common saying in the country that if ever there should be a quarrel between Shighnan and Roshán, whichever State first seizes this tower will keep possession of both countries. The river is here barely a gunshot across, and there is no path whatever on the other side.

This country of Shighnan would appear to be richer and of much more importance than Wakhan and other districts of Badakhshán with which we are acquainted. From Kuguz Parin to Darband Tower there are numerous villages scattered along both banks of the river.‡ These are surrounded with gardens, orchards and well cultivated lands. The chief town, Bar Panjah,§ is on the left bank, and with its suburbs probably contains about 1,500 houses. The palace is inside the fort, and is built of stone; the windows have shutters outside as in Cabul and Cashmere. The fort itself is square, each side being about 500 paces in length. The walls are very strong, and about 40 feet high, built of clay, stone, and wood. There are five loopholed towers, but these contain no big guns. There is a garrison of about 400 soldiers, who are mostly armed with swords manufactured in the country itself, and with guns, said to be made by the Kirgbiz, similar to those which are supplied to the Kashghar troops viz., heavy rifled weapons which are fired resting on the ground, the muzzle being supported on a prong attached to the barrel of the rifle. Lead and all the materials employed in the manufacture of gunpowder are found in the country. The valley at Bar Panjah is about four miles wide and contains a great many houses and gardens. The river runs in numerous channels separated by jungle covered islands. Short punt shaped boats, similar to those in Central India, are used at the ferry. In July and August, when there is much water in the river, all travellers have to cross at Bar Panjah, to the other bank, the road on the left bank being then impracticable.

In its passage through Shignán the Oxus receives two considerable affluents on the left bank, the Shewa and Vacherv River. The former is crossed by a good bridge, and was about 25 yards in width, and unfordable, when the Múnshi passed in May. It flows from a lake in the Shewá Pamir, a favored pasture ground much frequented by herds of horses, sheep, and cattle from Badakhshán. The owners of these flocks are said to make payments to the King of Shighuán for the right of grazing there. The Vacherv River is about the same size as the Shewa stream, and joins the Panjah to the south of Bar Panjah. Along it lies a much frequented road from Shighnan, over the Shewa Pámir, to Faizabad.

---

* This portion of the route is not improbably the *Tangi Badascani* of Benedict Goez.
† At the tower was a guard of soldiers from Wamur, who examines the passports of all travellers.
‡ The names of these villages and the distances apart will be found in the Appendix.
§ Or "above Panjah" so named from having been built originally over a stone similar to the one at Kila Panjah, which was supposed to bear the impress of the *Panjah* or *palm* of Hazrat Ali.

On its right bank the Oxus receives one very large river, the Suchán, formed by two large streams, the Shákhdara and the Ghund, which unite about half a mile before joining the Panjah. The two branches are of about equal size, and the united stream is about two-thirds of the size of the main river, which continues to be called the Ab-i-Panjah. The Suchán stream enters a few miles south of Bar Panjah. The valley opens opposite the junction to a width of about four miles, forming a beautiful well cultivated plain, with a good deal of pasture land, generally covered with horses and cattle from Bar Panjah, which place forms a most picturesque addition to the landscape, situated as it is on a white rock surrounded by trees and gardens, which extend uninterruptedly a distance of about two miles north of the fort.

Both the Shákhdara and the Ghund Rivers have numerous villages on their banks. On the former at two days' march from Bar Panjah is the large fort of Rách, the residence of the Governor (Hákim) of the Shakhdara district, which is said to contain about 500 houses. The Ghund valley, the chief place on which is Chársim, is said to contain about 700 houses. Roads lie up both these valleys to the Pámir steppes. The Pamír at the head of the Ghund valley goes by the name of Bugrúmál, and is possibly a continuation of, if not identical with, the Alichúr Pámir. The direct road to Kashghar up this valley is said to be a much easier road than that by Tashkúrghán.

At Sácharv, nine miles north of Bar Panjah, in the Shighnan valley, the river narrows and becomes turbulent and the road is very bad. Sixteen miles further on is the Darband Tower before described. Beyond it lies the territory of Roshán, a dependency of Shighnan, and ruled by the same King, Yusuf Ali Khan.

Two and a half miles beyond Darband is the junction of the Murghab River with the Panjah. This is the river I have already traced from its source in the Lake of Little Pamir under the name of Ak-su. It is also said to carry away water from Lakes Karakul* and Rang-kul. The Panjah valley, which at Darbaud is very narrow, rapidly widens to five miles, and would be fit for cultivation, but that the ground is frequently flooded by the Murghab River. The Munshi crossed the river about two hundred paces above its junction with the Panjah; the stream was in three channels, and the torrent was so rapid that most of the horses lost their footing. The Panjah stream was very clear, but the Murghab was red, thick, and muddy. The volume of the latter was considerably larger and its velocity greater than that of the Panjah.† From bank to bank the width of the river bed is about one and a half miles, and of this at least one mile was covered with water. The passage was effected with great difficulty. In the summer floods the water is said to extend from mountain to mountain, a distance of not less than five miles; it can then only be crossed by boats.

This river is generally called the Murghab, but it is also known by the name of the Darya-i-Bartang, so called from the district of that name through which it flows. Three miles below the junction, on the right bank of the now united rivers, which still bear the name of Panjah, is Wámur, the chief town of Roshán.

Wámur is a flourishing place; a large Fort‡ about the same size as that of Bar-Panjah, is surrounded by several hundred houses and orchards. Fruits and grain grow in abundance, and the soil is very fertile.

The Múnshi remained several days at Kila Wámur, where the King of Shighnán was residing.§ He was enabled to visit thence the *Fatíla Sang*,|| which together with the ruby mines are described in the *Sir*¶ as the two sights of Badakhshán. It is situated about three and a half miles down the river, underlying the mountains. He extracted

---

* I am myself by no means sure as to whether this river does really receive any water from Lake Karakul.
† This statement of the Múnshi is confirmed by other sources of information which I possess.
‡ With a garrison of about 200 men.
§ The King generally spends the winter months at Kila Wamur returning for the summer to Bar Panjah.
|| "The wick stone," probably *asbestos*.
¶ The "Sir" is a book written by Moulvi Imám Afzál, Khorassani.

some fragments from the rock *in situ* and brought them away. They consisted of a sort of soft fibrous stone which can be twisted into the shape of a wick, and when saturated with oil will burn almost for ever.* From the Fatíla stone he went two miles further down the river to the village of Pigish, the furthest point reached by him. At this point the *Oxus*, which from Ishkashim, a distance of about 100 miles, had been flowing due north, takes a sudden bend to the west, and going in that direction for a few miles turns apparently to the north.

The Roshán territory is divided into three districts—the Wámur on the right bank embracing the upper portion of the *Oxus* valley, and containing about 800 houses. The district of Pa-e-Khoja lies on the left bank of the *Oxus*, below the turn to the west before alluded to, and is said to contain about 1,000 houses. It is at a long day's journey below Wámur. This district is inhabited by *Khojahs*† who pay no tribute, but give their services as soldiers in time of war. The third district is that of Bartang,‡ which lies up the river of that name, and is said to contain about 500 houses. The direct approach to this district from the Panjah valley is very difficult, owing to the precipitous defiles through which the river passes; so that the most frequented road between Wamur and Sirich Fort, the chief place of the Bartang district, lies by the somewhat roundabout way of the Ghund valley.

The Múnshi gives the following particulars about Shighnán:—

"The country of Shighnán and Roshán is sometimes called Zuján (or two-lived); its climate and water being so good that a man on entering the district is said to have come into possession of two lives. The inhabitants state that their country is called Lubnán in the *Gulistan* of Sheikh Sádi of Shiraz, and that it is by this name that their country is known in Persia. Sheikh Sádi writes that 'there is one good Mussulman in Lubnán' (Ek-i-az-Sulhai Lubnán)."

"In time of war, the two countries combined can produce 7,000 armed men, which allowing three men from each two houses would give a present total of about 4,500 for the number of houses in Shighnan and Roshán together."

"The family of the Shah-i-Shighnán originally came from Persia. The first arrival from that country (said to have taken place about from 500 to 700 years ago) was the '*Shah-i-Khamosh*,' who was a Syud and a fakir. The country was at that time in the hands of the Zerdushtis, a very powerful and learned race. The Shah commenced to teach these people the Korán. There were already at this time Mussulmen in the neighbouring country of Darwáz, A.H. 665, and on the arrival of the Shah-i-Khamosh many people flocked thence into Shighnán. In about ten years' time he had converted large numbers of the people, and a civil war commenced which ended in the Shah-i-Khamosh wresting the kingdom from Kahakah, the then Governor of Shighnán and Roshán, under the Zerdushtis, the seat of whose Government was in Balkh. After another ten years the whole of the people were converted to the Shiah religion. The tomb of Shah-i-Khamosh now exists at Bar Panjah. Every Thursday people meet to worship there."

"The Chinese during their occupation of Kashghar used to pay to the surrounding countries a kind of subsidy, in return for which the States to whom the payments were made used to guarantee to keep the roads open, and safe for merchants. For this service the Shah-i-Shighnán used to receive an annual payment of ten *Yamboos*;§ the ruler of Sarikol used to receive six; the Kanjudis four; and the ruler of Wakhán three."

"At one period it is said that Wakhán and Darwaz and all the surrounding States were under the rule of the King of Shighnán."

The Múnshi did not succeed in bringing back much information about the course of the Oxus below Wámur. The furthest point down the river reached by him was Pigish, a village

---

* Probably *asbestos*.

† *i.e.*, whose ancestors are Syuds on one side only.

‡ Or "Above the Narrows."

§ A yamboo is a large piece of silver valued about Rupees 170 or seventeen pounds sterling.

four or five miles below Wámur. About five miles beyond Pigish on the right bank, is the village of Bar Roshán, on the frontier of Roshán. At one day's march beyond this, also on the right bank, is Waznud, the frontier village of Darwáz. Between Waznud and Bar Roshán the Pa-e-Khoja valley before alluded to enters the Panjah valley on the south. Five marches along the Panjah beyond Waznud is Kila Khúmb, the chief town of the country of Darwáz. The road to it along the river is very difficult, and impassable for laden horses, the valley being very narrow, and the banks of the river very precipitous. Kila Khúmb is said to lie in a northerly direction from Wámur and can be reached in three days by a short summer road, which lies up the small stream which enters the Panjah (right bank) at Wámur. The boundary between Darwaz and Shighnán is the water-shed at the head of the Wámur ravine.*

The country of Darwáz possesses villages on both banks of the river Panjah. At Khúmb itself the fort is on the right bank, but some houses are on the left bank of the river. Below Darwáz is said to be the country of Khatlán, the chief town of which is Koláb.

Part of this information, which was supplied by the Múnshi as the result of enquiries made by him, is directly contradictory to the existing ideas of the geography of these regions, and I was at one time disinclined to place much reliance on it. In plotting on paper the Múnshi's route survey, it was found that the course of the Panjah river lies much to the north of the position assigned to it in existing maps. I was at first unable to reconcile this with what little authentic information we have, either from English or Russian sources, but further consideration, and study of the subject, has to a certain extent cleared the matter up. While at Simla, immediately after my return to India, I was examining some old documents in the Quarter Master General's Office, and lighted on a paper of considerable importance. It was a copy of a document well known to students of Central Asian Geography, viz., the route from Khokand to Peshawur, by the Shahzada Sultan Mahomed, an Envoy who came from Khokand to India in 1854. The peculiarity of this individual copy is that it contains a marginal note that six of the halting places on the route, viz., "Faizbad, Naruk, Tootkul, Buljuwan, Kulab, and Surchushma, are on the banks of the River Hamoon, which is called Panj by the natives." In the margin was a note, bearing the initials of no less a person than the present Lord Lawrence stating that the Hamoon was the same as the Oxus. The significance of the document consists in the fact that Lord Lawrence (who was then Chief Commissioner for the Punjab) was the person who originally took down the statements of the Khokandian Ambassador, who, during his stay at Murree, "lived for some weeks within a few yards of the Chief Commissioner's residence, and had frequent and intimate intercourse with him." It is evident that the document I had lighted on was a copy of the original statement as taken down by Lord Lawrence, whereas all other versions that I have seen, of the same route, omit the note that the six places abovementioned are on the banks of the Oxus.

The deduction that I made from this note was, that the Surkháb River probably joined the Oxus or Panjah somewhere above Faizabad and Naruk, and consequently that the latter river took a very considerable detour to the North, as is shown on my Preliminary Map. There were many arguments in support of this view, which it is now unnecessary to enter upon, as one of the Trans Frontier explorers, "the Havildar," has just returned from a visit to Koláb and Darwáz, and although there has not yet been time to plot the details of his work, sufficient is known to prove that the *note* to which I have alluded must be erroneous, and consequently the portion of my map which was mainly founded thereon is also erroneous. The true course of the Oxus will, I believe, be found to occupy a position intermediate between those shown on my map and on all preceding ones.

Return to Yarkánd viâ the Great Pámir.

Our return route to Yárkand lay up the north branch of the Panjah River, which flows westwards from Wood's (Victoria) Lake through a portion of the Great Pámir. Leaving

---

* Four miles above Wámur on this stream is a mine from which a rich iron ore (**kurch**) is obtained. At Bar Roshán also iron is found in large quantities.

Panjah on the 26th of April (the day previous to which was the first warm day we had since leaving Yangi-Hissar, the thermometer in the shade going up to 74° and in the sun to 99°) we made a short march of only six miles to Langarkish (9,350 feet), the highest inhabited spot on the road up to the lake. We passed on the left the villages of Zang and Hissar, between which is a hot spring* (temperature 120°) enclosed in a stone building and said to possess valuable curative properties, for the sake of which the old Mír occasionally visits the spot. I may note that hot springs are of frequent occurrence in these mountains; some near Patur in the Sarhadd valley have a temperature of about 160°. These springs have a sensible influence on the temperature of the rivers they flow into, a fact which tends to neutralize any argument (such as that used by Wood) that the relative elevation of the sources of the two branches of the Oxus, may be estimated from the temperature of the streams at their junction.

Where the two Pámir streams meet opposite Zang, the united river was about 40 yards wide and one and a half feet deep, with a velocity of three and a half miles per hour. This measurement was taken at 11 A. M. at which period of the day the river had not attained its full size and velocity. In the hot weather at Panjah it cannot be forded, but is crossed by rafts made of skins.

Close by the village of Hissar (or Asshor) on a small isolated rocky hill, is the ancient fort (or kila or kalhai) of Zanguebar, which I examined in hopes of finding some relic of Zoroastrian worship. The ruined walls had, within memory, been used as dwelling-houses by the inhabitants of the neighbouring village, but I could discern no relics of antiquity, except fragments of a surrounding wall, and an arch formed by large slabs of stone resting, on either side, on solid rock.

At Langar Kish, a very picturesque village, a fair sized stream from the north joined the main stream, passing through one of those characteristic fissures I have before alluded to. I tried to ascend it, but was very soon stopped by enormous boulders lying in the bed of the stream which flows between perpendicular rocky banks. From this village we had to take all our supplies for the return journey to Sarikól, and as collecting sufficient even for a rapid journey was found to be a matter of considerable difficulty, we had here reluctantly to give up all idea of halting on the road or making any detour for exploration.

Our first march from Langar Kish was about 18 miles to Yumkhana (also called Jaugalik). The road follows the right bank of the river rising above it in several places as much as 1,000 feet. From both sides occasional small mountain streams help to swell the waters of the main river. We passed on our right several ruined huts formerly occupied by Kirghiz, who many years ago abandoned this part of the country. The descendants of the men who accompanied Wood on this same journey, driven away by the insecurity of life and property, are now many of them quietly settled, hundreds of miles away, in the neighbourhood of Kilian and Sanju, under the rule of the Amír of Kashghar. Not a single Kirghiz, I was given to understand, remains even under the nominal sway of the Mír of Wakhan. As we advanced the valley opened somewhat, and the mountains on the south appeared to decrease in height, radiating from a pointed peak situated between the two branches of the Panjah River. After a time we came to the Ab-i-Zer-i-Zamin, a stream flowing from the north-west through banks 1,000 feet in height. We had to descend to the bed of the stream, cross and ascend the opposite side, and then traverse a plain, formed by a broad terrace at the foot of the range on our left, and situate about 1,000 feet above the bed of the Oxus. Four miles after passing the Zer-i-Zamin River we reached our camp, where some springs and rich soil had combined to produce a profusion of grass and fire-wood. From our tents we had a very fine view down the valley, seeing in particular one very prominent snowy peak, probably 20,000 feet in height, situated near the head of the glacier opposite Panjah. Next day we continued along the right bank of the river, passing, after five miles, the Ab-i-Matz, along which

---

* Curiously enough a cold spring with a temperature of 60° F. issues from the ground within a few feet of the hot one.

is the summer road to Shighnan * from the head of the Wakhan valley. This road crosses the Joshmgaz, a very high and lofty pass closed by snow throughout the winter and spring, and proceeds down the Shakh Darah (valley) to Kila Rach, the residence of the Hákim of the Shakh Darah District of Shighnan. From Rách a road continues down the stream to Bar Panjah.

On our own road, two miles beyond Ab-i-Matz, is Boharak, an occasional halting place of caravans, stated by our guide to be the commencement of the Great Pámír. Here, the valley, hitherto half a mile across, widens into a large flat open plain, one and a half miles in width, said to have abounded in former years with the magnificent Pamír sheep (Ovis Poli). Of these we saw nothing but bones and skulls. Severe murrain has within the last few years carried off not only nearly the whole of the wild sheep, but also the ibex. Six miles beyond Boharak was our camp at Yol Mazár (road-side temple), two miles short of which is a large stream joining the river on its left bank, and of equal bulk with it. Near the camp a smaller stream entered on the right bank. I ascended this for some distance and found an open grassy valley in which there were some huts in ruins, and some obvious traces of former cultivation; it was doubtless once the residence of Kirghiz. At our camp, which was at an elevation of about 12,000 feet above the sea, there was plenty of fire-wood and grass, this was the highest point in the valley at which good fire-wood was found, although further up and throughout this Pámír there was abundance of "boortsee" and grass. Two inches of snow fell at night, but the morning, though cold, was fine.

We were now fairly in the Great Pámír; the grassy valley, about a mile broad, was bounded by terraces formed by low spurs coming down in gentle slopes from the mountain ranges on both sides. On the 29th April we continued our march along the Pámír to Bilaor Bas. The road was excellent throughout, as in fact it was the whole way, from Panjah to Ak-tásh, although at starting there are numerous steep ascents and descents. This day's march was along the right bank of the river, through a grassy plain, bounded on both sides by low undulating hills. The valley gradually widens, but the flat grassy portion is nowhere much more than a mile in width, the ascent was steady, and the road everywhere first-rate. Shortly before reaching camp we passed on our left the Ab-i-Khargoshi which flows from and through the Khargoshi plain, beyond which, at a day's journey from camp, is the Alichur Pámír, which nominally belongs to Wakhán, but practically to Shighnán.† In it lies a small salt lake "Tuz-kul" from which no water flows, and beyond which the drainage goes to Shighnán. Two days' march from this lake, i.e., three days from our camp, the Alichur stream is said to fall into the Murghábi. The Alichur Pámír is reported to be higher but smaller than the Great Pámír, and to possess roads going in every direction.

On the 30th we continued along the Great Pámír for 20 miles to Mázar Tupa, the plain getting gradually wider and wider as we advanced, until a breadth of six miles is attained. The valley is not so well defined, as that of the Little Pámír, where steep mountains bordered the plain on both sides. Here low spurs from the mountain ranges north and south run into and are hardly to be distinguished from the plain. The mountains on the south are considerably higher than those on the north, the former rise to about 5,000 feet‡ and the latter to about 2,500 feet above the river bed, giving absolute heights of 18,000 and 15,500 feet, respectively.

The next day five miles of very gentle ascent brought us to the west end of Wood's Victoria Lake, which, like its sister in the Little Pámír, was supposed to have two outlets. Of that to the west there could be no doubt; through a channel some 12 paces wide, a little stream 6 inches deep, and with a velocity of 2½ miles an hour, emerged from under the ice with which the lake was covered, and flowed steadily westward. The temperature of the water was 38°, and

---

* Vide Appendix. Section Routes.

† i.e., according to the statement of the Wakhis who accompanied us.

‡ Elevations of hills were measured with an "Abney's clinometer," which I always used to carry in my pocket. Their positions were fixed by the intersections of compass bearings taken at different points on the line of march; the heights of the latter were determined hypsometrically.

it was thus evident that the lake was partially supplied from warm springs. A few wild fowl were congregated near this end of the lake doubtless waiting for the rapidly approaching warm weather to melt the ice and enable them to proceed with their parental duties.

The lake runs nearly due east and west, is about ten miles long, and nowhere more than two miles in breadth.

The valley in which it lies is, opposite the lake, about four miles broad. The height of the hills to the north I estimated at 3,000 feet above the level of the lake, while those on the south were at least 2000 feet higher.

The only name by which the lake is *well known* to natives is " Kul-i-Pámír Kalan," *i.e.*, lake of the Great Pámír. I have once or twice heard it called " Airán Kul," or buttermilk lake. To avoid confusion, and to make as little possible change in existing nomenclature, I purpose calling it "Kul-i-Pámír Kalan," or "Victoria Lake," the last name being the one originally bestowed by its discoverer, Lieutenant Wood. Our camp, which was about two miles east of its head was called by the "Wákhis" Sar-i-kul (head of the lake), a camp in a corresponding position at the lower end being called "Bun-i-kul" (foot of the lake). This may account for the other name erroneously given to it by Lieutenant Wood (Sir-i-kól).

After reaching camp, a distance of 16½ miles, I went to the head of the lake to investigate its drainage and determine its limits (for from a little distance off it was impossible to discriminate between the ice and snow on the lake, and the snow on shore). I was soon convinced that all the water from the hills at the east end drained *into* the lake, which therefore like its neighbour in the Little Pámír has but one outlet, although in the former case the water flows west, and in the latter east. To the East of the lake the valley opens out, and forms a large basin which extends ten or twelve miles from West to East, and six miles from North to South. At the lower portion of this basin, surrounding the head of the lake, is a great deal of marshy ground formed by the drainage which enters from numerous side valleys,* coming from the hills on the South. At the time of our visit this marsh was covered with snow and ice; but later on in the season, when the snow is melting on the surrounding hills, there is much water, and the place is said to become the favoured breeding place of thousands of geese.

Our march from Sir-i-kul lay along the Northen side of the valley, the whole of which was deep in snow, and was so level that I experienced considerable difficulty in determining the correct position of the water-shed, which was crossed at a distance of twelve miles from the east end of the lake and at a height of 14,320 feet. A frozen stream here comes down from the North, divided into two portions by a low ridge of gravel, one flowing eastward into the Aksu River, the other westward into the lake.

Eastward from the water-shed the Great Pámír valley contracts. We followed down a rivulet which, shortly before passing the camp at Shásh Tupa, joins a considerable stream coming down a broad valley from the North. The name of our camp was derived from the "Shásh Tupa" or "six hills" by which it is surrounded, and between each pair of which roads issue to different parts of the Pámír steppes.

Our road from Shásh Túpa lay for nearly eight miles due north on the right bank of the stream, and then continued down it for ten miles in a north-east direction to the camp "Dahn-i-Isligh."† On our left we passed three broad open ravines, containing streams coming from the west; one of them was nearly as large as the river we were following, and before joining

---

* Up one of these valleys is a road across the hills to Langar in the Great Pamir. One good day's march takes the traveller over the Warram Kotal (Pass), another half day to Langar, and another half day to Sarhadd (horse marches). This is the road by which a very short time ago Jehandar Shah, the Ex-Mir of Badakhshan, when attacked by the Cabul troops, fled, accompanied by several hundred followers, to Yassin. His shorter route from Panjah would doubtless have been up the Sarhadd valley, but anticipating that he would be intercepted on that line, he made the long detour above mentioned, passing through uninhabited country the whole way from Langar Kish, and striking the Little Pamir at a considerable distance above Sarhadd, instead of having to fight his way up to the latter place.

† "Mouth of the Isligh."

(53)

it passed through a plain some six miles long and two broad. At Dahn-i-Isligh the river is joined by two more streams, the Kizil Robat coming from the south-east, and the Karasu from the west, both of which pass through broad grassy valleys. The ground is very open, and may be traversed in almost every direction. Two or three miles north-east of our Camp the Great Pámír terminates, having extended for a distance of some 90 miles from Boharak.

From Dahn-i-Isligh I took a path which follows the Isligh stream, until it emerges into the Aksu plain; this road is somewhat circuitous, and the rest of the party took a shorter line, going over a low pass, and rejoined the main stream about 16 miles from our starting point. The path I followed is rarely used by travellers; in summer it is quite impassable on account of floods. When I went down it (in April) the ice was breaking up, and travelling was somewhat dangerous, as the river had to be crossed many times. The hills on the north are very precipitous, and in places rise nearly perpendicularly to a height of some 2,000 feet above the river bed. Where the two paths unite, the valley opens, and down it a good road leads to the Aksu plain, which is crossed diagonally in a S.-E. direction. Prior to reaching our camp at Ak-tásh we had much difficulty in crossing the Aksu River, which was much swollen by melting snow. On this march (37 miles in length) I had the good fortune to shoot an "Ovis Poli," the only one that has fallen to the rifles of our party.

At Ak-tásh we rejoined the road we had followed on our outward journey, and returned by it, to Tashkurghán and Yárkand making the slight variations in our route, to which I have already alluded.

It appears from the foregoing narrative that although the name Pámír has been inaccurately employed as a generic term covering the whole of the elevated mass lying between the Hindu Kush and the mountains of Khokand, yet it is rightly applied to some of the *steppes* which occupy a large portion of this region. These steppes would appear to be a series of broad undulating grassy valleys, formed on the surface of an elevated plain, by lofty ridges running more or less parallel to the equator. The general slope of the plateau is from east to west. Its eastern portion is gently undulating, and comparatively flat, while its western edge merges into spurs, which slope down gradually to the west, and are separated by bold and precipitous defiles. On the east the Pámír steppes are bounded by a transverse ridge, which has been appropriately termed the Pámír range by Pundit Manphul. This ridge runs in a direction from south-south-west to north-north-east and is the true watershed between Eastern and Western Turkestan; at the Neza Tash Pass where we crossed it, the watershed is very clearly defined; the ridge was seen trending as far north as latitude 38° 15'; it appeared to sink gradually, and I was informed by Kirghiz that it eventually subsided to the level of the Kizil-art plains a little short of the Great Karákul (lake) in which vicinity a difference of level of a few feet may probably determine the flow of water, either into the Sea of Aral in Western Turkestan, or into the semi-mythical lake of Lop, on the confines of China.

To the east of the Pámír range there is an extensive plateau, which stretches from the Muztagh range of the Himalaya mountains up to the South Khokand range—the Trans-Alai of Fedchenko—in the parallel of $39\frac{1}{4}°$. Portions of it are designated in order from south to north as the Taghdumbásh Pámír, the Sarikol or Tashkurghan valley, the Tagharma, and the Kízil-art plains. This plateau is in turn bounded on the east by the range to which Hayward gave the name of the Kízil-art, the name by which it is known to the inhabitants of Kashghar, and which runs nearly parallel to Pandit Manphul's Pámír range. Fedchenko has questioned the existence of the Kízil-art range in the following words:—"Hayward's researches seem to point to a meridional range to the west of Kashgar, but he only saw these mountains in the distance, and covered entirely with winter snow, which is very misleading as regards direction. Therefore his statement regarding a meridional Kizil-art range with steep easterly declivities appears to me very untrustworthy. When you have the ends of a chain facing you they appear, when covered with snow and seen *en face* to form a consecutive chain running in a direction perpendicular to the line of sight of the beholder." But all the information I have obtained decidedly corroborates Hayward's views, which are also shared by Mr. Shaw I have every reason to believe that the magnificent line of snowy peaks which is viewed from Kashghar, constitutes a meridional chain of mountains, instead of being composed of the tail ends of a series of longitudinal chains. It is broken through nearly at right angles by the Yamunyar river, which brings down the drainage of the Little Karakul Lake and the contiguous portion of the Kizil-art plain, just as the Kuen Luen and many of the Himalayan ranges are broken through by rivers whose sources are in the upper table-lands.

The positions of several peaks of the Kizil-art range were fixed by numerous bearings, taken from points along the road between Yárkand and Káshghar, and the four most conspicuous ones, embracing a length of 52 miles were found to lie almost exactly in one straight line having a direction of about 30° west of the true meridian. The most southerly and the highest of these, the Tagharma peak * of Hayward I ascertained trigonometrically to be 25,350 feet above sea level, while two others are at least 22,500 feet high.

From the Tagharma peak southwards the range diminishes very much in height. On our return journey we crossed the Chichiklik mountains (which may be considered as a continuation of the same range) at the Kok-Mainák Pass at an elevation of 15,670 feet; whilst further south the same mountains are pierced by the Tashkurghan river at a height of about 10,000 feet. Little is known of the range further south, but it would seem to be a connecting link with the Himalayan ranges so that the old Chinese geographers, who did indeed link together the "Bolor" and the "Karakorum" under the common name of "Tsung Ling" or "Onion mountains" were not far wrong in their ideas.

I am inclined to agree with Mr. Fedchenko in considering the Pámír steppes, within the limits by which I have defined them, to be a portion of the Thien Shán. At all events they present a very similar physical formation, the main feature of which is the existence of ranges situated on a high table-land, and running more or less east and west. We have already seen that in the only portion of the Thien Shán system visited by us, i.e., to the north and northeast of Kashghar, the mountains consist entirely of parallel ranges having an easterly and westerly direction, and that the elevated plain on which they are situated rises rapidly higher and higher as it advances northwards. It is not always easy to detect the parallelism of these ranges. On the expedition to Chadyr Kul, where we continuously ascended the bed of the Toyanda stream, I did not fully realize the fact, and it was only after our subsequent journey towards Ush Turfán, where I had an opportunity of penetrating and crossing no less than four of these ranges, that I was convinced that this southern portion was of the same physical configuration as other portions of the Thien Shán as portrayed on the Russian maps. Fedchenko, proceeding apparently solely on the basis of this theory of the parallelism of ranges, has shown in his last map the country north-east of Káshghar † in much the same way as I have myself done, and he would doubtless have been much gratified, had he lived, to find his theories so soon verified.

An examination of the map accompanying this report will show the ideas I have myself formed of the ground lying between the Great Pámir and the Alai plateau, which last has been visited by M. Fedchenko. The position and extent of the Great and Little Pámirs have been accurately laid down, and it is hoped that the mapping of the ground between them and the Alai will be found to be not very far from correct; the geographical detail shown is the result of careful study.

On the construction of the Preliminary map accompanying this report.

The positions of all places in Eastern Turkestan, and Wakhan, that have been visited by members of the Mission, depend upon the astronomically fixed position of the Yangi-shahr or new city of Káshghar, for full details of which the appendix, Sections A. and B., may be consulted.

---

* The altitude and bearings of this peak I measured with great care, with my theodolite, from both Yapchan and Kashghar, and I thus obtained two independent results of 25,364 feet and 25,328 feet.

† M. Fedchenko was never there, and, as far as I am aware, the Russians possess no survey of the ground to the north-east of Káshghar.

The final positions in longitude of Yárkand and other important places have been determined as follows:—

The true longitude of KASHGHAR (Yangi-Shahr) is ...						76°	6'	47"
The difference of longitude between Kashghar and Yangi-Hissar as determined by Pandit Kishen Sing's pacing, corrected from latitude observations, is—								
On outward journey	...	+ 0°	6'	15"	} mean	6'	8"	+	6'	8"
On return journey	...	+ 0°	6'	0"					
Giving for longitude of Yangi-Hissar ...						76°	12'	55"
The difference of longitude between Yangi-Hissar and Yárkand, determined in the same manner—								
By outward journey is ...	...	1°	3'	0"				
By return journey ...	...	1°	4'	25"				

On the outward journey the survey was carried along the direct road, about 75 miles in length, and over a perfectly level country, whereas on the return journey the road followed a circuitous line of 180 miles, over one snowy pass and very rough ground. The first value is therefore accepted in preference, viz. ... ... 1° 3' 0"

Giving a final value for YARKAND (Yangi-Shahr) of ... ... 77° 15' 55"

which is 0° 3' 5" in defect of the astronomically determined value of the same place. I have determined to accept the value as deduced from Kashghar in preference to the independent results arrived at from observations to the moon.

Again, the final longitude of Yangi-Hissar (as above) is ... 76° 12' 55"
The difference between Yangi-Hissar and Tashkurghan by Pandit's pacing corrected for latitude is ... 53' 25" }
The difference ascertained chronometrically by Captain Trotter is ... ... 54' 23" } mean 53' 54"

Giving a final value for TASHKURGHAN of ... 75° 19' 1"

which is 4' 59" in defect of the value obtained from one night's observations to the moon at the same place.

The longitude of Kila Panjah (Wakhan) was determined chronometrically—

1. On outward journey, from Tashkurghan ... 72° 44' 18"
2. On return journey, from Ighiz-yar (near to and connected with Yangi-Hissar by a traverse survey)... 72° 46' 40"

Giving a final longitude for KILA PANJAH of . 72° 45' 29"

Whilst the observations for absolute longitude at the same place give a result of 72° 45' 30"
and a fourth entirely independent result obtained by Captain Trotter's route survey, corrected for latitude is 72° 44' 10"

The mean result obtained chronometrically is adopted for the final position. The wonderfully accordant results at Kila Panjah, although highly satisfactory, must perhaps to a certain extent be regarded as fortuitous, but the admirable *rates* obtained for the watch employed in the chronometric determinations, a silver *lever watch* by Brock of London specially made for explorations, are worth recording[*] and ought to give results in the accuracy of which great confidence may be placed.

[*] *Travelling rates obtained by Captain Trotter for Brock's lever watch, No. 1602, during journey from Yangi-Hissar to Kila Panjah, and return journey to Yarkand.*

Stage.	Dates.	No. of days from which rate was determined.	Rate per diem gaining in seconds of time.	Remarks.
Yangi-Hissar to Ak-tala.	18th to 22nd March	4	+ 6.0	(1) Rate obtained by comparing difference of observed times with difference of longitude as derived from Pandit's pacing, corrected for latitude.
Ak-tala to Tashkur-ghan.	22nd to 31st March	9	+ 6.1	(2) Ditto Ditto.

I am much gratified to be able to state that after all my computations were completed and the details of routes transferred for the first time on to a correct graticule, my position of the west end of Victoria Lake (the extreme east point visited by Wood in his travels) was latitude 37° 27' north and longitude* 73° 40' 38", which is practically identical with the independent determination of the same point by Lieutenant Wood which is given at page 232, new edition of Wood's Oxus, with essay by Colonel Yule, London, 1872.

I will now indicate how the positions of points on the road between Leh (Ladakh) and Yarkand have been determined. The position of Ak-tagh (2nd camp) was fixed by myself in lat. 36° 0' 11" and long. 78° 6' 20". It was the converging point of three different route surveys (by Pandits) starting from fixed points on the south, and is in the neighbourhood of a hill above Chibra whose position was satisfactorily fixed by intersection (on the plane-table) of several rays from trigonometrically fixed peaks of the Karakorum. The position of Ak-tagh in longitude with regard to these peaks may be looked on as correct within a mile, and its position in latitude is undoubtedly correct within a few hundred feet.

From this point three traverse lines have been carried by different Surveyors to Karghalik, which, when corrected and adjusted on the proper parallel (37° 53' 15"), had a maximum divergence of 3¾ miles, the mean of the three values gives a position in (true)† longitude of 77° 25' 30."

Between Karghalik and Yarkand I had also two independent traverses, i.e., on both outward and return journey, which differed from each other in the resulting longitude of Karghalik by less than a mile. The mean of these two when referred to the value of Yárkand as determined from Káshghar places Karghalik in longitude 77° 28' 30." A mean between

Travelling rates obtained by Captain Trotter for Brock's lever watch, &c., &c.—(Concluded).

STAGE.	DATES.	No. of days from which rate was determined.	Rate per diem gaining in seconds of time.	REMARKS.
Yangi-Hissar to Wakhan and back to Ighiz-yar.	18th March to 18th May.	61	+ 6.1	During these 61 days almost an entire circuit was made. The difference of longitude between Yangi Hissar and Ighiz-yar, viz., 1' 45" only, was determined by Pandit's pacing.
Kogachak to Ak-tash...	3rd April to 5th May	32	+ 5.7	During these 31 days a smaller circuit was made; the difference of longitude between Kogachak and Ak-tash is 1' 35". In both these circuits allowance has been made for the stationary rate (+ 7·8) obtained during our halt in Wakhan.
Kashghar to Ighiz-yar	15th to 18th May...	3	+ 5.5	Rate obtained in same manner as (1) & (2).

It should be noted that my watches and chronometers were always carried in a small box that I had specially made for them, carefully packed in cotton wool, and inserted in the middle of a large leather mule trunk, packed with clothes. They were thus kept at a tolerably uniform temperature and escaped in great measure the jerks and shakes they would otherwise have been exposed to. Of my pocket chronometers, having a regular chronometric escapement, one by Peter Birchall, London, No. 1096, was well suited for astronomical observations, keeping excellent time when stationary and beating half seconds very audibly. It was always used by me in my astronomical observations, but it required very careful handling, as a violent jerk was apt to make it gain several seconds suddenly A third watch, a pocket chronometer, by Dent, unfortunately got out of order before the Pamir trip, but I had found that while travelling, neither its rate nor that of Birchall compared favorably with that obtained from Brock's watch. It is perhaps needless to add that my watches were daily carefully compared together, and also both before and after observations of stars. An omission to do this on a single occasion prevented my getting a chronometric value for the differences of longitude between Yangi-Hissar and Kashghar.

* The position in longitude in the "Preliminary map" differs slightly from this, as the latter had to be prepared prior to the completion of the computations.

† True, i.e., depending on the most recent determination of the longitude of Madras. All the Indian Survey maps are based on the astronomically determined position of the Madras Observatory. Recent observations have shown that the old value, that is the one adopted by the Survey Department, is about 3 miles too much to the east. In my map I have been compelled to make allowance for this, and have shifted three miles to the west, the whole of the positions in Northern India taken from the existing maps.

this and the value previously deduced from the south gives 77° 27' 0" which has been assigned as its final position. The smallness of the amount of the adjustment necessary to connect my own work, depending on my own astronomical observations at Káshghar, and that depending on the Indian Survey derived from the astronomically fixed position of Madras is a gratifying proof of the general accuracy of the work.

This sketch would be incomplete without a few lines as to my connection on the north with the Russian Survey, which appears, I think, equally satisfactory with the above.

The only position in the Amir of Kashghar's dominions in Eastern Turkestan astronomically fixed by the Russians is that of Káshghar. This was done in 1872, the year prior to our own visit, by Colonel Scharnhorst of the Mission under General Baron Von Kaulbars. A comparison of results is given :—

Position of Yangi-Shahr (Káshghar) determined by English Mission, 1873—
    Latitude   ...   ... 39° 24' 26" North.
    Longitude ...   ... 76° 6' 47" East of Greenwich.

Position of Yangi-Shahr (Káshghar) determined by Russian Mission, 1872—
    Latitude   ...   ... 39° 24' 16" North.
    Longitude ...   ... 76° 4' 42" East of Greenwich.

As the quarters occupied by the British Mission, where the observations were made, lies outside and to the east of the fort, while those occupied by the Russians were in about the same latitude and nearly one mile to the west of the fort, the difference in longitude is reduced to about one mile, our latitudes being practically identical. I would have wished to take the mean between the two as the final position of Káshghar, but as our stay there was of much longer duration than that of the Russians, and I had opportunities of taking many more observations than they did, I prefer leaving my own values intact.* The slight discrepancy now noticed disappears on the road between Káshghar and Chadyr Kul, the only line of survey common both to the Russians and ourselves, and along which I carried a rough traverse survey in which the distances were estimated by the time occupied on the line of march. Prior to my departure from India Colonel Stubendorff, of the Russian War Office, had sent to Colonel Walker, the Superintendent of the Great Trigonometrical Survey, the positions of a number of points in Russian and in Khokandian territory that had been astronomically determined by Russian officers. Amongst them was the north-east corner of Lake Chadyr Kul. Bearing this in mind, when at the most northerly point on the road reached by us, I took a bearing tangential to the east end of the lake, which lay nearly due north at a distance of about three miles from us. On my return to India when I plotted in my work from my own astronomical position of Káshghar, I found that by adopting the Russian value of the east end of the lake, viz., latitude 40° 43' north, our positons in longitude† of the same point exactly coincided.

In determining the position of Khotan I have made use of Pandit Kishen Sing's route from Karghalik to Khotan, and thence viâ Keria back to Ladakh. As a result of this route survey our previously accepted value of the longitude of Khotan has been altered by more than thirty miles. It may appear bold to make this extensive change in the position of a place that has been visited by a European explorer (Mr. Johnson), but the route survey executed by this Pandit is so consistent, and the plotted results agree so closely with the observed latitudes throughout the whole of his work, that I have no hesitation in accepting it as correct. I may further add that I have been in communication with Mr. Johnson on the subject, and that he freely admits the possibility of a large error in his longitude of Khotan.

* Since the above was written Colonel Walker has heard from Colonel Stubendorff that the Russian astronomical observations at Káshghar which were taken by Colonel Scharnhorst were referred to the most northern angle of the Yangi-Shahr, a position almost identical in latitude with my own, and differing by two-fifths of a mile only in longitude. Colonel Stubendorff mentions that the Russian observations depend on the eclipse of the sun on the 6th June 1872, and that corrections for error in the lunar tables have not been applied. This last remark applies to my own observations also.—H. T.

† 75° 24' East of Greenwich.

P

He states that in commencing his reconnaissance from the Kuen Luen Mountains (which he carried on with the plane-table only), one of the three trigonometrically fixed points on which his work was based, turned out subsequently to have been incorrectly projected on his board. This, together with the doubt that must always exist when rapidly passing through an unknown country as to the identity of the different peaks visible from the line of march, is quite sufficient to account for the discrepancy. In my preliminary map I have assigned to Khotan a longitude of 79° 59' instead of 79° 26,' the position it has recently occupied on our maps. About its latitude there can be no doubt. Mr. Johnson took several observations there with a 14-inch theodolite and obtained a mean result of 37° 7' 35", whilst from Kishen Sing's observations with a sextant extending over nearly a month we have a mean result of 37° 7' 36". The points east of Khotan, *i.e.*, Keria and the Sorghak gold fields, are derived from Kishen Sing's route survey, combined with his latitude observations. We also have from the same source a complete survey for the first time of the road *viâ* Polu to Nob, and thence to Leh. As a specimen of the accuracy of this Pundit's work I may mention that when the road from Karghalik to Pal, a distance of 630 miles, was plotted out on the scale of 2,000 paces to the mile, without any correction or adjustment whatever (although 4½° were added to each magnetic bearing in order to allow for magnetic variation) starting from my own value of Karghalik, the plot closed at Pal (fixed by the Great Trigonometrical Survey) almost absolutely correct in latitude and only eight minutes out in longitude, and in no single portion of the whole route, which passes over elevations exceeding 17,000 feet in height, did the plotted value differ by as much as three miles from his own observed astronomical latitude (*vide* Appendix Section A.). Of this discrepancy of eight minutes in longitude it is possible that a portion may be due to error of position in the starting point (Karghalik), but it may be noted that the amount is no more than would be accounted for by an error of 1¼° in the assumed value of magnetic variation. It is not to be supposed that such accuracy is generally attainable, but in the present case, although the surveyor laboured under certain disadvantages from the absence of inhabitants, yet there were the compensating advantages that he was under no necessity for concealment; he was therefore able to take and record bearings when and where he pleased.

As regards the work executed to the north-east and east of Káshghar; the position of Maralbashi, on the road to Aksu, was fixed in latitude by Captain Biddulph (*vide* Appendix Section A.), and its position in longitude is roughly determined by a few bearings, and estimated distances taken by him on the road from Káshghar.

On the road to Ush Turfan I carried on a rough route survey wherever I went, and took observations for latitude and obtained chronometric determinations of longitude as far as Ui Bulák, in latitude 40° 26' north and longitude 77° 36' east. Thence by route survey I got a determination of the position of the Belowti Pass; calculating from this the probable position of Ush Turfan I place it about three-quarters of a degree to the east of the position given it in the last edition of Colonel Walker's Turkestan map. On examining the latest Russian map (1873) it appears that the position of Ush Turfan has been recently altered, and placed very near where I would myself locate it. I have therefore in my map adopted the last Russian values of Ush Turfan, Aksu, and all places to the east. It will be found that the cities of Aksu and Kuldja are more than twenty miles to the east of the places assigned them in all but the most recent maps.

The details inserted to the north of the map are taken almost exclusively from the Russian topographical map of Central Asia (corrected to 1873). The portion of ground to the south of Khokand, visited by Mr. Fedchenko, is derived from various maps purporting to be by that distinguished traveller, amongst others, one recently sent by Madame Fedchenko to Colonel Walker, differing materially from all others that I have seen. For the country between the Alai, visited by Mr Fedchenko on the north, and the scene of our own explorations in the Pamirs on the south, the map is compiled from all the limited sources available* which have

---

* Including the route survey carried on by Abdul Subhan from Panjah to Kila Wamur, the chief town of Roshán, and also including a sketch map prepared by Colonel Gordon and Captain Biddulph representing their joint ideas of the geography of the Pamír.

been bound together to the best of my ability. I am by no means yet satisfied with the result, and one of my first labours, when I have finished this report, will be the preparation of a map on a larger scale of the Pámir regions, when I doubt not that further considerations will induce some changes in the map as it at present stands.

Most of the details to the south of the map, with the exception of those portions north of Leh that have been traversed by members of the Mission, have been taken from the last edition of Colonel Walker's Map of Turkestan, but all the positions in the latter have been shifted three minutes to the west in longitude in order to allow for the most recently determined value of the longitude of Madras, viz., 80° 14′ 19.5″ East of Greenwich.

In the portion of country traversed by Members and Attachés of the Mission use has been made of all the material collected by them. The maps of Messrs. Shaw and Hayward have also been called into requisition.

The reductions of the astronomical observations, and the computations of heights, have all been made in the Office of Colonel Walker, R.E., the Superintendent of the Great Trigonometrical Survey, in whose Office also, the map compiled by myself has been drawn and photozincographed. A large amount of work has been got through in a moderate space of time, and I am deeply indebted to Colonel Walker for the facilities he has given, and to Messrs. Hennessey, Keelan, and Wood in the Computing Office, and Messrs. Atkinson and Sindon in the Drawing Office for the assistance afforded by them in their several departments.

Meteorological Observations.

Whilst on the march I always took readings of thermometers, and barometer or boiling point thermometer, at our camps, and on high passes, and at other places of interest. These were taken chiefly for the purpose of determining the height above sea level of the stations of observation and where used for this object are shown in Appendix C. Where they are not required for this I have not published them, as isolated observations at different places, taken under constantly varying conditions, are not of much use to the meteorologist.

While I was at Leh Mr. R. B. Shaw, the British Joint Commissioner, commenced a regular meteorological registry, which has since been continued under the superintendence of Captain Molloy, the recorder being the Native Doctor attached to the dispensary there. At my special request Mr. Shaw kindly took extra barometrical observations at the hours of 9 A.M. and noon, whilst I was on the journey to, and during my residence and travels in, Eastern Turkestan, these being considered the most likely hours at which I should myself be able to take barometrical observations for height on passes and in camp. I have thus throughout the whole of my absence from Leh got almost simultaneous readings at the fixed Observatory of Leh, whose height has been accurately determined by the Great Trigonometrical Survey. This circumstance combined with the use by myself of mercurial barometers, enable me to compute the height of the various passes and halting-places with an amount of accuracy superior to anything yet attainable. It is hardly necessary to add that I have made at Leh, both on the outward and return journeys, numerous comparisons between my own instruments and those in use at the Leh Observatory, and that my own were previously compared with the standards at Dehra Dún (and some of them at Kew).

While on the march to Yárkand I succeeded in taking numerous sets of observations with a Hodgkinson's actinometer. I took these at the special request of Mr. J. B. N. Hennessey of the Great Trigonometrical Survey, who supplied me with an instrument belonging to the Royal Society. They were chiefly taken at considerable altitudes, but owing to cloudy weather the Chang La (Pass), 17,600 feet above sea level, was the only very high point at which I was able to take sets extending over a period of several hours in the middle of the day. These actinometric observations have been handed over to Mr. Hennessey (now in England) for reduction, and they ought to give very interesting results, which will probably be communicated to the Royal Society.

(60)

At Leh in Ladákh advantage was taken of the presence of the Pundits to get a series of continuous hourly observations of the barometer. These extended over a period of six days during which there was no break in the observations. The height of the Observatory above the sea level (11,530 feet), coupled with the extreme dryness of the air of Ladákh, and its position in the interior of a large continent, combine to render the determination of the diurnal curve of considerable value.* In the diagram accompanying the vertical scale is ten times that of the natural scale, the exaggeration being necessary in order to show clearly the curve. The actual barometer readings† have been corrected for Index Error, and reduced to a temperature of 32°, before being projected on the diagram.

The curve indicates two maxima, viz., at 1 A.M. and at 8 A.M., and minima at between 2 and 3 A.M. and between 4 and 5 P.M., which differ considerably from results obtained in other parts of the world. The daily maximum and minimum is very much more clearly marked than the nightly one.

At Yárkand also, during the winter, sets of continuous hourly observations were taken on the 20th, 21st, and 22nd of each month. Several of these sets have been reduced to a curve, which I have also shown in the same diagram.‡ It so happens that on the days that were selected for hourly observations at Yárkand there was almost always a steady fall in the barometer, as will be seen by a glance at the monthly curves in the other plate. In order to allow for this constant fall, the effect of which is to distort the true daily curve, I have applied proportionate corrections, so that the dotted line represents the true diurnal curve. The mean of six days' hourly observations, viz., on 20th and 21st of December, 20th and 21st of January and 20th and 21st of February, have been employed in constructing the curve. It will be observed that at Yárkand the night maxima and minima are much more clearly marked than at Leh, but that there is much less difference between those of the day and night. The maxima occur at 10 A.M. and 11 P.M., the minima at 4 A.M. and 3 P.M. At Yárkand, where the Pandits passed the winter, meteorological observations were commenced on the 19th November and continued without a break until the 15th March. They consisted of the readings at 9 A.M., noon, 3 P.M., 6 P.M., and 9 P.M., of a mercurial barometer, an aneroid barometer, dry and wet bulb thermometers, and direction of the wind (N.B.—There was no rainfall, but a little snow fell in March); also the maximum and minimum temperatures in the shade during the 24 hours.

At Káshghar observations were commenced on the 12th December, but were not so complete or regular as those at Yárkand, as I had fewer observers to assist me, and I was myself absent for two periods, viz., from 31st December to 11th January, and again from 15th February to 3rd March. Observations were continued up to the 16th March, and generally consisted of readings of two aneroid barometers at the hours of 9 A.M., noon, and 3 P.M., and occasionally at 6 P.M. Readings of thermometer (dry) and direction of wind were taken at the same hours, besides the maxima and minima during the 24 hours. Readings of the wet bulb thermometer were also taken during the latter half of February and March. In addition to these a series of hypsometric observations were taken, with the object of determining the relative heights of Yárkand and Káshghar.

The whole of these observations are shewn in the Appendix, Section G., to which the reader is referred. I have prepared (plate 2) a set of curves showing the connection of the barometric wave between the stations of Káshghar, Yárkand, Leh, and Dehra Dún (at the foot of the southern slopes of the Himalayas). The curve represents the height of the corrected readings of the barometer at 9 A.M., during the four months for which I was able to obtain data, with the exception of Dehra, where 9 A.M. readings not being forthcoming I have taken the observations recorded at 10·30 A.M.

---

* The Schlagintweits took hourly observations at Leh during the day, and interpolated values for the night hours. The results thus obtained cannot have anything like the same value as those derived from observations taken throughout the 24 hours.

† The instrument employed was a mercurial barometer by Casella.

‡ These diagrams have been drawn by Mr. Keelan of the Great Trigonometrical Survey, who has also rendered me great assistance in the preparation of the Appendices of this report.

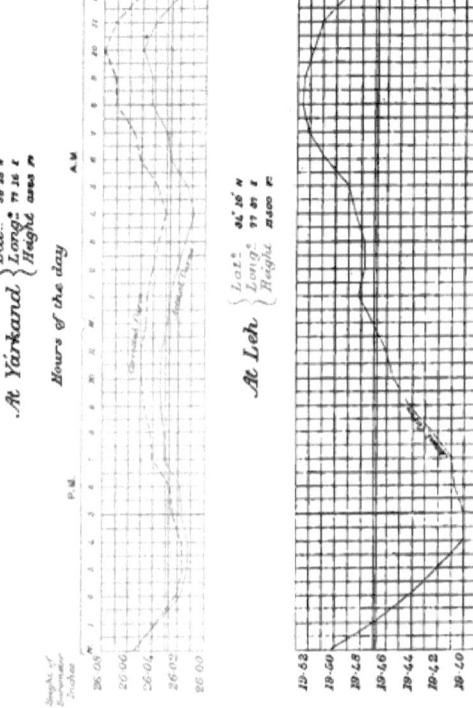

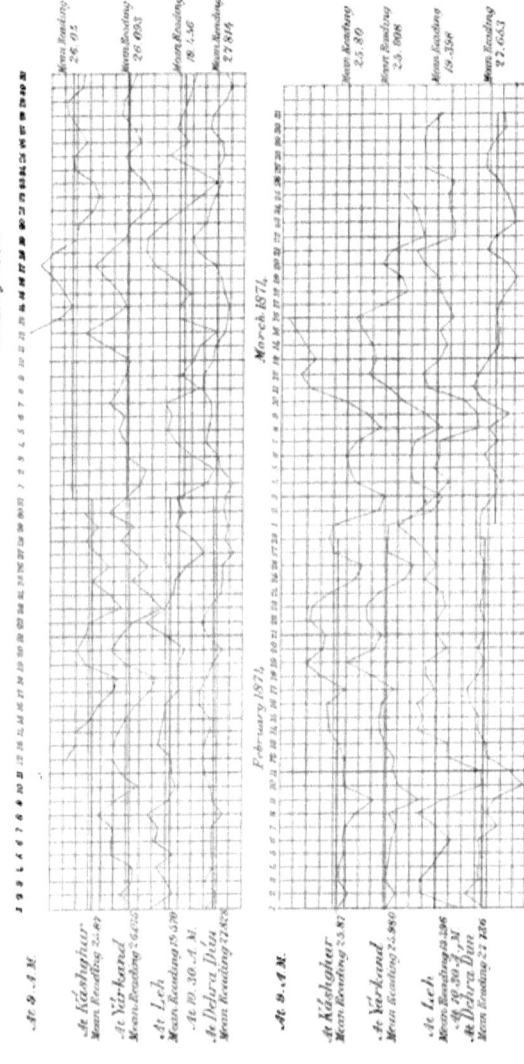

Magnetic Observations.

As has been mentioned in a previous portion of this report it was decided not to take from India a complete set of magnetic instruments. I took with me however a dip circle by Barrow with which observations for inclination were taken at Leh (in Ladakh), Chágra (in Ladakh), Yárkand, Káshghar, and Tashkurghán (in the Sarikol District). It has been laid down as an axiom by General Sabine, the great authority on matters of magnetism, that "the value of each new magnetic station is directly proportional to its distance from those where observations have already been made," and I may therefore hope that the record of results, vide Appendix, Section E., may prove of considerable value, as I am not aware that any magnetic observations have ever been taken within a very considerable distance of any of the three last named stations. The rules laid down by General Sabine were rigorously adhered to in taking the observations.

Observations for magnetic variation (declination) were taken at, and have been computed out for sixteen stations in, Ladakh, Turkestan, and Wakhan. The station furthest to the north-east was at Uï Bulák (latitude $40°\ 26'$ and longitude $77°\ 36'$) where the variation was $5°\ 40'$ east; the extreme western station was at Kila Panjah (latitude $37°$ longitude $72°\ 45'$) where the variation was $4°\ 17'$ east. Details of the results, which are very consistent *inter se*, are given in the Appendix. The instrument employed in the determination of declination was the six-inch transit theodolite, which has been described in the Appendix, Section B. It was fitted with a first-rate magnetic needle. Comparisons taken at Leh and at Dehra both prior to the departure of the Mission, and subsequent to its return, prove that no alteration has taken place in the position of its magnetic pole. The object observed was generally Polaris. In many instances, however, the sun, either near sunrise or sunset, was made use of; at important stations, such as Leh and Kashghar, the mean of several different independent determinations has been taken.

I cannot conclude this report without alluding to the sad loss we have all sustained by the recent and sudden death of our much lamented comrade, Dr. F. Stoliczka. Having been in almost daily intercourse with him from the day of leaving the Punjáb on our outward journey (through the Changchenmo, Chakmák, Artysh, and Pámír trips) up to the day of his death, and being naturally especially attracted to him as working always cordially with him to add my mite to the field of science, I most bitterly regret his loss. It is hard to think that he should not have been spared to give to the world the results of his laborious investigation and scientific research, and although he has left valuable notes behind him, yet owing to his unequalled knowledge of Himalayan geology there is probably no man living as competent as he was to do full justice to them; and it is unlikely that any one will go through his valuable zoological and other collections with the same minute care and attention that he would himself have bestowed upon them. I have special reason to regret the absence of his experience and advice while preparing my own report, in writing which I had confidently looked forward to receiving the benefit of his assistance.

(Sd.)   HENRY TROTTER, *Capt., R. E.*

GEOGRAPHICAL APPENDIX.

SECTION A.

LATITUDES.

Abstract of Observations for Latitude on road from LEH

Place of Observation.	Reference numbers.	Astronomical date.	Observer.	Instrument observed with.	Object observed.
Chang Lá or Sakti Pass...	3	15th Sept. 1873	Capt. Trotter...	Theodolite ...	Sun (U.L.) ...
Lukong Vil. Pang-gong-chu	7	19th Sept. 1873	Kalian Sing ...	Sextant No. 44	α Piscis Australis (Fomalhaut)
		,, ,,	Kishen Sing ...	,, 44	α Aquilæ (Altair) ...
		,, ,,	,, ...	,, 44	α Piscis Australis (Fomalhaut)
		20th ,,	,,	,, 44	Sun (U.L.) ...
		19th ,,	Capt. Trotter...	Theodolite	,, ,, ...
Chágrá	8	20th Sept. 1873	Kalian Sing ...	Sextant No. 44	α Piscis Australis (Fomalhaut)
		,, ,,	Kishen Sing ...	,, 44	α Ursæ Minoris (Polaris)
		21st ,,	,, ...	,, 44	α Aquilæ (Altair) ...
Gográ Camp	12	24th Sept. 1873	Kalian Sing ...	,, 8	α Aquilæ (Altair) ...
		25th ,,	,, ...	,, 8	α Piscis Australis (Fomalhaut)
		23rd ,,	Kishen Sing...	,, 44	α Aquilæ (Altair) ...
		24th ,,	,, ...	,, 44	α Piscis Australis (Fomalhaut)
		,, ,,	,,	,, 44	α Ursæ Minoris (Polaris)
E. Route viâ Ling-zi-thang. { Bhao (Shumallung) Camp.	13	26th Sept. 1873	Kishen Sing ...	,, 44	α Aquilæ (Altair) ...
		27th ,,	,, ...	,, 44	β Orionis (Rigel) ...
Changlung Nischu Camp.	15	27th Sept. 1873	Kishen Sing ...	,, 44	α Aquilæ (Altair) ...
		,, ,,	,, ...	,, 44	α Ursæ Minoris (Polaris)
Ling-zi-thang plain, camp on.	16	28th Sept. 1873	Kishen Sing ...	,, 44	α Aquilæ (Altair) ...
		,, ,,	,, ...	,, 44	α Ursæ Minoris (Polaris)
		29th ,,	,, ...	,, 44	β Orionis (Rigel) ...
Sumna Camp (E. of Kizil jilga).	18	30th Sept. 1873	Kishen Sing ..	,, 44	α Aquilæ (Altair) ...
		,, ,,	,, ...	,, 44	α Ursæ Minoris (Polaris)

(3)

to YARKAND via Chang-Chenmo and Sháhidúlla.

Double altitudes or zenith distances corrected for index and level errors.	Elements used in computation of refraction.		Deduced Latitudes.			Remarks.
	Barometer.	Ther. Faht.	By stars north of zenith.	By sun or stars south of zenith	Final latitudes north.	
° ′ ″	Inches.	Degrees.	° ′ ″	° ′ ″	° ′ ″	
Z. D. 30 47 40	15·8	44		34 4 49	34 4 49	In observations with the sextant the stars have been invariably taken on the meridian. In observations with the theodolite the stars have been taken on the meridian except where an asterisk has been affixed to the name of the star (in column 6). Where this occurs the numbers in the column of Remarks are the computed means of the true local times of observation used in the computation for latitude. The numbers in brackets in columns 7, 10, and 11, denote the number of pairs (face left and face right) of observations taken. The corresponding figures in column 7 give the corrected mean zenith distance.
D. A. 51 27 20	18·2	51		34 0 1		
,, 129 5 10	18·2	51		33 59 55		
,, 51 27 0	18·2	51		34 0 12		
,, 114 38 20	18·2	51		34 0 23		
Z. D. 32 17 12	18·0	61		33 59 57	34 0 6	
D. A. 51 17 20	17·6	33		34 5 4		
,, 70 55 50	17·6	33	34 5 6			
,, 128 55 40	17·6	33		34 4 40	34 4 59	
D. A. 128 24 10	17·0	44		34 20 24		
,, 50 47 10	17·0	44		34 20 4		
,, 128 23 0	17·0	44		34 21 1		
,, 50 41 40	17·0	44		34 22 40		
,, 71 27 30	17·0	44	34 21 1		34 21 4	The theodolite employed is described in the Geographical Appendix, Section B.
D. A. 128 7 0	16·3	44		34 28 59		
,, 94 21 10	16·3	44		34 29 13	34 29 6	
D. A. 127 55 53				34 34 33		
,, 71 56 33	,,	,,	34 35 32		34 35 3	
D. A. 127 29 33				34 47 45		
,, 72 23 13	,,	,,	34 48 54			
,, 93 47 23				34 46 10	34 47 54	
D. A. 126 32 43				35 16 9		
,, 73 19 43	,,	,,	35 17 9		35 16 39	

Abstract of Observations for Latitude on road from LEH

Place of Observation.		Reference numbers.	Astronomical date.	Observer.	Instrument observed with.	Object observed.
W. Route viâ head of Kárákásh River.	Kotajilga Camp...	19	26th Sept. 1873 " "	Capt. Trotter... " "	Theodolite ... " ...	α Ursæ Minoris (*Polaris*)* " " "
	Sumzumlung Pa ..	22	28th Sept. 1873 " 29th " " "	Capt. Trotter... " ... " ... " ...	Theodolite ... " ... " ... " ...	α Ursæ Minoris (*Polaris*)* " " " γ Aquilæ α Aquilæ (*Altair*)
	Dunglung or Shinglung.	26	3rd Oct. 1873 " " " "	Capt. Trotter... " ... " ...	Theodolite ... " ... " ...	α Piscis Australis (*Fomalhaut*) α Pegasi (*Markab*) ... γ Cephei ...
Kizil-jilga on bank of Kárákásh River.		27	5th Oct. 1873 " " 1st " 2nd " 5th " " "	Kalian Sing ... " ... Kishen Sing... " ... " ... " ...	Sextant No. 44 " 8 " 44 " 44 " 44 " 44	β Ceti ... α Ursæ Minoris (*Polaris*) α Aquilæ (*Altair*) α Orionis ... β Ceti ... α Ur. Min. (*Polaris*) ...
Chúng Tash		28	8th Oct. 1873	Capt. Trotter...	Theodolite ...	Sun U. L. ...
E. Route along Kárákásh River.	Dáktod Karpo Sumdo.	30	9th Oct. 1873 10th " " "	Kishen Sing ... " ... " ...	Sextant No. 44 " 44 " 44	α Aquilæ (*Altair*) ... α Orionis ... α Canis Majoris (*Sirius*)
	Dungnagu Camp	32	12th Oct. 1873 " " " "	Kishen Sing... " ... " ...	Sextant No. 44 " 44 " 44	β Orionis (*Rigel*) ... α Orionis ... α Canis Majoris (*Sirius*)...
	Sorá Camp	33	13th Oct. 1873 " " 14th "	Kishen Sing... " ... " ...	Sextant No. 44 " 44 " 44	β Ceti ... α Ursæ Minoris (*Polaris*) α Canis Majoris (*Sirius*)...

(5)

to YARKAND viâ *Chang-Chenmo and Sháhidúlla.*—(continued.)

Double altitudes or zenith distances corrected for index and level errors.			Elements used in computation of refraction.		Deduced Latitudes.			Remarks.			
			Barometer.	Ther. Faht.	By stars north of zenith.	By sun or stars south of zenith.	Final latitudes north.				
	°	′	″	Inches.	Degrees.	° ′ ″	° ′ ″	° ′ ″		H.	M.	S.
Z. D.	54	24	1(1)	18·0	16	34 20 22(1)			Mean time =	10	25	37
"	54	24	24(1)	18·0	16	34 29 27(1)		34 20 25	"	10	31	14
Z. D.	54	19	16(1)	15·9	9	34 40 39(1)			"	9	49	42
"	54	18	23(1)	15·9	9	34 40 45(1)			"	9	52	57
"	24	22	39	15·9	10		34 41 23					
"	26	8	38	15·9	10		34 41 8	34 40 59				
Z. D.	65	26	25	16·0	−3		35 10 13					
"	20	38	5	16·0	−3		35 9 53					
"	41	45	30	16·0	−5	35 9 38		35 9 51				
D. A.	71	59	0	16·5	18		35 20 33					
"	73	27	30	16·5	18	35 21 4						
"	126	25	3	16·5	18		35 19 58					
"	124	6	53	16·5	18		35 19 56					
"	71	59	33	16·5	18		35 20 10					
"	73	28	3	16·5	18	35 21 21		35 20 42				
Z. D.	41	16	37	17·0	34		35 36 56	35 36 56				
D. A.	125	33	33	...	...		35 45 45					
"	123	15	13	...	...		35 45 47					
"	75	25	13	...	...		35 45 52	35 45 48				
D. A.	91	37	3	...	...		35 51 22					
"	123	3	23	...	...		35 51 43					
"	75	13	43	...	...		35 51 37	35 51 34				
D. A.	70	39	33	...	...		36 0 22					
"	74	49	23	...	...	36 2 0		36 1 9				
"	74	56	33	...	...		36 0 12					

(6)

Abstract of Observations for Latitude on road from LEH

Place of Observation.		Reference numbers.	Astronomical date.	Observer.	Instrument observed with.	Object observed.
E. Route along Kárákásh River—(Contd.)	Jung Chidmo Camp	35	15th Oct. 1873	Kishen Sing ...	Sextant No. 44	β Ceti ... ...
			,, ,,	,, ...	,, 44	α Ursæ Minoris (Polaris)
			16th ,,	,, ,,	,, 44	β Orionis (Rigel) ...
			,, ,,	,, ,,	,, 44	α Orionis ... ...
			,, ,,	,, ...	,, 44	α Canis Majoris (Sirius)
	Gulbáshem	38	17th Oct. 1873	Kishen Sing ...	Sextant No. 44	β Ceti ... ...
			,, ,,	,, ,,	,, 44	α Ursæ Minoris (Polaris)
			18th ,,	,, ...	,, 44	α Canis Majoris (Sirius) ...
			17th ,,	Capt. Trotter...	Theodolite	α Ursæ Minoris (Polaris)*
W. Route viâ Aktágh.	Shorjilga	39	10th Oct. 1873	Capt. Trotter...	Theodolite	α Ursæ Minoris (Polaris)
	Kárátágh Pass ...	41	11th Oct. 1873	Capt. Trotter...	Theodolite ...	Sun (U. L.) ...
	Fotásh Pass (near Traverse Station No. 44.)	41A	19th Oct. 1873	Capt. Trotter...	Theodolite ...	Sun (U. L.) ...
	Aktágh (1st camp)	43	13th Oct. 1873	Nain Sing ...	Sextant No. 7..	α Ursæ Minoris (Polaris)
			14th ,,	Capt. Chapman	Theodolite ...	Sun (U. L.) ...
	Chíbra Camp ...	43A	15th Oct. 1873	Kalian Sing ...	Sextant No. 8...	β Ceti ...
			,, ,,	,, ...	,, 8...	α Ursæ Minoris (Polaris)...
	Sugét Camp	47	17th Oct. 1873	Kalian Sing ...	Sextant No. 8...	β Ceti ...
			,, ,,	,, ...	,, 8...	α Ursæ Minoris (Polaris)
	Sugét Pass	45	16th Oct. 1873	Capt. Trotter...	Theodolite ...	Sun (L. L.) ...
Sháhidúlla Camp		48	22nd Oct. 1873	Kalian Sing ...	Sextant No. 8...	β Ceti ...
			,, ,,	,, ...	,, 8...	α Ursæ Minoris (Polaris)
			21st ,,	Nain Sing ...	,, 7...	,, ,, ,,
			,, ,,	,,	,, 7...	α Canis Minoris (Procyon)

(7)

to YARKAND viâ *Chang-Chenmo and* **Sháhidúlla.**—(continued.)

Double altitudes or zenith distances corrected for index and level errors.	Elements used in computation of refraction.		Deduced Latitudes.			Remarks.
	Barometer.	Ther. Faht.	By stars north of zenith.	By sun or stars south of zenith.	Final latitudes north.	
	Inches.	Degrees	° ′ ″	° ′ ″	° ′ ″	
D. A. 70 19 43	...	...		36 10 19		
„ 75 8 33	...	...	36 11 36			
„ 90 59 3	...	...		36 10 14		
„ 122 26 3	...	...		36 10 24		
„ 74 36 43	...	...		36 10 9	36 10 32	
D. A. 70 6 13	19·4	25		36 17 5		
„ 75 22 13	19·4	25	36 18 26			
„ 74 23 3	19·4	18		36 17 1		*H. M. S.*
Z. D. 52 42 13(3)	19·0	25		36 17 19(3)	36 17 28	Mean time = 8 36 36
Z. D. 53 47 56(3)	16·5	6	35 41 2		35 41 2(3)	Mean time = 7 27 27
Z. D. 42 30 58	15·7	30		35 42 54	35 42 54	
Z. D. 45 58 4	17·4	40		35 56 31	35 56 31	
D. A. 74 43 20	17·2	12	35 59 0			.
Z. D. 43 54 37	16·6	25		35 59 6	35 59 3	
D. A. 70 26 30	15·6	25		36 6 46		
„ 75 0 20	15·6	25	36 7 38		36 7 12	
D. A. 70 3 40	18·0	25		36 18 20		
„ 75 23 40	18·9	25	36 19 10		36 18 45	
Z. D. 45 22 5	15·7	30		36 9 53	36 9 53	
D. A. 69 52 30	19·5	30		36 23 55		
„ 75 35 20	19·5	30	36 25 2			
D. A. 75 37 20	19·5	30	36 26 4			
„ 118 17 10	19·5	30		36 24 48	36 24 57	

(8)

Abstract of Observations for **Latitude** on road from *LEH*

Place of Observation.	Reference numbers.	Astronomical date.	Observer.	Instrument observed with.	Object observed.
Kárákorum Camp	48A	25th Oct. 1873 " "	Kalian Sing "	Sextant No. 8 " 8	β Ceti α Ursæ Minoris (*Polaris*)
Giazgia Camp	48B	29th Oct. 1873 30th " 24th " " "	Kishen Sing " Nain Sing "	Sextant No. 44 " 44 " 7 " 7	α Ursæ Minoris (*Polaris*) α Canis Minoris (*Procyon*) α Canis Majoris (*Sirius*) α Canis Minoris (*Procyon*)
Tám Langar	51	25th Oct. 1873 " " " "	Capt. Trotter Nain Sing "	Theodolite Sextant No. 7 " 7	α Ursæ Minoris (*Polaris*)* " " " α Canis Minoris (*Procyon*)
Khewaz Langar	51A	26th Oct. 1873	Nain Sing	Sextant No. 7	α Canis Minoris (*Procyon*)
Sanjú Bazar	52	1st Nov. 1873 28th Oct. 1873 29th " 30th "	Capt. **Trotter** Nain **Sing** " "	Theodolite Sextant No. 7 " 7 " 7	α Ursæ Minoris (*Polaris*)* " " " α Canis Majoris (*Sirius*) α Ursæ Minoris (*Polaris*)
Khushtagh Village	52A	2nd Nov. 1873 " " " "	Capt. Trotter Nain Sing "	Theodolite Sextant No. 7 " 7	α Ursæ Minoris (*Polaris*)* " " " α Canis Minoris (*Procyon*)
Oi Toghrák Village	53	3rd Nov. 1873	Capt. Trotter	Theodolite	α Ursæ Minoris (*Polaris*)*
Boíra Village	54	3rd Nov. 1873 4th " " "	Capt. Trotter Nain Sing "	Theodolite Sextant No. 7 " 7	α Ursæ Minoris (*Polaris*)* β Ceti α Ursæ Minoris (*Polaris*)
Karghalik Bazar	55	6th Nov. 1873 26th May 1874 6th Nov. 1873 " " " " 29th Mar. 1874 " " 30th "	Capt. Trotter " Nain Sing " " " " "	Theodolite " Sextant No. 7 " 7 " 7 " 7 " 7 " 7	α Ursæ Minoris (*Polaris*)* α Libræ α Ursæ Minoris (*Polaris*) β Orionis (*Rigel*) α Orionis Sun (*U. L.*) Jupiter Sun (*U. L.*)

(9)

to YARKAND viâ *Chang-Chenmo and Sháhidúla.*—(continued.)

Double altitudes or zenith distances corrected for index and level errors.	Elements used in computation of refraction.		Deduced Latitudes.			Remarks.
	Barometer.	Ther. Faht.	By stars north of zenith.	By sun or stars south of zenith.	Final latitudes north.	
	Inches.	*Degrees*	° ′ ″	° ′ ″	° ′ ″	
D. A. 69 26 30	20·4	25		36 36 59		
,, 76 1 20	20·4	25	36 38 0		36 37 30	
D. A. 76 12 43	20·2	32	36 43 46			
,, 117 36 33	20·2	32		36 45 7		
,, 73 25 50	19·9	30		36 45 37		
,, 117 36 0	19·9	30		36 45 24	36 44 59	
						H. M. S.
Z. D. 51 52 38(2)	21·9	32	36 52 5(2)			Mean time = 9 19 12
D. A. 76 30 20	21·1	30	36 52 29			
,, 117 23 10	21·1	30		36 51 51	36 52 4	
D. A. 117 1 20	22·5	37		37 2 47	37 2 47	
Z. D. 51 30 22(3)	24·3	19	37 11 4(3)			Mean time = 9 15 57
D. A. 77 8 0	24·5	25	37 11 12			
,, 72 33 50	24·5	25		37 11 52	37 11 17	
,, 77 7 30	24·5	25	37 10 58			
Z. D. 51 15 34(3)	24·7	21	37 21 40(3)			Mean time = 10 22 46
D. A. 77 28 30	23·4	33	37 21 34			
,, 116 25 50	23·4	33		37 20 33	37 21 5	
Z. D. 51 12 15(3)	24·8	16	37 30 20(3)		37 30 20	Mean time = 8 58 7
Z. D. 51 2 23(3)	25·2	21	37 36 55(3)			Mean time = 11 8 11
D. A. 67 25 50	24·4	33		37 37 29	37 37 19	
,, 78 0 10	24·4	33	37 37 22			
Z. D. 50 47 19(3)	26·1	22	37 53 9(3)			Mean time = 9 5 2
,, 53 23 35	23·6	70		37 53 23		
D. A. 78 32 0	25·3	54	37 53 20			
,, 79 35 30	25·3	54		37 52 19		
,, 110 1 0	25·3	54		37 53 2		
,, 111 26 50	24·9	40		37 53 43		
,, 110 49 20	24·9	40		37 53 39		
,, 112 13 50	24·9	40		37 53 30	37 53 15	

(10)

Abstract of Observations for Latitude on road from LEH

Place of Observation.	Reference numbers.	Astronomical date.	Observer.	Instrument observed with.	Object observed.
Posgiám Bazar	56	7th Nov. 1873	Capt. Trotter	Theodolite	α Ursæ Minoris (*Polaris*)*
		,, ,,	Nain Sing	Sextant No. 7	,, ,, ,,
		27th Mar. 1874	,,	,, 7	α Canis Minoris (*Procyon*)
		,, ,,	,,	,, 7	Jupiter
YARKAND. At Elchi Kháná near the centre of the Yangi-Shahr or new city of Yárkand.	57	8th Nov. 1873	Capt. Trotter	Theodolite	α Ursæ Minoris (*Polaris*)*
		11th ,,	,,	,,	Sun (*L.L.*)*
		,, ,,	,,	,,	α Cephei
		,, ,,	,,	,,	ε Pegasi
		,, ,,	,,	,,	α Aquarii
		12th ,,	,,	,,	α Ursæ Minoris (*Polaris*)
		27th ,,	,,	,,	,, ,, ,,
		9th Nov. 1873	Nain Sing	Sextant No. 7	,, ,, ,,
		10th ,,	,,	,, 7	
		26th ,,	,,	,, 7	α Canis Majoris (*Sirius*)
		30th ,,	,,	,, 7	α Canis Minoris (*Procyon*)
		,, ,,	,,	,, 7	α Hydræ
		5th Dec. 1873	,,	,, 7	α Tauri (*Aldebaran*)
		,, ,,	,,	,, 7	β Orionis (*Rigel*)
		13th ,,	,,	,, 7	β Ursæ Minoris
		14th ,,	,,	,, 7	
		16th ,,	,,	,, 7	β Ceti
		,, ,,	,,	,, 7	Jupiter
		18th ,,	,,	,, 7	α Orionis (*Rigel*)
		,, ,,	,,	,, 7	α Canis Majoris (*Sirius*)
		19th ,,	,,	,, 7	Sun (*U.L.*)
		,, ,,	,,	,, 7	α Ursæ Minoris (*Polaris*)
		20th ,,	,,	,, 7	α Orionis
		,, ,,	,,	,, 7	α Canis Majoris (*Sirius*)
		,, ,,	,,	,, 7	α Canis Minoris (*Procyon*)
		,, ,,	,,	,, 7	α Leonis (*Regulus*)
		21st ,,	,,	,, 7	Sun (*U.L.*)
		,, ,,	,,	,, 7	α Tauri (*Aldebaran*)
		22nd ,,	,,	,, 7	Sun (*U.L.*)
		27th ,,	,,	,, 7	α Hydræ
		,, ,,	,,	,, 7	α Leonis (*Regulus*)
		6th Jan. 1874	,,	,, 7	α Ursæ Minoris (*Polaris*)
		,, ,,	,,	,, 7	Sun (*U.L.*)
		11th ,,	,,	,, 7	,, ,,
		13th ,,	,,	,, 7	,, ,,
		17th ,,	,,	,, 7	Jupiter
		,, ,,	,,	,, 7	α Virginis (*Spica*)
		19th ,,	,,	,, 7	β Ursæ Minoris
		28th ,,	,,	,, 7	α Ursæ Minoris (*Polaris*)
		30th ,,	,,	,, 7	β Orionis (*Rigel*)
		,, ,,	,,	,, 7	α Orionis
		,, ,,	,,	,, 7	α Canis Majoris (*Sirius*)
		20th Mar. 1874	,,	,, 7	Sun (*U.L.*)

(11)

to YARKAND via Chang-Chenmo and Shahidúlá.—(Concluded.)

Double altitudes or zenith distances corrected for index and level errors.			Elements used in computation of refraction.		Deduced Latitudes.			Remarks.			
			Barometer. Inches.	Ther. Faht. Degrees.	By stars north of zenith.	By sun or stars south of zenith.	Final latitudes north.				
	°	′	″			°	′	″	°	′	″		H.	M.	S.
Z. D.	50	25	21(2)	26·3	29	38 11 53(3)			Mean time = 10	4	44
D. A.	79	8	30	25·4	35	38 11 32					
„	114	42	40	25·4	35		38 12 11				
„	110	1	0	25·8	51		38 12 1	38 11 54			
Z. D.	50	13	58(1)	26·5	28	38 24 48(1)		⎫			
„	56	9	37(5)	26·4	47			⎪	Mean time = 10	45	0
„	23	37	58	26·4	40	38 24 55	38 25 16(5)	⎬ 38 24 57	„ = 12	2	29
„	29	6	39	26·4	40			⎪			
„	39	20	19	26·4	40		38 24 59	⎪			
„	50	21	50(3)	26·5	35	38 24 48(3)	38 25 5	⎪	Mean time = 11	34	50
„	50	13	21(4)	26·5	31	38 24 40(4)		⎭	„ = 9	14	51
D. A.	79	36	20	26·2	40	38 25 28					
„	79	36	40	26·2	40	38 25 38					
„	70	7	30	26·2	22		38 25 4	⎫			
„	114	16	50	„	22		38 25 5	⎪			
„	86	58	30	„	22		38 25 7	⎪			
„	135	43	40	„	22		38 23 52	⎪			
„	86	30	10	„	22		38 25 3	⎪			
„	46	14	10	„	22	38 24 59		⎪			
„	46	14	10	„	22	38 24 59		⎪			
„	65	51	10	„	22		38 24 55	⎪			
„	105	9	40	„	22		38 24 57	⎪			
„	86	29	0	„	22		38 25 36	⎪			
„	70	7	30	„	22		38 24 59	⎪			
„	56	53	0	„	32		38 25 16	⎪			
„	79	35	40	„	22	38 25 16		⎪			
„	117	55	50	„	22		38 25 36	⎬ 38 25 8	Final latitude of Yárkand 38° 25′ 2″·5		
„	70	7	0	„	22		38 25 14	⎪			
„	114	16	10	„	22		38 25 22	⎪			
„	128	21	0	„	22		38 24 55	⎪			
„	56	50	10	„	32		38 25 18	⎪			
„	135	40	40	„	22		38 25 22	⎪			
„	56	52	30	„	32		38 24 9	⎪			
„	86	58	50	„	22		38 24 51	⎪			
„	128	21	30	„	22		38 24 39	⎪			
„	74	10	0	„	18	38 25 16		⎪			
„	58	43	0	„	28		38 25 22	⎪			
„	60	6	40	„	28		38 24 57	⎪			
„	60	45	20	„	28		38 25 11	⎪			
„	104	18	20	„	18		38 25 6	⎪			
„	82	12	30	„	18		38 24 37	⎪			
„	46	14	10	„	18	38 25 7		⎪			
„	74	9	40	„	18	38 25 5		⎪			
„	86	30	0	„	18		38 25 0	⎪			
„	117	56	10	„	18		38 25 24	⎪			
„	70	7	0	„	18		38 25 6	⎪			
„	103	19	40	„	19		38 25 15	⎭			

(12)

Abstract of Observations for Latitude on road from LEH

Place of Observation.	Reference numbers	Astronomical date.	Observer.	Instrument observed with.		Object observed.
Panamik Village	59A	4th Oct. 1873	Nain Sing	Sextant No.	7	α Piscis Australis (*Fomalhaut.*)
		,, ,,	,,	,,	7	α Ursæ Minoris (*Polaris*)
Chánglung Village	59B	6th Oct. 1873	Nain Sing	Sextant No.	7	Saturn
		,, ,,	,,	,,	7	α Piscis Australis (*Fomalhaut*)
		,, ,,	,,	,,	7	α Ursæ Minoris (*Polaris*)
		,, ,,	,,	,,	7	α Canis Majoris (*Sirius*)
		16th May 1874	,,	,,	7	α Ursæ Minoris (*Polaris*)
		17th ,,	,,	,,	7	Jupiter
		,, ,,	,,	,,	7	α Virginis (*Spica*)
		,, ,,	,,	,,	7	β Ursæ Minoris
Tútialák Camp (*Pang-dong-sú.*)	59D	7th Oct. 1873	Nain Sing	Sextant No.	7	α Aquilæ (*Altair*)
		15th May 1874	,,	,,		Jupiter
		,, ,,	,,	,,	7	α Ursæ Minoris (*Polaris*)
Sausér-polu...	59F	8th Oct. 1873	Nain Sing	Sextant No.	7	α Canis Majoris (*Sirius*)
		13th May 1874	,,	,,		Jupiter
		14th ,,	,,	,,	7	α Ursæ Minoris (*Polaris*)
		,, ,,	,,	,,	7	β Ursæ Minoris
		20th June 1874	Capt. Trotter..	Theodolite		Sun (Centre)
Brúchso	83	17th June 1874	Capt. Trotter..	Theodolite		α Serpentis ...
		,, ,,	,,	,,		ζ Ursæ Minoris
		,, ,,	,,	,,		δ Ophiuchi ...
		,, ,,	,,	,,		β Ursæ Minoris
Khúmdán Camp	60	12th May 1874	Nain Sing	Sextant No. 7		α Ursæ Minoris (*Polaris*)
Giapshan Kizil	60A	11th May 1874	Nain Sing	Sextant No. 7		Jupiter
		,, ,,	,,	,,		α Virginis (*Spica*)
		,, ,,	,,	,,		α Ursæ Minoris (*Polaris*)
Daolatbeg-uldi	61	11th Oct. 1873	Nain Sing	Sextant No. 7		β Orionis (*Rigel*)
Bálti or Kárákorum polu	62B	10th May 1874	Nain Sing	Sextant No.	7	Jupiter
		,, ,,	,,	,,	7	α Virginis (*Spica*)
		,, ,,	,,	,,	7	α Ursæ Minoris (*Polaris*)

(13)

to *YARKAND* viâ *Karakoram and Kugiar.*

Double altitudes or zenith distances corrected for index and level errors.			Elements used in computation of refraction.		Deduced Latitudes.		Final Latitudes north.	Remarks.
			Barometer.	Ther. Faht.	By stars north of zenith.	By sun or stars south of zenith.		
	°	′ ″	Inches.	Degrees.	° ′ ″	° ′ ″	° ′ ″	
D. A.	49	54 40	20·7	44		34 46 34		
,,	72	21 10	20·7	44	34 47 45		34 47 10	
D. A.	67	29 30	20·3	44		34 55 50		
,,	49	36 20	20·3	44		34 55 42		
,,	72	38 20	20·3	44	34 56 23			
,,	77	5 40	20·3	44		34 55 40		
,,	67	9 30	20·2	50	34 55 40			
,,	119	14 40	20·2	50		34 56 38		
,,	89	8 30	20·2	50		34 56 1		
,,	100	29 30	20·2	50	34 54 23		34 55 43	
D. A.	127	6 0	17·4	30		34 59 31		
,,	119	6 30	17·4	35		35 0 46		
,,	67	18 50	17·4	35	35 0 26		35 0 17	
D. A.	76	52 0	17·1	21		35 2 25		
,,	119	1 40	17·3	30		35 2 58		
,,	67	24 0	17·3	30	35 2 59			
,,	100	45 10	17·3	30	35 2 15			
Z. D.	11	35 53	16·6	42		35 3 4	35 2 43	
Z. D.	28	15 33	16·6	42		35 5 6		
,,	43	5 58	16·6	42	35 4 23			
,,	38	27 27	16·6	42		35 5 39		
,,	39	35 35	16·6	42	35 4 16		35 4 51	
D. A.	67	34 0	17·0	30	35 8 1		35 8 1	
D. A.	118	30 40	16·7	19		35 17 58		
,,	88	24 0	16·7	19		35 18 14		
,,	67	53 0	16·7	19	35 17 30		35 17 54	
D. A.	92	35 10	16·2	15		35 22 16	35 22 16	
D. A.	118	16 30	16·5	17		35 24 41		
,,	88	9 40	16·5	17		35 25 24		
,,	68	5 40	16·5	17	35 23 49		35 24 26	

(14)

Abstract of Observations for Latitude on road from LEH

Place of Observation.	Reference numbers.	Astronomical date.	Observer.	Instrument observed with.	Object observed.
Nain Sing's Camp near Kárá-korum Pass.	62A.	25th April 1874	Nain Sing	Sextant No. 7	Jupiter
		,, ,,	,,	,, 7	α Virginis (*Spica*)
		,, ,,	,,	,, 7	α Ursæ Minoris (*Polaris*)
		,, ,,	,,	,, 7	β Ursæ Minoris
		9th May 1874	,,	,, 7	Jupiter
		,, ,,	,,	,, 7	α Ursæ Minoris (*Polaris*)
Kárákorum Brangsa	62	15th June 1874	Capt. Trotter	Theodolite	Sun (Centre)
		,, ,,	,,	,,	α Virginis (*Spica*)
		,, ,,	,,	,,	ζ Virginis
		,, ,,	,,	,,	α Libræ
		,, ,,	,,	,,	β Ursæ Minoris
		8th May 1874	Nain Sing	Sextant No. 7	Jupiter
		,, ,,	,,	,, 7	α Virginis (*Spica*)
		,, ,,	,,	,, 7	α Ursæ Minoris (*Polaris*)
Aktágh (2nd Camp) This camp is about one mile to the north of Aktágh 1st on the *Shéhidúla* route.	79	13th June 1874	Capt. Trotter	Theodolite	α Viginis (*Spica*)
		,, ,,	,,	,,	α Libræ
		,, ,,	,,	,,	β Ursæ Minoris
		,, ,,	,,	,,	β Libræ
Khufelong Camp	78	12th June 1874	Capt. Trotter	Theodolite	Sun (Centre)
Káshmír-jilga Camp	77	17th Oct. 1873	Nain Sing	Sextant No. 7	Saturn
		,, ,,	,,	,, 7	α Piscis Australis (*Fomalhaut*)
		,, ,,	,,	,, 7	α Ursæ Minoris (*Polaris*)
Kirghiz Camp (near Kirghiz jangal.)	76A	18th Oct. 1873	Nain Sing	Sextant No. 7	β Orionis (*Rigel*)
		,, ,,	,,	,, 7	α Orionis
		,, ,,	,,	,, 7	α Canis Majoris (*Sirius*)
Tupa Diwán Camp	76B	20th Oct. 1873	Nain Sing	Sextant No. 7	Saturn
		,, ,,	,,	,, 7	α Piscis Australis (*Fomalhaut*)
		,, ,,	,,	,, 7	α Ursæ Minoris (*Polaris*)
		,, ,,	,,	,, 7	α Canis Majoris (*Sirius*)

(15)

to *YARKAND* viâ *Karakoram and Kugiar*.—(Continued.)

Double altitudes or zenith distances corrected for index and level errors.	Elements used in computation of refraction.		Deduced Latitudes.			Remarks.
	Barometer.	Ther. Faht.	By stars north of zenith.	By sun or stars south of zenith.	Final latitudes north.	
° ′ ″	Inches.	Degrees.	° ′ ″	° ′ ″	° ′ ″	
D. A. 117 32 20	15·6	30		35 32		
,, 87 54 40	15·6	30		35 32 50		
,, 68 24 30	15·6	30	35 33 15			
101 47 30	15·6	30	35 33 22			
117 58 30	16·1	25		35 33 14		
68 23 50	16·1	25	35 32 56		35 33 4	
Z. D. 12 18 56	15·6	45		35 38 8		
,, 46 7 33	15·6	45		35 37 42		
,, 35 34 33	15·6	45		35 37 43		
,, 51 8 37	15·6	45		35 37 33		
,, 39 2 17	15·6	45	35 37 36			
D. A. 117 48 10	17·4	15		35 37 55		
,, 87 45 10	17·4	15		35 37 41		
,, 68 32 40	17·4	15	35 37 16		35 37 42	
Z. D. 46 30 21	16·9	31		36 0 35		
,, 51 30 46	16·9	31		36 0 15		
,, 38 40 5	16·9	31	35 59 44			
,, 44 54 45	16·9	31		36 0 9	36 0 11	
Z. D. 12 59 3	17·4	52	36 8 34		36 8 34	
D. A. 64 51 40	17·5	30		36 16 42		
,, 47 1 30	17·5	30		36 13 2		
,, 75 15 0	17·5	30	36 14 55		36 14 54	
D. A. 90 35 50	17·7	20		36 21 59		
,, 122 2 30	17·7	20		36 22 10		
,, 74 12 20	17·7	20		36 22 19	36 22 9	
D. A. 64 38 0	18·1	31		36 24 31		
,, 46 40 30	18·1	31		36 23 35		
,, 75 36 40	18·1	31	36 25 45			
,, 74 9 30	18·1	31		36 23 43	36 24 24	

Abstract of Observations for Latitude on road from LEH

Place of Observation.	Reference numbers.	Astronomical date.	Observer.	Instrument observed with.	Object observed.
Kirghiz Jangul Camp	76	10th June 1874 ,, ,, ,, ,, ,, ,,	Capt. Trotter ,, ,, ,,	Theodolite ,, ,, ,,	α Virginis (*Spica*) α Libræ β Ursæ Minoris β Libræ
Sasak bulák Camp	78A	17th April 1874 ,, ,, ,, ,, ,, ,, ,, ,, ,, ,,	Nain Sing ,, ,, ,, ,, ,,	Sextant No. 7 ,, 7 ,, 7 ,, 7 ,, 7 ,, 7	α Hydræ α Leonis (*Regulus*) Jupiter α Virginis (*Spica*) α Ursæ Minoris (*Polaris*) β Ursæ Minoris
Teshek Tásh Camp	73A	13th April 1874 ,, ,, ,, ,, ,, ,,	Nain Sing ,, ,, ,,	Sextant No. 7 ,, 7 ,, 7 ,, 7	α Hydræ Jupiter α Ursæ Minoris (*Polaris*) β Ursæ Minoris
Duba Camp	73	5th June 1874 ,, ,,	Capt.Trotter ,,	Theodolite ,,	α Coronæ α Serpentis
Mazár Khoja	65	12th April 1874 ,, ,, ,, ,, ,, ,,	Nain Sing ,, ,, ,,	Sextant No. 7 ,, 7 ,, 7 ,, 7	Sun (Upper Limb) α Leonis (*Regulus*) Jupiter α Ursæ Minoris (*Polaris*)
Chiklik	65A	31st May 1874 ,, ,, ,, ,, ,, ,,	Capt.Trotter ,, ,, ,,	Theodolite ,, ,, ,,	α Libræ α Bootis (*Arcturus*) β Ursæ Minoris β Libræ
Ak-Masjid	63	8th April 1874 ,, ,, 9th ,, ,, ,, ,, ,,	Nain Sing ,, ,, ,, ,,	Sextant No. 7 ,, 7 ,, 7 ,, 7 ,, 7	α Leonis (*Regulus*) Jupiter Sun (Upper Limb) α Hydræ Jupiter
Fusár Village	63A	6th April 1874 7th ,, ,, ,,	Nain Sing ,, ,,	Sextant No. 7 ,, 7 ,, 7	Sun (Upper Limb) ,, ,, Jupiter

(17)

to YARKAND viâ Karakoram and Kugiar.—(Continued.)

Double altitudes or zenith distances corrected for index and level errors.	Elements used in computation of refraction.		Deduced Latitudes.			Remarks.
	Barometer.	Ther. Faht.	By stars north of zenith.	By sun or stars south of zenith.	Final latitudes north.	
	Inches.	*Degrees.*	° ′ ″	° ′ ″	° ′ ″	
Z. D. 46 55 35	18·2	26		36 25 54		
,, 51 56 12	18·2	26		36 25 46		
,, 38 14 10	18·2	26	36 25 37			
,, 45 20 23	18·2	26		36 25 40	36 25 44	
D. A. 90 52 30	18·3	18		36 27 28		
,, 132 14 50	18·3	18		36 27 47		
,, 115 16 10	18·3	18		36 27 7		
,, 86 5 40	18·3	18		36 27 30		
,, 70 13 10	18·3	18	36 27 25			
,, 103 36 20	18·3	18	36 27 41		36 27 30	
D. A. 90 19 20	19·9	24		36 44 6		
,, 114 24 50	19·9	24		36 44 26		
,, 70 46 50	19·9	24	36 44 11			
,, 104 10 0	19·9	24	36 44 27		36 44 18	
Z. D. 0 38 13	20·2	55	36 46 37			
,, 29 56 53	20·2	55		36 46 30	36 46 34	
D. A. 124 8 20	20·9	39		36 50 50		
,, 131 30 20	20·9	30		36 50 3		
,, 114 7 30	20·9	30		36 50 52		
,, 70 59 20	20·9	30		36 50 24	36 50 32	
Z. D. 52 33 15	21·8	52		37 2 54		
,, 17 12 42	21·8	52	37 3 11			
,, 37 37 2	21·8	52	37 2 40			
,, 45 57 18	21·8	52		37 2 49	37 2 54	
D. A. 130 54 20	21·3	33		37 8 4		
,, 113 15 0	21·3	33		37 7 38		
,, 121 20 50	21·3	40		37 8 17		
,, 89 31 0	21·3	33		37 8 18		
,, 113 17 30	21·3	33		37 8 50	37 8 13	
D. A. 118 41 10	22·7	47		37 20 40		
,, 119 24 0	22·7	47		37 21 51		
,, 112 46 40	22·7	44		37 19 20	37 20 37	

(18)

Abstract of Observations for Latitude on road from LEH

Place of Observation.	Reference numbers	Astronomical date.	Observer.	Instrument observed with.	Object observed.
Kugiár Village	60	29th May 1874	Capt. Trotter ..	Theodolite ...	η Ursæ Majoris ...
		"	"	"	β Ursæ Minoris ...
		2nd April 1874	Nain Sing ...	Sextant No. 7	Jupiter ...
		3rd "	" ...	" 7	Sun (Upper Limb) ...
		"	" ...	" 7	α Leonis (*Regulus*) ...
		4th "	" ...	" 7	Sun (Upper Limb) ...
		"	" ...	" 7	α Hydræ ...
		"	" ...	" 7	α Leonis (*Regulus*) ...
		5th "	" ...	" 7	Sun (Upper Limb) ...
		"	" ...	" 7	α Leonis (*Regulus*) ...
Yolárik Village	68	27th May 1874	Capt. Trotter ..	Theodolite ...	β Ursæ Minoris ...
		"	" ...	" ...	β Libræ ...

(19)

to YARKAND viâ *Karakoram and Kugiar*.—(Concluded.)

Double altitudes or zenith distances corrected for index and level errors.	ELEMENTS USED IN COMPUTATION OF REFRACTION.		DEDUCED LATITUDES.			REMARKS.
	Barometer.	Ther. Faht.	By stars north of zenith.	By sun or stars south of zenith.	Final latitudes north.	
° ′ ″	Inches.	Degrees.	° ′ ″	° ′ ″	° ′ ″	
Z. D. 12 32 43	23·4	63	37 23 43			
„ 37 15 29	23·4	63	37 24 11			
D. A. 112 10 40	23·2	40		37 24 11		
„ 116 15 40	23·2	45		37 25 1		
„ 130 23 40	23·2	40		37 23 25		
„ 117 1 20	23·2	45		37 25 6		
„ 88 59 40	23·2	40		37 24 2		
„ 130 23 10	23·2	40		37 23 40		
„ 117 47 0	23·2	45		37 25 4		
„ 130 22 40	23·2	40		37 23 55	37 24 14	
Z. D. 37 12 41	23·6	70	37 26 59			
„ 46 21 40	23·6	70		37 27 13	37 27 6	

(20)

Abstract of Observations for Latitude on road from LEH

Place of Observation.	Reference numbers	Astronomical date.	Observer.	Instrument observed with.	Object observed.
Angche Chortan, R. bank of Nischu River.	108A.	28th July 1874 29th „	Kishen Sing... „	Sextant No. 8.. „	α Scorpii (*Antares*) ... β Ceti ... ...
Sumzi Ling Camp ...	108	26th July 1874 27th „ „ „ „ „	Kishen Sing... „ „ „	„ „ „ „	α Aquilæ (*Altair*) ... α Piscis Australis (*Fomalhaut*) β Ceti ... ...
Chumik Lhákmo Camp ...	107	23rd July 1874 „ „ 24th „ „ „	Kishen Sing... „ ... „ ... „	„ „ ... „ „	α Scorpii (*Antares*) ... α Aquilæ (*Altair*) ... Saturn ... ... α Piscis Australis (*Fomalhaut*)
Táshliák Khiol, lake bank of.	106	22nd July 1874 „ „	Kishen Sing... „	„ „	Saturn ... ... α Piscis Australis (*Fomalhaut*)
Arash Camp, on right bank of Kiria river.	103	14th July 1874 15th „ „ „	Kishen Sing... „ ... „	„ „ „	α Scorpii (*Antares*) ... α Piscis Australis (*Fomalhaut*) α Scorpii (*Antares*) ...
Ghubolik Camp, bank of Ulokshahí Khiol Lake.	102	12th July 1874 13th „	Kishen Sing... „ ...	„ „	α Aquilæ (*Altair*) ... Saturn ... ...
Polu Village	101	2nd July 1874 4th „ „ „ 7th „ 8th „ 9th „ „ „	Kishen Sing... „ ... „ „ „ „ „	„ „ „ ... „ ... „ ... „ ... „ ...	α Scorpii (*Antares*) .. α Aquilæ (*Altair*) ... Saturn ... ... α Aquilæ (*Altair*) ... α Scorpii (*Antares*) ... „ „ „ α Aquilæ (*Altair*) ...
Kiria Bazar	99	18th June 1874 26th „ 27th „ 28th „ 29th „ „ „	Kishen Sing... „ ... „ ... „ ... „ „	„ ... „ ... „ ... „ ... „ ... „ ...	β Ursæ Minoris ... α Aquilæ (*Altair*) ... Saturn ... ... β Ursæ Minoris ... α Aquilæ (*Altair*) ... Saturn ...

(21)

to YARKAND viâ *NOH,* ***POLU,*** *and* ***KHOTAN.***

Double altitudes or zenith distance corrected for index and level errors.	Elements used in computation of refraction.		Deduced Latitudes.			Remarks.
	Barometer.	Ther. Faht.	By stars north of zenith.	By sun or stars south of zenith.	Final latitudes north.	
° ′ ″	Inches.	Degrees.	° ′ ″	° ′ ″	° ′ ″	
D. A. 60 20 40	17·6	42		33 41 23		
„ 75 15 50	17·6	42		33 42 24	33 41 54	
D. A. 129 2 10	17·1	42		34 1 26		
„ 51 26 0	17·1	42		34 1 1		
„ 74 37 50	17·1	42		34 1 26	34 1 18	
D. A. 58 58 10	16·3	41		34 22 38		
„ 128 18 0	16·3	41		34 23 31		
„ 75 5 10	16·3	41		34 21 6		
„ 50 42 50	16·3	41		34 22 37	34 22 28	
D. A. 74 36 0	16·4	40		34 38 19		
„ 50 9 0	16·4	40		34 39 29	34 38 54	
D. A. 56 44 0	16·0	38		35 29 49		
„ 48 28 40	16·8	38		35 29 49		
„ 56 43 30	16·8	38		35 30 3	35 29 54	
D. A. 125 41 40	16·8	40		35 41 40		
„ 72 55 20	17·3	40		35 40 10	35 40 55	
D. A. 55 20 40	21·8	65		36 11 42		
„ 124 39 40	23·0	65		36 12 43		
„ 72 16 50	23·0	65		36 10 13		
„ 124 29 30	22·1	65		36 12 49		
„ 55 20 50	22·0	65		36 11 37		
„ 55 21 0	21·9	65		36 11 32		
„ 124 39 20	21·9	65		36 12 53	36 11 56	
D. A. 104 24 30	25·0	69	36 51 57		36 51 26	
„ 123 22 0	25·0	69		36 51 35		
„ 71 11 40	25·1	69		36 50 24		
„ 104 24 50	25·0	69	36 52 8			
„ 123 22 0	25·2	69		36 51 35		
„ 71 9 10	25·2	69		36 49 37		

(22)

Abstract of Observations for **Latitude** *on road from* **LEH**

Place of Observation.	Reference numbers.	Astronomical date.	Observer.	Instrument observed with.	Object observed.
Sorghák Khiang Shahi Bazar.	100	22nd June 1874 23rd ,,	Kishen Sing ... ,,	Sextant No. 8. ,,	β Ursæ Minoris α Aquilæ (*Altair*)
Chíra Bazar ...	98	11th June 1874 ,, ,, 12th ,, 13th ,, 14th ,,	Kishen Sing... ,, ,, ,, ,,	,, ,, ,, ,, ,,	α Virginis (*Spica*) β Ursæ Minoris α Aquilæ (*Altair*) β Ursæ Minoris α Aquilæ (*Altair*)
KHOTAN CITY. Observations taken in Shamál Bagh in nearly the same latitude as the centre of the city.	93	19th May 1874 ,, ,, ,, ,, 20th ,, ,, ,, ,, ,, 21st ,, ,, ,, ,, ,, ,, ,, 26th ,, ,, ,, 27th ,, 28th ,, ,, ,, 29th ,, 30th ,, ,, ,, ,, ,, 3rd June 1874 4th ,, ,, ,, ,, ,, 5th ,,	Kishen Sing... ,,	,, ,,	α Virginis (*Spica*) α Ursæ Minoris (*Polaris*) β Ursæ Minoris α Virginis (*Spica*) α Ursæ Minoris (*Polaris*) β Ursæ Minoris α Scorpii (*Antares*) α Virginis (*Spica*) α Ursæ Minoris (*Polaris*) β Ursæ Minoris α Ursæ Minoris (*Polaris*) β Ursæ Minoris α Aquilæ (*Altair*) α Scorpii (*Antares*) α Aquilæ (*Altair*) β Ursæ Minoris α Aquilæ (*Altair*) α Virginis (*Spica*) α Ursæ Minoris (*Polaris*) β Ursæ Minoris α Virginis (*Spica*) α Aquilæ (*Altair*) α Virginis (*Spica*) α Ursæ Minoris (*Polaris*) β Ursæ Minoris α Aquilæ (*Altair*)
Kárákásh Bazar	94	23rd May 1874 24th ,, ,, ,, ,, ,,	Kishen Sing... ,, ,, ,,	,, ,, ,, ,,	α Virginis (*Spica*) α Virginis (*Spica*) α Ursæ Minoris (*Polaris*) β Ursæ Minoris
Gúmá Bazar	90	12th May 1874	Kishen Sing...	,,	Jupiter

(23)

to YARKAND via NOH, POLU, and KHOTAN.—(Concluded.)

Double altitudes or zenith distances corrected for index and level errors.			Elements used in computation of refraction.		Deduced Latitudes.			Remarks
			Barometer. Inches.	Ther. Faht. Degrees.	By stars north of zenith.	By sun or stars south of zenith	Final latitudes north.	
	°	′	″		°	′	″	°	′	″	°	′	″	
D. A.	104	0	40	22·9	66	36 40 5			
,,	123	45	50	22·9	66		36 39 37	36 39 51	
D. A.	85	1	20	25·4	69		36 59 49		
,,	104	41	40	25·4	69	37 0 30			
,,	123	3	50	25·4	69		37 0 37		
,,	104	41	50	25·4	69	37 0 35			
,,	123	4	0	25·4	69		37 0 32	37 0 26	
D. A.	84	47	0	25·2	70		37 6 58		
,,	71	35	0	25·2	70	37 8 20			
,,	104	56	40	25·2	70	37 7 55			
,,	84	46	50	25·2	70		37 7 3		
,,	71	34	40	25·2	70	37 8 10			
,,	104	56	50	25·2	70	37 8 0			
,,	53	29	40	25·2	70		37 7 29		
,,	84	47	10	25·2	70		37 6 53		
,,	71	34	40	25·2	70	37 8 10			
,,	104	56	40	25·2	70	37 7 55			
,,	71	34	50	25·5	70	37 8 16			
,,	104	56	30	25·5	70	37 7 51			
,,	122	50	50	25·5	70		37 7 4		
,,	53	29	10	25·5	70		37 7 43		
,,	122	50	40	25·5	70		37 7 9		
,,	104	56	30	25·5	70	37 7 51			
,,	122	50	40	25·5	70		37 7 10		
,,	84	46	40	25·5	70		37 7 8		
,,	71	34	10	25·5	70	37 7 58			
,,	104	56	20	25·5	70	37 7 48			
,,	84	46	40	25·5	70		37 7 9		
,,	122	50	20	25·5	70		37 7 22		
,,	84	46	30	25·5	70		37 7 14		
,,	71	34	10	25·5	70	37 7 59			
,,	104	56	30	25·5	70	37 7 55			
,,	122	50	30	25·5	70		37 7 17	37 7 36	
D. A.	84	29	0	25·7	70		37 15 59		
,,	84	28	30	25·7	70		37 16 14		
,,	71	54	0	25·7	70	37 17 49			
,,	105	15	0	25·7	70	37 17 5		37 16 47	
D. A.	113	52	30	25·5	60		37 37 31	37 37 31	

Abstract of Observations for Latitude on road from

Place of Observation.	Reference numbers.	Astronomical date.	Observer.	Instrument observed with.	Object observed.
Kok Robát	109	20th May 1874 „ „ „ „	Capt. Trotter „ „	Theodolite „ „	Jupiter β Leonis α Virginis (*Spica*)
Kizil Village	110	30th Nov. 1873 „ „	Capt. Trotter „	Theodolite „	α Ursæ Minoris (*Polaris*)* „ „ „*
Yangi Hissar Town	111	1st Dec. 1873 18th Mar. 1874	Capt. Trotter „	Theodolite „	α Ursæ Minoris (*Polaris*)* α Leonis (*Regulus*)
Yapchan Village	112	3rd Dec. 1873 „ „	Capt. Trotter „	Theodolite „	α Ursæ Minoris (*Polaris*)* γ Pegasi (*Algenib*)*
KASHGHAR—Yangi-Shahr. In Embassy Quarters just outside the gate of the Yangi-Shahr.	113	4th Dec. 1873 19th „ 24th „ „ „ „ „ 27th „ „ „ „ „ 29th Jan. 1874 „ „ „ „ 3rd Feb. 1874 „ „ 13th „ „ „ „ „	Capt. Trotter „ „ „ „ „ „ „ „ „ „ „ „ „ „ „	Theodolite „ „ „ „ „ „ „ „ „ „ „ „ „ „ „	α Ursæ Minoris (*Polaris*)* „ „ „* „ „ „* α Tauri (*Aldebaran*) β Orionis (*Rigel*) ε Orionis β Orionis (*Rigel*) ε Orionis α Ursæ Minoris (*Polaris*)* δ Orionis ε Orionis α Orionis* α Canis Minoris (*Procyon*)* α Ursæ Minoris (*Polaris*)* α Canis Majoris* α Ursæ Minoris (*Polaris*)* „ „ „* „ „ „*

(25)

YARKAND to KASHGHAR.

Double altitudes or zenith distances corrected for index and level errors.	Elements used in computation of refraction.		By stars north of zenith.	By sun or stars south of zenith.	Final latitudes north.	Remarks.		
	Barometer.	Ther. Faht.	Deduced Latitudes.					
	Inches.	Degrees.	° ′ ″	° ′ ″	° ′ ″		H. M. S.
Z. D. 33 53 20	25·3	71		38 26 11				
„ 23 9 29	25·3	71		38 26 2				
„ 48 56 25	25·3	71		38 26 2	38 26 5			
Z. D. 50 11 57(3)	26·4	20	38 39 26(3)			Mean time = 6	19	48
„ 50 7 33(2)	26·3	20	38 39 20(2)		38 39 23	„ = 6	44	5
Z. D. 49 48 24(3)	26·3	37	38 55 58(3)			Mean time = 6	50	27
„ 26 20 59	25·2	33		38 56 17	38 56 8			
Z. D. 49 32 48(3)	25·5	38	39 13 32			Mean time = 6	36	15
„ 24 44 53(2)	25·5	38		39 13 30(2)	39 13 31	„ = 7	38	48
Z. D. 49 34 40	25·6	24	39 24 16(3)			Mean time = 11	7	4
„ 49 38 39(4)	25·6	14	39 24 19(4)			„ = 10	18	28
„ 49 13 25	25·5	17	39 24 5					
„ 23 8 40	„	„		39 24 23				
„ 47 44 30	„	„		39 24 36				
„ 40 40 44	„	„		39 24 31				
„ 47 44 19	„	„		39 24 24				
„ 40 40 34	„	„		39 24 21				
„ 49 55 38(5)	„	20	39 24 22(3)			Mean time = 10	51	8
„ 39 47 55	„	17		39 25 0				
„ 40 41 14	„	„		39 24 57				
„ 32 1 31(4)	25·7	19		39 24 26(4)		Mean time = 9	35	47
„ 33 52 43(4)	25·5	14		39 24 19(4)		„ = 7	25	33
„ 50 51 16(4)	„	„	39 24 13(4)			„ = 11	1	45
„ 55 56 32(6)	25·5	20		39 24 32(6)		„ = 5	53	42
„ 50 44 10(2)	„	„	39 24 14(2)			„ = 10	2	5
„ 50 47 47(2)	„	„	39 24 26(2)			„ = 10	12	48
„ 50 49 18(2)	„	„	39 24 33(2)		39 24 26	„ = 10	17	34

(26)

Abstract of Observations for Latitude on road from

Place of Observation.	Reference numbers.	Astronomical date.	Observer.	Instrument observed with.	Object observed.	
Osten Artysh (Besak Village).	115	10th Jan. 1874	Capt. Trotter...	Theodolite ...	δ Orionis ...	...
Chung Tirik Village ...	116	9th Jan. 1874	Capt. Trotter...	Theodolite ...	α Ursæ Minoris (*Polaris*)	
Chakmák Fort ...	118	8th Jan. 1874	Capt. Trotter...	Theodolite ...	Sun (U. L.)	...
Chakmák Station, three miles north of fort.	118A	3rd Jan. 1874	Capt. Trotter...	Theodolite ...	,, ,,	
Torgat Belá ...	110	7th Jan. 1874	Capt. Trotter...	Theodolite ...	α Ursæ Minoris (*Polaris*)	

Observations for Latitude on road

Viâ Uch Turfan. {	Ayák Soghon ...	126	20th Feb. 1874	Capt. Trotter...	Theodolite ...	ε Orionis ...	..
			,, ,,	,,	,, ...	α Orionis ...	
	Kyr Bulák ...	127	27th Feb. 1874	Capt. Trotter...	Theodolite ...	α Ursæ Minoris (*Polaris*)*	
	Ui Bulák ...	120	25th Feb. 1874	Capt. Trotter...	Theodolite ...	β Orionis (*Rigel*)	...
			,, ,,	,, ...	,, ...	δ Orionis ...	...
			,, ,,	,,	,, ...	ε Orionis ...	...
Viâ Marálbáshi. {	Faizabád ...	132	2nd March 1874	Capt. Trotter ...	Theodolite ...	δ Orionis	...
			,, ,,	,, ...	,, ...	ε Orionis	...
			,, ,,	,,	,, ...	α Orionis ...	
	Marálbáshi ...	137	11th Jan. 1874 17th ,,	Capt. Biddulph ,, ...	Six-inch Sextant. ,,	Sun (L. L.) ,,	... ...

Observations for Latitude taken in

Tangitár ...	139	17th Feb. 1874	Capt. Trotter...	Theodolite ...	α Canis Minoris (*Procyon*)	
		,, ,,	,, ...	,, ...	β Geminorum (*Pollux*)	...
Tughamati	140	18th Feb. 1874	Capt. Trotter...	Theodolite ...	β Orionis (*Rigel*)	...
		,, ,,	,, ...	,, ...	δ Orionis ...	...
		,, ,,	,, ...	,, ...	ε Orionis ...	...
Kizil-boia or Shamba Bazar	140A.	3rd Jan. 1874	Kishen Sing ...	Sextant No. 44	α Orionis ...	...
		4th ,,	,, ...	,, 44	α Canis Majoris (*Sirius*)	...
		,, ,,	,, ...	,, 44	α Canis Minoris (*Procyon*)	
Khánárik or Kháuárik Shamba Bazar.	140B.	5th Jan. 1874	Kishen Sing ...	Sextant No. 44	β Orionis (*Rigel*)	...
		,, ,,	,, ...	,, 44	α Orionis ...	
		6th ,,	,, ...	,, 44	α Canis Majoris (*Sirius*)	...
		,, ,,	,, ...	,, 44	α Canis Minoris (*Procyon*)	

KASHGHAR to CHADYRKUL.

Double altitudes or zenith distances corrected for index and level errors.	Elements used in computation of refraction.		Deduced Latitudes.			Remarks.
	Barometer.	Ther. Faht.	By stars north of zenith.	By sun or stars south of zenith.	Final latitudes north.	
	Inches.	Degrees.	° ′ ″	° ′ ″	° ′ ″	
Z. D. 39 59 34	25·0	20		39 36 50	39 36 50	
Z. D. 48 50 36	23·0	2	39 47 0		39 47 0	
Z. D. 62 3 11	21·5	32		40 5 9	40 5 9	
Z. D. 62 41 14	21·5	10		40 8 28	40 8 28	
Z. D. 48 13 51	19·4	−10	40 23 53		40 23 53	

from KASHGHAR to AKSU.

Z. D. 41 17 5	25·5	23		40 0 47		
„ 32 35 56	25·5	23		39 59 25	40 0 6	
						H. M. S.
Z. D. 50 7 31(3)	25·2	29	40 6 7(3)		40 6 7	Mean time = 9 21 21
Z. D. 48 46 1	23·8	25		40 25 57		
„ 40 49 22	23·8	25		40 26 24		
„ 41 42 41	23·8	25		40 26 20	40 26 14	
Z. D. 39 52 31	26·0	42		39 29 34		
„ 40 45 51	26·0	42		39 29 30		
„ 32 6 15	26·0	42		39 29 42	39 29 35	
Z. D. 61 50 7	26·2	28		39 46 1		
„ 60 47 12	26·3	29		39 46 46	39 46 24	

neighbourhood of KASHGHAR.

Z. D. 34 23 22	23·9	32		39 56 41		
„ 11 36 53	23·9	32		39 56 51	39 56 46	
Z. D. 48 22 0	23·7	30		40 1 54		
„ 40 24 56	23·7	30		40 1 57		
„ 41 18 8	23·7	30		40 1 46	40 1 52	
D. A. 116 1 33	25·0	20		39 22 44		
„ 68 11 23	25·0	20		39 22 59		
„ 112 21 23	25·0	20		39 22 44	39 22 49	
D. A. 84 48 33	26·0	20		39 15 46		
„ 116 16 13	26·0	20		39 15 24		
„ 68 25 53	26·0	20		39 15 44		
„ 112 35 3	26·0	20		39 15 53	39 15 42	

(28)

Abstract of Observations for Latitude on road from YANGI to KILAH

Place of Observation.	Reference numbers.	Astronomical date.	Observer.	Instrument observed with.	Object observed.
Aktala Camp	149	22nd March 1874 ,, ,,	Capt. Trotter ,,	Theodolite ,,	α Hydræ α Leonis (Regulus)
Kasha-sú Camp	151	15th May 1874 ,, ,, ,, ,, ,, ,,	Capt. Trotter ,, ,, ,,	Theodolite ,, ,, ,,	α Virginis (Spica) ζ Virginis η Ursæ Majoris α Bootis (Arcturus)
Tárbáshí Camp	156	27th March 1874	Capt. Trotter	Theodolite	α Leonis (Regulus)
TÁSHKURGHÁN, Camp near the Fort.	160	31st March 1874 ,, ,, ,, ,, ,, ,,	Capt. Trotter ,, ,, ,,	Theodolite ,, ,, ,,	α Leonis (Regulus)* α Ursæ Minoris (Polaris)* α Ursæ Majoris* ,, ,, ,,
Kogachak Camp	163	3rd April 1874 ,, ,,	Capt. Trotter ,,	Theodolite ,,	α Hydræ α Leonis
Aktásh Camp	183	5th May 1874	Capt. Trotter	Theodolite	β Corvi
Shash Tipá Camp	181	2nd May 1874. ,, ,, ,, ,,	Capt. Trotter ,, ,,	Theodolite ,, ,,	α Ursæ Majoris δ Leonis β Corvi
Pámir-kul, Camp on N. edge of Oi-kul or lake of Little Pámir.	165	5th April 1874 ,, ,, ,, ,, ,, ,,	Capt. Totter ,, ,, ,,	Theodolite ,, ,, ,,	ε Ursæ Majoris α Hydræ α Leonis α Ursæ Majoris
Daráz Diwán Camp	167	7th April 1874 ,, ,, ,, ,,	Capt. Trotter ,, ,,	Theodolite ,, ,,	ε Ursæ Majoris α Hydræ θ Ursæ Majoris
Mazár Tipá Camp	178	30th April 1874	Capt. Trotter	Theodolite	γ Leonis

(20)

PANJAH (WAKHAN) viâ *TASHKURGHAN and return journey to* **YARKAND**.

Double altitudes or zenith distances corrected for index and level errors.	Elements used in computation of refraction.		Deduced Latitudes.			Remarks.
	Barometer.	Ther. Faht.	By stars north of zenith.	By sun or stars south of zenith.	Final latitudes north.	
° ′ ″	Inches.	Degrees.	° ′ ″	° ′ ″	° ′ ″	
Z. D. 46 35 44	22·2	29		38 29 38		
" 25 53 42	22·2	29		38 28 57	38 29 18	
Z. D. 48 41 45	19·7	26		38 12 8		
" 38 8 44	19·7	26		38 12 3		
" 11 44 50	19·7	26	38 11 34			
" 18 21 49	19·7	26	38 12 16		38 12 0	
Z. D. 25 30 55	19·0	15		38 6 8	38 6 8	
						H. M. S.
Z. D. 25 12 7(3)	20·2	23		37 46 59(3)		Mean time = 9 23 37
25 11 37	20·2	23		37 46 50		
53 11 31(3)	20·2	23	37 46 30(3)			" = 9 30 20
24 40 40(4)	20·2	23	37 46 55(4)			" = 10 17 48
" 24 38 49	20·2	23	37 46 48		37 46 49	
Z. D. 45 43 37	18·2	9		37 37 23		
" 25 1 46	18·2	9		37 36 58	37 37 11	·
Z. D. 60 16 18	18·6	26	37 35 13		37 35 13	
Z. D. 24 54 9	26·0	18	37 31 36			
" 16 18 32	26·0	18		37 31 32		
" 60 13 2	26·0	18	37 31 54		37 31 39	
Z. D. 11 17 55	18·0	4		37 14 14		
" 45 21 48	18·0	4		37 15 33		
" 24 38 58	18·0	4		37 14 10		
" 25 11 49	18·0	4		37 13 49	37 14 27	
Z. D. 11 31 49	19·6	27	37 0 20			
" 45 6 30	19·6	27		37 0 16		
" 15 14 59	19·6	27		37 0 1	37 0 9	
Z. D. 16 59 59	1·79	20		37 28 53	37 28 53	

8

Abstract of Observations for Lat. on road from YANGI HISSAR to KILAH PANJAH

Place of Observation.	Reference numbers.	Astronomical date.	Observer.	Instrument observed with.	Object observed.
Yol Mazár Camp ...	176	28th April 1874	Capt. Trotter...	Theodolite ...	α Leonis ... ...
Kilah Panjah (WAKHAN)	174	18th April 1874 22nd ,, ,, ,, ,, ,, ,, ,, ,, ,,	Capt. Trotter... ,, ... ,, ... ,, ... ,, ...	Theodolite ... ,, ... ,, ... ,, ... ,, ...	α Ursæ Minoris (*Polaris*) α Virginis (*Spica*) ... ζ Virginis ... ... η Ursæ Majoris ... α Libræ ... ... α Libræ ... ...

(31)

(WAKHAN) viâ *TASHKURGHAN and return journey to YARKAND.*—(Concld.)

Double altitudes or zenith distances corrected for index and level errors.	Elements used in computation of refraction.		Deduced Latitudes.			Remarks.
	Barometer.	Ther. Faht.	By stars north of zenith.	By sun or stars south of zenith.	Final latitudes north.	
° ′ ″	Inches.	Degrees.	° ′ ″	° ′ ″	° ′ ″	
Z. D. 24 42 54	19·0	32		37 18 7	37 18 7	
Z. D. 54 19 43	21·3	25	37 0 14			
,, 47 30 3	21·3	25		37 0 28		
,, 36 57 2	21·3	25		37 0 21		
,, 12 56 8	21·3	25	37 0 8			
,, 52 30 30	21·3	25		37 0 23		H. M. S.
,, 52 33 35(2)	21·3	25		37 0 25 (2)	37 0 18	Mean time = 12 51 4

GEOGRAPHICAL APPENDIX.

SECTION B.

LONGITUDES.

THE method of observation employed in the determination of absolute longitudes was that of lunar zenith distances, as being best adapted to the largest instrument carried with the expedition, *viz.*, a six-inch transit theodolite, with micrometer eye-piece. This method of observation has not hitherto occupied a prominent position in English astronomical works, and as the results at *Kashghar* cannot but be considered satisfactory, I have thought advisable to enter somewhat at length into the subject and to give an example of the computation of a single night's observations there, drawn up on a form specially prepared from Chauvenet's *formulæ* by J. B. N. Hennessey, Esq., of the Great Trigonometrical Survey.

The subject is gone into somewhat fully in an article furnished by Colonel Walker, R.E., to *Hints to Travellers*, a publication of the Royal Geographical Society (3rd Edition, December 1871), to which the reader is referred.

The instrument employed at Kashghar is furnished with two micrometers, each moving a separate wire, the eye-piece being so arranged that the micrometer wires may be placed parallel either to the fixed vertical or to the fixed horizontal wire of the diaphragm, according as transits or zenith distances are required to be observed.

The distance between the micrometer and centre wires is adjustable at pleasure, and may be set according to the rate of motion of the celestial body observed. A complete observation of the moon, on one face of the instrument, consists in noting the chronometer times of passage of the moon's limb across each of the wires in succession and the corresponding reading of the vertical verniers; a complete pair of observations on both faces gives, altogether, six *times* and four *readings* of the vertical arc. The readings of the ends of the bubble of the level attached to the telescope, object and eye ends being alternately directed towards the object observed, give a correction to be applied to the mean of the readings of the vertical arc which gives a final zenith distance corresponding to the mean of the six chronometer times.

In the example I have given it took me just three quarters of an hour to observe ten complete pairs of zenith distances as before described. A quarter of an hour may be allowed for the observation of three pairs of zenith distances to a star for time, prior to the observations to moon, and an equal time for similar observations after. To complete the observations in the time above mentioned, however, the observer must be thoroughly familiar with his instrument, must have a good recorder, and have his lamps and apparatus in perfect order.

The weak point of the system is that it is only applicable at certain times when the moon is favorably situated for observation; still, however, even in this respect it contrasts favorably with all other methods, excepting that of "lunar distances," for determining longitudes. I give some rules which have been laid down on this subject by Colonel Walker in the *Hints to Travellers*, modified by subsequent experience: they may I hope be of use to future explorers.

"Take pairs of observations of zenith distance on a star for the determination of the local time and chronometer error, then take other pairs of observations of zenith distance on the moon; in each instance adopt the mean of the chronometer times as that of the 'complete observation' of zenith distance. Both moon and star should be as nearly easterly or westerly as possible, and not very near (say within 10° of) the horizon. The operations should commence and close with star observations, in order that the chronometer rate may be duly ascertained and allowed for. The effect of instrumental errors will be materially reduced when the stars and the moon are on the same side of the meridian and at nearly the same zenith distance, if time permits, observations should be taken both east and west of the meridian, and both before and after full moon. In north latitudes, when the moon is going from south to north in declination on any day, she is most favorably situated for observing when west of the meridian; if moving in declination from north to south, she should be observed east of the meridian. The best time for observation is *when the direction of the proper motion* of the moon is towards the zenith of the observer. The sidereal time when this occurs may be readily found, graphically, by drawing on a chart of the heavens a tangent to the moon's orbit, at some point near the mean position of the moon on the day of observing, and producing it to cut the declination circle passing through the observer's zenith; then the hour circle passing through the point of intersection gives the sidereal time of observation. For practical purposes it will suffice to drop a perpendicular from the point indicating the moon's mean position on to the ecliptic, and drawing through that point a line at right angles with the perpendicular, and prolonging it to cut the declination circle. It will be found that the most favorable times occur when the moon is on the observer's prime vertical, and the least favorable when she is on the meridian. Whenever possible a few observations should be taken daily on several days rather than a large number on a single day."

An examination of the results of the observations now published shows, at a glance, that those at Kashghar are both much more complete and satisfactory in every way than those taken at Yarkand and elsewhere. This is easily accounted for by several reasons:—

My stay at Yarkand was limited to twenty days in all, many of which were cloudy and unfavorable for observing; whereas I was at Kashghar on and off for more than two months, during which time I was enabled to select the most favorable days for observing; I was at Yarkand during the early portion of our stay in the country, and not knowing what opportunities I should have, if any, for further observations, there or elsewhere, I observed the moon whenever I could get an opportunity quite irrespective of its position being favourable or otherwise. The observations were taken in a small court-yard, where the paved flooring gave anything but a stable footing to the instrument and caused great difficulty with the levels. The noise in the small court of people moving about during the operation was, it may well be imagined, highly detrimental to such delicate work as observations for longitude, particularly where a pocket chronometer had to be used.

At Kashghar, on the other hand, the court-yard was much larger and quieter and the ground more stable, and altogether the surroundings were very much more favorable.

These circumstances, combined with the results obtained from the computations, have induced me to employ the longitude of *Kashghar* as the origin for all my positions in Turkestan.

I have merely employed the other observed longitudes as checks upon the general accuracy of the positions of those points as determined by other methods, for which *vide* the details on the construction of the map which are given in the body of the report.

(Sd.)   HENRY TROTTER, *Capt., R.E.*

(36)

Observations for Time, and resulting Chronometer corrections employed in determining Local Mean Time for the calculation of Longitude from Lunar Zenith Distances.

Place of Observation.	Astronomical date.	Object observed.	E. or W. of Meridian	Elements employed in computation of refraction.		No. of pairs of observations.	Mean of observed Z. Ds corrected for dislevelment.	Mean of Chronometer Times.	Computed correction to Chronometer Time to find corresponding Mean Time.
				Baro.	Ther. (Fahrt.)		° ′ ″	H. M. S.	H. M. S.
	1873.			In.					
KASHGHAR (Yangi-Shahr.)	6th Dec.	γ Geminorum	E.	25·7	24	3	53 8 29	10 8 32·0	−0 22 22·0
	„ „	β „	„	...	...	3	41 15 19	11 43 27·3	−0 22 21·6
	7th „	β „	„	25·8	...	3	47 21 5	11 7 57·6	−0 22 19·2
	„ „	α Leonis	„	...	15	3	66 7 53	12 40 2·6	−0 22 19·3
	27th „	α Androm.	W.	5·5	20	3	42 46 7	9 21 31·1	−0 22 19·2
	28th „	α Arietis	„	25·6	18	2	50 11 53	11 39 11·7	−0 22 20·7
	„ „	α „	„	...	...	2	52 26 18	11 50 45·6	−0 22 20·1
	1874.								
	29th Jan.	β Geminorum	E.	...	31	3	47 13 25	7 40 17·9	−0 22 22·0
	„ „	α Leonis	„	...	16	3	49 40 49	10 38 33·6	−0 22 22·4
	31st „	α „	„	25·5	15	4	49 34 17	6 56 31·0	+3 12 25·5
	1873.								
YARKAND	8th Nov.	β Tauri	E.	26·25	28	3	46 4 26	10 45 45·7	−0 18 25·7
	„ „	β Geminorum	„	...	...	3	48 57 41	12 50 17·0	−0 18 26·2
	9th „	„ „	„	26·25	23	3	39 3 6	13 36 52·9	−0 18 23·2
	„ „	„ „	„	...	...	3	22 15 22	15 3 56·5	−0 18 22·6
	1874.								
TASHKURGHAN.	31st March.	α Bootis (Arcturus)	E.	20·2	23	3		58 51 15	9 10 9·9	+0 2 34·4
KILA PANJAH	24th April	β Geminorum	W.	21·4	41	3	58 26 41	10 18 29·2	−0 10 5·2
	„ „	α Leonis (Regulus)	„	...	...	4	55 26 9	11 45 13·2	−0 10 4·9

(37)

Observations of Lunar Zenith Distances and resulting determination of Longitude.

Place of Observation.	Astronomical date.	E. or W. of Meridian.	Upper or Lower Limb.	Mean of each pair of observed Z. Ds corrected for dislevelment	Mean of Chronometer Times.	Resulting Longitude. Value from each pair of observations.			Mean of each day's observations.			Approx. sidereal time of observations.
				° ′ ″	H. M. S.	H.	M.	S.	H.	M.	S.	H. M.
KASHGHAR (Yangi-Shahr). The station of observation was in the centre of the Embassy Buildings just outside of and to the north of the YangiShahr or New City.	6th Dec. 1873.	E.	L.	48 30 3 47 48 47 46 40 26 46 3 40 43 59 14 43 16 48 42 25 11 41 45 4	10 27 19·3 30 59·0 37 4·4 40 19·9 51 24·4 55 9·3 59 45·2 11 3 18·2	5 4 4 4 3 4 4 4	4 	9 25 6 15 51 16 0 25	5	4	11	3 45
	7th „	E.	L.	49 1 13 48 7 59 47 2 24 46 23 50 45 7 4 44 27 30 43 33 28 42 51 23	11 24 3·1 28 46·8 34 37·3 38 2·3 44 52·1 48 23·3 53 12·9 56 58·0	5 4 3 4 4 4 4 4	3 	59 10 56 19 20 21 7 5	5	4	10	4 45
	27th „	W.	L.	53 13 22 54 2 16 57 16 20 58 0 11 59 4 2 59 42 29	9 47 18·0 52 17·1 10 11 34·9 15 52·1 22 2·4 25 44·6	5 4 4 4 4 4	4 	14 11 23 17 32 24	5	4	20	4 40
	28th „	W.	L.	46 56 38 47 43 14 48 33 30 49 43 0 50 17 58 51 17 43 51 53 54 52 45 57 53 23 12 54 25 40	10 25 34·8 30 10·9 35 5·8 41 48·7 45 10·3 50 52·7 54 18·5 59 13·6 11 2 44·2 8 34·2	5 4 4 4 4 4 4 4 4 4	4 	42 34 28 41 40 36 42 36 23 34	5	4	36	5 15
	29th Jan. 1874.	E.	U.	42 31 24 41 49 33 41 1 42 40 14 34 39 13 27	6 33 49·5 37 32·2 41 46·0 45 57·1 51 22·2	5 4 4 4 4	4 	41 36 48 41 44	5	4	47	3 25

10

(38)

Observations of Lunar Zenith Distances and resulting determination of Long.—(contd·)

PLACE OF OBSERVATION.	Astronomical date.	THE MOON.		Mean of each pair of observed Z. Ds corrected for disilvrelment.	Mean of Chronometer Times.	RESULTING LONGITUDE.		Approx. sidereal time of observations.
		E. or W. of Meridian.	Upper or Lower Limb.			Value from each pair of observations.	Mean of each day's observations.	
				° ′ ″	H. M. S.	H. M. S.		
KASHGHAR (Yangi-Shahr)—concluded.	29th Jan. 1874.	E.	U.	38 36 19 37 53 53 37 12 17	54 39·8 58 25·6 7 2 7·9	4 51 4 59 4 54		
	31st Jan. 1874.	E.	U.	42 21 6 41 39 0 40 2 49 38 29 9 37 54 22 36 36 42	8 31 25·7 35 12·4 43 48·7 52 15·4 55 23 6 9 2 25·1	5 4 44 4 24 4 51 4 29 4 34 4 50	5 4 39	H. M. 5 30
	Arithmetical Mean of Longitude from six days' observations, which is the value finally adopted.						H. M. S. 5 4 27·2 or ° ′ ″ 76 6 47·5	
YARKAND Station of observation in the Embassy Quarters in the centre of the Yangi-Shahr or New City.	8th Nov. 1873.	E.	L.	54 59 57 53 48 30 53 7 19 52 21 38 51 34 9 48 19 50 47 38 27 46 26 52 45 30 28	11 10 35·0 16 54·7 20 33·2 24 35·1 28 44·9 45 50·8 49 28·3 55 44·5 12 0 41·2	5 8 30 8 30 8 35 8 45 9 13 8 58 9 6 9 8 9 0	H. M. S. 5 8 51	H. M. 2 40
Ditto	,, ,,	W.	U.	57 55 21 58 32 13 59 15 55 60 10 58 60 47 38 61 29 37 62 16 38 63 29 22	20 22 51·3 26 7·9 30 1·8 34 58·4 38 15·6 42 2·2 46 16·0 52 50·8	5 9 40 10 0 10 7 9 50 9 55 9 52 10 4 9 59	5 9 56	11 50

(39)

Observations of Lunar Zenith Distances and resulting determination of Long.—(concld.)

Place of Observation.	Astronomical date.	E. or W. of Meridian.	Upper or Lower Limb.	Mean of each pair of observed Z. Ds corrected for disdevelopment.	Mean of Chronometer Times.	Resulting Longitude.		Approx. sidereal time of observations.
						Value from each pair of observations.	Mean of each day's observations.	
				° ′ ″	H. M. S.	H. M. S.	H. M. S.	H. M.
YARKAND Station of observation in the Embassy Quarters in the centre of the Yangi-Shahr or New City.	9th Nov. 1873.	E.	L.	38 17 7 37 25 58 36 35 26 35 39 54 31 57 45 31 6 19 30 6 53 29 11 7	13 36 28·9 40 58·1 45 25·9 50 19·5 14 10 4·3 14 41·2 20 2·9 25 5·8	5 8 52 9 11 8 55 9 7 9 8 9 2 8 50 9 1	5 9 1	5 15
	Arithmetical mean of longitude from three days' observations*						5 9 16 or ° ′ ″ 77 19 0	
	Final longitude adopted for Yarkand, *vide* body of Report						° ′ ″ 77 15 55	
TASHKURGHAN... Station of observation about 300 yards to the east of the Fort.	31st March 1874.	E.	U.	61 44 7 60 37 23 59 50 7 59 16 52 58 4 33 57 17 40	7 27 42·3 33 51·1 37 24·3 41 20·9 48 7·2 52 32·7	5 2 16 2 4 1 44 1 26 1 7 1 1	H. M. S. 5 1 36 or ° ′ ″ 75 24 0	8 15
	Which gives the Astronomical longitude from one night's observations.							
	Final longitude adopted for Tashkurghan, *vide* body of Report						° ′ ″ 75 19 1	
KILA PANJAH Station of observation about 300 yards to south of principal Fort of Kila Panjah.	24th April 1874.	W.	L.	44 0 53 45 13 15 46 15 41 47 3 46 50 52 43 51 40 43 52 24 10 53 3 42 55 9 16	10 23 21·7 31 0·5 34 53·5 38 59·7 58 28·8 11 2 32·8 6 13·8 9 34·9 20 14·1	4 50 55 51 17 51 7 51 2 50 43 50 57 51 8 51 9 50 56	H. M. S. 4 51 2 or ° ′ ″ 72 45 30	13 0
	Which gives the Astronomical longitude from one night's observations.†							
	Final longitude adopted for Kila Panjah, *vide* Geographical Chapter.						72 45 29	

* Observations were also taken at Yarkand on three other nights, when the moon was so unfavorably situated that these have not been employed.
† Observations were made on another night at Kila Panjah, but it appeared from the resulting time computations that the chronometer employed had been going irregularly.

(40)

SPECIMEN COPY OF COMPUTATION OF ONE DAY'S

Computation of Longitude fr

At Kashghar (Yangi-Shahr) Station, on

Moon { West of Meridian, Lower Limb observed. Lat. N. $= \phi =$ 39° 24′ 32″ Assumed

Ref. No.	No. of observation (Mean of F. L. and F. R.)				1			2			3		
(1)	Chronometer Time of observation	...	...		10	47	55·2	10	52	31·3	10	57	26·2
(2)	,, Correction	...	...	−		22	20·4		22	20·4		22	20·4
(3)	Local Mean Time (Ast. D.) = 28 days	...	+	10	25	34·8	10	30	10·9	10	35	5·8
(4)	Approx. Gr. Mean Time = (3) + L_1 = 28 days		+	5	20	34·8	5	25	10·9	5	30	5·8
(5)	☾ 's observed Zenith Distance	...	...	$= \zeta_0$	46	56	38	47	43	14	48	33	30
(6)	Refraction (for B and T) = r	...	$=+$				57			59		1	0
(7)	☾ 's Semi-diameter at (4) from N. A. = S	...	−		16	2		16	2		16	2
(8)	From Table I	ΔS	...	−			11			11			11
(9)	(5) + (6) + (7) + (8)	...	...	$= \zeta_2$	46	41	22	47	28	0	48	18	17
(10)	☾ 's Horizontal Parallax at (4) from N. A. = π″	+			58	45		58	44		58	44
(11)	From Table II	$\Delta \pi$″	+			5			5			5
(12)	Log. π_1″ = log. $(\pi + \Delta \pi)$″	..	...	{	3·54777			3·54765			3·54765		
(13)	Log. sin ζ_2	...	...	...	1·86192			1·86740			1·87314		
(14)	(12) + (13) = log. $(\pi_1 \sin \zeta_2)$″	...	(	3·40969			3·41505			3·42079		
(15)	$\pi_1 \sin \zeta_2$	...	...		42	49		43	20		43	55
(16)	(9) − (15) = $\zeta_2 - \pi_1 \sin \zeta_2$ =	...	ζ_1	45	58	33	46	44	40	47	34	22
(17)	☾ 's Declination at (4) from N.A. = δ	...	+	11	57	8·	11	58	15	11	59	27
(18)	$\Delta \delta$ from Table III	...	...	+			15			15			15
(19)	(17) + (18) = $\delta + \Delta \delta = \delta_1$	...	+	11	57	23	11	58	30	11	59	42
(20)	$\phi - (19) = (\phi - \delta_1)$	...	...		27	27	9	27	26	2	27	24	50
(21)	(16) + (20) = $\zeta_1 + (\phi - \delta_1) = 2 \sigma_1$	...		73	25	42	74	10	42	74	59	12
(22)	(16) − (20) = $\zeta_1 - (\phi - \delta_1) = 2 \sigma_2$	...		18	31	24	19	18	38	20	9	32
(23)	σ_1	...	...		36	42	51	37	5	21	37	29	36
(24)	σ_2	...	...		9	15	42	9	39	19	10	4	46
(25)	Log. sin σ_1	...	...		1·7765729			1·7803585			1·7848813		
(26)	Log. sin σ_2	...	...		1·2066735			1·2245847			1·2430716		
(27)	Log. sec ϕ	...	...		0·1120256			0·1120256			0·1120256		
(28)	Log. sec δ_1	...	...		0·0095255			0·0095554			0·0095876		
(29)	(25) + (26) + (27) + (28) = log. sin $\tfrac{1}{2} t$			1·1047975			1·1265242			1·1490661		
(30)	Log. sin $\tfrac{1}{2} t$				1·5523988			1·5632621			1·5745331		
(31)	t (in arc)	...	...	+	41	48	18	42	54	56	44	6	8
(32)	S. T. Gr. Mean Noon on 28 days (see (4))	...		18	28	5·8	18	28	5·8	18	28	5·8
(33)	Local Mean Time (same as (3))	...		10	25	34·8	10	30	10·9	10	35	5·8
(34)	Acceleration for (4)	...	...				52·7			53·4			54·2
(35)	(32) + (33) + (34) = local S. T. of observation = θ		4	54	33·3	4	59	10·1	5	4	5·8
(36)	t (in time) deduced from (31)	...	+	2	47	13·2	2	51	39·7	2	56	24·5
(37)	☾ 's Right Ascension or AR = $\theta - t$	...		2	7	20·1	2	7	30·4	2	7	41·3
(38)	Greenwich Mean Time for (37) from N. A.	...		5	21	1·1	5	25	47·8	5	30	51·2
(39)	(38) − (33) = Approx. Long. = L_2	...	−	5	4	33·7	5	4	23·1	5	4	14·6
(40)	(39) − $L_1 = L_2 - L_1$	...	...	+			26·3			36·9			45·4
(41)	At (38) change in ☾ 's A R for increment of $1^m = \lambda^s$ +		2·155			2·155			2·156		
(42)	Do. Do. Decn. Do. $= \beta''$ +		14·621			14·615			14·609		
(43)	Log. cos ϕ (see (27))	...	...		1·8880			1·8880			1·8880		
(44)	Log. sin t (see (31))	...	...		1·8239			1·8331			1·8426		
(45)	Log. cosec ζ_1 (see (16))	...	...		0·1432			0·1377			0·1319		

(41)

OBSERVATIONS FOR *LONGITUDE* AT KASHGHAR.

om *Lunar Zenith Distances.*

28th December 1873 *(Civil Date,* P.M.)

Long. E. $= L_1 = -$ 76° 15′ | Barometer = B = 25·6 Inches.
$=$ 5h. 5m. in time | Thermometer = T = 18° (Fahrenheit.)

4	5	6	7	8	9	10
11 4 9·1	11 7 30·7	11 13 13·1	11 16 38·9	11 21 34·0	11 25 4·6	11 30 54·6
22 20·4	22 20·4	22 20·4	22 20·4	22 20·4	22 20·4	22 20·4
10 41 48·7	10 45 10·3	10 50 52·7	10 54 18·5	10 59 13·6	11 2 44·2	11 8 34·2
5 36 48·7	5 40 10·3	5 45 52·7	5 49 18·5	5 54 13·6	5 57 44·2	6 3 34·2
49 43 0	50 17 58	51 17 43	51 53 54	52 45 57	53 23 12	54 25 40
1 3	1 4	1 5	1 8	1 10	1 12	1 14
16 2	16 2	16 2	16 2	16 2	16 2	16 2
11	11	10	10	10	10	10
49 27 50	50 2 49	51 2 36	51 38 50	52 30 55	53 8 12	54 10 42
58 44	58 44	58 44	58 44	58 44	58 44	58 44
5	5	5	5	5	5	5
3·54765	3·54765	3·54765	3·54765	3·54765	3·54765	3·54765
1·88081	1·88455	1·89077	1·89443	1·89956	1·90313	1·90894
3·42846	3·43220	3·43842	3·44208	3·44721	3·45078	3·45659
44 42	45 5	45 44	46 7	46 40	47 3	47 41
48 43 8	49 17 44	50 16 52	50 52 43	51 44 15	52 21 9	53 23 1
12 1 5	12 1 55	12 3 18	12 4 7	12 5 19	12 6 10	12 7 36
15	15	15	15	15	15	15
12 1 20	12 2 10	12 3 33	12 4 22	12 5 34	12 6 25	12 7 51
27 23 12	27 22 22	27 20 59	27 20 10	27 18 58	27 18 7	27 16 41
76 6 20	76 40 6	77 37 51	78 12 53	79 · 3 13	79 39 16	80 39 42
21 19 56	21 55 22	22 55 53	23 32 33	24 25 17	25 3 2	26 6 20
38 3 10	38 20 3	38 48 56	39 6 27	39 31 37	39 49 38	40 19 51
10 39 58	10 57 41	11 27 57	11 46 17	12 12 39	12 31 31	13 3 10
1·7898535	1·7925646	1·7971396	1·7998761	1·8037582	1·8065019	1·8110386
1·2673721	1·2790905	1·2983804	1·3096455	1·3253301	1·3362001	1·3538172
0·1120256	0·1120256	0·1120256	0·1120256	0·1120256	0·1120256	0·1120256
0·0096314	0·0096539	0·0096912	0·0097132	0·0097457	0·0097687	0·0098076
1·1788826	1·1933346	1·2172368	1·2312004	1·2508596	1·2644963	1·2866890
1·5894413	1·5906673	1·6086184	1·6156302	1·6254298	1·6322482	1·6433445
45 43 41	46 32 24	47 55 6	48 44 55	49 56 11	50 46 55	52 11 38
18 28 5·8	18 28 5·8	18 28 5·8	18 28 5·8	18 28 5·8	18 28 5·8	18 28 5·8
10 41 48·7	10 45 10·3	10 50 52·7	10 54 18·5	10 59 13·6	11 2 44·2	11 8 34·2
55·3	55·9	56·8	57·4	58·2	58·8	59·7
5 10 49·8	5 14 12·0	5 19 55·3	5 23 21·7	5 28 17·6	5 31 48·8	5 37 39·7
3 2 54·7	3 6 9·6	3 11 40·4	3 14 59·7	3 19 44·7	3 23 7·7	3 28 46·5
2 7 55·1	2 8 2·4	2 8 14·9	2 8 22·0	2 8 32·9	2 8 41·1	2 8 53·2
5 37 15·4	5 40 38·6	5 46 26·6	5 49 44·2	5 54 47·7	5 58 35·9	6 4 10·2
5 4 33·3	5 4 31·7	5 4 26·1	5 4 34·3	5 4 25·9	5 4 8·3	5 4 24·0
26·7	28·3	33·9	25·7	34·1	51·7	36·0
2·156	2·156	2·156	2·156	2·157	2·157	2·157
14·603	14·598	14·593	14·588	14·583	14·578	14·572
1·8880	1·8880	1·8880	1·8880	1·8880	1·8880	1·8880
1·8549	1·8608	1·8705	1·8761	1·8838	1·8892	**1·8977**
0·1241	0·1203	0·1140	0·1102	0·1050	0·1014	**0·0955**

11

SPECIMEN COPY OF COMPUTATION OF ONE DAY'S

Computation of Longitude fr

At Kashghar (Yangi-Shahr) Station, on

Moon { West of Meridian. Lower Limb observed. } | Lat. N. $= \phi =$ 39° 24′ 32″ | Assumed

Ref. No.	No. of observation (Mean of F. L. and F. R.)			1	2	3
(46)	(43) + (44) + (45) = Log. sin q	...	...	1·8551	1·8588	1·8625
(47)	Log. tan q from (46)	...	...	0·0114	0·0190	0·0269
(48)	Log. cos c_1 (see (28))	...	...	1·9905	1·9904	1·9904
(49)	Log. λ (see (41))	...	...	0·3334	0·3334	0·3336
(50)	Log. 15	...	...	1·1761	1·1761	1·1761
(51)	Log. sum = (47) + (48) + (49) + (50)	...		1·5114	1·5189	1·5270
(52)	Log. β	...	...	1·1650	1·1648	1·1646
(53)	(52) − (51) = log. a (see Table IV.)	...	+	1·6536	1·6459	1·6376
(54)	1 + a	...	...	1·450	1·442	1·434
(55)	$\frac{L_q - L_1}{1 + a} = \Delta L_1$	...	... +	18s.	26s.	32s.
(56)	$L = L_1 + \Delta L_1$	...	... −	5h. 4m. 42s.	4m. 34s.	4m. 28s.

Explanation of Symbols adopted.

Ast. D. stands for Astronomical Date.
Gr: do. Greenwich.
S. T. do. Sidereal Time.
N. A. do. Nautical Almanac.
Approx: do. Approximate.

Rules for Computation.

Compute δ for each observation, *i.e.*, for Nos. 1, 2, 3 ... 8.
Do. $\Delta \delta$ }
Do. S } for middle observation, and adopt this value as constant for all the other observations.
Do. $\Delta \pi$ }
Do. π and ΔS for No. 1 and No. 8, and interpolate for Nos. 2 to 6 with change in Gr. Mean Time for argument.

NOTE.—S and ΔS have the same sign and are both $\pm$ when $\frac{upper}{lower}$limb of ☾ is observed; $\Delta \delta$ is + in N. Latitude; t is $\pm$ if ☾ is $\frac{W}{E}$ of Meridian; λ is always +; β is $\pm$ when ☾ is moving in Declination from $\frac{S.\ to\ N.}{N.\ to\ S.}$: sign of a = sign of β × sign of t.

OBSERVATIONS FOR *LONGITUDE* AT KASHGHAR.—*(Continued.)*
on *Lunar Zenith Distances.*
28th *December* 1873 *(Civil Date,* P.M. *)*

Long. E. $= L_1 = -$ 76° 15′
5h. 5m. in time

Barometer $= B =$ 25·6 Inches.
Thermometer $= T =$ 18° (Fahrenheit.)

4	5	6	7	8	9	10
1·8670	1·8691	1·8725	1·8743	1·8768	1·8786	1·8812
0·0366	0·0412	0·0488	0·0528	0·0586	0·0627	0·0689
T.9904	1·9903	1·9903	1·9903	1·9903	1·9902	1·9902
0·3336	0·3336	0·3336	0·3336	0·3339	0·3339	0·3339
1·1761	1·1761	1·1761	1·1761	1·1761	1·1761	1·1761
1·5367	1·5412	1·5488	1·5528	1·5589	1·5629	1·5691
1·1644	1·1643	1·1641	1·1640	1·1638	1·1637	1·1635
1·6277	1·6231	1·6153	1·6112	1·6040	1·6008	1·5944
1·424	1·420	1·412	1·409	1·403	1·399	1·393
19s.	20s.	21s.	18s.	24s.	37s	26s.
4m. 41s.	4m. 40s.	4m. 36s.	4m. 42s.	4m. 36s.	4m. 23s.	4m. 31s.

Mean resulting longitude from **observations on 28th December 1873**—5h. 4m. 36s. or 76° 9′ 0″.

Table used to facilitate the computation.

TABLE I for Δ S			TABLE II for Δ π			TABLE III for Δ δ $= D (1-f)$				
C's Apparent Zenith Distance.	Horizontal semi-diameter.		Latitude.	Equatorial Parallax.		Latitude.	D		δ	f
	14′ 0″	17′ 0″		53′	61′		53′	61′		
°	″	″	°	″	″	°	″	″	°	
0	12·7	18·8	0	0·0	0·0					
10	12·5	18·6	10	0·3	0·4					
20	12·0	17·7	20	1·2	1·4	0	0·0	0·0	0	·00
30	11·0	16·3	30	2·7	3·1	5	1·8	2·1	5	·00
40	9·7	14·4	40	4·4	5·1	10	3·7	4·2	10	·02
50	8·2	12·1	50	6·2	7·2	15	5·5	6·3	15	·03
60	6·4	9·5	60	8·0	9·2	20	7·2	8·3	20	·06
70	4·4	6·5	70	9·4	10·8	25	8·9	10·3	25	·09
80	2·3	3·4	80	10·3	11·9	30	10·6	12·1	30	·13
90	0·1	0·2	90	10·6	12·2	35	12·1	13·9		
						40	13·6	15·6		
						45	14·9	17·2		
						50	16·2	18·6		

Example. $\phi = 30°·5′$
$\pi = 56'·7, \; \delta = 7°$
From Tables
$D =$ 11″·5
$-fD =$ $-1·2$
$\Delta \delta = 10$

GEOGRAPHICAL APPENDIX,

SECTION C.

HEIGHTS.

ABSTRACT OF OBSERV

Observations on road from LEH *to* YAR

Number in Alphabetical List.	Place of Observation.	Date.	Observer.	At Station — Reading of barometer or boiling point thermometer corrected for index error.
				Inches or Degrees.
1	Chimray village	13th Sept. 1873	Capt. Trotter	19·340(2)
2	Zingral Camp	14th ,,	,,	16·776(4)
3	Chang La (or Sakti Pass)	15th ,,	,,	15·635(6)
4	Tsultak village	,, ,,	,,	16·680(2)
5	Tankse village	16th & 17th Sept. 1873	,,	18·650(6)
6	Chakr Talao Camp	18th Sept. 1873	,,	18·022(2)
7	Lukong village (on Pangong Lake)	19th & 20th Sept. 1873	,,	17·851(7)
8	Chágrá Camp	21st Sept. 1873	,,	17·217(8)
9	Lankar La (or Marsimik Pass)	22nd ,,	,,	15·135(2)
10	Rimdi Camp	,, ,,	,,	15·727(4)
11	Pamzal Camp	23rd ,,	,,	17·388(4)
12	Gogra Camp	24th ,,	,,	16·864(4)
13	East Route *viá* Lingzi Thung. — Shummal Lung pa or Bhao	26th ,,	Capt. Biddulph	15·897
14	Changlung Burma Pass	27th ,,	,,	14·596
15	Nischu (Camp near)	,, ,,	,,	14·912
16	Lingzi Thung plain (south side of)	28th ,,	,,	15·534
17	Lingzi Thung plain (camp on)	,, ,,	,,	15·560
18	Súmná Camp east of Kiziljilga	30th ,,	,,	15·720
19	West Route, *viá* Head of Karakash River. — Kotajilga Camp	26th ,,	Capt. Trotter	16·149(1)
20	Pangtung Camp	28th ,,	,,	15·725(1)
21	Pangtung or Chang Lung Pass	,, ,,	,,	14·805(1)
22	Sumzum Lung pa Camp	29th ,,	,,	15·714(4)
23	Debra Compass Camp	30th ,,	,,	15·309(1)
24	Compass Wala's Pass	1st Oct. 1873	,,	A 15·18(1)
25	Karakash River near Compass La	,, ,,	,,	15·625(1)
26	Shinglung, or Dunglung Camp	2nd & 3rd Oct. 1873	,,	15·844(8)
	Ditto	,, ,,	,,	181·60(2)
27	Kiziljilga Camp	1st, 2nd ,,	,,	16·098(2)
28	Chungtash Camp	8th ,,	,,	16·786

NOTE.—The figures in column (5) when given in inches are the corrected readings of a mercurial mountain barometer unless the letter A. is The numbers in brackets preceding the figures in column (5) indicate the number of sets of observations, the corrected mean of which has been employed

(47)

ATIONS FOR HEIGHT.

KAND viâ *Changchenmo* and *Shahidúla*.

OF OBSERVATION.		AT BASE STATION LEH.*			Resulting height above mean sea level.	REMARKS.
Temperature of mercury (Fahrenheit).	Temperature of air (Fahrenheit).	Corrected reading of barometer.	Temperature of mercury (Fahrenheit).	Temperature of air (Fahrenheit).		
Degrees.	Degrees.	Inches.	Degrees.	Degrees.	Feet.	
63	61	19·580	60	56	11,890	
57	51	19·580	60	56	15,780	
43	31·3	19·617	58·3	54	17,590	By Captain Biddulph, 17,395 feet.
51	38	19·617	58	54	15,950	
51	48	19·617	58	54	12,000	
61	58	19·617	58	54	13,890	
56	55	19·617	58	54	14,130	
52·3	48·8	19·617	58·3	54	15,090	
45	25	19·617	58·3	54	18,420	By Captain Biddulph, 18,530 feet.
41	42	19·617	58	54	17,500	
58	54	19·569	56	52	14,790	
47·3	45·5	19·569	56·3	54	15,570	
...	48·2	19·424	...	57·6	17,020	
...	32	19·478	...	56·5	19,280	
...	35·3	19·396	...	57·8	18,630	
...	33·3	19·522	...	56·3	17,680	
...	29·0	19·522	...	56·3	17,610	
...	22·0	19·443	...	54·2	17,150	
47	44	19·569	56	52	16,730	
24	22	19·569	56	52	17,250	
33	26	19·569	56	52	18,910	
32	28	19·569	56	52	17,330	
21	15	19·569	56·3	49·3	17,890	
...	23	19·537	49	40·6	18,160	
33	30	19·572	49	40·6	17,440	
25	25	19·572	49	40·6	17,030	} Mean height = 17,030 feet.
..	18	19·537	49	40·6	17,030	
...	26·5	19·508	...	43·1	16,590	
...	37·8	19·659	...	43·5	15,590	

attached, in which case an aneroid barometer has been used; when given in degrees the figures are the corrected means of hypsometrical readings, in determining the height.
* The height of the observatory at Leh is taken as 11,538 feet above sea level.

(48)

Observations on road from LEH to YAR

Number in Alphabetical List.		Place of Observation.			Date.		Observer.	AT STATION. Reading of barometer or boiling point thermometer corrected for index error.
								Inches or Degrees.
29	East Route along Karakash River.	Karakash River, Captain	Biddulph's Camp		9th Oct. 1873	...	Capt. Biddulph	16·898
30		Ditto	ditto	...	10th ,,	...	,, ...	17·233
31		Ditto	ditto	...	11th ,,	...	,, ...	17·450
32		Ditto	ditto	...	12th ,,	...	,, ...	17·656
33		Ditto	ditto (Sora)	...	13th ,,	...	,, ...	17·796
34		Ditto	ditto	...	14th ,,	...	,, ...	18·036
35		Ditto	ditto	...	15th ,,	...	,, ...	18·376
36		Ditto	ditto	...	16th ,,	...	,, ...	18·491
37		Fotash Camp	...	...	18th ,,	...	Capt. Trotter	18·890(2)
38		Gulbashem	...	...	17th ,,	...	Capt. Biddulph	18·804
38		Ditto	...	...	17th & 18th Oct. 1873		Capt. Trotter	19·057(1)
39	West Route viâ Aktagh.	Shorjilga Camp	...	...	10th Oct. 1873	...	Capt. Trotter	16·322(3)
39		Ditto	...	...	,, ,,	...	,, ...	182·75(2)
40		Top of hill above Camp	...	...	,, ,,	...	,, ...	A 15·35(1)
41		Karatagh Pass	...	...	11th ,,	...	,, ...	180·80(2)
42		Karatagh Lake	...	...	,, ,,	...	,, ...	182·15(2)
43		Aktagh 1st	...	...	13th ,,	...	,, ...	16·571(2)
44		Chibra Hill	...	...	15th ,,	...	,, ...	A 15·36(1)
45		Suget Pass	...	...	16th ,,	...	,, ...	15·399(1)
46		Suget Hill	...	...	,, ,,	...	,, ...	A 15·36(1)
47		Suget Camp	...	...	17th ,,	...	,, ...	18·575(1)
48		Shahidúla	...	...	21st ,,	...	,, ...	19·477(1)
49		Sirki Angár	...	...	22nd ,,	...	,, ...	18·290(1)
50		Sanju Pass (or Grim Pass)	...	...	23rd ,,	...	,, ...	16·106(1)
51		Tam village	...	...	25th ,,	...	,, ...	21·700(1)
52		Sanju village	...	...	28th ,,	...	,, ...	24·010(2)
53		Oi Tughrak village	...	...	2nd Nov. 1873	...	,, ...	24·425(1)
54		Boira village	...	...	4th ,,	...	,, ...	24·856(1)
56		Posgiam village	...	...	7th ,,	...	,, ...	25·931(1)
55		Karghalik Town	...	...	6th ,,	...	,, ...	25·711(3)
57		YARKAND, Yangishahr	...	...	Dec. 1873 to March 1874.*		......	25·992 *

* The mean height of the barometer, derived from four months' observations at Yárkand, has here

(49)

KAND viâ *Changchenmo and Shahidúla.*—(Concluded.)

OF OBSERVATION.		AT BASE STATION LEH.			Resulting height above mean sea level.	REMARKS.
Temperature of mercury (Fahrenheit).	Temperature of air (Fahrenheit).	Corrected reading of barometer.	Temperature of mercury (Fahrenheit).	Temperature of air (Fahrenheit).		
Degrees.	Degrees.	Inches.	Degrees.	Degrees.	Feet.	
...	30·0	19·637	...	51.5	15,540	
...	42·9	19·572	...	53·5	14,980	
...	45	19·563	...	49·2	14,620	
...	36·5	19·471	...	50·7	14,160	
...	34·0	19·529	...	41·7	14,000	
...	47·4	19·513	...	50·5	13,670	
...	43·6	19·490	...	47·7	13,120	
...	43	19·453	...	50·7	12,910	
38	36	19·615	47	43·8	12,520	
...	41	19·512	...	51·0	12,530	} Mean height = 12,385 feet.
28	21·5	19·615	47	43·8	12,240	
29	29	19·655	49	44	16,410	} Mean height = 16,490 feet.
...	31	19·619	49	44	16,570	
...	31	19·619	49	44	18,050	
...	30	19·620	48·5	44	17,710	
...	26	19·620	48·5	44	16,890	
22	...	19·655	48·5	44	15,960	
...	20	19·583	47	43·8	17,910	
32	13	19·615	46·5	43·8	17,610	
...	20	19·583	47	43·8	17,990	
38	38	19.615	47	43·8	12,970	
53	40	19·615	46·5	43·8	11,780	
28	30	19·615	47	43·8	13,340	
...	48	19·558	43.6	39·5	16,760	
54	52	19·584	44	39·5	8,790	
...	39	19·558	43·6	39·5	6,070	
53	49	19·666	40	36	5,760	
34	33	19·666	40	36	5,340	
36	36	19·666	40	36	4,210	
46·9	48	19·666	40·1	36·4	4,370	
32	32·6	19·439	24·6	32	3,923	

been employed; and the corresponding mean of the barometer during these same months at Leh.

(50)

Observations on road from *LEH* to *YAR*

Number in Alphabetical List.	Place of Observation.	Date.	Observer.	At Station Reading of barometer or boiling point thermometer corrected for index error.
				Inches or Degrees.
58	Sasser La (Pass)	8th October 1873	Nain Sing	15·419(1)
59	Sasser Pulu Camp	8th ,,	,,	17·009(1)
60	Khumdán	9th ,,	,,	16·983(1)
61	Daolatbeguldi Camp	12th ,,	,,	16·057(1)
62	Karakoram Brangsa	13th ,,	,,	15·855(1)
63	Ak Masjid	9th April 1874	,,	21·636(5)
64	Tupa or Akoram Pass	10th ,,	,,	20·392(1)
65	Mazar Khoja Camp	11th ,,	,,	21·325(2)
66	Yangi Diwan Pass	16th ,,	,,	16·672(1)
55	Karghalik Town	6th Novr. 1873	Captain Trotter	25·711(3)
55	Karghalik do.	27th May 1874	,,	203·65 25·286
68	Yolaregh	28th ,,	,,	200·90 23·901
69	Kugiar Village	29th ,,	,,	200·20 23·559
64	Tupa or Akoram Pass	1st June 1874	,,	193·19(3)
70	Tiznaf River, Camp on	2nd ,,	,,	196·47 21·799
71	Skatlich Camp	2nd ,,	,,	196·82 21·959
65	Mazar Khoja Camp	3rd ,,	,,	195·32 21·277
73	Dubá Camp	3rd ,,	,,	193·67 20·547
74	Uch Ughaz or Chiragsaldi	8th ,,	,,	185·72 17·321
66	Yangi Diwan Pass	8th ,,	,,	183·10(2)
75	Kulunaldi on Yarkand River	9th ,,	,,	188·62 18·445
76	Kirghiz jangal Camp	10th ,,	,,	187·92 18·168
77	Kashmir Jilga Camp	11th ,,	,,	186·92 17·779
78	Khufelong Camp	12th ,,	,,	185·97 17·415
79	Aktagh, 2nd Camp	13th ,,	,,	184·67(2)
80	Wahabjilga Camp	14th ,,	,,	183·12 16·362
62	Karakoram Brangsa	15th ,,	,,	181·72 15·867
81	Karakoram Pass	16th ,,	,,	179·32(4)
61	Daolatbeguldi Camp	17th ,,	,,	181·92(2)

(51)

KAND viâ Karakorum and Kugiar.

Of Observation.		At Base Station LEH.			Resulting height above mean sea level.	Remarks.
Temperature of mercury (Fahrenheit).	Temperature of air (Fahrenheit).	Corrected reading of barometer.	Temperature of mercury (Fahrenheit).	Temperature of air (Fahrenheit).		
Degrees.	Degrees.	Inches.	Degrees.	Degrees.	Feet.	
28	18	19·655	48·5	44	17,840 a	a Mean height = 17,820 feet.
21	15	19·655	48·5	44	15,240	
28	15	19·655	48·5	44	15,290	
15	12	19·655	48·5	44	16,700 b	b Mean height = 16,790 do.
5	15	19·655	48·5	44	17,030 c	c Do. = 17,180 do.
47	45·3	19·589	43·8	43·9	8,870	
37	35	19·589	43·8	43·9	10,450 d	d Mean height = 10,465 do.
30	30·5	19·589	43·8	43·9	9,250 e	e Do. = 9,355 do.
23	18	19·575	46	46·1	15,690 f	f Do. = 16,000 do.
46·9	48	19·666	40·1	36·4	4,370	} Do. = 4,440 do.
...	69	19·689	60	59·2	4,510	
...	60	19·689	60	59·2	6,150	
...	78	19·689	60	59·2	6,450	
...	66	19·587	63·1	60·0	10,480 d	
...	56	19·750	63·1	60·0	8,800	
...	70	19·750	63·1	60·0	8,350	
...	62	19·750	63·1	60·0	9,460 e	
...	60	19·750	63·1	60·0	10,440	
...	43	19·614	62·9	60·1	14,940	
...	49	19·451	62·9	60·1	16,310 f	
...	35	19·614	62·9	60·1	13,210	
...	35	19·614	62·9	60·1	13,620	
...	50	19·614	62·9	60·1	14,250	
...	49	19·614	62·9	60·1	14,810	
...	40	19·451	62·9	60·1	15,330	
...	42	19·614	62·9	60·1	16,490	
...	40	19·628	61·4	57·0	17,330 c	
...	40	19·469	61·4	57·0	18,550	
...	22	19·628	61·4	57·0	16,880 b	

(52)

Observation on road from LEH to YAR

Number in Alphabetical List.	Place of Observation.	Date.			Observer.		AT STATION Reading of barometer or boiling-point, thermometer corrected for index error.
							Inches or Degrees.
82	Dipsang Col ...	17th June 1874		...	Capt. Trotter	...	A15·11[1]
83	Bruchse	17th	,,	...	,,	...	183·72[2]
84	Murghi	18th	,,	...	,,	...	185·02[2]
58	Sasser Pass ...	21st	,,	...	,,	...	180·52[2]
85	Changlung spur, **top of**	22nd	,,	...	,,	...	184·97
							17·039
86	Changlung village	22nd	,,	...	,,	...	192·32[1]
87	Panamik **village**	23rd	,,	...	,,	...	192·57
							20·071
88	Shyok **and Nubra Rivers (junction of)**	23rd	,,	...	,,	...	192·72
							20·136
89	Digar **La Pass**	27th	,,	...	,,	...	180·42[3]

(53)

KAND viâ *Karakoram and Kugiar.*—Concluded.

OF OBSERVATION.		AT BASE STATION LEH.			Resulting height above mean sea level.	REMARKS.
Temperature of mercury (Fahrenheit).	Temperature of air (Fahrenheit).	Corrected reading of barometer.	Temperature of mercury (Fahrenheit).	Temperature of air (Fahrenheit).		
Degrees.	Degrees.	Inches.	Degrees.	Degrees.	Feet.	
...	42	19·628	61·4	57·9	18,450	
...	42	19·469	61	57·9	15,920	
...	55	19·469	61·4	57·9	15,190	
...	36	19·469	61·4	57·9	17,800 a	
...	27	19·586	69·0	66·6	15,310	
...	52	19·413	69·0	66·6	10,760	
...	78	19·586	69·0	66·6	10,840	
...	60	19·586	69·0	66·6	10,760	
...	50	19·413	69·0	66·6	17,930	

(54)

Observations on road from YARKAND to

Number in Alphabetical List.	Place of Observation.	Date.	Observer.	At Station Reading of barometer or boiling point thermometer corrected for index error.
				Degrees.
90	Guma village	12th and 13th May 1874	Kishen Sing	203·51(5)
91	Muji village	14th May 1874	,,	204·0(1)
92	Zawa Kurghan	16th ,, ,,	,,	203·28(1)
93	KHOTAN City	18th ,, ,,	,,	203·24(6)
93	Ditto	19th ,, ,,	,,	203·03(3)
93	Ditto	31st ,, ,,	,,	203·16(3)
94	Karakash town	23rd ,, ,,	,,	203·78(1)
95	Borezen Yotkan village	29th ,, ,,	,,	203·40(2)
93	KHOTAN City	7th June ,,	,,	203·50(3)
96	Yurungkash town	8th ,, ,,	,,	203·30(3)
97	Dol Langar village	9th ,, ,,	,,	203·00(1)
98	Chira village	11th ,, ,,	,,	203·38(3)
98	Ditto	13th ,, ,,	,,	203·45(3)
99	Keria Town	18th ,, ,,	,,	202·57(5)
100	Sorghak Khiang Shahi Bazaar	22nd ,, ,,	,,	198·42(3)
99	Keria Town	29th ,, ,,	,,	202·92(3)
101	Polu village	8th July ,,	,,	196·33(5)
102	Ghubolik Camp, bank of Ulok Shahi Kul	12th and 13th July 1874	,,	182·1(2)
103	Arash Camp, bank of Keria River	15th July 1874	,,	183·92(3)
104	Keria River at Bas Kul	16th ,, ,,	,,	182·25(1)
105	Yeshil Kul (Lake)	18th and 19th July 1874	,,	183·58(2)
106	Tashliak Kul (bank of)	22nd July 1874	,,	182·67(4)
107	Chumik Lhakmo Camp	23rd and 24th July 1874	,,	182·63(2)
108	Sumzi Ling Camp	26th July 1874	,,	184·50(1)

LEH viâ Khotan, Polu and Noh.

OF OBSERVATION.		AT BASE STATION LEH.				
Temperature of mercury (Fahrenheit).	Temperature of air (Fahrenheit).	Corrected reading of barometer.	Temperature of mercury (Fahrenheit).	Temperature of air (Fahrenheit).	Resulting height above mean sea level.	REMARKS.
Degrees.	Degrees.	Inches.		Degrees.	Feet.	
...	75·3	19·509		51·4	4,340	
...	72·5	19·465		53·6	4,290	
...	70·0	19·465		53·6	4,430	
...	72·6	19·496		51·9	4,500 a	a Mean height = 4,490 feet.
...	76·6	19·496		51·9	4,590 a	
...	80·2	19·530	The quantities given in the preceding column have been reduced to a temperature of 32°.	60·0	4,480 a	
...	82·0	19·481		62·4	4,010	
...	84·9	19·502		62·5	4,240	
...	77·8	19·586		60·0	4,380 a	
...	67·3	19·451		60·1	4,370	
...	68·0	19·388		64·8	4,420	
...	75·8	19·451		60·1	4,260	Mean height = 4,220 feet.
...	81·2	19·451		60·1	4,180	
...	67·0	19·469		57·9	4,830 b	b Mean height = 4,575 feet.
...	77·2	19·413		66·6	7,060	
...	90·8	19·413		66·6	4,320 b	
...	70·0	19·477		65·4	8,430	
...	45·0	19·477		65·4	16,960	
...	59·7	19·533		68·5	16,020	
...	47·0	19·454		70·7	16,880	
...	54·3	19·494		71·1	16,160	
...	49·0	19·463		65·8	16,020	
...	41·3	19·463		65·8	16,000	
...	73·0	19·428		68·1	15,570	

(56)

Observations on road from

Number in Alphabetical List.	Place of Observation.	Date.	Observer.	AT STATION — Reading of barometer or boiling point thermometer corrected for index error.
				Inches or Degrees.
109	Kok Robát ...	28th **Nov.** 1873	Capt. Trotter	205·64(2)
110	Kizil village	29th ,, ,,	,,	205·64(2)
111	Yangi Hissar town	30th Nov., 1st & 2nd Dec. 1873.	,,	204·71(6)
112	Yapchan village	4th Dec. 1873	,,	204·64(2)
112	Ditto	17th March 1874, 1873.	,,	204·33(2)
113	KASHGHAR (Yangi Shahr)	11th Dec., 3-30 P.M.	,,	25·968
		14th ,, 9 A.M.	,,	25·026
		17th ,, 9 ,,	,,	25·764
		18th ,, 3 P.M.	,,	25·680
		21st ,, 3 ,,	,,	25·971
		25th ,, 3 ,,	,,	25·754
		21st Jan., noon	,,	25·816
		8th Feb. 3 P.M.	,,	25·576

NOTE.—The values given above as barometrical readings at Káshghar are actually the readings

| | KASHGHAR (Yangi Shahr) | Dec. 1873 to March 1874. | Capt. Trotter | Corrected mean reading. A. 25·880 |

NOTE.—This mean reading of 25·880 inches is obtained from the reduction of

Observations on road from **KASH**

114	Artysh River, bed of	31st Dec. 1873	Capt. Trotter	A. 25·07(1)
115	Besak village (Osten Artysh)	31st ,, and 1st Jan. 1874	,,	203·33(1)
116	Chungterek, Kirghiz village	1st and 2nd **Jan.**	,,	199·13(1)
117	Balghun Bashi Camp	3rd Jan. ...	,,	194·98(1)
117	Ditto	7th ,, ...	,,	A. 21·13(1)
118	Chakmak Fort	3rd ,, ...	,,	196·18(1)
119	Turgat Bela Camp	5th ,, ...	,,	191·83(1)
119	Ditto Ditto	6th ,, ...	,,	192·03(2)
120	Turgat Pass	6th ,, ...	,,	188·83(2)

(57)

YARKAND to KASHGHAR.

OF OBSERVATION.		AT BASE STATION LEH OR YARKUND.			Resulting height above mean sea level.	REMARKS
Temperature of mercury (Fahrenheit).	Temperature of air (Fahrenheit).	Corrected reading of barometer.	Temperature of mercury (Fahrenheit).	Temperature of air (Fahrenheit).		
Degrees.	Degrees.	Inches.	Degrees.	Degrees.	Feet.	
...	47	19·720	40	32·5	3,830	
...	38	19·720	40	32·5	3,910	Mean height = 4,030 feet.
...	34	19·660	39	36	4,320	See Station No. 110, page 21.
...	42	19·547	...	36·5	4,140	Mean height = 4,210 feet.
...	22	19·353	...	27·3	4,280	
		Base Station Yarkand 3,923 feet above sea level.				
...	33	26·100	43	39	4,056	⎫
...	26	26·173	24	20	4,068	⎪
...	23	25·195	23	20	4,074	⎪
...	47·5	25·837	52	50	4,088	⎬ Mean value deduced from Yarkand 4,060 feet.
...	32	26·089	34	32	4,041	⎪
...	33	25·950	36	33	4,123	⎪
...	33	25·923	30	31	4,032	⎪
...	39	25·648	41	40	3,997	⎭

corresponding to the corrected mean of several boiling point observations.
Base Station Leh 11,538 feet above sea level.

	33·8	19·446	24·6	32·2	4,027	From Leh 4,027
						From Yárkand ... 4,060
						Final value ... 4,043 feet.

several hundreds of observations.

GHAR to CHADYRKUL.

	23	26·000	22	19	4,860	
...	28	25·976	22	20	5,290	Mean height = 5·160 feet.
...	30	25·051	21	19·5	7,000	
	...	26·071	21	19	9,180 ⎫	
	−8	26·199	20	19	9,230 ⎬	Mean height = 9·205 feet.
	10	19·449	...	16·6	8,830 ⎭	
	−5	19·449	...	16·6	11,150 ⎫	
	20	19·449	...	16·6	11,030 ⎬	Mean height = 11·090 feet.
	12	19·449	...	16·6	12,760 ⎭	

Observations on road from KASHGHAR

Number in Alphabetical List.	Place of Observation	Date.	Observer.	AT STATION Reading of barometer or boiling-point thermometer corrected for index error.
				Inches & Degrees.
121	Bibi Miriam village	14th Feb. 1874	Capt. Trotter.	A 25·84[2]
121	Ditto	22nd & 24th Feb. 1874	,,	A 25·52[s]
122	Artysh Altyn village	15th & 16th ,,	,,	A 25·79[5]
122	Ditto	Ditto	,,	A 25·88
123	Besh Kerim village	26th Feb. 1874	,,	A 25·57[1]
124	Kalti Ailak village	24th & 25th Feb. 1874	,,	A 25·77[2]
124	Ditto	1st March 1874	,,	204·72[2]
125	Bash Sogon Camp	19th & 20th Jan. 1874	,,	200·63[2]
125	Ditto	19th & 20th Feb. 1874	,,	A 23·84[2]
126	Ayak Sogon Camp	21st Feb. 1874	,,	A 24·97[1]
126	Ditto	Ditto	,,	202·94
127	Kyr Bulak Camp	28th Feb. 1874	,,	202·48
127	Ditto	Ditto	,,	202·48
128	Jai Tupa Camp	22nd Feb. 1874	,,	A 25·14[1]
129	Ui Bulak	23rd ,,	,,	200·12
129	Ditto	26th ,,	,,	199·54[2]
130	Jigda Camp	23rd ,,	,,	202·88[1]
130	Ditto	27th ,,	,,	202·94[2]
131	Belowti Pass	24th ,,	,,	191·28[2]
131	Ditto	24th ,,	,,	191·28

* The height of Kashghar is taken

(59)

to *AKSU* viâ *Ush Turfan*.

Of Observation.		At Base Station LEH or KASHGHAR.*			Resulting height above mean sea level.	Remarks.
Temperature of mercury (Fahrenheit).	Temperature of air (Fahrenheit).	Corrected reading of barometer.	Temperature of mercury (Fahrenheit).	Temperature of air (Fahrenheit).		
Degrees.	Degrees.	Inches.	Degrees.	Degrees.	Feet.	
	37	25·88		34	4,070	} Mean height = 4,270 feet.
	31	25·96		32	4,470	
	38	25·91		29	4,150	} ,, = 4,100 ,,
	33	19·386(LEH)		20·2	4,050	
	54	25·67		35	4,130	
	45	25·79		32	4,050	} ,, = 4,000 ,,
	20	25·913	41	30·4	3,950	
	8	19·460(LEH)		21·5	6,490	} ,, = 6,390 ,,
	20	26·00		31	6,290	
	22	25·93		31	5,010	} ,, = 5,025
	19	26·037	40	40·2	5,040	
	20	19·436(LEH)		27·2	5,380	} ,, = 5,335 ,,
	20	25·92		34	5,290	
	24	26·128	38	38·2	4,910	
	16	26·05		40	6,680	} ,, = 6,650 ,,
	16	25·811	44	42·8	6,620	
	26	19·454(LEH)		22·2	5,190	} ,, = 5,095 ,,
	25	25·986	42	40·7	5,000	
	10	19·446(LEH)		22·0	11,430	} ,, = 11,355 ,,
	10	25·88		38	11,280	

* 4,043 feet above sea level.

Observations on road from KASHGHAR

Number in Alphabetical List.	Place of Observation.	Date.	Observer.	AT STATION Reading of barometer or boiling point thermometer corrected for index error.
				Inches & Degrees.
132	Faizabad town	1st Jan. 1874	Capt. Biddulph	A 26·04
133	Yangi Awat village	2nd ,,	,,	,, 26·10
134	Kashmir village	3rd ,,	,,	,, 26·37
135	Tojha Sulukh village	4th ,,	,,	,, 26·45
136	Shujeh village	6th ,,	,,	,, 26·60
137	Maralbashi town	8th ,,	,,	,, 26·56(3)
138	Charwagh village	15th ,,	,,	,, 26·57

Points in *neighbourhood*

139	Tangitar Kurghan	17th & 18th Feb.	Capt. Trotter	A 24·31(3)
139	Ditto	18th Feb.	,,	202·04(2)
140	Tughamati	18th & 19th Feb.	,,	A 24·05(3)
140	Ditto	19th Feb.	,,	201·54(2)

(61)

to *AKSU* viâ *Maralbashi*.

OF OBSERVATION.		AT BASE STATION KASHGHAR.			Resulting height above mean sea level.	REMARKS.
Temperature of mercury (Fahrenheit).	Temperature of air (Fahrenheit).	Corrected readings of barometer.	Temperature of mercury (Fahrenheit).	Temperature of air (Fahrenheit).		
Degrees.	*Degrees.*	*Inches.*	*Degrees.*	*Degrees.*	*Feet.*	
...	28·5	A 26·00	...	28·5	3,090	As these results mostly depend upon single readings of an Aneroid Barometer, they can only be looked upon as approximate.
...	28·5	,, ...	...	28	3,030	
...	22	,, ...	...	22	3,670	
...	24	,, ...	...	24	3,590	
...	26·3	,, ...	...	26	3,440	
...	27	,, ...	...	27	3,480	
...	24	,, ...	...	24	3,470	

of *KASHGHAR.*

...	32	25·88	...	33	5,670 }	Mean height = 5,730 feet.
...	27	26·29	42	39·7	5,790 }	
...	29	26·02	...	33	6,090 }	Mean height = 5,975 feet.
...	4	26·14	33·6	33	5,860 }	

Observations on road from YANGI-HISSAR

Number in Alphabetical List.	Place of Observation.	Date.	Observer.	AT STATION. Reading of barometer or boiling-point thermometer corrected for index error.
				Inches & Degrees.
148	Ighizyar village	22nd March 1874	Capt. Trotter	201·38(2)
149	Aktala Camp	,, ,,	,,	198·19(2)
150	Sasak Taka Camp	23rd ,,	,,	A 20·02(2)
152	Kaskasu Pass	25th ,,	,,	188·60(1)
153	Chehil Gumbaz Camp	,, ,,	,,	193·17(2)
154	Turat Pass	26th ,,	,,	188·07(2)
155	Past Robat Camp	,, ,,	,,	195·02(2)
156	Tarbashi Camp	27th ,,	,,	191·24(2)
157	Chichiklik Plain (pass leading into)	28th ,,	,,	185·67(2)
158	Balghun Camp	,, ,,	,,	192·72(2)
159	Chushman village	29th ,,	,,	193·57(2)
160	TASHKURGHAN, fort and town	31st ,,	,,	193·27(2)
		1st & 2nd April 1874	,,	193·62(4)
161	Kanshubar Camp	2nd ,,	,,	188·64(4)
162	Neza Tash Diwan (Pass)	3rd ,,	,,	185·18(2)
163	Kogachak Camp	,, ,,	,,	189·00(4)
164	Unkul Camp	4th & 5th ,,	,,	188·62(4)
165	Oikul, Káz-kul or lake of Little Pamir, north side	6th ,,	,,	188·17(2)
166	Langar Camp	6th & 7th ,,	,,	189·39(4)
167	Daráz Diwan Camp	7th & 8th ,,	,,	192·62(5)
168	Sarhadd village	8th ,,	,,	192·67(2)
168	Sarhadd village	9th ,,	,,	192·07(2)
169	Baroghil Pass		Capt. Biddulph	......
170	Patuch village	9th & 10th ,,	Capt. Trotter	192·59(4)
171	Yur village	10th & 11th ,,	,,	193·19(4)
172	Babatangi (Patur) village	11th & 12th ,,	,,	194·00(5)
173	Zung village	12th & 13th ,,	,,	195·65(4)
174	Kila Panjah (Wakhán)	13th, 14th, & 25th ,,	,,	195·67(6)
174A	Langarkish village	27th ,,	,,	195·17(2)
175	Yumkhana or Jangalik Camp	,, ,,	,,	191·47(2)
	Ditto ditto	28th ,,	,,	A 19·65(2)
176	Yol Mazar Camp	28th & 29th ,,	,,	189·08(4)
177	Bilaor Bas Camp	29th ,,	,,	188·65(2)

(63)

to *PANJAH (WAKHAN)*.

OF OBSERVATION.		AT BASE STATION YARKAND.				REMARKS.
Temperature of mercury (Fahrenheit).	Temperature of air (Fahrenheit).	Corrected readings of barometer.	Temperature of mercury (Fahrenheit).	Temperature of air (Fahrenheit).	Resulting heights above mean sea level.	
Degrees.	*Degrees.*	*Inches.*	*Degrees.*	*Degrees.*	*Feet.*	
...	24	25·736	48	48·5	5,580 a	a Mean height = 5,600 feet.
...	30	25·736	48	48·5	7,350 b	b Ditto = 7,345 ,,
...	36	25·753	46	43·8	9,430 c	c Ditto = 9,455 ,,
...	26	19·386	...	33·7	12,850 d	d Ditto = 12,930 ,,
...	14	19·386		33·7	10,310	
...	16	19·386		33·7	13,130	
...	25	19·386		33·7	9,280 h	h Ditto = 9,370 ,,

At Base Station LEH.

...	17	19·395	37·5	33·7	11,370 e	e Ditto = 11,515 ,,
...	20	19·395	37·5	33·7	14,180	
...	25	19·395	37·5	33·7	10,540	
...	10	19·395	37·5	33·7	10,100	
...	31	19·380	37·5	33·7	10,230 f	f Ditto = 10,230 ,,
...	32	19·504	39·3	38·4	10,160 f	
...	34	19·504	39·3	38·4	12,980	
...	25	19·486	39·3	38·4	14,930 g	g Ditto = 14,915 ,,
...	4	19·487		38·4	12,740	
...	19	19·504	39·3	38·4	12,970	
...	8	19·486	39·3	38·4	13,200	
...	18	19·504	39·3	38·4	12,530	
...	20	19·517	41·6	41·2	10,780	
...	31	19·562	43·8	43·9	10,800	} Ditto = 10,975 ,,
...	31	19·589	43·8	43·9	11,150	
...	...	......	Approximate.		12,000	
...	28	19·589	43·8	43·9	10,850	
...	30	19·589	43·8	43·9	10,510	
	30	19·589	43·8	43·9	10,060	
	37	19·589	43·8	43·9	9,110	
	37	19·562	43·8	43·9	9,090	
	43	19·589	47·5	46·9	9,350	
	40	19·589	47·5	46·9	11,470	} Ditto = 11,440 ,,
	24	19·589	47·5	46·9	11,410	
	29	19·589	47·5	46·9	12,320	
	54	19·589	47·5	46·9	13,120	

Observations on road from *YANGI-HISSAR.*

Number in Alphabetical List.	Place of Observation.	Date.	Observer.	AT STATION Reading of barometer or boiling-point thermometer corrected for index error.
				Inches & Degrees.
178	Mazar Tupa Camp	30th April 1874	Capt. Trotter	187·48[6]
179	Victoria Lake (or Lake of Great Pamir)	1st & 2nd May 1874	,,	187·03[4]
180	Watershed on Great Pamir	2nd ,,	,,	186·52[1]
181	Shash Tupa Camp	2nd & 3rd ,,	,,	187·42[2]
182	Dahn-i-Isligh Camp	3rd ,,	,,	188·32[1]
183	Aktash Camp (on Aksu River)	5th & 6th ,,	,,	189·42[2]
184	Tagharma Plain	10th ,,	,,	A 20·42[1]
185	Neza Tash Diwan	6th ,,	,,	185·52[2]
160	TASHKURGHAN, fort and town	10th ,,	,,	193·42[2]
186	Balghun (Darschatt River)	,, ,,	,,	190·02[3]
187	Kok Mainak Pass	12th ,,	,,	184·17[2]
156	Tarbashi	13th ,,	,,	191·02[3]
155	Past Robat Camp	14th ,,	,,	194·87[2]
152	Kaskasu Pass	15th ,,	,,	188·70[2]
151	Kaskasu Camp	,, ,,	,,	192·22[2]
150	Sasak Taka Camp	16th ,,	,,	194·82[2]
149	Aktala Camp	17th ,,	,,	198·47[2]
148	Ighizyar village	18th ,,	,,	201·42[2]
110	Kizil village	19th ,,	,,	203·94[4]

to *PANJAH (WAKHAN).*—(Concluded.)

OF OBSERVATION.		AT BASE STATION LEH.				REMARKS.
Temperature of mercury (Fahrenheit).	Temperature of air (Fahrenheit).	Corrected readings of barometer.	Temperature of mercury (Fahrenheit).	Temperature of air (Fahrenheit).	Resulting height above mean sea level.	
Degrees.	Degrees.	Inches.	Degrees.	Degrees.	Feet.	
...	32	19.556	47.5	46.9	13,760	
...	23	19.524	49.7	49.5	13,950	
...	46	19.524	49.7	49.5	14,320	
...	33	19.524	49.7	49.5	13,760	
...	24	19.561	49.7	49.5	13,220	
...	29	19.524	49.7	49.5	12,600	
...	35	19.548	51.3	51.4	10,310	
...	42	19.524	49.7	49.5	14,900g	
...	51	19.508	52.8	51.9	10,270f	
...	30	19.548	51.3	51.4	12,240	
...	40	19.548	51.3	51.4	15,670	
...	35	19.548	51.3	51.4	11,060e	
...	36	19.548	51.3	51.4	9,460h	
...	55	19.495	52.8	51.9	13,010d	
...	30	19.537	52.8	51.9	106,60	
...	30	19.537	52.8	51.9	9,480c	
...	50	19.495	53.0	51.9	7,340b	
...	60	19.495	53.0	51.9	5,610a	
...	65	19.495	53.0	51.9	4,150	

GEOGRAPHICAL APPENDIX.

SECTION D.

ALPHABETICAL LIST of LATITUDES, LONGITUDES, & HEIGHTS.

(68)

Alphabetical List of Latitudes,

Reference number.	Name of Place.	Latitude.			Longitude.			Height.
		°	′	″	°	′	″	*Feet.*
64	Akkoram (or Tupa) Pass	......			......			10,465
63	Ak Masjid Camp	37	8	13	......			8,870
43	Aktagh, 1st Camp	35	59	3	......			15,960
79	Aktagh, 2nd Camp	36	0	11	78	3	20	15,330
149	Aktala Camp	38	29	18	......			7,345
183	Aktash Camp on Aksu River	37	35	13	74	53	44(c)	12,600
108a	Angche Chortan	33	41	54	......			
103	Arash Camp, bank of Keria river	35	29	54	......			16,020
115	Artysh Osten (Besak village)	39	36	50	......			5,160
114	Artysh River (bed of)	......			......			4,800
122	Artysh (Altyn)	......			......			4,100
126	Ayak Sogon Camp	40	0	6	76	40	32(c)	5,025
172	Babatangi (Pater) village	......			......			10,000
186	Balghun (Darschatt River)	......			......			12,240
158	Balghun Camp	......			......			10,540
117	Balghun Bashi	......			......			9,205
62b	Balti Polu or Karakoram Polu	35	24	26	......			
169	Baroghil Pass	......			......			12,000
125	Bash Sogon Camp	......			......			6,390
131	Belowti Pass	40	40	20	77	50	0	11,355
115	Besak village (Osten Artysh)	......			......			5,160
123	Besh Kerim village	......			......			4,130
13	Bhao or Shusmal Lung Pa	34	29	6	......			17,020
121	Bibi Miriam Khan's village	......			......			4,270
177	Bilaor Bas Camp	......			......			13,120
54	Bohira village	37	37	19	......			5,340
95	Borezen Yotkan village	......			......			4,240
83	Bruchse Camp	35	4	51	......			15,920
8	Chagra Camp	34	4	59	......			15,090
118	Chakmak Fort	40	5	9	......			8,830
118a	Chakmak, three miles north of Fort	40	8	28	......			
6	Chakr Talao Camp	......			......			13,890
3	Changla or Sakti Pass	34	4	49	......			17,590
14	Changlung Burma Pass	......			......			19,280
15	Do. Nischu Camp	34	35	3	......			18,630
15a	Do. or Pangtung Pass	......			......			18,910
85	Do. spur (top of)	......			......			15,310
86 & 59b	Do. village	35	55	43	......			10,760
138	Charwagh village	......			......			3,470
43a	Chibra Camp	36	7	12	......			
44	Do. Hill	......			......			17,910
153	Chehil Gumbaz Camp	......			......			10,310
157	Chichiklik plain (pass leading into)	......			......			14,480
65a	Chiklik Camp	37	2	54	......			
1	Chimray village	......			......			11,890
98	Chira village	37	0	26	......			4,220
107	Chumik Lhakmo Camp	34	22	28	......			16,600
28	Chung Tash	35	36	56	......			15,590
116	Chungtirik (Kirghiz village)	39	47	0	......			7,000
159	Chushman village	......			......			10,100
24	Compass Wala's Pass	......			......			18,160

(c) denotes that the longitude has been

(69)

Longitudes, and Heights.

Reference number.	Name of Place.	Latitude. ° ′ ″	Longitude. ° ′ ″	Height. Feet.
182	Dahn-i-Isligh Camp	......	......	13,220
30a	Daktod Karpo Sumdo	35 45 48	......	......
167	Daraz Diwan Camp	37 0 9	73 46 7(c)	10,780
61	Daulat Beguldi Camp	35 22 16	......	10,790
23	Dehra Compass Camp	......	......	17,890
89	Digar La Pass	......	......	17,930
82	Dipsang Col	......	......	18,450
97	Dol Langar village	......	......	4,420
73	Duba Camp	36 46 34	......	10,440
26	Dunglung (or Shinglung)	35 9 51	......	17,030
32	Dungnagu Camp	35 51 34		
132	Faizabad town	39 29 36	76 46 10(c)	3,990
37	Fotash Camp	......	......	12,520
41a	Do. Pass	35 56 31		
63a	Fusar village	37 20 37		
165	Gazkul (see Oikul)	......		13,200
102	Ghubolik Camp	35 40 55		16,960
60a	Giapchan Kizil	35 17 54		
486	Giazgia Camp	36 44 59		
12	Gogra Camp	34 21 4		15,570
38	Gulbashem Camp	36 17 28		12,385
90	Guma village	37 37 31		4,340
148	Ighiz Yar village			5,600
	Ishkashm			9,500 (Approximate.)
128	Jai Tupa Camp	......		4,910
130	Jigda Camp	......		5,095
35	Jung Chidmo Camp	36 10 32		
124	Kalti Ailak village	......		4,000
161	Kanshubar Camp	......		12,980
25	Karakash River near Compass La			17,440
94	Do. town	37 16 47		4,010
29	Do. river, Captain Biddulph's Camp	......		15,540
30	Do. do.	......		14,980
31	Do. do.	......		14,620
32	Do. do.	......		14,160
33	Do. Sora do.	......		14,000
34	Do. do.	......		13,670
35	Do. do.	......		13,120
36	Do. do.	......		12,910
62	Karakoram Brangsa	35 37 42		17,180
48a	Do. Camp	36 37 30		
81	Do. Pass	......		18,550
62a	Do. Nain Sing's Camp near Pass	35 33 4		
42	Karatagh Lake	......		16,890
41	Do. Pass	35 42 54	......	17,710
55	Karghalik town	37 53 15	77 27 0	4,440
113	KASHGHAR—(Yangi-shahr)	39 24 26	76 6 47	4,043

deduced chronometrically from Káshghar.

(70)

Alphabetical List of

Reference number.	NAME OF PLACE.	Latitude.			Longitude.			Height.
		°	′	″	°	′	″	*Feet.*
134	Kashmir village	......			......			3,670
77	Kashmir Jilga Camp	36	14	54	......			14,250
151	Kaskasu Camp	38	12	0	......			10,960
152	Kaskasu Pass	......			......			12,930
104	Keria River at Bas Khiol	......			......			16,880
99	Keria Town	36	51	26	......			4,575
140b	Khanarik or Do Shamba Bazar	39	15	42				
51a	Khewaz Langar	37	2	47				
93	KHOTAN (City centre of)	37	7	36	79	59	0	4,490
78	Khufelong Camp	36	8	34	......			14,810
60	Khumdan Camp	35	8	1	......			15,290
52a	Khushtagh village	37	21	5				
174	Kila Panjah (Wakhan)	37	0	18	72	45	29(c)	9,090
76	Kirghiz jangal Camp	36	25	44	......			13,620
76a	Kirghiz Camp near Kirghiz jangal	36	22	9				
110a	Kizil Boia or Shamba Bazar	39	22	49				
27	Kizil Jilga Camp	35	20	42	......			16,500
110	Kizil village	38	39	23				4,030
163	Kogachak Camp	37	37	11	74	55	19(c)	12,740
187	Kok Mainak Pass	......			......			15,670
109	Kok Robat	38	26	5				3,830
19	Kotajilga Camp	34	29	25	......			16,730
69	Kugiar village	37	24	14	......			6,450
75	Kulu Naldi (on Yarkand River)	......			......			13,210
127	Kyr Bulak Camp	40	6	7	76	52	26(c)	5,335
166	Langar Camp	......			......			12,530
174a	Langarkish village	......			......			9,350
9	Lankar La (or Marsimik La)	......			......			18,420
	Leh Observatory	......			......			11,538
17	Lingzi Thung Plain (Camp on)	34	47	54	......			17,610
16	Lingzi Thung Plain (south side of)	......			......			17,680
7	Lukong village (on Pangong Lake)	34	0	6	......			14,130
137	Maralbashi Town	39	46	24	(78	11	20 Approximate.)	3,480
9	Marsimik La (or Lankar La)	......			......			18,420
65	Mazar Khoja Camp	36	50	32	......			9,355
178	Mazar Tupa Camp	37	28	53	73	34	41(c)	13,760
91	Muji village	......			......			4,290
84	Murghi Camp	......			......			15,190
185	Neza Tash Diwan	......			......			14,915
15	Nischu (Camp near)	......			......			18,630
165	Oi Kul or Lake of Little Pamir (Camp on north side)	37	14	27	74	19	40(c)	13,200
53	Oi Tugrak village	37	30	20	......			5,760
115	Osten Artysh (Besak village)	39	36	50	......			5,290
	Pamir Great, Lake of, see Victoria Lake	......			......			13,950
165	Pamir Little, Lake of, see Oi Kul	37	14	27	......			13,200
11	Pamzal Camp	......			......			14,790
59a & 87	Panamik village	37	47	10	......			10,840
20	Pangtung Camp	......			......			17,250
21	Pangtung or Chung Lung Pass	......			......			18,910
174	Panjah Kila (Wakhan)	37	0	18	72	45	29(c)	9,090
157	Pass to Chichiklik Plain	......			......			14,480
155	Past Robat Camp	......			......			9,370

(71)

Latitudes, &c.—(Continued.)

Reference number.	NAME OF PLACE.	Latitude.			Longitude.			Height.
		°	′	″	°	′	″	Feet.
170	Patuch village	......						10,850
101	Patūr village	36	11	56				8,430
56	Posgiam village	38	11	54				4,210
10	Rimdi Camp							17,500
50	Sanju (or Grim Pass)	......						16,760
52	Sanju village	37	11	17				6,070
168	Sarhadd village	......						10,975
78a	Sasak Bulak	36	27	30				
150	Sasak Taka Camp	......			......			9,455
58	Sasser La Pass	......			......			17,820
59	Sasser Pelu Camp	35	2	43	......			15,240
48	Shahidulla (old fort and town)	36	24	57	......			11,780
181	Shash Tupa Camp	37	31	39	74	15	23(c)	13,760
26	Shinglung (or Dunglung Camp)	......			......			17,030
39	Shorjilga Camp	35	41	2	......			16,490
40	Shorjilga (top of hill)	......			......			18,050
136	Shujeh village	......			......			3,440
13	Shummal Lungpa or Bhao	......			......			17,020
88	Shyok River at junction with **Nubra River**	......			......			10,760
40	Sirki Angar	......			......			13,340
71	Skatlich Camp	......			......			8,550
33	Sora Camp	36	1	9	......			14,000
100	Sorghak Khiang Shahi	36	39	51	......			7,060
47	Suget Camp	36	18	45	......			12,970
46	Suget hill	......			......			17,990
45	Suget Pass	36	9	53	......			17,610
108	Sumji Ling Camp	34	1	18	......			15,570
18	Sumna Camp east of Kizil Jilga	35	16	39	......			17,150
22	Sumzumlung Pa	34	41	10	......			17,330
	Tagharma or Muztagh Peak	38	35	15	75	22	47	25,350
184	Tagharma Plain	......			......			10,310
51	Tam village	36	52	4	......			8,790
139	Tangitar Kurghan	39	56	46	......			5,730
5	Tanks	......			......			12,900
156	Tarbashi Camp	38	6	8	......			11,515
160	TASHKURGHAN Fort and Town	37	46	49	75	19	1(c)	10,230
106	Tashliak Kul (bank of Lake)	34	38	54	......			16,620
73a	Teshektash	36	44	18				
70	Tiznaf River **(Camp on)**	......						8,800
135	Tojha Sulukh village	......						3,590
4	Tsultak village	......						15,950
140	Tughamati	40	1	52				5,975
173	Tung village	......						9,110
64	Tupa or Akkorum **Diwan**	......						10,465
76b	Tupa Diwan Camp	36	24	24				
154	Turat Pass	......						13,130
119	Turgat Bela Camp	40	23	53				11,090
120	Turgat Pass	......						12,760
59d	Tutialak Camp	35	0	17				
74	Uch Ugbaz or Chiraghsaldi	......			......			14,940
129	Ui Bulak	40	26	14	77	35	47 (c)	6,650
164	Unkul Camp	......			......			12,970

Alphabetical List of

Reference number.	NAME OF PLACE.	Latitude.			Longitude.			Height.
		°	′	″	°	′	″	Feet.
179	Victoria Lake, or Lake of Great Pamir (West end)	37	27	0	73	40	38	13,950
80	Wahabjilga Camp	......			......			16,490
	Wamar Fort (Junction of Murghabi and Panja River)	......			......			(Appe.) 7,500
180	Water-shed on Great Pamir	......			......			14,320
133	Yangi Awat village	......			......			3,930
66	Yangi Diwan Pass	......			......			16,000
111	Yangi Hissar Town	38	56	8	76	12	55	4,320
112	Yapchan village	39	13	31	......			4,210

Latitudes, &c.—(Concluded.)

Reference number.	NAME OF PLACE.	Latitude.			Longitude.			Height.
		°	′	″	°	′	″	*Feet.*
57	YARKAND (Yangi-shahr)	38	25	1	77	15	55	3,923
105	Yeshil Kul (Lake)	......			......			16,160
68	Yolarik	37	27	6	......			6,150
176	Yol Mazar Camp	37	18	7	73	5	49(c)	12,320
175	Yumkhana or Jangalik Camp	......			......			11,440
171	Yur village	......			......			10,510
96	Yurungkash town	......			......			4,370
2	Zingral Camp	......			......			**15,780**
92	Zawa Kurghan	......			......			**4,430**

GEOGRAPHICAL APPENDIX.

SECTION E.

MAGNETIC OBSERVATIONS.

(76)

MAGNETIC

Abstract of results of observations taken by Captain H. Trotter, R.E.,

Station of observation.		Date of observation.	Approximate.		
			North Latitude.	Longitude east of Greenwich.	Height above sea level.
		1873.	° ′	° ′	Feet.
On road from LEH to KASH-GHAR.	LEH ...	1st and 3rd September	34 10	77 37	11,540
	Chagra Camp... ...	21st September ...	34 5	78 30	15,000
	Chung Tash Camp ...	8th October ...	35 37	78 40	15,590
	Sanju village	1st November ...	37 11	78 31	6,070
	Oi Toghrak village	3rd ,, ...	37 30	78 3	5,760
	Karghalik town ...	6th ,, ...	37 53	77 41	4,370
	YARKUND (Yangi-shahr)	27th ,, ...	38 25	77 16	3,923
	Yangi Hissar town	1st December ...	38 56	76 13	4,320
	Yapchan village	3rd ,, ...	39 14	76 7	4,210
	KASHGHAR (Yangi-shahr) ...	4th and 19th December and 13th February 1874.	39 24	76 7	4,043
On road from KASHGHAR to WAKHAN.	Ui Bulak. (On road to Ush Turfan and Aksu)	25th February ...	40 26	77 36	6,650
	Ighizyar ...	18th May	38 40	76 12	5,600
	TASHKURGHAN	31st March ...	37 47	75 29	10,230
	Aktash ...	5th May	37 35	74 54	12,000
	Yol Mazar Camp	28th April ...	37 18	73 6	12,320
	Panjah (Wakhan)	18th ,, ...	37 0	72 45	9,090

The observations for Magnetic Dip were taken with Dip Circle No. 2 by Barrow (belonging to the Great "Admiralty Manual of Scientific Enquiry. The rules laid down therein were rigorously adhered to.

The observations for declination were taken with the 6-inch Transit Theodolite (by Troughton and Simms). parisons at Dehra and at Leh, both before the start and after the return of the Mission, proved that no sensible

OBSERVATIONS.

for Magnetic Inclination (Dip) and Declination (Variation) 1873-74.

Magnetic Dip north.	Magnetic Variation east.	REMARKS.	
° ′	° ′		
47 21·5 (Mean of two sets.)	3 43	From observations to Sun. (Two sets.)	
47 22·7	3 50	From observations to Sun and to Polaris.	General Cunningham, R.E., took magnetic observations at Leh in October 1847 when the dip was found to be ... 46° 43′·15. and the declination ... 2° 46′· 87 E. The Schlagintweits in July and September 1856 made dip ... 46° 51′· 88 and the declination on July 31st ... 3° 24′· 1 ⎱ E. on September 30th ... 3° 21′· 1 ⎰
	3 51	From observations to Polaris.	
	4 32	Ditto ditto.	
	4 32	Ditto ditto.	
	4 53	Ditto ditto.	
53 8·0 (Mean of two sets.)	4 58	Ditto ditto.	
	4 57	Ditto ditto.	
	4 55	Ditto ditto.	
54 31·7	5 1	Ditto ditto and to Sun. (Four sets.)	
	5 40	From observations to Sun.	
	4 20	From observations to β *Ursæ Minoris*. (Two sets.)	
52 3·3	4 34	From observation to Sun ditto.	
	4 24	Ditto to Polaris ditto.	
	4 12	Ditto Ditto ditto.	
	4 16	From observation to do. and to β *Ursæ Minoris*.	

Trigonometrical Survey Department). The method of observation was that recommended by General Sabine in the

The needle attached to the Instrument was re-magnetized prior to the departure of the expedition from India, and com- displacement had taken place in the position of its magnetic pole.

GEOGRAPHICAL APPENDIX.

SECTION F.

METEOROLOGICAL OBSERVATIONS.

Meteorological Observations recorded by the Great Trigonometrical

Date.		Mercurial Barometer No. 720 corrected for index error.	Temperature of mercury.	Reading of aneroid barometer Solomon's uncorrected.	Temperature of Air.	
					Dry Bulb.	Wet Bulb.
		Inches.	Degrees.	Inches.	Degrees.	Degrees.
Nov. 12th, 1873,	9 A.M.	26·112	46	26·46	42	38·5
	Noon	·107	55	·46	52	47·5
	3 P.M.	·077	50	·43	48·5	44·5
	6 ,,	·007	46·5	·46	45	41
	9 ,,	·007	44·5	·47	42	39·5
,, 13th ,,	9 A.M.	·132	44	·51	42	38·5
	Noon	·127	55	·49	45	39
	3 P.M.	·077	49·5	·44	48	44
	6 ,,	·087	45	·46	45	41
	9 ,,	·087	42	·46	41	38
,, 14th ,,	9 A.M.	·147	44	·52	42	39
	Noon	·127	52	·48	48	45
	3 P.M.	·087	47·5	·45	46	42
	6 ,,	·062	46	·46	44	39·5
	9 ,,	·125	42	·50	40·8	36·5
,, 15th ,,	9 A.M.	·157	48·5	·54	41·0	37·0
	Noon	·167	58·0	·53	48	41
	3 P.M.	·142	51·5	·52	48·5	40
	6 ,,	·197	49·5	·56	43	36
	9 ,,	·237	47·5	·61	38	32
,, 16th ,,	9 A.M.	·282	47·5	·68	36	33
	Noon	·277	60·0	·66	45·3	38·8
	3 P.M.	·227	55·8	·62	50·5	43
	6 ,,	·207	48	·63	46	41·3
	9 ,,	·237	43·5	·66	42	37
,, 17th ,,	9 A.M.	·187	44·5	·61	38	34
	Noon	·157	46·5	·56	42	37·5
	3 P.M.	·107	48	·52	45·5	39
	6 ,,	·117	45	·51	40	35
	9 ,,	·037	41·5	·54	38	33
,, 18th ,,	9 A.M.	·187	43	·59	39	36
	Noon	·197	55·5	·56	47	40·3
	3 P.M.	·157	51·5	·55	48·5	41
	6 ,,	·137	47	·56	42·5	37
	9 ,,	·207	43	·58	39	34
,, 19th ,,	9 A.M.	·207	44	·63	35·5	34
	Noon	·192	57	·59	46·5	41
	3 P.M.	·162	53·5	·55	49·5	42
	6 ,,	·137	47·0	·59	45	39
	9 ,,	·187	45·0	·60	40·5	36
,, 20th ,,	Noon	·217	55·5	·61	47·5	42
	3 P.M.	·187	51·0	·57	46	39
	6 ,,	·197	45·0	·59	45	39
	9 ,,	·197	44·0	·60	41	37
,, 21st ,,	9 A.M.	·237	45·0	·65	38	32·5
	Noon	·227	47·5	·63	47	42·5
	3 P.M.	·197	52·0	·61	51	44
	6 ,,	·197	48·0	·62	42·5	38
	9 ,,	·217	43·0	·64	39	34
,, 22nd ,,	9 A.M.	·157	44·0	·58	41	36
	Noon	·127	50·5	·55	50	45

(81)

Survey Pandits at YARKAND during the winter of 1873-74.

MINIMUM IN SHADE.	MAXIMUM IN SHADE.	Direction of wind.	REMARKS.
During preceding 24 hours.			
Degrees.	*Degrees.*		At Yárkand the thermometers were placed in a courtyard—in the open—against a wall and at a height of five feet above the ground. The wall faced north, and the sun's rays never fell on or near it. The aneroid barometer was also suspended against the same wall. The mercurial barometer was placed in complete shade, in a porch which opened towards the north. On the 20th, 21st, and 22nd of every month continuous hourly observations were taken extending over a period of 48 hours, *i.e.*, from noon on the 20th up to noon on the 22nd of each month. These observations having been reduced to diagrams, *vide* body of Report, it has not been thought necessary to reproduce them here. The thermometers were all graduated on **Fahrenheit's** scale.
......	......	W.	
......	......	W.	
......	......	W.	
......	......	N.	
......	......	N.	
......	......	W.	
......	......	N.W.	
......	......	W.	
......	......	E.	
......	......	S.W.	
......	......	W.	
......	......	S.	
......	......	N.	
......	......	S.	
......	......	E.	
......	......	E.	
......	......	N.E.	
......	......	S.	
......	......	E.	
......	......	N.	
......	......	S.	
......	......	S.	
......	......	N.	
......	......	E.	
......	......	W.	
......	......	N.	
......	......	N.	
......	......	W.	
......	......	E.	
......	......	E.	
......	......	S.	
......	......	E.	
......	......	W.	
......	......	N.	
......	......	E.	
......	......	S.	
......	......	E.	
......	......	S.	
......	......	E.	
......	......	S.	
......	......	W.	
......	......	S.	
......	......	S.	
......	......	N.	
......	......	S.	
......	......	N.	
......	......	N.	

(82)

Meteorological Observations recorded by the Great Trigonometrical Survey

Date.			Mercurial Barometer No. 720 corrected for index error.	Temperature of mercury.	Reading of aneroid barometer Solomon's uncorrected.	Temperature of Air.	
						Dry Bulb.	Wet Bulb.
			Inches.	Degrees.	Inches.	Degrees.	Degrees.
Nov 22nd, 1873,	3 P.M.	...	26·087	53·0	26·50	52	46
	6 ,,	...	·087	52·5	·50	46	41
	9 ,,	...	·107	49·0	·53	42	38
,, 23rd ,,	9 A.M.	...	·127	47·0	·55	40	37
	Noon	...	·117	60·0	·51	53	46
	3 P.M.	...	·047	57·0	·46	57	49
	6 ,,	...	·037	50·0	·45	48	42
	9 ,,	...	·047	47·0	·49	44	40
,, 24th ,,	9 A.M.	...	·047	43·0	·50	42·3	38
	Noon	...	·037	58·0	·45	52	46
	3 P.M.	...	·002	63·0	·38	53·5	46
	6 ,,	...	25·962	51·0	·37	44·5	39
	9 ,,	...	·952	45·0	·38	40	36
,, 25th ,,	9 A.M.	...	·922	43·0	·35	34	31
	Noon	...	·932	55	·31	46·5	41
	3 P.M.	...	·882	52	·30	51	43
	6 ,,	...	·902	49	·30	45	40
	9 ,,	...	·942	45	·34	39	34·5
,, 26th ,,	9 A.M.	...	·902	45·5	·32	39	36
	Noon	...	·922	58	·31	45	41
	3 P.M.	...	·952	54	·32	49	44
	6 ,,	...	·952	50·5	·37	44	40·5
	9 ,,	...	·972	45	·40	37·5	34
,, 27th ,,	9 A.M.	...	26·122	45·5	·52	36	34
	Noon	...	·102	57	·50	49	43·3
	3 P.M.	...	·092	53	·49	52	44
,, 28th ,,	Noon	...	·422	43	·04	40	33
	3 P.M.	...	·427	48	·02	45	37
	6 ,,	...	·442	42	·06	36	32
	9 ,,	...	·452	37	·09	31·5	27·5
,, 29th ,,	9 A.M.	...	·462	28	·03	26	23
	Noon	...	·322	35	25·96	33	29
	3 P.M.	...	·272	37	·87	34	31
	6 ,,	...	·222	35·5	·85	28	24
	9 ,,	...	·212	35	·84	25	22
,, 30th ,,	9 A.M.	...	·102	27·5	·75	24	24
	Noon	...	·052	37·5	·65	36	33
	3 P.M.	...	·002	39·0	·63	36	32
	6 ,,	...	25·997	37	·62	30	27
	9 ,,	...	26·042	33	·66	26	25

(83)

Pandits at YARKAND during the winter of 1873-74.—(Continued.)

Minimum in shade.	Maximum in shade.	Direction of wind.	Remarks.
During preceding 24 hours.			
Degrees.	Degrees.		
......	......	E.	
......	......	W.	
......	......	S.	
......	......	N.	
......	......	N.	
......	......	E.	
......	......	S.	
......	......	W.	
......	......	E.	
......	......	W.	
......	......	S.	
......	......	N.	
......	......	N.	
......	......	W.	
......	......	W.	
......	......	S.	
......	......	N.	
......	......	N.	
......	......	S.	
......	......	W.	*For the month of November* 1873.
......	......	E.	9 a.m. Noon. 3 p.m. 6 p.m. 9 p.m.
......	......	N.	
......	......	N.	Mean of Mercurial
......	......	W.	barometer No. 720
......	......	W.	corrected to $32°$... 26·143 26·149 26·115 26·109 26·126
33·5	42·5	N.E.	
......	......	N.E.	Mean of Dry Bulb
......	......	N.	Thermometer .. 37·4 45·9 48·0 42·2 38·1
......	......	N.	
16·5	44	E.	Mean of Wet Bulb
......	......	S.	Thermometer ... 34·2 40·6 41·6 37·4 34·1
......	......	E.	
......	......	W.	
......	......	S.	
14	34·8	S.W.	
......	......	W.	
......	......	E.	
......	......	N.	

Meteorological Observations recorded by the Great Trigonometrical

Date.		Mercurial Barometer No. 720 corrected for index error.	Temperature of mercury.	Reading of aneroid barometer Solomon's uncorrected.	Temperature of Air.	
					Dry Bulb.	Wet Bulb.
		Inches.	Degrees.	Inches.	Degrees.	Degrees.
Dec. 1st, 1873,	9 A.M.	26·022	26	25·66	22	21
	Noon	·052	34·5	·68	34	31
	3 P.M.	·042	39·5	·63	37	33
	6 ,,	·042	37	·68	30	29
	9 ,,	·082	33	·71	25	24
,, 2nd ,,	9 A.M.	·152	27	·80	25	23
	Noon	·102	38	·72	36	32
	3 P.M.	·062	39	·69	36·5	34
	6 ,,	·052	36	·68	31	30
	9 ,,	·027	33	·66	25·3	25
,, 3rd ,,	9 A.M.	·042	26	·67	23	22·2
	Noon	·042	37	·67	34	30
	3 P.M.	·002	44	·64	38	35
	6 ,,	·022	39·8	·62	33	30
	9 ,,	·022	57	·65	29	26
,, 4th ,,	9 A.M.	·052	28	·68	24·5	22·3
	Noon	·027	37·5	·67	35	32
	3 P.M.	·042	42·8	·61	37·5	36
	6 ,,	·022	38	·62	30	27
	9 ,,	·032	34	·64	24	23
,, 5th ,,	9 A.M.	·022	26	·63	23	22
	Noon	......	......	·65	33	30
	3 P.M.	·027	42	·63	38	36
	6 ,,	·082	38	·69	29·5	28·3
	9 ,,	·102	33	·71	24·5	24
,, 6th ,,	9 A.M.	·202	26·5	·85	24	23
	Noon	......	......	·83	33	30
	3 P.M.	·162	40	·78	36·5	34
	6 ,,	·177	37	·80	29	28·5
	9 ,,	·167	32	·98	25	24
,, 7th ,,	9 A.M.	·192	26·3	·83	24	24
	Noon	·222	39	·86	35	32
	3 P.M.	·212	44	·83	38	34
	6 ,,	·242	40	·87	32	29
	9 ,,	·242	35·5	·88	27	24·2
,, 8th ,,	9 A.M.	·312	26·5	·95	24	23
	Noon	·307	38·5	·94	36	32
	3 P.M.	·302	44	·91	40·3	35
	6 ,,	·322	34·5	·90	34	31
	9 ,,	·282	27	·92	30	27
,, 9th ,,	9 A.M.	·182	27	·83	25	23
	Noon	·152	36	·78	34	30·8
	3 P.M.	·112	40	·70	38	34
	6 ,,	·062	37·5	·68	32·5	29
	9 ,,	·052	35	·67	29	27
,, 10th ,,	9 A.M.	·002	24	·62	21	20
	Noon	25·992	33	·61	29	26·5
	3 P.M.	·962	39·5	·57	37	32
	6 ,,	·977	36·0	·60	28	26·5
	9 ,,	26·012	32·5	·63	25·5	25·0
,, 11th ,,	9 A.M.	·122	26	·77	24	23
	Noon	·132	38	·79	32	29

(85)

Survey Pandits at YARKAND during the winter of 1873-74.—(Continued.)

Minimum in shade.	Maximum in shade.	Direction of wind.	Remarks
During preceding 24 hours.			
Degrees.	*Degrees.*		
13·5	38·8	S.W.	
......	......	W.	
......	......	E.	
......	......	N.	
......	......	N.	
15·5	38·5	E.	
......	......	S.	
......	......	E.	
......	......	S.	
......	......	W.	
15·8	39·8	N.	
......	......	N.W.	
......	......	S.	
......	......	N.	
......	......	E.	
16	38	N.	
......	......	W.	
......	......	S.W.	
......	......	N.	
......	......	N.	
12	37·5	W.	
......	......	N.	
......	......	S.E.	
......	......	N.E.	
13	41	N.	
......	......	N.W.	
......	......	N.	
......	......	N.W.	
......	......	S.	
12·5	35	W.	
......	......	E.	
......	......	N.	
......	......	S.W.	
......	......	W.	
11·5	37	E.S.	
......	......	N.E.	
......	......	E.	
......	......	N.	
......	......	N.	
12	38	S.E.	
......	......	W.N.	
......	......	N.E.	
......	......	W.	
......	......	E.	
10	42·5	S.	
......	......	E.	
......	......	W.	
......	......	N.	
......	......	W.	
12	34	S.W.	
......	......	S.E.	

(86)

Meteorological Observations recorded by the Great Trigonometrical Survey

Date.		Mercurial Barometer No. 720 corrected for index error.	Temperature of mercury.	Reading of aneroid barometer Solomon's uncorrected.	Temperature of Air.	
					Dry Bulb.	Wet Bulb.
		Inches.	*Degrees.*	*Inches.*	*Degrees.*	*Degrees.*
Dec. 11th, 1873, 3 p.m.		26·134	43	25·64	39·3	35
6 "		·142	38	·78	31·5	28·5
9 "		·162	32·5	·80	26	24
" 12th " 9 a.m.		·202	28	·85	27	25
Noon		·232	37	·86	37	34·3
3 p.m.		·202	38·8	·82	37	33
6 "		·202	36	·83	33	31
9 "		·222	33	·84	27	26
" 13th " 9 a.m.		·192	24	·84	22	21·5
Noon		·182	35	·82	32	39·5
3 p.m.		·152	40	·79	36	33·5
6 "		·162	37	·78	30·5	29·5
9 "		·172	32·5	·81	27·0	25·0
" 14th " 9 a.m.		·162	24·5	·81	20	19·5
Noon		·152	35·0	·78	32	32
3 p.m.		·102	39·0	·72	36	32
6 "		·132	35·5	·73	27	26
9 "		·102	32·0	·72	25	22·5
" 15th " 9 a.m.		·082	21	·71	16·5	16·0
Noon		·002	33	·75	30	27
3 p.m.		·002	39	·68	26	33
6 "		·052	35	·67	26	25
9 "		·042	30	·66	22	21·3
" 16th " 9 a.m.		·022	25	·65	21	20
Noon		25·997	36	·61	31·5	29·5
3 p.m.		·952	40·5	·58	35	33
6 "		·972	35	·59	30	29
9 "		·952	32	·60	23	22
" 17th " 9 a.m.		·902	23	·54	20	19
Noon		·877	30·5	·53	31	29
3 p.m.		·857	33·5	·59	31·3	28·5
6 "		·862	33·0	·59	29	28
9 "		·862	32·0	·58	28	26
" 18th " 9 a.m.		·892	33·0	·51	30	28
Noon		·902	49·3	·52	47	38
3 p.m.		·892	52	·51	50	41·5
6 "		·902	44	·52	33	31
9 "		·927	37	·57	33	32
" 19th " 9 a.m.		26·077	20·5	·72	17·5	16
Noon		·112	32	·74	30	27
3 p.m.		·102	36	·72	34	31
6 "		·112	32	·76	25	24
9 "		·122	26·5	·77	21	19
" 20th " 9 a.m.		·202	23·5	·85	22	21
Noon		·192	35	·84	33	30
3 p.m.		·162	37	·80	36	31
6 "		·152	32	·80	28	25
9 "		·177	31	·82	24	22
" 21st " 9 a.m.		·132	21	·79	17·5	16
Noon		·132	30·5	·78	28	25·5
3 p.m.		·102	34·5	·75	32	29
6 "		·102	31	·72	25	23

(87)

Pandits at YARKAND during the winter of 1873-74.—(Continued.)

Minimum in shade. During preceding 24 hours. Degrees.	Maximum in shade. Degrees.	Direction of wind.	Remarks.
......	......	N.	
......	......	N.	
......	......	N.	
18	45	S.	
......	......	N.W.	
......	......	N.E.	
......	......	N.	
......	......	S.	
10	41	N.	
......	......	N.	
......	......	S.E.	
......	......	S.	
......	......	E.	
12	34	N.	
......	......	N.W.	
......	......	N.	
......	......	W.	
......	......	S.E.	
10	33	N.W.	
......	......	W.	
......	......	E.	
......	......	W	
......	......	S.	
10	36·5	W.	
......	......	E.	
......	......	E.	
......	......	N.	
......	......	W.	
9·8	36	N.	
......	......	S.W.	
......	......	N.	
......	......	S.	
......	......	S.	
19	35·5	S.E.	
......	......	N.	
......	......	W.	
......	......	E.	
......	......	S.	
10	49	N.E.	
......	......	N.	
......	......	N.E.	
......	......	W.	
......	......	S.	
9·5	31·5	N.	
......	......	N.	
......	......	W.	
......	......	E.	
·6	14	N.	
......	......	N.E.	
......	......	S.E.	
......	......	N.	

(88)

Meteorological Observations recorded by the Great Trigonometrical Survey

Date.			Mercurial Barometer No. 720 corrected for index error.	Temperature of mercury.	Reading of aneroid barometer Solomon's uncorrected.	Temperature of Air.	
						Dry Bulb.	Wet Bulb.
			Inches.	*Degrees.*	*Inches.*	*Degrees.*	*Degrees.*
Dec. 21st, 1873,	9 P.M.		26·002	27	25·75	21	20
„ 22nd	„	9 A.M.	·067	20·5	·75	17·5	16·0
		Noon	·042	31·5	·67	30	27
		3 P.M.	·012	35	·65	32	29
		6 „	25·977	31	·61	26	24
		9 „	·952	28	·59	21	19·9
„ 23rd	„	9 A.M.	·822	19·5	·48	19·5	18·5
		Noon	·772	30	·40	29	26
		3 P.M.	·712	33	·35	31	28
		6 „	·702	31	·35	22	20
		9 „	·752	30	·40	26·5	24
„ 24th	„	9 A.M.	·942	36	·57	34·5	29·5
		Noon	·932	48	·55	47	47
		3 P.M.	·952	47	·56	47	40
		6 „	·952	36	·59	33	32
		9 „	26·002	30·5	·62	26·5	25·5
„ 25th	„	9 A.M.	·042	19·0	·66	17	16
		Noon	·027	32	·64	31	28
		3 P.M.	25·967	36	·59	33	31
		6 „	·962	31·5	·58	26	24
		9 „	·972	28	·61	24	23
„ 26th	„	9 A.M.	·922	20	·56	17	15·5
		Noon	·952	34	·57	32	28
		3 P.M.	·922	35	·56	32·3	29·3
		6 „	·952	32	·59	26	24
		9 „	·982	26·5	·65	21	19
„ 27th	„	9 A.M.	26·017	24	·65	24	21·8
		Noon	·002	32	·63	31·5	28·5
		3 P.M.	25·952	36	·58	34	32
		6 „	·922	32	·56	27	26
		9 „	·942	27	·59	20	19
„ 28th	„	9 A.M.	26·097	16	·75	12	11
		Noon	·127	29·5	·77	28	24·3
		3 P.M.	·107	33	·75	30	27
		6 „	·102	29·5	·73	24	22
		9 „	·097	24	·72	18	15·5
„ 29th	„	9 A.M.	·022	18·5	·67	14	13
		Noon	·007	31·5	·65	29	27
		3 P.M.	·012	36	·65	33	31
		6 „	·027	30	·70	26	24·5
		9 „	·077	27	·75	21	20
„ 30th	„	9 A.M.	·192	10	·86	9	8
		Noon	·182	23	·85	21	19
		3 P.M.	·142	28	·80	26	23
		6 „	·122	25	·77	18	17
		9 „	·102	21	·74	13	12
„ 31st	„	9 A.M.	·052	10	·70	14	14
		Noon	·007	24·5	·66	22	21
		3 P.M.	25·952	28	·61	24	22
		6 „	·952	26	·61	19	18
		9 „	·962	22	·62	16	14

(89)

Pandits at YARKAND during the winter of 1873-74.—(Continued.)

Minimum in shade. During preceding 24 hours.	Maximum in shade.	Direction of wind.	Remarks.
Degrees.	*Degrees.*		
......	......	S.W.	
8·0	29·8	W.	
......	......	S.	
......	......	N.	
......	......	N.	
......	......	W.	
10	33	S.E.	
......	......	E.	
......	......	S.W.	
......	......	N.	
......	......	N.	
15	29·5	W.	
......	......	W.	
......	......	E.	
......	......	S.W.	
......	......	N.	
10·5	47	W.	
......	......	N.W.	
......	......	E.	
......	......	E.	
......	......	N.	
7	46·5	W.	
......	......	W.	
......	......	S.E.	
......	......	W.	
......	......	N.	
11·8	33·3	S.W.	
......	......	N.	
......	......	E.	
......	......	W.	
......	......	E.	
5	34	N.W.	
......	......	W.	For the month of December 1873.
......	......	S.E.	
......	......	N.	
......	......	E.	
2·5	28	E.	
......	......	N.E.	
......	......	N.	
......	......	E.	
......	......	E.	
3	30	W.	
......	......	N.W.	
......	......	N.	
......	......	N.	
......	......	N.W.	
2	24	W.	
......	......	N.	
......	......	S.E.	
......	......	W.	
......	......	N.	

For the month of December 1873.

	9 P.M.	Noon.	3 P.M.	6 P.M.	9 P.M
Mean of Mercurial Barometer No. 720	26·075	26·067	26·042	26·047	26·050
Mean of Dry Bulb Thermometer	21·0	32·3	35·3	28·3	24·1
Mean of Wet Bulb Thermometer	19·7	29·5	32·1	26·4	23·3
Mean of Minimum Thermometer	...	...	...	...	10·8
Mean of Maximum Thermometer in shade				...	35·2

Meteorological Observations recorded by the Great Trigonometrical

Date.		Mercurial Barometer No. 720 corrected for index error.	Temperature of mercury.	Reading of aneroid barometer Solomon's uncorrected.	Temperature of Air.	
					Dry Bulb.	Wet Bulb.
		Inches.	Degrees.	Inches.	Degrees.	Degrees.
Jan. 1st, 1874,	9 A.M.	25·952	10	25·61	10·3	9·3
	Noon	·952	24·8	·61	25	23
	3 P.M.	·927	28	·57	27	25
	6 ,,	·922	26	·55	21	20
	9 ,,	·932	23	·58	17·5	16
,, 2nd ,,	9 A.M.	·927	12	·60	13	12
	Noon	·932	21·5	·61	22	20
	3 P.M.	·927	26·5	·60	24·5	22
	6 ,,	·922	23	·60	19	18·5
	9 ,,	·942	20·5	·63	16	15
,, 3rd ,,	9 A.M.	26·052	11	·72	12·5	12
	Noon	·052	22·5	·72	22	19·5
	3 P.M.	·042	28·5	·70	26	23
	6 ,,	·052	24·5	·72	18·5	17
	9 ,,	·072	21	·74	15·5	14
,, 4th ,,	9 A.M.	26·062	11	25·73	11	10
	Noon.	·052	25	·71	23	21
	3 P.M.	·047	28	·71	26	23
	6 ,,	·072	25	·73	21	19
	9 ,,	·082	21	·76	15	14
,, 5th ,,	9 A.M.	·117	10	·80	11	10
	Noon	·107	25	·78	23	21
	3 P.M.	·072	27·5	·72	25	23
	6 ,,	·062	25	·74	20	19
	9 ,,	·072	21	·76	16	15
,, 6th ,,	9 A.M.	·067	10	·83	8	7
	Noon	·152	23·5	·82	22	19
	3 P.M.	·127	27	·78	24	21
	6 ,,	·152	25	·80	20	18
	9 ,,	·152	22	·80	17	16
,, 7th ,,	9 A.M.	·192	11	·87	13	12
	Noon	·192	21	·86	21·5	19·5
	3 P.M.	·167	25	·81	24	21
	6 ,,	·172	23	·84	20	19
	9 ,,	·197	22	·86	19	18
,, 8th ,,	9 A.M.	·152	18·8	·81	17	16
	Noon	·117	25·8	·78	25	22·5
	3 P.M.	·077	27	·73	25·5	23
	6 ,,	·082	23·3	·74	19	18
	9 ,,	·062	20	·73	16	15
,, 9th ,,	9 A.M.	·067	10	·73	10	9
	Noon	·052	25	·70	23	21
	3 P.M.	25·992	28	·66	26	23
	6 ,,	26·007	25	·68	21	19
	9 ,,	·012	21	·69	18	16
,, 10th ,,	9 A.M.	·027	11·5	·70	10	9
	Noon	·022	26·5	·67	26	23
	3 P.M.	25·972	31	·63	29	27
	6 ,,	·972	27	·63	24	23
	9 ,,	·952	24	·61	21	19
,, 11th ,,	9 A.M.	26·202	13	·87	13	12
	Noon	·302	25	·95	23·5	20

Survey Pandits at YARKAND during the winter of 1873-74.—(Continued).

Minimum in shade. During preceding 24 hours.	Maximum in shade.	Direction of wind.	Remarks.
Degrees.	*Degrees.*		
0	23	N.	
......	......	S.E.	
......	......	W.	
......	......	N.	
......	......	S.	
7·5	19	W.	
......	......	S.	
......	......	S.	
......	......	N.W.	
......	......	W.	
6	29·5	S.W.	
......	......	N.	
......	......	S.E.	
......	......	W.	
......	......	N.	
2	23	N.	
......	......	N.W.	
......	......	N.	
......	......	N.	
......	......	W.	
1·8	24	N.	
......	......	N.E.	
......	......	E.	
......	......	N.	
......	......	S.E.	
1·3	25	E	
......	......	N.E.	
......	......	E.	
......	......	W.	
......	......	W.	
3	22·5	N.W.	
......	......	W.	
......	......	S.W.	
......	......	N.E.	
......	......	N.W.	
9	26	S.W.	
......	......	E.	
......	......	S.E.	
......	......	E.	
......	......	N.	
1	29·5	S.W.	
......	......	N.E.	
......	......	E.	
......	......	E.	
......	......	W.	
3	23	S.	
......	......	N.	
......	......	W.	
......	......	W.	
......	......	N.	
4	31·5	W.	
......	......	N.E.	

(92)

Meteorological Observations recorded by the Great Trigonometrical Survey

Date.			Mercurial Barometer No. 720 corrected for index error.	Temperature of mercury.	Reading of aneroid barometer Solomon's uncorrected.	Temperature of Air.	
						Dry Bulb.	Wet Bulb.
			Inches.	*Degrees.*	*Inches.*	*Degrees.*	*Degrees.*
Jan. 11th	1874,	3 P.M. ...	26·352	28·3	26·01	26	23
		6 ,, ...	·382	24	·05	19	18
		9 ,, ...	·412	21	·08	14	13
,, 12th	,,	9 A.M. ...	·402	17·5	·05	15	14
		Noon ...	·342	26	·01	26	21
		3 P.M. ...	·302	28·5	25·94	26	23
		6 ,, ...	·262	23·5	·93	20	18
		9 ,, ...	·252	20	·90	14	13
,, 13th	,,	9 A.M. ...	·192	10	·85	10	8
		Noon ...	·152	25	·80	23·5	20
		3 P.M. ...	·102	28	·76	27	23
		6 ,, ...	·092	24·5	·75	20	17
		9 ,, ...	·072	19·8	·73	15	14
,, 14th	,,	9 A.M. ...	·052	10	·72	10	9
		Noon	·042	25	·70	24	21
		3 P.M. ...	·022	29	·67	27	24
		6 ,,	·032	25	·70	21	19
		9 ,,	·042	20·3	·71	17	14·5
,, 15th	,,	9 A.M. ...	·112	11	·80	11	10
		Noon	·107	25	·77	24	21
		3 P.M. ...	·102	29	·74	27	23·5
		6 ,,	·122	25	·78	20	18
		9 ,,	·152	21	·80	16	15
,, 16th	,,	9 A.M. ...	·207	11	·88	10	9
		Noon	·222	27	·89	26	22
		3 P.M.	·202	30	·87	28	25
		6 ,,	·242	26·5	·90	22	20
		9 ,, ...	·257	21	·92	17	15
,, 17th	,,	9 A.M. ...	26·312	12·5	26·01	13	11
		Noon ...	·327	27	25·98	26	22
		3 P.M. ...	·302	31	·95	29	26
		6 ,, ...	·302	27	·95	25	23
		9 ,, ...	·292	24	·94	20	18
,, 18th	,,	9 A.M. ...	·207	11	·88	13	12
		Noon ...	·202	27·5	·87	28	24
		3 P.M. ...	·107	32	·73	30	27
		6 ,, ...	·107	28	·77	24	22
		9 ,, ...	·102	24	·74	20	18
,, 19th	,,	9 A.M. ...	·077	12	·73	13	11
		Noon ...	·072	27	·72	27	23
		3 P.M. ...	·052	31	·69	31	28
		6 ,, ...	·057	28	·70	23	20
		9 ,,	·082	23	·72	18	16
,, 20th	,,	9 A.M. ...	·062	18·5	·71	12	10
		Noon	·052	31	·70	30	26
		3 P.M.	·052	33	·71	33	31
		6 ,,	·052	30	·73	31	28
		9 ,,	·027	27·5	·68	22	20
,, 21st	,,	9 A.M.	25·932	22	·58	21	18·5
		Noon	·927	30	·56	30·5	27·5
		3 P.M.	·862	32	·51	31	28·5
		6 ,,	·867	30	·54	28	26

(93)

Pandits at YARKAND during the winter of 1873-74.—(Continued.)

Minimum in shade.	Maximum in shade.	Direction of wind.	Remarks.
During preceding 24 hours.			
Degrees.	*Degrees.*		
......	......	N.W.	
......	......	W.	
......	......	S.	
3	24	S.E.	
......	......	W.	
......	......	E.	
......	......	W.	
......	......	E.	
1	23	E.	
......	......	S.E.	
......	......	N.E.	
......	......	N.W.	
......	......	N.	
0·5	23·5	S.W.	
......	......	N.E.	
......	......	S.E.	
......	......	N.	
......	......	N.	
1	25·5	W.	
......	......	N.W.	
......	......	W.	
......	......	S.	
......	......	N.	
1	25	N.	
......	......	S.	
......	......	E.	
......	......	E.	
......	......	S.	
1	25	N.W.	
......	......	S.E.	
......	......	N.E.	
......	......	E.	
......	......	N.	
2·5	27	S.W.	
......	......	W.	
......	......	S.E.	
......	......	E.	
......	......	N.	
4	30	E.	
......	......	N.W.	
......	......	S.	
......	......	E.	
......	......	N.E.	
7·5	33	S.W.	
......	......	S.	
......	......	E.	
......	......	S.	
......	......	W.	
10·8	34·8	S.	
......	......	N.	
......	......	N.E.	
......	......	W.	

(94)

Meteorological Observations recorded by the Great Trigonometrical

Date.			Mercurial Barometer No. 720 corrected for index error.	Temperature of mercury.	Reading of aneroid barometer Solomon's uncorrected.	Temperature of Air.	
						Dry Bulb.	Wet Bulb.
			Inches.	*Degrees.*	*Inches.*	*Degrees.*	*Degrees.*
Jan. 21st, 1874,	9 P.M.	...	·892	29	·56	20·5	22·5
„ 22nd „	9 A.M.	...	·902	25	·55	24	21
	Noon	...	·912	31	·56	32	28
	3 P.M.	...	·912	34	·56	33·5	27
	6 „	...	·942	30	·60	26	23
	9 „	...	·947	27	·64	22·5	20·5
„ 23rd „	9 A.M.	...	·952	23	·62	22	19
	Noon	...	·947	31·5	·58	32	27·5
	3 P.M.	...	·917	33	·57	33	30
	6 „	...	·952	31·8	·62	28	26
	9 „	...	·972	28·5	·67	25	24
„ 24th „	9 A.M.	...	26·062	20·5	·72	19	27·3
	Noon	...	·062	33·5	·72	32·5	29
	3 P.M.	...	·052	37·5	·69	36	34·5
	6 „		·057	34·0	·73	29	28
	9 „	...	·072	30	·75	26	23
„ 25th „	9 A.M.	...	·092	21	·75	20·5	19·5
	Noon	...	·042	35	·67	34·5	30·3
	3 P.M.	...	25·982	38	·62	37	34·5
	6 „	...	·972	34	·62	30	29
	9 „	...	·972	32	·61	29	25
„ 26th „	9 A.M.	...	·992	28	·62	27	25
	Noon	...	·977	39	·62	40	36
	3 P.M.	...	·972	40	·60	38	33·5
	6 „	...	26·002	36	·65	31	29
	9 „	...	·007	30·5	·68	26	24
„ 27th „	9 A.M.	...	·022	22	·69	21	19
	Noon	...	·042	32	·69	33	29
	3 P.M.	...	·017	38	·66	37	34
	6 „	...	·022	33·5	·69	30	28·5
	9 „	...	·032	29	·70	24·5	23
„ 28th „	9 A.M.	...	26·132	21	·80	19	17
	Noon	...	·132	34	·80	33	31
	3 P.M.	...	·112	37·5	·75	35	30
	6 „	...	·122	33·5	·79	28	25
	9 „	...	·172	32	·84	29·5	25·3
„ 29th „	9 A.M.	...	·142	28	·80	29	26
	Noon	...	·142	35	·81	36	32
	3 P.M.	...	·082	38	·73	36	31
	6 „	...	·102	33	·77	29	26
	9 „	...	·007	30	·76	24	22
„ 30th „	9 A.M.	...	26·062	22·5	25·78	21	19
	Noon	...	·032	35·5	·68	35	31
	3 P.M.	...	·002	38	·64	37	31
	6 „	...	·007	34·5	·65	31	26
	9 „	...	·012	31	·66	27	24
„ 31st „	9 A.M.	...	·032	22	·69	21	19
	Noon	...	·022	34·8	·67	33·5	29
	3 P.M.	...	25·997	38·5	·63	36·8	33·5
	6 „	...	26·002	34	·65	31	27
	9 „	...	·007	32	·67	29	26

(95)

Survey Pandits at YARKAND during the winter of 1873-74.—(Continued.)

Minimum in shade. During preceding 24 hours.	Maximum in shade.	Direction of wind.	Remarks.
Degrees.	*Degrees.*		
......	......	N.W.	
19	34	S.W.	
......	......	N.W.	
......	......	N.	
......	......	W.	
......	......	N.E.	
17	38	S.W.	
......	......	S.	
......	......	E.	
......	......	N.E.	
......	......	N.	
9	39	N.W.	
......	......	E.	
......	......	E.	
......	......	N.W.	
......	......	N.	
9	33·8	N.W.	
......	......	N.E.	
......	......	S.W.	
......	......	E.	
......	......	N.	
14	34·5	S.W.	
......	......	E.	
......	......	S.E.	
......	......	S.	
......	......	W.	
11	43·5	W.	
......	......	N.	
......	......	N.	
......	......	E.	*For the month of January* 1874.
......	......	N.E.	
7·8	42	N.W.	9 A.M. Noon. 3 P.M. 6 P.M. 9 P.M.
......	......	N.E.	Mean of Mercurial 26·063 26·087 26·060 26·068 26·074
......	......	N.	Barometer No. 720
......	......	S.	corrected to 32°.
......	......	E.	
17	34	W.	Mean of Dry Bulb 15·5 27·8 30·0 24·2 20·4
......	......	E.	Thermometer.
......	......	S.W.	
......	......	N.	Mean of Wet Bulb 14·0 24·5 26·8 22·2 18·5
......	......	N.E.	Thermometer.
11	41	S.W.	
......	......	N.E.	Mean of minimum thermometer ... 6°·2 6°·2
......	......	N.E.	Mean of maximum thermometer in shade ... 29°·7 29°·7
......	......	S.	
......	......	E.	
8	34·5	S.W.	
......	......	S.E.	
......	......	S.E.	
......	......	N.	
......	......	E.	

Meteorological Observations recorded by the Great Trigonometrical Survey

Date.			Mercurial Barometer No. 720 corrected for index error.	Temperature of mercury.	Reading of Aneroid Barometer Solomon's uncorrected.	TEMPERATURE OF AIR.	
						Dry bulb.	Wet bulb.
			Inches.	*Degrees.*	*Inches.*	*Degrees.*	*Degrees.*
Feb.	1st, 1874,	9 A.M.	25·982	26	25·63	25·5	23
		Noon	·977	35	·62	36	32
		3 P.M.	·907	38	·56	37	32·5
		6 ,,	·912	34	·58	30	26
		9 ,,	·917	31	·59	26	23
,,	2nd ,,	9 A.M.	·902	20	·58	19	17
		Noon	·897	36	·56	35	31·5
		3 P.M.	·872	42	·52	41	35
		6 ,,	·892	38	·53	34	32
		9 ,,	·912	33·5	·59	28	25
,,	3rd ,,	9 A.M.	·982	24	·65	24	21
		Noon	·977	36	·62	36	32
		3 P.M.	·952	42	·58	41	35
		6 ,,	·942	38·5	·57	31	28
		9 ,,	·962	33	·62	29	26
,,	4th ,,	9 A.M.	·962	25	·62	24	21
		Noon	·962	37	·62	37	32·5
		3 P.M.	·927	42·5	·56	41	36
		6 ,,	·927	39	·58	32	28
		9 ,,	·947	33·3	·60	27	25
,,	5th ,,	9 A.M.	·952	26·5	·61	27·5	22·5
		Noon	·952	37·5	·60	37	31·5
		3 P.M.	·923	42	·55	42	36
		6 ,,	·927	39	·58	32	28
		9 ,,	·952	32·5	·61	26	23
,,	6th ,,	9 A.M.	·932	26·5	·62	26	23
		Noon	·927	36	·00	36	31
		3 P.M.	·902	42	·55	41	36
		6 ,,	·902	37·5	·55	33	29
		9 ,,	·907	33	·58	29	26
,,	7th ,,	9 A.M.	·907	25·5	·58	24	22
		Noon	·922	38	·59	38	32
		3 P.M.	·892	42·5	·52	41	34·5
		6 ,,	·892	38	·52	32	28
		9 ,,	·897	34	·55	29	26
,,	8th ,,	9 A.M.	·952	24	·50	23	20·5
		Noon	·792	36	·42	36	31
		3 P.M.	·677	41	·31	40	36
		6 ,,	·702	36	·36	33	32
		9 ,,	·722	34	·37	30	26
,,	9th ,,	9 A.M.	·732	31	·41	31·5	28
		Noon	·712	38	·36	38	33
		3 P.M.	·712	41	·37	40	34
		6 ,,	·752	38	·40	35	31
		9 ,,	·757	35	·41	33	30
,,	10th ,,	9 A.M.	·897	31·8	·55	31	28
		Noon	·927	40·3	·57	41	36·3
		3 P.M.	·922	39	·57	38·5	34·5
		6 ,,	·947	35·5	·63	33	31
		9 ,,	·952	32	·64	31	29
,,	11th ,,	9 A.M.	·937	31·5	·59	33	31·5
		Noon	·902	37	·56	38	35·3

Pandits at *YARKAND* during the month of 1873-74.—(Continued).

MINIMUM IN SHADE.	MAXIMUM IN SHADE.	Direction of wind.	REMARKS.
During preceding 24 hours.			
Degrees.	*Degrees.*		
14·3	36	S.	
......	......	S.W.	
......	......	E.	
......	......	N.E.	
......	......	N.	
8·5	42	N.W.	
......	......	W.	
......	......	E.	
......	......	W.	
......	......	N.	
12·8	38·5	N.	
......	......	W.	
......	......	S.	
......	......	W.	
......	......	E.	
13	39	N.W.	
......	......	N.E.	
......	......	W.	
......	......	E.	
......	......	N.	
16·5	40	S.W.	
......	......	S.W.	
......	......	W.	
......	......	W.	
......	......	N.	
12·8	38·5	W.	
......	......	N.E.	
......	......	E.	
......	......	N.	
......	......	S.	
11	43	N.W.	
......	......	N.	
......	......	N.E.	
......	......	E.	
......	......	N.	
9·8	45	N.E.	
......	......	W.	
......	......	N.E.	
......	......	N.	
......	......	N.	
16·5	49	S.W.	
......	......	N.E.	
......	......	W.	
......	......	N.	
......	......	W.	
24·5	49·5	N.W.	
......	......	E.	
......	......	E.	
......	......	W.	
......	......	W.	
22	48	N.E.	Clouds and snow.
......	......	N.	

(98)

Meteorological Observations recorded by the Great Trigonometrical

Date.			Mercurial Barometer No. 720 corrected for index error.	Temperature of mercury.	Reading of Aneroid Barometer Solomon's uncorrected.	Temperature of Air.	
						Dry bulb.	Wet bulb.
			Inches.	Degrees.	Inches.	Degrees.	Degrees.
Feb. 11th, 1874,	3 p.m.	...	25·872	37·5	25·52	37	35
	6 ,,	...	·892	34	·55	32	30
	9 ,,	...	·902	30	·57	28	27
,, 12th ,,	9 a.m.	...	·942	30	·61	29·5	27
	Noon	...	·937	37	·59	35	32
	3 p.m.	...	·902	39·5	·54	39·3	34
	6 ,,	...	·902	36	·57	30	27
	9 ,,	...	9·12	31	·60	27	25
,, 13th ,,	9 a.m.	...	9·92	28	·66	26·5	25
	Noon	...	26·002	36	·67	35	31
	3 p.m.	...	25·977	45·5	·66	38	34
	6 ,,	...	·952	37·5	·65	30·5	28
	9 ,,	...	·972	31·3	·67	26·3	25
,, 14th ,,	9 a.m.	...	26·027	29	·68	27·5	25·5
	Noon	...	·002	38	·65	37	33
	3 p.m.	...	25·952	41	·58	39	36
	6 ,,	...	·912	38	·56	33	28
	9 ,,	...	·952	34	·63	31	26·5
,, 15th ,,	9 a.m.	...	26·052	34	·71	34	32
	Noon	...	·027	41	·69	41·3	35
	3 p.m.	...	·022	43	·67	41	35
	6 ,,	...	·022	40	·67	36	31
	9 ,,	...	·012	35	·67	31	27
,, 16th ,,	9 a.m.	...	·027	26	·71	25	22
	Noon	...	·042	38·5	·66	37	32
	3 p.m.	...	·022	43	·60	41	35
	6 ,,	...	25·952	40	·59	33	28
	9 ,,	...	·952	34	·59	30	26
,, 17th ,,	9 a.m.	...	·942	34·5	·57	34	31
	Noon	...	·927	41·5	·55	42·5	37
	3 p.m.	...	·912	45·5	·54	46	38·5
	6 ,,	...	·932	40·5	·60	35	30
	9 ,,	...	·972	38	·65	38	28·5
,, 18th ,,	9 a.m.	...	26·102	36·3	·79	36·3	31
	Noon	...	·102	44·5	·70	44	34
	3 p.m.	...	·092	48	·69	48	38
	6 ,,	...	·082	42	·73	39	31
	9 ,,	...	·102	37	·78	31·5	26
,, 19th ,,	9 a.m.	...	·172	26	·83	25·5	23·5
	Noon	...	·162	34	·76	35·5	32·3
	3 p.m.	...	·127	38·5	·78	38	33
	6 ,,	...	·127	36	·78	34	29
	9 ,,	...	·132	33·5	·79	32	28
,, 20th ,,	9 a.m.	...	·092	33·5	·74	34	30·5
	Noon	...	·072	40	·72	42	36
	3 p.m.	...	·017	43	·63	44·3	38
	6 ,,	...	25·997	39	·64	35	30
	9 ,,	...	26·002	35	·65	30	26
,, 21st ,,	9 a.m.	...	·042	31·5	·68	32	29
	Noon	...	·052	41	·70	42	35
	3 p.m.	...	·017	43·5	·65	43	36
	6 ,,	...	·032	41	·69	38	31

(99)

Survey Pandits at *YARKAND* during the winter of 1873-74.—(Continued).

Minimum in shade.	Maximum in shade.	Direction of wind.	Remarks.
During preceding 24 hours.			
Degrees.	*Degrees.*		
......	......	S.	
......	......	E.	
		S.	
19·8	48	N.-W.	
......	......	N.	
......	......	N.-E.	
......	......	S.	
......	......	S.-W.	
11	41	N.	
......	......	S.	
......	......	E.	
......	......	N.	
		S.	
17·5	36	N.-W.	
......	......	S.-W.	
......	......	N.-E.	
......	......	S.	
		S.	
22	37	N.-W.	
......	......	N.-E.	
......	......	S.	
......	......	S.-E.	
		N.	
16	47	N.	
......	......	E.	
......	......	W.	
......	......	E.	
		E.	
22	40	W.	
......	......	S.-W.	
......	......	S.-E.	
......	......	N.	
		S.	
21	50·5	W.	
......	......	N.	
......	......	S.-E.	
......	......	E.	
		E.	
18	52	N.-W.	
......	......	W.	
......	......	S.-W.	
......	......	S.-E.	
		S.	
24·5	41·5	N.-E.	
......	......	N.-E.	
......	......	S.-E.	
......	......	S.	
		E.	
20	50	W.	
......	......	S.-E.	
......	......	E.	
......	......	W.	

Meteorological Observations recorded by the Great Trigonometrical

Date.			Mercurial Barometer No. 720 corrected for index error.	Temperature of mercury.	Reading of aneroid barometer Solomon's uncorrected.	Temperature of Air.	
						Dry Bulb.	Wet Bulb.
			Inches.	Degrees.	Inches.	Degrees.	Degrees.
Feb. 21st,	1874,	9 P.M.	26·062	37	25·74	35	27
,, 22nd	,,	9 A.M.	·147	34·5	·82	35	31·5
		Noon	·152	39	·82	40·5	35·5
		3 P.M.	·107	38	·72	38·5	35
		6 ,,	·02	36	·75	35	32
		9 ,,	·112	33·5	·77	32	30
,, 23rd	,,	9 A.M.	·162	33·5	·80	33	31
		Noon	·142	37	·77	37·5	34
		3 P.M.	·092	40·3	·75	40	32
		6 ,,	·082	37·3	·73	33·5	29
		9 ,,	·077	32·5	·74	30	27
,, 24th	,,	9 P.M.	·052	30·5	·72	30·5	28
		Noon	·002	38	·65	37	34
		3 P.M.	25·932	40	·57	41	34
		6 ,,	·912	38·5	·56	36	30·5
		9 ,,	·902	36	·55	33	28·5
,, 25th	,,	9 A.M.	·852	32·5	·52	31·5	28
		Noon	·812	40	·47	39	34
		3 P.M.	·757	42	·39	42	35
		6 ,,	·752	39	·39	36	29
		9 ,,	·752	35	·39	31	26·5
,, 26th	,,	9 A.M.	·802	36·8	·46	36	32·5
		Noon	·802	48	·43	47	39
		3 P.M.	·772	51	·37	50·5	40·5
		6 ,,	·802	45·5	·44	44·5	36
		9 ,,	·877	40	·53	36·0	31
,, 27th	,,	9 A.M.	26·002	36·8	·66	36	31·5
		Noon	·002	44	·64	44	38
		3 P.M.	25·952	47	·62	46	37
		6 ,,	·972	44	·63	41	33
		9 ,,	26·002	39·8	·65	36·5	31·5
,, 28th	,,	9 A.M.	·002	38	·67	38	33
		Noon	·017	46	·66	46	37·5
		3 P.M.	25·992	48	·62	49	39·5
		6 ,,	26·002	45	·68	40	34
		9 ,,	·052	40	·70	37·5	31

(101)

Survey Pandits at **YARKAND** *during the winter of* **1873-74.**—(Continued.)

Minimum in shade.	Maximum in shade.	Direction of wind.	Remarks.
During preceding 24 hours.			
Degrees.	Degrees.		
......	......	W.	
26·8	47·8	E.	
......	......	N.W.	
......	......	S.W.	
......	......	E.	
......	......	W.	
27	43	N.E.	
......	......	N.E.	
......	......	S.E.	
......	......	W.	
......	......	W.	
21·8	45	S.E.	
......	......	W.	
......	......	N.W.	*For the month of February* 1874.
......	......	W.	
		N.E.	
17·5	48·0	W.	
......	......	W.	
......	......	S.	
......	......	E.	
......	......	N.	
20·8	44·5	S.	
......	......	S.	Mean of dry bulb
......	......	S.W.	Thermometer
......	......	S.	Mean of wet bulb
......	......	W.	Thermometer
19·8	50·5	S.E.	Mean of Minimum Thermometer
......	......	W.	Mean of Maximum Thermometer in shade
......	......	W.	
......	......	W.	
......	......	N.E.	
22	45	W.	
......	......	N.	
......	......	S.E.	
......	......	W.	
......	......	E.	

	9 A.M.	Noon.	3 P.M.	6 P.M.	9 P.M.
Mean of Mercurial Barometer No. 720.	25·980	25·971	25·935	25·936	25·952
Mean of dry bulb Thermometer	29·7	38·9	41·6	34·5	30°·7
Mean of wet bulb Thermometer	26·8	33·8	35·5	30·0	27°·0
Mean of Minimum Thermometer					18°·2
Mean of Maximum Thermometer in shade					44°·1

(102)

Meteorological Observations recorded by the Great Trigonometrical Survey

DATE.		Mercurial Barometer No. 720 corrected for index error.	Temperature of mercury.	Reading of aneroid barometer Solomon's uncorrected.	TEMPERATURE OF AIR.	
					Dry Bulb.	Wet Bulb.
		Inches.	Degrees.	Inches.	Degrees.	Degrees.
March 1st, 1874,	9 A.M.	25·997	36·5	·65	36·8	32·3
	Noon	·992	45·5	·61	45·5	40
	3 P.M.	·882	50·5	·50	50·5	41
	6 ,,	·802	45·8	·43	41	34
	9 ,,	·802	41	·43	36·5	30·5
,, 2nd ,,	9 A.M.	·662	38	·32	39	33
	Noon	·612	48·3	·25	48·3	41·3
	3 P.M.	·562	52·5	·18	54	45
	6 ,,	·552	49	·16	42	35·5
	9 ,,	·542	44	·15	39	33
,, 3rd ,,	9 A.M.	·582	39	·23	40	35
	Noon	·597	48·5	·24	50·3	44
	3 P.M.	·582	50	·22	50	40·8
	6 ,,	25·652	49	25·28	47	39
	9 ,,	·682	45	·33	42	36
,, 4th ,,	9 A.M.	·832	45	·48	45	37
	Noon	·827	50	·46	51	41
	3 P.M.	·802	49·8	·43	49·3	40·8
	6 ,,	·842	46·5	·48	43	37·5
	9 ,,	·807	43	·45	40	35
,, 5th ,,	9 A.M.	·822	40	·46	39·8	35·5
	Noon	·797	49	·44	50	42
	3 P.M.	·767	51·8	·36	52	42
	6 ,,	·777	49	·45	47	39·5
	9 ,,	·782	45	·46	43	38
,, 6th ,,	9 A.M.	·832	40·5	·48	40	36
	Noon	·852	48·8	·49	50	42
	3 P.M.	·792	51	·42	51·3	41·3
	6 ,,	·767	48·8	·40	46	38
	9 ,,	·752	45	·36	43	36
,, 7th ,,	9 A.M.	·792	40·3	·44	41·5	32
	Noon	·752	47·3	·36	50	42
	3 P.M.	·652	50	·28	52	42·3
	6 ,,	·612	45·8	·22	43	37
	9 ,,	·607	42	·25	40·5	36
,, 8th ,,	9 A.M.	·597	40	·23	36	33
	Noon	·577	42	·20	43	37
	3 P.M.	·552	41·3	·18	41·3	36·8
	6 ,,	·602	40·5	·23	38	34
	9 ,,	·607	38·3	·25	36·5	33·5
,, 9th ,,	9 A.M.	·697	38	·35	39	33·5
	Noon	·692	41	·33	41	37
	3 P.M.	·677	42·8	·32	43	37·5
	6 ,,	·727	41	·36	38·5	34
	9 ,,	·772	36	·41	33	30
,, 10th ,,	9 A.M.	·877	36·5	·52	37	31·3
	Noon	·892	45·8	·53	46	39·5
	3 P.M.	·892	47·5	·53	47·3	37
	6 ,,	·932	42·5	·58	40·3	35
	9 ,,	26·002	37·5	·64	37·3	30·5
,, 11th ,,	9 A.M.	·137	34·5	·77	34	30·3
	Noon	·152	41	·82	43	40

Pandits at YARKAND during the winter of 1873-74.—(Continued.)

Minimum in shade.	Maximum in shade.	Direction of wind.	Remarks.
During preceding 24 hours.			
Degrees.	*Degrees.*		
19·8	49	N.W.	
......	......	N.E.	
......	......	S.	
......	......	N.	
......	......	N.	
22·3	55·5	S.W.	
......	......	S.E.	
......	......	E.	
......	......	S.	
......	......	S.W.	
24·8	56·8	W.	
......	......	W.	
......	......	S.E.	
......	......	W.	
......	......	S.E.	
34·8	57·5	N.E.	
......	......	N.E.	
......	......	N.E.	
......	......	W.	
......	......	E.	
32	57·5	W.	
......	......	S.E.	
......	......	N.	
......	......	N.E	
......	......	W.	
37	55·5	W.	
......	......	N.E.	
......	......	N.E.	
......	......	E.	
......	......	S.E.	
33·5	55·	N.E	
......	......	S.E.	
......	......	E.	
......	......	S.W.	
......	......	N.W.	
36	58·5	W.	
......	......	E.	
......	......	N.E.	
......	......	N.E.	
......	......	N.E.	
29	44·3	W.	One inch of snow at night.
......	......	N.	
......	......	W.	
......	......	N.E.	
......	......	S.	
21	49	N.E.	
......	......	S.E.	
......	......	W.	
......	......	W.	
......	......	W.	
29	52	W.	
......	......	E.	

(104)

Meteorological Observations recorded by the Great Trigonometrical

Date.			Mercurial Barometer No. 720 corrected for index error.	Temperature of mercury.	Reading of aneroid barometer Solomon's uncorrected.	Temperature of Air.	
						Dry Bulb.	Wet Bulb.
			Inches.	Degrees.	Inches.	Degrees.	Degrees.
March 11th, 1874,	3 P.M.	...	26·142	45	25·76	45	38·5
	6 ,,	...	·152	40·5	·81	37·5	33
	9 ,,	...	·162	39	·83	36	33
,, 12th ,,	9 A.M.	...	·147	36	·82	35·8	33
	Noon	...	·152	38·5	·83	39	37
	3 P.M.	...	·112	37·3	·77	37·8	35
	6 ,,		·107	35·3	·78	34	35
	9 ,,		·102	34·5	·77	33	30·5
,, 13th ,,	9 A.M.		·102	35	·73	36	32
	Noon		·072	41·8	·71	44	40
	3 P.M.		·057	43·5	·67	43·5	38·5
	6 ,,		·062	41	·69	37	34·5
	9 ,,		·092	39	·75	37	33·0
,, 14th ,,	9 A.M.	...	·122	38·8	·78	39	35
	Noon	...	·112	43·5	·76	45·3	40
	3 P.M.	...	·082	47	·71	49	42
	6 ,,	...	·102	42·5	·73	40·5	35·3
	9 ,,	...	·117	39	·76	36	33
,, 15th ,,	9 A.M.		·202	39	·86	41	37
	Noon		·197	47	·85	47·5	40
	3 P.M.		·177	48·8	·82	47	40·3
	6 ,,		·202	41·8	·84	38	34·3
	9 ,,		·207	39	·85	36	33
,, 16th ,,	9 A.M.		·247	37	·89	38	32
	Noon		·212	42	·85	43	36·3
	3 P.M.		·152	43·3	·74	43	36
	6 ,,	...	·152	41·5	·74	37	31
	9 ,,	...	·122	36·3	·73	34	30
,, 17th ,,	9 A.M.		·032	37	·67	37·5	33·5
	Noon		·002	42·5	·64	46	39·3
	3 P.M.		25·927	47	·53	49	40
	6 ,,		·902	43	·51	39	33
	9 ,,	...	·907	39·8	·52	37	31
,, 18th ,,	9 A.M.	...	·862	37·5	·52	39	34·5
	Noon	...	·852	46·5	·48	48	40
	3 P.M.	...	·807	39·3	·42	51	41
	6 ,,	...	·812	46·5	·44	43	36
	9 ,,	...	·817	42·5	·45	38·5	33
,, 19th ,,	9 A.M.	...	·897	39	·53	39·8	35·8
	Noon	...	·892	50	·52	51	41·5
	3 P.M.	...	·872	52·5	·49	54	44
	6 ,,	...	·887	50	·52	45	38
	9 ,,	...	·892	44·5	·53	38·5	34
,, 20th ,,	9 A.M.		26·052	39·5	·09	41	36
	Noon	...	·052	50·8	·69	53·3	42
	3 P.M.	...	·032	54·8	·65	55	43
	6 ,,	...	·047	51·5	·68	47	38
	9 ,,	...	·057	44·8	·70	43	37
,, 21st ,,	9 A.M.		25·982	43	·64	44	37
	Noon	...	·882	52	·58	53·5	41·5
	3 P.M.	...	·817	56	·47	56·3	44
	6 ,,	...	·762	49	·40	47	37·5

(105)

Survey Pandits at YARKAND *during the winter of* 1873-74.—(Continued.)

Minimum in shade. During preceding 24 hours.	Maximum in shade.	Direction of wind.	Remarks.
Degrees.	Degrees.		
......	......	S.E.	
......	......	N.	
......	......	N.	
29	52	N.	A fall of half an inch of snow at night.
......	......	N.	
......	......	S.W.	
......	......	E.	
......	......	S.E.	
28	43·5	E.	
......	......	S.W.	
......	......	W.	
......	......	N.	
......	......	E.	
29	51·5	N.W.	
......	......	W.	Cloudy and slight snow.
......	......	N.E.	
......	......	N.	
......	......	W.	
29	56·3	W.	
......	......	S.E.	
......	......	E.	
......	......	W.	
......	......	E.	
29·5	54·8	E.	
......	......	S.E.	
......	......	W.	
......	......	N.W.	
......	......	N.	
24·8	49	N.E.	
......	......	S.E.	
......	......	N.	
......	......	N.	
......	......	N.E.	
35·5	55·0	E.	
......	......	N.	
......	......	E.	
......	......	N.	
......	......	N.	
35·5	50·5	W.	
......	......	N.E.	
......	......	N.E.	
......	......	E.	
......	......	E.	
27·5	57·3	E.	
......	......	N.E.	
......	......	N.W.	
......	......	S.W.	
......	......	S.	
27	......	N.E.	
......	......	E.	
......	......	N.W.	
......	......	S.	

(106)

Meteorological Observations recorded by the Great Trigonometrical Survey

Date.			Mercurial Barometer No. 720 corrected for index error.	Temperature of mercury.	Reading of aneroid barometer Solomon's uncorrected.	Temperature of Air.	
						Dry Bulb.	Wet Bulb.
			Inches.	Degrees.	Inches.	Degrees.	Degrees.
March 21st,	1874,	9 P.M. ...	25·752	46	25·41	43	36
,, 22nd	,,	9 A.M.	·727	42	·34	42	37
		Noon ...	·752	46·5	·38	47·5	40
		3 P.M. ...	·742	53	·35	53	43
		6 ,, ...	·747	50	·35	46	39
		9 ,, ...	·757	44·5	·38	41	35
,, 23rd	,,	9 A.M. ...	·762	43·8	·41	44·5	39·8
		Noon ...	·762	50	·38	53	44·5
		3 P.M. ...	·742	52·5	·35	44·5	45
		6 ,, ...	·747	49	·37	45	39
		9 ,, ...	·752	45·8	·41	41	36
,, 24th	,,	9 A.M. ...	·822	49	·48	50	44
		Noon ...	·817	56·5	·46	60·5	50
		3 P.M. ...	·797	58·3	·47	60	49
		6 ,, ...	·802	53·8	·49	50	43
		9 ,, ...	·802	48	·49	43	37·5
,, 25th	,,	9 A.M. ...	·902	46	·53	·47	42
		Noon ...	·872	57·8	·50	60·3	50·5
		3 P.M. ...	·852	60	·45	61	50
		6 ,, ...	·852	57	·47	54	45

(107)

Pandits at YARKAND during **the winter of** 1873-74.—(Concluded.)

Minimum in shade.	Maximum in shade.	Direction of wind.	Remarks.
During preceding 24 hours.			
Degrees	*Degrees.*		
......	......	S.	
34·5	......	S.E.	
......	......	W.	
......	......	N.W.	
......	......	N.W.	*For the month of March* 1874.
......	......	W.	9 A.M. Noon. 3 P.M. 6 P.M. 9 P.M.
35·5	......	W.	
......	......	W.	Mean of Mercurial 25·908 25·894 25·858 25·862 25·662
......	......	N.W.	Barometer No. 720
......	......	N.W.	corrected to 32°.
......	......	W.	
30·8	......	W.	Mean of Dry Bulb 40·1 48·4 49·6 42·7 37·1
......	......	N.E.	Thermometer.
......	......	W.	
......	......	N.	Mean of Wet Bulb 35·1 41·1 41·3 36·4 33·8
......	......	E.	Thermometer.
31	......	W.	
......	......	S.W.	Mean of Minimum Thermometer ... 29°·8
......	......	W.	Mean of Maximum Thermometer in shade ... 52°·5
......	......	W.	

(108)

Meteorological Observations at KASHGHAR during

Date.		Aneroid Barometer No. V., by Troughton and Simms, corrected for index error.	Aneroid Barometer by Dixey, corrected for index error.	Temperature of Air.		Maximum in Shade.	Minimum in Shade.	Minimum in Open.
				Dry bulb.	Wet bulb.	During preceding 24 hours.		
		Inches.	Inches.	Degrees.	Degrees.	Degrees.	Degrees.	Degrees.
Dec. 12th, 1873,	9 A.M.	26·07	26·09	...	...	44·0	...	15·8
	Noon	·02	·06	34·5	...	...	...	...
	3 P.M.	25·95	·02	34·5	...	...	...	...
	6 ,,	26·02	·07	...	...	...	...	...
,, 13th ,,	9 A.M.	·00	·06	...	...	38	...	53
	Noon	25·98	·04	33	...	...	...	...
	3 P.M.	·92	25·99	37	...	...	...	...
	6 ,,	·98	26·02	...	...	...	...	...
,, 14th ,,	9 A.M.	26·00	·05	26	...	38·5	...	10·5
	6 P.M.	25·93	25·98	...	...	...	...	...
,, 15th ,,	9 A.M.	·89	·95	20	...	37·5	...	7
	Noon	·86	·92	32	...	...	...	...
	3 P.M.	·80	·88	36	...	...	...	...
	6 ,,	·87	·90	...	...	...	...	...
,, 16th ,,	9 A.M.	·82	·88	19·5	...	37	...	6·5
	Noon	·78	·83	36·0	...	...	...	...
	3 P.M.	·74	·78	36·0	...	...	...	...
	6 ,,	·77	·80	...	...	...	...	...
,, 17th ,,	9 A.M.	·70	·76	23	...	38	...	11
	Noon	·67	·70	33	...	...	...	...
	3 P.M.	·66	·69	33	...	...	...	...
	6 ,,	·69	·72	...	...	...	...	...
,, 18th ,,	9 A.M.	·67	·74	23	...	35	...	11·5
	Noon	·67	·72	45·5	...	...	...	...
	3 P.M.	·65	·69	47·5	...	...	...	...
	6 ,,	·69	·73	...	...	...	...	...
,, 19th ,,	9 A.M.	·92	·99	...	...	50	30·5	7
	Noon	·92	·99	...	·\.	...	...	...
	3 P.M.	·89	·95	...	...	...	...	...
	6 ,,	·89	·95	...	...	...	...	...
,, 20th ,,	9 A.M.	·99	26·04	20	·\.	...	...	11
	Noon	·99	·05	36	...	...	...	...
	3 P.M.	·95	·01	32	...	...	...	...
	6 ,,	·97	·03	26·5	...	...	...	...
,, 21st ,,	9 A.M.	·93	·00	28	...	...	...	7·5
	Noon	·92	25·98	35	...	...	...	...
	3 P.M.	·89	·94	32	...	...	...	...
	6 ,,	·90	·95	27	...	...	...	...
	9 ,,	·94	·99	24	...	...	...	...
,, 22nd ,,	9 A.M.	·88	·94	25·5	...	29·5	...	8·5
	Noon	·84	·89	35	...	...	...	...
	3 P.M.	·80	·84	33	...	...	...	...
	6 ,,	·78	·82	26	...	...	...	...
,, 23rd ,,	9 P.M.	·63	·67	22	...	29	...	8·5
	Noon	·58	·60	31	...	...	...	...
	3 P.M.	·50	·54	28·5	...	...	...	...
	6 ,,	·52	·54	25·5	...	...	...	...
,, 24th ,,	9 A.M.	·72	·74	38	...	40	...	15
	Noon	·73	·75	44	...	...	...	...
	3 P.M.	·74	·76	38	...	...	...	...
	6 ,,	·80	·82	28·5	...	...	...	...
,, 25th ,,	9 A.M.	·87	·90	27	...	35	...	11·5
	3 P.M.	·78	·81	33	...	...	...	...
	6 ,,	·77	·80	26·5	...	...	...	...

(109)

the winter of 1873-74 *by Captain H. Trotter,* **R.E.**, *and his Native Assistants.*

Boiling point Thermometer No. 17970, corrected for index error.	Boiling point Thermometer No. 17972, corrected for index error.	Boiling point Thermometer No. 17974, corrected for index error.	Boiling point Thermometer No. 17975, corrected for index error.	Direction of wind.	REMARKS.
Degrees.	*Degrees.*				
205·20	205·20	......	......	W.	At Kashghar the aneroid barometers and the thermometers (with the exception of the *minimum in open*) were placed in a covered porch, opening into a large court-yard and facing the east; they were completely protected from the direct rays of the sun.
......	......			W.	
205·07	205·07	......	......	S.	
......	......			W.	
205·17	205·15	......	......	W.	
......	......			E.	
205·07	205·05	......	......	N.E.	
				N.	
205·12	205·10	205·07	205·07	W.	The *minimum in open* was placed on the surface of a table, raised three feet above the ground, and placed near the centre of the large court-yard.
				E.	
205·02	205·00	205·02	205·02	W.	
......	......	......		W.	
204·87	204·85	204·77	204·77	S.W.	
......	......	......			The thermometers were **all graduated on Fahrenheit's scale.**
204·87	204·85	204·77	204·77	S.E.	
......	......	......		W.	
204·72	204·70	204·62	204·62	W.	
......	......	......		E.	
204·62	204·60	204·57	204·57	W.	
......	......	......		E.	
204·52	204·50	204·52	204·52	S.	
......	......	......		E.	
204·54	204·52	204·42	204·42	S.W.	
......	......	......		S.	
204·42	204·40	204·37	204·37	S.E.	
......	......	......	......	W.	
......	......	......	......	S.W.	
......	......	......	......	W.	
......	......	......	......	S.W.	
......	......	......	......	S.W.	
205·22	205·20	......	......	E.	
......	......			S.	
205·07	205·05	205·02	205·02	W.	
......	......	......	......	E.	
205·12	205·10	204·97	204·97	W.	
......	......	......	......	S.E.	
205·02	205·00	204·92	204·92	E.	
......	......	......	......	E.	
......	......	......	......	S.W.	
204·97	204·95	204·92	204·92	S.E.	
......	......	......	......	W.	
204·72	204·70	204·57	204·57	W.	
......	......	......	......	S.E.	
204·39	204·40	204·27	204·27	W.	
......	......	......		S.E.	
204·17	204·15	......	......	S.	
......	......	......	......	N.	
......	......	......	......	S.	
......	......	......	......	S.W.	
......	......	......	......	N.E.	
......	......			N.	
204·92	204·90	204·79	204·82	W.	
204·72	204·73	204·62	204·62	S.E.	
......	......	......	......	S.	

Meteorological Observations at KASHGHAR during the winter

Date.		Aneroid Barometer No. V., by Troughton and Simms, corrected for index error.	Aneroid Barometer by Dixey, corrected for index error.	Temperature of air.		Maximum in shade.	Minimum in shade.	Minimum in open.
				Dry bulb.	Wet bulb.	During preceding 24 hours.		
		Inches.	Inches.	Degrees.	Degrees.	Degrees.	Degrees.	Degrees.
Dec. 26th, 1873,	9 A.M.	25·74	25·77	23	...	29	...	7
	Noon	·75	·78	33	...	...	...	...
	3 P.M.	·72	·74	33	...	...	...	...
	6 ,,	·78	·80	26	...	...	...	...
,, 27th ,,	9 A.M.	·83	·86	22	...	30	...	10·5
	Noon	·78	·82	34·5	...	...	...	...
	3 P.M.	·73	·76	33	...	...	...	...
	6 ,,	·72	·76	32	...	...	...	...
,, 28th ,,	9 A.M.	·92	·97	23	...	30	...	2·5
	6 P.M.	·88	·94	26	...	...	...	...
,, 29th ,,	9 A.M.	·82	·88	24	...	29	...	0·0
	3 P.M.	·80	·85	30·5	...	...	...	...
	6 ,,	·88	·91	24·5	...	...	...	...
,, 30th ,,	9 A.M.	25·93	26·08	24	...	28·5	...	4·5
	Noon	·97	·02	29	...	...	...	...
	3 P.M.	·93	25·98	27	...	...	...	...
,, 31st ,,	9 A.M.	......	......	22·5	...	31·5	9·5	...
	Noon	......	......	30	...	...	...	...
	3 P.M.	......	......	26	...	...	...	...
	6 ,,	......	......	22	...	...	...	...

of 1873-74 *by Captain H. Trotter,* **R.E.,** *and his Native Assistants.*—(Continued.)

Boiling point Thermometer No. 17970, corrected for index error.	Boiling point Thermometer No. 17972, corrected for index error.	Boiling point Thermometer No. 17974, corrected for index error.	Boiling point Thermometer No. 17975, corrected for index error.	Direction of wind.	Remarks.
Degrees.	*Degrees.*				
204·72	204·67	204·59	204·62	W.	
				E.	*For the month of* December 1873.
204·64	204·62	204·57	204·57	S.W.	
				S.E.	Mean of Aneroid Barometer No. Y., by Troughton and Simms corrected for index error. — 9 A.M. 25·87 | Noon. 25·83 | 3 P.M. 25·80 | 6 P.M. 25·82
				W.	
				S.	
				S.W.	
				S.	
				W.	
				S.	Mean of Aneroid Barometer by Dixey corrected for index error. — 9 A.M. 25·90 | Noon. 25·88 | 3 P.M. 25·84 | 6 P.M. 25·86
				N.	
				S.E.	
				E.	
				N.	
				N.W.	Mean of Dry Bulb Thermometer. — 9 A.M. 24·1 | Noon. 34·7 | 3 P.M. 33·5 | 6 P.M. 26·4
				S.E.	
					Mean of Maximum Thermometer in shade ... 35·0
				W.	Mean of Minimum in open ... 8·9
				S.W.	
				S.	
				E.	

(112)

Meteorological Observations at *KASHGHAR* during the

Date.		Aneroid Barometer No. V., by Troughton and Simms, corrected for index error.	Aneroid Barometer by Dixey corrected for index error.	Temperature of air.		Maximum in shade.	Minimum in shade.	Minimum in open.
				Dry bulb.	Wet bulb.	During preceding 24 hours.		
		Inches.	*Inches.*	*Degrees.*	*Degrees.*	*Degrees.*	*Degrees.*	*Degrees.*
Jan. 1st, 1874,	9 A.M.	...	...	15·5	...	31·5	12·5	...
„ 8th „	9 A.M.	...	...	18	...	30·5	7·5	...
	Noon	...	...	26·5	...	...	...	...
	3 P.M.	...	...	24·5	...	...	...	...
	6 „	...	...	20	...	...	...	...
„ 9th „	9 A.M.	...	...	20	...	28·5	10	...
„ 10th „	9 A.M.	...	...	17·5	...	29	12·5	...
	Noon	...	...	26	...	...	...	...
	3 P.M.	...	...	25	...	...	...	...
	6 „	...	...	20	...	...	...	...
„ 11th „	9 A.M.	...	...	19	...	28·5	7·5	...
	Noon	...	...	24·5	...	...	...	...
	3 P.M.	...	...	24	...	...	...	...
	6 „	...	...	20·5	...	...	...	...
„ 12th „	9 A.M.	26·35	26·34	16·5	...	25	6	...
	Noon	·31	·30	28·5	...	...	...	...
	3 P.M.	·25	·22	26·0	...	...	...	...
„ 13th „	9 A.M.	·14	·13	18	...	24·5	5	...
	Noon	·08	·08	28	...	...	...	...
	3 P.M.	·06	·02	25·5	...	...	...	...
	6 „	·06	·02	21	...	...	...	...
„ 14th „	9 A.M.	·04	·00	20·5	...	28·5	7·5	...
	Noon	·01	25·97	29	...	...	...	...
	3 P.M.	25·97	·93	26·5	...	...	...	...
	6 „	26·01	·97	19	...	...	...	...
„ 15th „	9 A.M.	·08	26·07	20	...	29	7·5	...
	Noon	·05	·03	27·5	...	...	...	...
	3 P.M.	·03	·02	26·5	...	...	...	...
	6 „	·06	·05	19·5	...	...	...	...
„ 16th „	9 A.M.	·17	·17	23	...	28·5	5	...
	6 P.M.	·20	·20	21	...	...	...	...
„ 17th „	9 A.M.	·28	·29	25	...	30·5	6·5	—5·5
	Noon	·26	·27	28	...	...	...	...
„ 18th „	9 A.M.	·17	·18	23·5	...	31·5	10	+1·5
	Noon	·10	·12	31·5	...	...	...	...
	3 P.M.	·04	·05	29	...	...	...	...
	6 „	·05	·06	...	...	...	...	...
„ 19th „	9 A.M.	·00	·02	22·5	...	29·5	12	+2
„ 20th „	9 A.M.	25·99	·00	26·5	...	28	14·5	+5
	Noon	·97	25·97	36·5	...	...	...	...
	3 P.M.	·96	·96	33	...	...	...	...
	6 „	·96	·96	...	...	...	...	...
„ 21st „	9 A.M.	·87	·87	24	...	36	20	+10
	Noon	·82	·82	33	...	...	...	...
	3 P.M.	·77	·77	32	...	...	...	...
	6 „	·81	·81	27·7	...	...	...	...
„ 22nd „	9 A.M.	·83	·84	26·5	...	39·5	22·5	17
	Noon	·83	·84	36	...	...	...	...
	3 P.M.	·85	·86	34	...	...	...	...
	6 „	·86	·87	29	...	...	...	...
„ 23rd „	9 A.M.	·87	·88	23·5	...	36	19·5	...
„ 24th „	9 A.M.	26·01	26·01	33	...	35	21·5	16
	Noon	·00	·00	37·5	...	...	...	...
	6 „	·00	·00	...	...	...	...	...

winter of 1874-75, *by Captain H. Trotter, R.E., and his Native Assistants.*

Boiling point Thermometer No. 17450, corrected for index error.	Boiling point Thermometer No. 17972, corrected for index error.	Boiling point Thermometer No. 17974, corrected for index error.	Boiling point Thermometer No. 17975, corrected for index error.	Direction of wind.	REMARKS.
Degrees.	Degrees.				
......	......	......	......	S.W.	The break in the observations from 1st to 11th January caused by Captain Trotter's absence on the expedition to Chadyr-Kul.
......	......	......	......	N.E.	
......	......	......	......	S.	
......	......	......	......	N.	
......	......	......	......	N.W	
......	......	......	......	S.	
......	......	......	......	N.	
......	......	......	......	S.	
......	......	......	......	S.W.	
......	......	......	......	W.	
......	......	......	......	N.	
......	......	......	......	N.E.	
......	......	......	......	W.	
......	......	......	......	S.	
......	......	......	......	S.	
......	......	......	......	W.	
......	......	......	......	E.	
......	......	......	......	N.W.	
......	......	......	......	S.	
......	......	......	......	S.	
......	......	......	......	N.E.	
......	......	......	......	S.W.	
......	......	......	......	S.E.	
......	......	......	......	S.	
......	......	......	......	S.W.	
......	......	......	......	S.W.	
......	......	......	......	S.E.	
......	......	......	......	S.W.	
......	......	......	......	S.W.	
......	......	......	......	W.	
......	......	......	......	S.E.	
......	......	......	......	N.E.	
......	......	......	......	W.	
......	......	......	......	S.W.	
......	......	......	......	S.	
......	......	......	......	S.E.	
......	......	......	......	S.W.	
......	......	......	......	W.	
......	......	......	......	S.	
......	......	......	......	S.W.	
......	......	......	......	N.	
......	......	......	......	W.	
204·57	204·55	204·57	204·62	S.W.	
......	......	......	......	S.E.	
......	......	......	......	W.	
......	......	......	......	S.W.	
......	......	......	......	E.	
......	......	......	......	N.E.	
......	......	......	......	S.	
......	......	......	......	N.	
......	......	......	......	W.	
......	......	......	......	S.W.	
......	......	......	......	W.	

(114)

Meteorological Observations at KASHGHAR during the winter of 1874-75,

Date.		Aneroid Barometer No. V., by Troughton and Simms, corrected for index error.	Aneroid Barometer by Dixey corrected for index error.	TEMPERATURE OF AIR.		MAXIMUM IN SHADE.	MINIMUM IN SHADE.	MINIMUM IN OPEN.
				Dry Bulb.	Wet Bulb.	During preceding 24 hours.		
		Inches.	*Inches.*	*Degrees.*	*Degrees.*	*Degrees.*	*Degrees.*	*Degrees.*
Jan. 25th, 1874,	9 A.M.	26·03	26·03	28	...	39	14·5	—5
	Noon	25·97	25·97	38·5	...	...	...	...
	6 P.M.	·92	·92	...	...	...	...	...
,, 26th ,,	9 A.M.	·93	·93	28	...	40·5	22	13
	Noon	·90	·90	35·5	...	...	...	...
	3 P.M.	·89	·89	35	...	...	...	...
	6 ,,	·92	·92	26	...	35	19·5	7·2
,, 27th ,,	9 A.M.	·99	·99	26·0	...	35	19·5	7·2
	Noon	·96	·96	34	...	...	...	...
	3 P.M.	·92	·93	35	...	...	...	...
	6 ,,	·93	·94	27	...	...	...	...
,, 28th ,,	9 A.M.	26·07	26·08	28·5	...	37·5	20	8·5
	3 P.M.	·04	·05	37	...	...	...	...
	6 ,,	·08	·08	...	...	...	...	...
,, 29th ,,	9 A.M.	·08	·10	32·5	...	42	22·5	14·5
	Noon	·02	·06	42	...	...	...	...
	3 P.M.	25·98	·02	38	...	...	...	...
	6 ,,	·98	·02	...	...	...	...	...
,, 30th ,,	9 A.M.	·96	·00	22	...	44	17·5	6·2
	Noon	·91	25·96	34·5	...	...	...	...
	3 P.M.	·90	·91	34·5	...	...	...	...
	6 ,,	·91	·92	...	...	...	...	...
,, 31st ,,	9 A.M.	·95	·98	29	...	37·5	17·5	6
	Noon	·91	·94	39	...	...	...	...
	6 P.M.	·89	·92	...	...	...	...	...

by Captain H. Trotter, R.E., and his Native Assistants.—(Continued.)

Boiling point Thermometer No. 17970, corrected values.	Boiling point Thermometer No. 17972, corrected values.	Boiling point Thermometer No. 17974, corrected values.	Boiling point Thermometer No. 17975, corrected values.	Direction of wind.	Remarks.
Degrees.	Degrees.				
......	......	......	......	W.	*For the month of January* 1874.
......	......	......	......	S.W.	
......	......	......	......	N.	
......	......	......	......	N.E.	
......	......	......	......	N.E.	
......	......	......	......	S.E.	
......	......	......	......	S.	
......	......	......	......	N.W.	
......	......	......	......	W.	
......	......	......	......	S.	
......	......	......	......	...	
......	......	......	......	W.	
......	......	......	......	W.	
......	......	......	......	S.	
......	......	......	......	S.E.	
......	......	......	......	E.	
......	......	......	......	W.	
......	......	......	......	S.	
......	......	......	......	N.E.	
......	......	......	......	S.E.	
......	......	......	......	W.	
......	......	......	......	S.W.	
......	......	......	......	W.	
......	......	......	......	S.	
......	......	......	......	N.	

Mean of Aneroid Barometer No. V. by Troughton & Simms, corrected for index error.

	9 A.M.	Noon.	3 P.M.	6 P.M.
	26·04	26·01	25·97	25·98

Mean of Aneroid Barometer by Dixey corrected for index error.

	9 A.M.	Noon.	3 P.M.	6 P.M.
	26·04	26·01	25·97	25·98

Mean of Dry Bulb thermometer. 23·5 32·4 30·3 22·5
Mean of minimum thermometer in shade. 13°·6
Mean of maximum thermometer in shade. 33°·0
Mean of minimum in open 7°·6

(116)

Meteorological Observations at KASHGHAR during the winter

Date.		Aneroid barometer No. V. by Troughton and Simms corrected for index error.	Aneroid barometer by Dixey corrected for index error.	Temperature of air.		Maximum in shade.	Minimum in shade.	Minimum in open.
				Dry Bulb.	Wet Bulb.	During preceding 24 hours.		
		Inches.	Inches.	Degrees.	Degrees.	Degrees.	Degrees.	Degrees.
Feb. 1st, 1874	9 A.M.	25·88	25·86	29	...	40·5	22	13·5
	Noon	·81	·82	38	...	...	...	...
	3 P.M.	·82	·79	35	...	...	...	...
	6 P.M.	·82	·78	...	...	...	...	...
,, 2nd ,,	9 A.M.	·82	·78	32·5	...	38·5	13·5	4
	Noon	·79	·75	38	...	...	...	...
	3 P.M.	·77	·73	38·5	...	...	...	...
	6 P.M.	·80	·77	...	...	...	...	...
,, 3rd ,,	9 A.M.	·89	·86	27·5	...	41·5	19·5	8
	Noon	·88	·85	40	...	...	...	...
	3 P.M.	·84	·80	37	...	...	...	...
	6 P.M.	·86	·82	...	...	...	...	...
,, 4th ,,	9 A.M.	·90	·86	35	...	42	19·7	9
	Noon	·86	·83	40·5	...	...	...	...
	3 P.M.	·83	·79	39	...	...	...	...
	6 P.M.	·84	·80	...	...	...	...	...
,, 5th ,,	9 A.M.	·86	·82	31	...	42	23	15
	Noon	·85	·81	41	...	...	...	...
	3 P.M.	·82	·78	40	...	...	...	...
	6 P.M.	·85	·81	...	...	...	...	...
,, 6th ,,	9 A.M.	·84	·83	32·5	...	41·5	20·5	11
	Noon	·79	·78	43·5	...	...	...	...
	3 P.M.	·76	·73	40·5	...	...	...	...
	6 P.M.	·80	·77	32	...	...	...	...
,, 7th ,,	9 A.M.	·84	·81	37	...	47·5	19·7	6·5
	Noon	·83	·80	45	...	...	...	...
	3 P.M.	·76	·75	40	...	...	...	...
	6 P.M.	·77	·76	31	...	...	...	...
,, 8th ,,	9 A.M.	·72	·73	29·5	...	44·5	20	10
	Noon	·67	·66	28	...	...	...	...
	3 P.M.	·58	·58	39	...	...	...	...
,, 9th ,,	9 A.M.	·61	·59	33·5	...	40·5	28·5	19·5
	Noon	·60	·58	39	...	...	...	...
	3 P.M.	·58	·57	39	...	...	...	...
	6 P.M.	·60	·59	34	...	...	...	...
,, 10th ,,	9 A.M.	·81	·81	39·5	...	41·5	29	24
	Noon	·83	·83	37	...	...	...	...
	3 P.M.	·81	·81	39	...	...	...	...
,, 11th ,,	9 A.M.	·80	·82	31·5	...	43·5	28·5	24·5
	Noon	·79	·79	38	...	...	...	...
	3 P.M.	·75	·76	40	...	...	...	...
	6 P.M.	·80	·81	31	...	...	...	...
,, 12th ,,	9 A.M.	·79	·82	33·5	...	46	24	15·5
	Noon	·78	·79	38·5	...	...	...	...
	3 P.M.	·76	·77	36	...	...	...	...
	6 P.M.	·76	·77	30	...	...	...	...
,, 13th ,,	9 A.M.	·83	·86	29·5	...	39·5	12·5	2
	Noon	·85	·88	36·5	...	...	...	...
	3 P.M.	·83	·84	35·5	...	...	...	...
	6 P.M.	·86	·87	31	...	...	...	...
,, 14th ,,	9 A.M.	·90	·93	30	...	38·5	21·5	12·5
	Noon		·89	39·5	...	...	...	...
	3 P.M.		·82	38	...	...	...	...

(117)

of 1874-75 *by Captain H. Trotter, R. E.*—(Continued.)

Boiling point thermometer No. 17970 corrected values.	Boiling point thermometer No. 17972 corrected values.	Boiling point thermometer No. 17974.	Boiling point thermometer No. 17975.	Direction of wind.	REMARKS.
Degrees.	Degrees.				
......	......	......	......	W.	
......	......	......	......	N.E.	
......	......	......	......	S.E.	
......	......	......	......	S.E.	
......	......	......	......	W.	
......	......	......	......	S.W.	
......	......	......	......	W.	
......	......	......	......	N.W.	
......	......	......	......	N.W.	
......	......	......	......	N.E.	
......	......	......	......	N.	
......	......	......	......	S.	
......	......	......	......	W.	
......	......	......	......	N.E.	
......	......	......	......	W.	
......	......	......	......	N.	
......	......	......	......	W.	
......	......	......	......	S.	
......	......	......	......	E.	
......	......	......	......	S.	
......	......	......	......	S.W.	
......	......	......	......	S.E.	
......	......	......	......	S.W.	
......	......	......	......	S.	
......	......	......	......	N.E.	
......	......	......	......	S.E.	
......	......	......	......	S.E.	
......	......	......	......	S.E.	
......	......	......	......	S.W.	
......	......	......	......	E.	
......	......	......	......	E.	
......	......	......	......	S.W.	
......	......	......	......	S.	
......	......	......	......	S.E.	
......	......	......	......	S.	
......	......	......	......	N.E.	
......	......	......	......	E.	
......	......	......	......	E.	
......	......	......	......	N.W.	
......	......	......	......	N.E.	
......	......	......	......	N.E.	
......	......	......	......	N.	
......	......	......	......	W.	
......	......	......	......	N.W.	
......	......	......	......	W.	
......	......	......	......	N.W.	
......	......	......	......	N.W.	
......	......	......	......	N.E.	
......	......	......	......	N.	
......	......	......	......	N.W.	
......	......	......	......	W.	The break in the readings of aneroid No. V. caused by Captain Trotter's absence in the Artysh Districts.
......	......	......	......	N.W.	
......	......	......	......	W.	

(118)

Meteorological Observations at KASHGHAR during the winter of

Date.		Aneroid barometer No. V., by Troughton and Simms corrected for index error.	Aneroid barometer by Dixey corrected for index error.	Temperature of air.		Maximum in shade.	Minimum in shade.	Minimum in open.
				Dry Bulb.	Wet Bulb.	During preceding 24 hours.		
		Inches.	Inches.	Degrees.	Degrees.	Degrees.	Degrees.	Degrees.
Feb. 15th, 1874	9 A.M.	......	25·94	31	...	42·8	25	12·5
	Noon	......	·90	42	28	...	...	...
	3 P.M.	......	·88	41	30	...	...	...
,, 16th ,,	9 A.M.	......	·95	37	33	44	23	17
	Noon	......	·91	41	33	...	...	...
	3 P.M.	......	·87	39·5	33·5	...	...	...
,, 17th ,,	9 A.M.	......	·80	34	32	42	27	15·5
	Noon	......	·79	42	33	...	...	...
	3 P.M.	......	·77	42·5	34	...	...	...
,, 18th ,,	9 A.M.	......	·99	41	32·5	44	23·5	21·5
	Noon	......	·96	45	35·6	...	...	...
	3 P.M.	......	·94	40	35	...	...	...
,, 19th ,,	9 A.M.	......	26·10	32·5	29	36·5	20	15
	Noon	......	·08	33	32	...	...	...
	3 P.M.	......	·03	31·5	32	...	...	...
,, 20th ,,	9 A.M.	......	25·98	41	31	42	22	19
	Noon	......	·93	43	32	...	...	...
	3 P.M.	......	·87	39	32	...	...	...
,, 21st ,,	9 A.M.	......	·96	32·5	29	44	22·5	14
	Noon	......	·92	42	32	...	...	...
	3 P.M.	......	·91	40	32	...	...	...
,, 22nd ,,	9 A.M.	......	26·08	31	34	42	30	12
	Noon	......	·04	34·5	32	...	...	...
	3 P.M.	......	·00	32	32	...	...	...
,, 23rd ,,	9 A.M.	......	·06	32·5	31	36	29	14
	Noon	......	·04	40	32·6	...	...	...
,, 24th ,,	9 A.M.	......	25·93	39	31	42	20	20·5
	Noon	......	·86	39·6	32·8	...	...	...
	3 P.M.	......	·84	36	32	...	...	...
,, 25th ,,	9 A.M.	......	·74	45	33	45	26	21
	Noon	......	·69	40	32	...	...	...
	3 P.M.	......	·64	32	32	...	...	...
,, 26th ,,	9 A.M.	......	·69	44	33	45	28	22
	Noon	......	·68	48	35	...	...	...
	3 P.M.	......	·67	40	36	...	...	...
,, 27th ,,	9 A.M.	......	·90	42·5	35	48	31	19
	Noon	......	·91	41	36	...	...	...
	3 P.M.	......	·89	40	36	...	...	...
,, 28th ,,	9 A.M.	......	·94	41	32	48·5	28	22
	Noon	......	·94	49	36·2	...	...	...
	3 P.M.	......	·87	45·8	35·5	...	...	...

1873-74, by *Captain H. Trotter, R.E., and his Assistants.*—(Continued.)

Boiling point thermometer No. 17970 corrected values.	Boiling point thermometer No. 17972 corrected values.	Boiling point thermometer No. 17974.	Boiling point thermometer No. 17975.	Direction of wind.	REMARKS.
Degrees.	Degrees.				
......	......	......	......	E.	
......	......	......	......	E.S.	
......	......	......	......	W.	
......	......	......	......	W.	
......	......	......	......	N.E.	
......	......	......	......	N.	
......	......	......	......	N.E.	
......	......	......	......	W.S.	
......	......	......	......	N.E.	
......	......	......	......	S.W.	
......	......	......	......	N.W.	
......	......	......	......	S.W.	
......	......	......	......	S.W.	
......	......	......	......	E.	
......	......	......	......	S.W.	
......	......	......	......	S.	
......	......	......	......	S.	
......	......	......	......	S.E.	
......	......	......	......	S.	
......	......	......	......	E.	
......	......	......	......	S.W.	
......	......	......	......	N.E.	Slight fall of snow.
......	......	......	......	N.E.	*For the month of February* 1874.
......	......	......	......	E.	
......	......	......	......	N.	
......	......	......	......	N.	
......	......	......	......	N.W.	
......	......	......	......	N.S.	
......	......	......	......	N.S.	
......	......	......	......	N.	
......	......	......	......	N.E.	
......	......	......	......	E.	
......	......	......	......	N.	
......	......	......	......	N.E.	
......	......	......	......	S.	
......	......	......	......	E.	
......	......	......	......	S.	
......	......	......	......	N.	
......	......	......	......	N.	
......	......	......	......	S.	

	9 A.M.	Noon.	3 P.M.	6 P.M.
Mean of Aneroid Barometer No. V. by Troughton and Simms ...	25·83	25·80	25·78	25·79
Mean of **Aneroid** Barometer by Dixey ...	25·87	25·84	25·81	25·78
Mean of Dry **Bulb** Thermometer ...	34·8	40·4	38·4	31·5
Mean of Wet Bulb Thermometer ...	31·9	32·8	33·2	
Mean of Minimum Thermometer in shade ...				23°·5
Mean of Maximum Thermometer in shade ...				42°·5
Mean of Minimum in open ...				15°·0

(120)

Meteorological Observations at KASHGHAR *during the winter of* 1874-75,

Date.		Aneroid barometer No. V. by Troughton and Simms corrected for index error.	Aneroid barometer by Carpenter, Westley, and Dixey corrected for index error.	Temperature of Air.		Maximum in Shade.	Minimum in Shade.	Minimum in Open.
				Dry Bulb.	Wet Bulb.	During preceding 24 hours.		
		Inches.	*Inches.*	*Degrees.*	*Degrees.*	*Degrees.*	*Degrees.*	*Degrees.*
Mar. 1st, 1874,	9 A.M.		25·91	49	39	49	27	29
	Noon		·86	51	38	...	...	...
	3 P.M.		·84	47	36	...	...	...
„ 2nd „	9 A.M.		·55	45·5	39	51·5	28	27
	Noon		·51	53·6	40	...	...	...
	3 P.M.		·44	51	41	...	...	...
„ 3rd „	9 A.M.		·50	40	36	55	32	21·5
	Noon		·49	42	38	...	...	...
	3 P.M.		·50	44	39	...	...	...
„ 4th „	9 A.M.		·74	43	40	47	36	24
	Noon		·71	48·5	39	...	...	...
	3 P.M.		·69	49·5	41	...	...	...
„ 5th „	9 A.M.	25·79	·79	43	39	50·5	37	24
	Noon	·74	·73	50	40	...	...	...
	3 P.M.	·72	·70	48·3	41	...	...	...
„ 6th „	9 A.M.	·82	·80	38·5	36	52	31	20
	Noon	·82	·78	49	41	...	...	...
	3 P.M.	·73	·73	45·5	40	...	...	...
„ 7th „	9 A.M.	·72	·73	41·2	38	54·5	37·5	...
	3 P.M.	·60	·58	45	39	...	...	...
„ 8th „	9 A.M.	·55	·54	34·5	33	48·5	34·0	28·0
	Noon	·53	·52	37·5	36	...	...	...
	3 P.M.	·51	·50	40·5	36	...	...	...
	6 P.M.	·55	·54	38	36	...	...	...
„ 9th „	9 A.M.	·63	·63	35	32·5	42	33·5	27·5
	Noon	·63	·62	40	35	...	...	...
	3 P.M.	·62	·61	44	37	...	...	...
	6 P.M.	·67	·66	37·5	34	...	...	...
„ 10th „	9 A.M.	·80	·80	43·5	36·5	44·5	27·5	22·0
	Noon	·82	·83	47	36	...	...	...
	6 P.M.	·87	·88	39·5	36	...	...	...
„ 11th „	9 A.M.	26·08	26·09	44	39	48·5	26·5	17·0
„ 12th „	9 A.M.	·12	·15	32·5	30	50	29	25
	Noon	·12	·15	39	35	...	...	...
	3 P.M.	·08	·10	40	36	...	...	...
	6 P.M.	·07	·08	37·5	36	...	...	...
„ 13th „	9 A.M.	·03	·05	39	35·5	47	30·5	26
	Noon	25·98	·00	44	38	...	...	...
	3 P.M.	·97	25·99	40	38	...	...	...
	6 P.M.	·97	·99	36·5	36	...	...	...
„ 14th „	9 A.M.	26·09	26·11	37·5	36	45	33·5	27·5
	Noon	·07	·08	46	40	...	...	...
	3 P.M.	·02	·04	41	39·5	...	...	...
	6 P.M.	·06	·08	39	37·5	...	...	...
„ 15th „	9 A.M.	·16	·19	34·5	32	47	31·5	27·5
	Noon	·15	·19	40·5	35	...	...	...
	6 P.M.	·14	·17	37·5	34·5	...	...	...
„ 16th „	9 A.M.	·20	·24	34	30	44	31·5	27
	Noon	·17	·19	41	34	...	...	...
	3 P.M.	·11	·12	44	34	...	...	...
	6 P.M.	·07	·08	38·5	35	...	...	...

(121)

by Captain H. Trotter, R.E., and his Native Assistants.—(Concluded.)

Boiling point thermometer No. 17970 corrected values.	Boiling point thermometer No. 17972 corrected values.	Boiling point thermometer No. 17974.	Boiling point thermometer No. 17975.	Direction of wind.	REMARKS.
Degrees.	Degrees.				
......	......	......	......	S.	*For the month of March* 1874.
......	......	......	......	N.	
......	......	......	......	S.	Mean of Aneroid
......	......	......	......	N.	Barometer No. 9 A.M. Noon. 3 P.M. 6 P.M.
......	......	......	......	S.	V. by Troughton
......	......	......	......	N.E.	and Simms .. 25·92 25·90 25·82 25·93
......	......	......	......	N.	Mean of Aneroid
......	......	......	......	N.	Barometer by
......	......	......	......	S.	Dixey and Car-
......	......	......	......	N.E.	penter and
......	......	......	......	N.	Westley ... 25·80 25·78 25·72
......	......	......	......	S.	Mean of Dry Bulb
......	......	......	......	S.	Thermometer... **39·7 44·9 44·6 38·0**
......	......	......	......	N.	Mean of Wet Bulb
......	......	......	......	N.	Thermometer... 35·7 37·5 38·3 35·6
......	......	......	......	S.E.	Mean of minimum thermometer ... **31°·6**
......	......	......	......	S.	Mean of maximum do. in shade **48°·5**
......	......	......	......	N.	Mean of minimum rod in open ... **24°·9**
......	......	......	......	NW.	
......	......	......	......	S.	
......	......	......	......	N.E.	
......	......	......	......	N.E.	Snow falling.
......	......	......	......	S.E.	
......	......	......	......	S.	
......	......	......	......	N.E.	Snow at night.
......	......	......	......	N.E.	
......	......	......	......	N.	
......	......	......	......	N.	
......	......	......	......	N.W.	
......	......	......	......	N.W.	
......	......	......	......	N.W.	
......	......	......	......	S.W.	
......	......	......	......	N.	
......	......	......	......	N.	
......	......	......	......	N.	
......	......	......	......	N.W.	Heavy fall of snow during night of about
......	......	......	......	N.W.	five inches.
......	......	......	......	N.W.	
......	......	......	......	N.W.	
......	......	......	......	N.W.	
......	......	......	......	N.	
......	......	......	......	N.	
......	......	......	......	N.W.	
205·25	205·25	......	......	N.W.	
......	......	......	......	N.E.	Fall of snow during night.
......	......	......	......	N.E.	
......	......	......	......	N.E.	
......	......	......	......	N.E.	
......	......	......	......	N.E.	
......	......	......	......	N.E.	
......	......	......	......	N.E.	

GEOGRAPHICAL APPENDIX.

SECTION G.

ROUTES.

GEOGRAPHICAL APPENDIX.

SECTION G.—ROUTES.

INDEX.

PART I.—*Routes traversed by members and employés of the Mission.*

Number of Route.	From.	To.	Remarks.	Authority.
I.	Yárkand	Leh (Ladakh)	*Viâ* Sánjú and Karakorum Pass.	Dr. Bellew.
II.	Ditto	Leh	*Viâ* Kugiar and Karakorum Pass.	Ditto.
III.	Leh	Shahidúlá (No. 12 of Route I.)	*Viâ* Changchenmo	Captain Biddulph.
IIIa.	Gogra	Ditto	Variation on No. III.	,, Trotter.
IV.	Yárkand	Káshghar	......	,, ,,
V.	Káshghar	Maralbáshi	......	,, Biddulph.
VI.	Ditto	Chadyr Kul	......	,, Trotter.
VII.	Ditto	* Belowti Pass	On road to Ush Turfán.	,, ,,
VIII.	Yangi Hissar (No. 3 of Route IV.)	Kila Panjah (Wakhan)	*Viâ* Tashkúrghán and Little Pámír.	,, Biddulph.
IX.	Kila Panjah	Aktásh (No. 11 of Route VIII.)	*Viâ* Great Pámír.	,, ,,
X.	Táshkúrghán (No. 9 of Route VIII.)	Yárkand	*Viâ* Charling River	,, Trotter (from Pundit Kishen Sing).
XI.	Kila Panjah	Kila Wámur (Roshan)	......	,, Trotter (from Abdul Subhan).
XII.	Yárkand	Aksú	*Viâ* Maralbáshi	,, Chapman (from Bhao Sing).
XIII.	Aksú	Kuchár	......	,, ditto.
XIV.	Karghálik (No. 2 of Route I.)	Tanksé (No. 5 of Route III.)	*Viâ* Khotan, Keria, and Polu, *vide*	,, Trotter (from Kishen Sing).
XIVa.*	Yárkand	Khotan	*Viâ* Karghálik	,, Chapman (from Ramchaud).

PART II.—*Routes in Turkestan derived from verbal information supplied by natives.*

Number of Route.	From.	To.	Remarks.	Authority.
XV.	Kuchár (Route XIII.)	Káráshahr		Compiled by Captain Trotter.
XVI.	Kuchár	Túrfan		Ditto ditto.
XVII.	Túrfan	Kámul, Khámil, or Hámi.		Ditto Dr. Bellew.
XVIIa.	Túrfan	Orúmchí or Orumtsi		Ditto ditto.
XVIII.	Urúmtsí or Orúmchí	Manás		Ditto ditto.
XIX.	Munas	Yulduz		Ditto ditto.
XX.	Yulduz	Ghúljá, or Kuldjá, or Ili.		Ditto ditto.
XXI.	Kurla (No. 8 of Route XV.)	Lob		Ditto ditto.
XXII.	Káráshahr (Route XV.)	Yuldúz Valley		Ditto ditto.
XXIII.	Khotan (Route XIV.)	Aksú (Route XII.)		Ditto Captain Chapman.
XXIV.	Khotan	Polu (No. 14 of Route XIV.)		Ditto ditto.

* This itinerary includes some notes on Khotan, compiled by Captain Chapman.—H. T.

PART II.—*Routes in Turkestan derived from verbal information supplied by natives.*

Number of Route.	From.	To,	Remarks.	Authority.
XXV.	Khotan	Charchand		Compiled by Captain Trotter.
XXVI.	Kila Wamar (Roshan), Route XI.	Kila Khumb (Darwaz)		Ditto ditto (from Abdul Subhan.)
XXVII.	Bar Panjah (Shighnan), No. 10 of Route XI.	Káshghar (Route IV.)		Ditto ditto.
XXVIII.	Bughrumal Pamir (No. 4 of Route XXVII.)	Khokand		Ditto ditto.
XXIX.	Yúr (near Kila Panjah Route VIII.)	Chitrál		Ditto Captain Biddulph.
XXX.	Túshkúrghan (No. 9 of Route VIII.)	Hanza (Kanjud)		Ditto Dr. Bellew.
XXXI.	Sarhadd (No. 14 of Route VIII.)	Kanjud		Ditto ditto.
XXXII.	Yárkand	Shahidúla	*Viâ* Kilik Pass	Ditto Captain Trotter.

GEOGRAPHICAL APPENDIX.

SECTION G.

ROUTES TRAVERSED BY MEMBERS AND EMPLOYÉS OF THE MISSION.

ROUTE I.

YÁRKAND TO LEH *viâ* SÁNJÚ AND KARAKORAM PASS (DR. BELLEW, OCTOBER AND NOVEMBER 1873).

1. Yárkand to Posgám (height* 4,210 feet), 17 miles.—Across a cultivated plain covered thickly with farmsteads and traversed by numerous irrigation streams. Trees along the water-courses, and orchards round the farmsteads. Cultivation interrupted by meadows and marshes. At three miles from Posgám cross the Zarafshán river, which flows in two channels separated by patches of tamarisk jangal. Ford across a firm pebbly bed between low sandy banks four to five hundred yards apart. Posgám is a market town of about 600 houses. Called also Chársbamba Bázár.

2. Kárghalik (height 4,370 feet), 24 miles.—Cultivated plain, farmsteads and fields, with marshes and jangal patches between. At eight miles cross Tiznáf river. Ford firm and pebbly between low sandy banks 80 to 100 yards apart. At five miles on pass through Yakshamba Bazar, 300 houses. Then across thin cultivation between patches of saline encrustation, marsh, and waste to Kárghalik, 1,000 houses. A market town with widespread farmsteads. Many trees and many water-courses.

3. Borá (height 5,340 feet), 25 miles.—Soon pass beyond cultivation across a stony desert waste six miles to Besharik, or "five streams," a populous settlement of farms on the water-courses in a wide hollow running from west to east. Then cross an arid and wide waste of coarse gravel to another hollow, deeper and narrower. In this is the settlement of Borá, 30 to 40 homesteads on the course of the stream from which the cultivation is irrigated. Trees in plenty.

4. Oi-toghrák (height 5,760 feet), 12 miles.—Across an arid desert of undulating surface, coarse gravel, and wind blown ridges of sand, very scanty herbal vegetation, to a deep and winding drainage gully in which, on course of its stream, is the Oi-toghrák settlement of 15 to 20 farmsteads. Trees few.

5. Khushtagh, 19 miles.—Across an arid, undulating desert waste of sandy gravel for 18 miles; then cross a wide boulder strewn hollow with thin tamarisk jangal, and pass through a belt of tall reeds to Khushtagh settlement in a wide hollow. Farmsteads for some miles along the course of the Kilián stream which flows eastward to Gúmá.

6. Sánjú (height 6,070 feet), 25 miles.—Cross arid strip of desert as before, eight miles to a dry ravine in which are four or five farmsteads watered from springs; this is Langar, and here is a roadside rest-house and tank of water under the shade of tall poplars. From this up a steep bank and across a ridgy desert as before for 16 miles to the Sánjú valley down a steep sandy slope. The road to Gúmá branches off north-east on this desert. Sánjú is a populous settlement along the course of a river which flows towards Khotan, and is forded on a rough boulder bed. Farmsteads, orchards, and fields here extend in unbroken succession for eight or ten miles along the river.

7. Kiwaz, 13½ miles.—Pass through Sánjú settlement five or six miles to high banks of gravel and red sand; then up a narrowing valley along the Sirikia river, which runs in three or four streams and is crossed twice *en route* on a boulder bottom, to Kiwaz; six or eight scattered huts on a limited flat amongst hills.

* The heights throughout these routes are supplied by Captain Trotter.

(128)

8. Tám (height 8,790 feet), 16½ miles.—Up course of Sirigkya river, through a gradually narrowing valley which winds between high and bare hills of schistose slate. River crossed repeatedly *en route* on a stony bed. Banks fringed with bushes and patches of pasture grass. At 11 miles pass the Chúchú glen to the left; a narrow defile which conducts over the Chúchú ridge to Shahídula, and is taken as an alternative route when the river is unfordable during the summer floods. At Tám two houses on a small flat leave habitation behind.

9. Gachga, 10 miles.—Up narrow winding valley, and cross river repeatedly as in last stage. No cultivation or habitation. Kirghiz camps in glens and hollows in the vicinity.

10. Kichik Karákoram, 14 miles.—Up by a rapid rise through a widening and branching defile to foot of Sanjú Dawán, a sharp ridge of mica slate 16,650 feet high. Then up a steep zigzag, through a narrow and rough gap, and down another on opposite side into a very narrow, deep, rough gorge descending to Kichik Karákoram; a narrow strip of turf on a trickling stream between lofty vertical cliffs. No fuel nor pasture.

11. Pillátághách, 11¼ miles.—Descend narrow, winding, dismal gorge over masses of landslip rock, down course of rivulet for four miles. Then enter valley of Kárákásh river at Mírzá Abábakar camp ground at a cluster of graves on the river bank. Then follow up stream six miles by a very rough road, fording river twice *en route* to Pillátághách camp ground on a limited flat of brushwood and pasture on the river bank. Valley very narrow; hills high and bare.

12. Shahídula Khoja (height 11,780 feet), 15 miles.—Up stream by rough road in winding valley, with brushwood and forage along river course; their patches interrupted by projecting moraine banks. At four miles cross Kilyán stream from the right to Korghán, a solitary mud castle at foot of a rock abutting on the river bank. At five miles on cross Toghrá stream from the right, then cross Karákásh river three times *en route* to the Fort of Shahídula Khoja, garrison 30 men; frontier post of Káshghar at the junction of the Kizil jangal glen with Karákásh valley. Fuel and forage here, and Kirghiz camps around.

13. Sugat (height 12,970 feet), 8 miles.—Up course of Karákásh river four miles. Then up course of the Sugat river to the right four miles, and, crossing several times, camp on turfy flat on right bank. Hills on left bank steep down to the river; on right bank rolling away in wide slopes to high mountains; everywhere bare schistose slate, and trap. Vegetation confined to river course.

14. Chibra, 21 miles.—Rise out of river channel and pass across wide slopes of hill to a narrow defile coming down from the left. Then up its course between bare banks of shale through a tortuous channel to foot of Sugat Pass, 17,600 feet high. Ascend by a steep path, and follow a gradual slope six miles down to camp ground at Chibra. No vegetation here. Water very scanty. Snow on Pass from September to April as on Sánjú Pass.

15. Aktágh (height 15,590 feet), 10 miles.—Over an elevated, arid, stony plateau, perfectly desert, by a path skirting banks of shale to the right. Breathing oppressed on this march. At ten miles turn slowly to right and slope down to Aktágh camping ground on a patch of turf in the wide, shallow, shingly bed of its stream. The whole region a bleak, desolate, and inhospitable waste. From this down stream is the Yangi Diwán and Kugiár route to Yárkand.

16. Brangsa Karákoram, 28 miles.—Up a wide, shallow, shingly drainage bed gradually ascending between low banks of shale that roll away in wide sweeps to the mountain tops. Vegetation most scanty in herbal tufts. A few antelopes met with. At half-way pass camp ground of Wahábjilga, where the Aktágh stream flows through a cutting in slate rocks. Then continue over the drainage bed to the Brangsa camp ground at the entrance of a narrow defile. No fuel and no forage in all this region. This Brangsa is also called Bálti Brangsa.

17. Daulatbeg Uldi (height 16,880 feet), 22 miles.—Through a narrow gorge up course of a little torrent for a mile; then enter a wide gully branching off amongst the hills. Soil soft and spongy, slate detritus. Rise gradually to foot of Karákoram Pass, 18,550 feet high, then up a short ascent and down a steep descent over soft clay to a hill slope along the course of a rivulet, and cross it several times *en route* to camp. The pass is half-way on this march. Breathing affected by the elevation on this wide plateau. Surface bare gravel and clay. From Daulatbeg there are two routes towards Ladakh. One by Kúmdán, the other by Dipsang, and both meet at the Sháyok River opposite Brangsa Saser. The first is only practicable in winter, and is traversed in three stages, *viz.*—(1.) Across an undulating ravine cut plateau to Gyapshan on the upper course of the Sháyok, 15 miles. (2.) Down the bed of the stream in and out of the water repeatedly, and through a narrow straight where the river bed is very nearly blocked by a vast glacier which has slid down across it, on to a bank of loose pebbles and shingle at the foot of a lofty vertical cliff like a wall. This is Kúmdán, nine miles. (3.) Brangsa Saser. Down the river course, and through another very narrow and winding straight between a great glacier and the opposite cliffs and then down a wide river channel to camp. The passage of the straight is done on the ice or through the stream where it is broken. A difficult road under any conditions. The second and usual route is the following in continuation from Daulatbeg Uldi.

18. Kizil Langar, 20 miles.—Over the Daulatbeg plateau, across a shallow stream in a wide deep gully with muddy soft bottom in which cattle stick, and rise up to the Dipsang plain; wide undulating plateau from which the world around subsides, the highest hill tops only peering above the horizon. Soil soft and spongy, gravel and clay mixed, and, where water logged, boggy. No vegetation. Approximate altitude 17,800 feet. Breathing distressed. From this descend a steep and stony gully into a very narrow, tortuous gorge between high cliffs of red clay; and travelling along in and down its torrent half a mile, enter a wider river bed of rolled pebbles over which the stream flows in a net-work of channels. Rocks roll from the hill tops on either side into the channel. Camp at Kizil Langar, where this channel joins a wider one from the north-west. There is no fuel or forage in all this region.

19. Murghi (height 15,190 feet), 16 miles.—Route down a net-work of shallow streams on a loose pebbly bottom, crossing them continually. At four miles pass Borsa camping ground on a gravelly talus shelving to the stream bed. At a mile beyond quit river, and pass over projecting bluffs, and again meet it as a raging torrent rolling over great boulders in a tight, winding gorge, and crossing from side to side by narrow fords camp at Murghi on turfy ground, where a gully from the west joins. Road very narrow and difficult, and risk from stone avalanches.

20. Brangsa Saser, 10 miles.—Up the dry, stony gully to the west. At two miles pass Chungtásh, "Great Rock," camp ground at a great erratic boulder on a turfy flat. Then descend rapidly into a deep, dark gully and follow down its winding course till it opens into the Sháyok River; pass up its stream a mile and ford opposite Brangsa.

21. Tútyálák, 15 miles.—Up a rough gully and across a glacier at its water-shed for two or three miles. Then up and down by an extremely difficult path between the side of a vast glacier and the opposite hills, a narrow pass full of angular rocks and snow drifts, and in summer purling with torrents on all sides. At half-way pass Sartang camp ground, an open space menaced by half a dozen glaciers around. Beyond, pass along a widening valley over stretches of turf fringing the stream and sloping up the hill sides, and at a glacier projecting from a valley to the west descend into the bed of the stream flowing from it, and camp on a gravelly flat close under the glacier. Fuel scanty; pasture in plenty here. An extremely difficult march.

22. Changlung (height 10,760 feet), 11 miles.—Down left bank of river amidst granite rocks for three miles. Then cross river by a wood bridge, and pass along a steep hill slope of loose gravel and sand above the river course and rise quickly up to the Lamsa crest at eight miles on. From this descent to the secondary ridge of Karáwal Dawan,

and look down on the **Nubra** valley, the first green spot and inhabited country since leaving Sánjú. Drop down to it by a very steep zigzag path and **camp** at Changlang, a small cluster of eight or ten Tatar huts with fields around.

23. **Panámik, 11 miles.**—Down the valley over two long strips of gravel talus cut by the deep boulder bed of the Tútyálák River, where it joins the Nubra stream, and is **crossed** by a timber bridge. Then along patches of turf and brushwood jangal of buckthorn, tamarisk, myricaria, and rose to the cultivation and village of Panámik—to **comfort and supplies.**

24. **Tagar, 13 miles.**—Down the left bank of the river as in last stage. Midway cross a rocky ridge abutting on the stream, with the populous village of Chirása on the opposite bank.

25. **Sati, 15 miles.**—Down the river course, as in last stage passing villages and cultivation, to its junction with the Sháyok River. Then up the right bank of the latter to Sati passing villages and cultivation with patches of brushwood and pasture between on the way. From Sati there are two routes to Leh. First, the direct route by the Khardung Pass. Second, the river route by the Digar Pass. The first is in three stages, *viz.*— (1.) Cross the Sháyok by ford or boat according to the season, and pass up the narrow defile of Rong, crossing its torrent several times, four miles; then rise up to a high cultivated plateau, and at three miles more camp at Khardung village. (2.) Polú, 15 miles. Up the course of a mountain torrent, cross a tributary from the right, and pass over moraine banks to an upland turfy slope. Continue up its winding and narrowing course to the foot of the Pass. Then pass a pool and glacier, and rise over latter by very steep ascent to the crest of the Khardung Pass, nearly 18,000 feet high, and descend by a very stony, steep zigzag to Polú camp ground on a turfy flat, cut by a rivulet coming down from a glacier at the head of a glen to the right. (3.) Leh, 7 miles. Down a winding gully, and over moraine banks, the road gradually improving to the cultivation of Leh, and then to the town itself. This is a very difficult route. The other continues down the river from Sati.

26. **Digar** (height 13,080 feet), **17 miles.**—Cross river, and then up its left bank for 12 miles. Then rise out of river bed up to a high flat talus of bare clay and gravel. Cross it and pass round a hill spur, and ascend to fields and houses of Digar in an amphitheatre of granite hills.

27. **Polú Digar, 14 miles.**—Up a rising **moorland amongst granite** boulders and across peat beds and bogs for five miles to Polú camp **ground** on a spur where the ascent increases. Then up a long stony slope covered with snow patches at end of June, and rise suddenly to crest of Digar Pass, 17,900 feet high. **Pass through** a narrow gap, and drop by a very steep and rough path to the other side; follow a winding, turfy glen and camp at Polú huts **near** a thin rivulet. Some pasture **here;** but **no** fuel. Pass very difficult.

28. **Leh** (height 11,538 feet) or Ladákh, **10 miles.**—Down the glen, across its stream to cultivation **and homesteads** of Sabú, and **then up the valley** to Leh.

ROUTE II.

YÁRKAND TO LADÁKH *viâ* **KUGIÁR.** (AUTHORITY, DR. BELLEW, JUNE 1874.)

1. **Yárkand to Yangichik, 12 miles.**—Across a **populous and** cultivated plain well stocked with trees, mostly willow, poplar, mulberry, alsaguns, and orchard trees. **At** five miles cross Zilchak stream by rustic bridge, and at six miles on ford the Zarafshán **or** Yárkand river, and camp another mile on at the Yangichik Settlement.

2. **Yakshamba Bázár, 18 miles.**—Over cultivated plain **with** farmsteads, meadows, and marshes. At 13 miles pass through Posgám, and on to **camp over** freely irrigated tract **of** cultivation.

3. Kárghalik, 16 miles.—At six miles cross Tiznáf river. Country as on last stage.
4. Beshterek, 20 miles.—At three miles out quit cultivation, and cross a wide gravelly waste of arid desert, strewed with boulders and coursed from west to east by sandy ridges. Pass through a gap in these to Beshterek or "Five poplars," a cluster of 8 or 10 huts.
5. Yólarik, 12 miles.—Pass out of Beshterek gully on to a wide wind swept desert of coarse sand traversed by gravelly ridges. Camp in settlement of Yólarik, a long stretch of farmsteads on the course of a small river.
6. Kugiár, 13 miles. Cross a wide, shallow, pebbly water-run; pass over a high ridge of loose sand on summit of which is the half buried shrine of Sicheáulúe Mazár; and descend to the Kugiár gully. Follow up its course seven miles past farmsteads to camp in the centre of the settlement.
7. Ak Masjid (height 8,870 feet), 24 miles.—Continue up the gully, and cross its stream to hamlet of Fusar, six miles. Here leave cultivation and habitation behind, and enter hills up a narrow winding gully to camp ground on banks of a stream running down an open glade. Hills of shale. Vegetation scanty.
8. Chiklik, 11 miles. Up a narrow winding gully by a very steep rise between hills of loose dust, six miles, to the top of the Tupa Dawán or "Dust Pass." Then descend by a steep, dusty path down a widening gorge to the bed of the Tiznáf river, and camp on a grassy flat, under an overshading bank of rock on its right bank, near a clump of willow and poplar trees.
9. Khoja Mazár (height 9,250 feet), 14 miles.—Up the bed of the river, crossing it girth deep 24 times *en route* on a rough boulder bottom (June), in a deep winding defile, and camp on a turfy slope on its left bank. Brushwood and forage in plenty. In winter the road is over the frozen river; in summer through it, and dangerous from sudden floods. Road difficult.
10. Dúba, 6 miles.—As last stage. Camp on turfy flat at angle of junction of two torrents. Banks fringed with willow and poplar forest. Pakhpo camps in the vicinity.
11. Gurunj Káldi, 9 miles.—Up the main stream as before, crossing two tributaries from the right, and camp on turfy slope amidst boggy springs. Hills of schist and granitic trap, and perfectly bare. Marmots here.
12. Chirágh Sáldí, 11 miles.—Up stream as before through a gradually widening valley. At eight miles pass ruins of Kirghiz Tam, a former outpost of the Chinese rulers, and beyond it cross a projecting spur into the wider bed of the river, which in June is covered with a deep layer of snow over which the road passes. Camp in a patch of brushwood at junction of a tributary from the right.
13. Kúlanaldí, 11 miles.—Up a winding and narrowing gully by easy ascent to the top of Yangi Dawán, 15,800 feet high, three miles. Then down an easy descent for two miles to where a gully joins from the left. Beyond this down an extremely difficult, narrow, tortuous, and deep gorge which is blocked till June by a glacier that melts away in the next month. The passage over it very difficult down to a wider and less steep channel, of loose shingle between steep banks of moraine rubble, which opens into that of the Yárkand river. Cross the river and camp in tamarisk jangal on opposite shore. River channel half a mile wide.
14. Kúkát Aghzí, 15 miles.—Up course of Yárkand river through extensive patches of tamarisk and myricaria crossing the river girth deep five or six times *en route* on a shingly and sandy bottom, and camp in tamarisk jangal. Channel wide with high hills draining to it on each side.
15. Kashmír Jilga, 25 miles.—Up stream as before. At three miles pass ruins of an outpost fort called Nazar Beg Kurghán, at entrance to a glen on the left which leads in two stages to Shahídula by Kirghiz jangal. Beyond this through an alternately widening,

and narrowing valley to a long stretch of brushwood also called Kirgbiz Jangal; and through this to camp.

16. Khufelung, 11 miles.—Up stream four miles, then rise up to a shelving slope of slate and shale on right hand; follow it seven miles and drop into junction point of a stream from the right; cross its pebbly wide bed and camp on the left bank of Yárkand river in tamarisk jangal.

17. Aktágh, 20 miles.—Up course of river leaving vegetation, and passing over snow fields filling its channel (June) to Aktágh. From this onwards the route is the same as that by Sánjú.

ROUTE III.

LEH TO SHAHIDULA (No. 12 OF ROUTE I) BY THE CHANGCHENMO ROUTE. AUTHORITY CAPTAIN BIDDULPH, SEPTEMBER AND OCTOBER 1873.

1. Tikshe, 10 miles.—Along Indus valley, road good. The village of Tikshe contains about 600 inhabitants.

2. Chimray (height 11,890 feet), 15 miles.—Along Indus valley for 10 miles, road indifferent in places. This Indus fordable in September after first six miles, turning up valley to north for five miles of pathways through cultivation to Chimray, village of about 500 inhabitants with monastery. Bad camping ground.

3. Zingral (height 15,780 feet), 8 miles.—Up valley about three miles till it forks. Up valley to eastward for 1½ miles to village of Sakti; beyond this the ascent gets steeper to Zingral; no village; good camping ground. At Zingral the valley forks to the Chang-la and Kay-la Passes, the latter saves about six miles, but is more difficult for loaded animals.

4. Tsultak (height 15,950 feet), 8 miles.—Up most northerly of the two valleys an easy but stony ascent of two miles to top of the Chang-la Pass, 17,600 feet. A very gradual descent of four miles, then turning abruptly to the east to Isultah, a small lake; no village; good camping ground. Though the Pass is not formidable either in height or steepness, it must always prove difficult to loaded animals on account of the badness of the road which is a mere track winding through rocks and boulders.

5. Tankse (height 12,900 feet), 14 miles.—Down valley for 6½ miles easy road, cross shoulder of hill into valley with stream running from south-east pass Durgu a small village, continue up valley to large village of Tankse, supplies of all sorts procurable, the residence of headman of the district. Behind the village is the valley coming in from the Kay-la.

6. Chakar-talab, 14 miles.—Valley above Tankse narrows to a gorge for six miles, then turns to the south and opens out, two miles further is Muglib, very small village; for three miles the valley is a grassy swamp, then narrows for two miles of gentle ascent among rocky boulders. At Chakar-talab is a small shallow pond, sometimes dry in summer; coarse grass on further side of it.

7. Lukong (height 14,130 feet), 7¼ miles.—Five miles up valley to north-west end of Pangong lake, water salt, 2 miles due north from end of the lake to Lukong small patch of cultivation with stream running into lake.

8. Chagra (height 15,090 feet), 8 miles.—1½ miles above Lukong, valley forks up one to north-east-summer pasture ground of Tartars, one or two stone huts, grass plentiful, and fish in the stream.

9. Rimdi (height 17,500 feet), 13 miles.—A short steep ascent out of valley half a mile due east into broad valley running east and west. Continue for 5½ miles very slight

ascent to Lunkur, stone hut, uninhabited, a little water, then steeper ascent, but not difficult to top of Lunkur-la or Marsimik Pass, 18,400 feet. Gradual descent down valley turning due north, at 3½ miles joins valley from west. Rimdi camping ground at junction; fuel scarce; water and grass plentiful.

10. Pamzal (height 14,790 feet), 13 miles.—Down valley to east; stony and narrow track for two miles along face of steep hill, valley then bends to north and road improves slightly. At nine miles, bed of stream narrows to stony gorge for a few paces, then opens out into quarter mile breadth. Very stony, brushwood plentiful, strike Changchenmo stream running east and west. Camping ground to west of junction. Fuel abundant; grass plentiful, half mile further down valley.

11. Gogra (height 15,570 feet), 12¼ miles.—Up Changchenmo valley into Kugrang valley, north north-west road good; fuel plentiful; grass scarce.

12. Shummal Lungpa (height 17,020 feet), 12 miles.—Cross valley, and up Chunglung valley to north-east stream runs in narrow gorge. At 4½ miles narrow steep descent and ascent across gorge coming from north. At six miles hot springs in river bed, valley bends round to north road, winds in narrow track on hill side, several steep ascents and descents. Three miles above hot springs is large ravine leading east, up which is road over Changlung Yokma Pass on to Lingzi Thung Plain; one mile beyond is Shummal Lungpa ravine, running east; first half mile narrow and stony, then opens out; camping ground 1¼ mile from entrance; water and fuel plentiful; grass very scarce.

13. Camp near Nischu (height 18,630 feet), 14¼ miles.—Up valley about 3½ miles to fork, up ravine to eastward at head of which appears a practicable pass. At half a mile take up ravine north by west up steepish ascent across Changlung Burma Pass, 19,300 feet high. Descend low hill into broad shallow valley due east, down valley, which bends to north, and camp near black jagged hill. No grass or fuel; march throughout good for laden animals.

14. Camp Lingzi Thung (height 17,680 feet), 16½ miles.—Down main valley which makes a great sweep round to north-east, and at 6¼ miles opens out into Shumshul Plain by Kala Pahar. Due north across plain for six miles cross low ridge with 200 feet rise and 700 feet descent on north side into Lingzi Thung Plain, due north for five miles and camp in water-course; fuel and water to be got by digging; no grass. From low ridge above mentioned, rocky peak at head of Kizil Jilga ravine bears 349°.

15. Jungle Camp, 17 miles.—Across plain for 9 miles, straight for rocky peak, across low ridges for 8 miles, and camp by small pond. No grass or fuel, but the latter can be collected on north side of plain where it is plentiful.

16. Camp Sumna (height 17,150 feet), 21¼ miles.—Among low hills for 3 miles into broad valley running north in which is plenty of water; keep up valley northwards for 2 miles towards smooth round hill, and turn up broad valley running in from west for 11 miles to red rock, and cross the Kizil Diwan (height 17,290 feet) at foot of it into Kizil Jilga ravine. Water, grass, and fuel obtainable 3 miles down, and more plentiful still further on.

17. Kizil Jilga (height 16,360 feet), 9 miles.—Down valley to Karakash river flowing between two huge red rocks, camping ground under southern one. Grass and fuel plentiful.

18. Khushk Maidan, 17 miles.—Down Karakash valley, at 5 miles water disappears in the ground. None to be found for 11 miles, where are numerous springs. Camp on south side of valley. Fuel abundant; grass scarce. Road excellent all the way.

19. Chung Tash (height 15,740 feet), 7 miles.—Down valley, which narrows. Huge rock on right bank. No fuel or grass. Road good.

20. Camp Sumnal (height 15,540 feet), 13 miles.—Down valley, which at 3½ miles bends round to north, and valley leading to Aktagh comes in west. The Karakash then flows

in narrow gorge and at 6 miles from Chung Tash are hot springs on right bank. A little fuel, but no grass. One mile above hot springs valley opens for a mile then closes again. Road in parts stony and bad. River has to be crossed frequently; small patches of fuel in side nullahs. Good camping ground at bend of river to east, where large nullah from west joins. Fuel and grass abundant.

21. Camp Tak Marpo (height 15,000 feet), 11 miles.—Valley opens out for 3 miles. Zinchin on right bank. Fuel and grass. Valley then narrows; road encumbered by huge boulders and masses of rubbish; very difficult for laden animals; camp under yellow rock on left bank. Fuel and grass at intervals all the way.

22. Camp Polong Karpo (height 14,600 feet), 21 miles.—Valley opens out and travelling good. At 8 miles is broad valley on left with abundant fuel, after which fuel is to be found all along in main valley; grass very scarce. At 16 miles valley narrows and turns to north, fuel becomes more plentiful. At Polong Karpo is a huge rock in bed of valley on left bank; good camping ground; grass abundant.

23. Camp Sora (height 14,000 feet).—At 5 miles river takes sharp bend to north-west into broad valley at foot of Kuen Luen. For 2 miles on either side of the bend is no fuel or grass. Ground at Sora covered with natural salt pans. Good camping ground. Fuel and grass abundant.

24. Jungle Camp, 17 miles.—Camp at mouth of small ravine. Opposite mouth of Karajilga ravine. Fuel and grass abundant.

25. Gulbashem, (height 12,390 feet), 42¼ miles.—Road down valley good; and grass and fuel abundant everywhere, except for 2 miles above Gulbashem. 12 miles above Gulbashem the river is much increased by springs. Gulbashem is a favourite Kirghiz camping ground.

26. Balakchi, 10 miles.—Grass and fuel.

27. Shahidúla (height 11,780 feet), 13 miles.—Small deserted fort on left bank of the Kara-kash. Grass and fuel abundant. At 6 miles strike road from Sugat Pass; road good.

Though parts of the road are practicable for guns and wheeled carriage, it is on the whole only available for camels or horses.

ROUTE IIIa.

Variation on No. III. (Captain Trotter, September and October 1873). From Gogra (Station 11 of Route III) to Shahidula (No. 27 of Route III).

1. Kotajilga (height 16,730 feet), 8 miles.—Road up stream the whole way good, but somewhat difficult for loaded ponies, as there are several steep ascents and descents in crossing tributary streams, which in the autumn contain only a few inches of water. Pass ravine on right leading to Nischu as per Captain Biddulph's route. At the camp, grass, water, and wood procurable.

2. Pangtong (height 17,250 feet), 7½ miles.—Steady and gentle ascent through a broad stony ravine for four miles, then somewhat steeper. Camping ground covered with snow, but grass and an inferior fuel said to be plentiful.

3. Sumzungling (height 17,310 feet), 15 miles.—Steady and not very steep ascent to the Changlung Pass (18,910 feet). The road then passes over a high table-land for about a mile, after which it enters a ravine along which it passes for 9½ miles of execrable road, crossing the stream in numerous places before reaching the camping ground at the junction of three nullas. Water and a little grass on a neighbouring hill, but no fuel, one of the worst marches on the whole road, as the number of recently dead animals that strewed the road too surely testified.

(135)

4. **Debra Kompás** (height 17,890 feet), 19 miles.—Road runs nearly due north up a gentle ascent for about 5 miles, road fair, then for several miles of good road across the west edge of the Ling-zi-thang plains; crosses several easy open ravines draining eastwards descends into and crosses a branch of the Karakash river and camp at foot of a low pass; very little water to be obtained by digging; and no grass or wood.

5. **Shinglung or Dunglung** (height 17,030 feet), 18 miles.—Across pass, and down a ravine for 5½ miles into Karakash river, where plenty of boortsee and water, but no grass. Road follows river, which after 3 miles turns up sharp in a northerly direction, road good, but stony; boortsee abundant.

6. **Kiziljilga** (height 16,360 feet), 14½ miles.—Bad stony road down bed of Karakash River for the first mile, then between about two or three miles of ice bed have to be traversed, the bed extending right across the ravine, here about ¼ mile in breadth; road very slippery and difficult for laden animals. Near camp passage of Karakash difficult (in October) owing to admixture of ice and water. Fuel (boortsee), grass and water, within reach of camp down Karakash River.

7. **Chungtash or Chung Tásh** (height 15,740 feet), 23½ miles.—Road down Karakash River generally good but stony and bad in the latter portion. Camp badly situated, as there is neither wood nor grass both of which might have been had at Khushk Maidan, a few miles further back. Camp under a big rock near where the bed of the Karakash is very much narrowed by precipitous hills coming down near the river bank.

8. **Shorjilga**, 14 miles.—Road for two miles down Karakash, which takes another sudden curve to the north-east, the road goes up a tributary stream containing nearly as much water as the Karakash itself. Road bad for two or three miles owing to the number of times the frozen stream has to be crossed and recrossed, it then passes over a tolerably level plain up to a gorge at the mouth of which is Shoorjilga. In October there was no water there and camp had to be pitched half mile up the gorge at a place where the river water disappears into the ground; not a stick of wood or blade of grass.

9. **Kárátágh** (height 16,890 feet), 9 miles.—Up ravine for several miles, snow and ice nearly the whole way and road bad; short but sharp descent from Karatagh Pass (17,710 feet) into large flat open plain, covered with several inches of snow. Lake frozen over, but water obtained by making hole in ice; plenty of boortsee, but no grass visible.

10. **Aktágh** (height 15,590 feet), 22½ miles.—Road the whole way good, over a level plain, which was entirely covered by snow. About half way at east foot of low double-topped hill is a place called Tamba* sometimes used as a camping ground. Ak-tagh is at the junction of the Karakoram and Changchenmo Routes.

11. **Chibra** 10 miles.—Road crosses stream and goes up ravine, steady ascent with fair but stony road. No grass or wood at camp.

12. **Suget** (height 12,970 feet), 18 miles.—Up ravine to top of Suget Pass (17,600 feet), 4 miles. Steady ascent and road good. Descent steep through the snow down zigzag, then straight down ravine for eight miles due north. Road stony, but descent gentle. Road then turns eastward and soon leaves the nullah, which has a very rapid fall; an alternative road goes right down the nullah in which there is plenty of wood and grass, abundance of both at camp.

13. **Shahidula** (height 1,780 feet), 8 miles.—The road descends to Karakash River (two miles) and follows the river to camp, crossing it twice *en route*. Passage somewhat difficult. Plenty of wood and grass a few miles up the Karakash River. Shahidula is the same as Station No. 12 of Route I.

---

* On this march we lost our road and had perforce to halt at Tamba, where we found boortsee; melted snow served for water, which is not procurable here in summer.

(136)

ROUTE IV.

YARKAND TO KASHGHAR (CAPTAIN TROTTER), NOVEMBER 1873.

1. Kok Robát or "Blue Hostelry" (height 3,830 feet), 22 miles.—Pass through cultivated tracts and at 4½ miles cross the Opo or Arpi canal (from the Yárkand river) by a good bridge. A little distance beyond is the village of Kárákoram, after which the road passes through grassy swamps, followed by a desert waste. Occasional small villages are passed before reaching Kok Robát, a scattered village of about 200 houses.

2. Kizil (height 3,910 feet), 26 miles.—Pass over sandy desert, without habitations or cultivation, to Ák Robát or "White Hostelry," where are two small wells whose surface water is 98 feet below the ground level; another 13½ miles over flat waste to Kizil, a large village of about 500 houses. The dry bed of the Kizil stream is passed, coming from the Kizil Tagh on the west. The country is irrigated by small canals taken higher up from the Kizil River which in summer contains a fair supply of water.

3. Yangi Hissar or "New Fort" (height 4,320 feet), 28¼ miles. Over a flat plain irrigated by small water-courses from the Kinkol River, the scattered villages of Chemalung, Kudok, Kosh-gombaz, Tuplok and Kalpín are passed. Low sand hills on right before reaching the Yangi Hissar River, which has its chief source in springs a few miles south-west of the town of the same name, which lies two half miles beyond it. Yangi Hissar is a large town with strong fort, and contains about 4,000 houses. The Yangi Hissar River* is crossed by a two-spanned timber bridge, about 60 feet long. A low ridge of hills separates it from the town. The fort is about 600 yards to the north of the town.

4. Yapchan (height 4,210 feet), 23½ miles.—Pass at four miles the Zaikásh stream fed from springs on the west, further on cross two branches of the Sailik canal from Kusánk. After passing the villages of Khánka Sorgoluk, and Tuglok cross by a wooden bridge a large canal from the Kusán River, and then cross the main stream of the Kusán itself by a wooden bridge. The road follows the lower bridge of the stream for about a mile, and is much cut up by branch canals. Soil generally sandy.

5. Yangi-shahr or new city of Kashghar (14½ miles).—Road passes through cultivated country and crosses several streams and canals, the largest of which are the Tazgún or Khanarik or Yamunyar and the Karasú (chiefly fed from springs). Pass the villages of Tazgún, Turmalak, and Kasr Robát. The old city of Kashghar lies about five miles from the Yangi-shahr in a north-west direction.

ROUTE V.

KASHGHAR TO MARALBASHI (AUTHORITY, CAPTAIN BIDDULPH) JANUARY 1874.

1. Sang, 19 miles. Through cultivation; at six miles village of Barin; 7½ miles Arowah, junction of road from city of Káshghar; nine miles village of Yandumba, from where goes cart road to Kizil Boia to east; cross rivers Yamunyar and Chokanak flowing into Kizil, both bridges swift streams. Sang large village.

2. Faizabad (height 4,000 feet), 16 miles.—Large village, through cultivation; at two miles cross small river; no bridge.

3. Yangi-awat, 11 miles.—Small village, cultivation almost ceases from Faizabad; at seven miles small village of Shagiat.

4. Kashmir, 28 miles.—Through bush jangal and plain; at 20 miles cross river Kizil; bridge used in summer; ice bears carts, &c. in winter. Kashmir a small post-house, no village.

5. Togha Sulukh, 13 miles.—Through tree jangal and white grass; a small post-house.

* Which I have known called by no less than nine different names.—H. T.

(137)

6. Shugeh, 18 miles.—A small post-house; road all the way through tree jangal.
7. Maralbashi (height 3950), 14 miles.—Small village and fort; road through tree jangal and high grass. Maralbashi is at the junction of Kashghar road, with road from Yárkand to Aksu. Carts travel freely all the way.

ROUTE VI.
KASHGHAR TO CHADYRKUL, CAPTAIN TROTTER.

Kashghar (Yangi-shahr) to—

1. Besák, Upper Artysh (height 5,290 feet), 26 miles.—Road leaves on left at 5½ miles the old city of Káshghar, and then crosses the Tuman (Káshghar) river by a good bridge; passes through numerous gardens into an open stony plain, and then through a gap in a low range of hills, beyond which lies the district of Osten Artysh, consisting of numerous scattered townships.

2. Chung Terek, or "Big poplar tree, (height 7,000 feet), 20 miles.—Road passes over level plain and then up the gently sloping Toyanda valley. Road good but stony; pass *en route* the old Chinese outpost of Teshektash and the small village of Tupa; a small Kirghiz village at camp.

3. Chakmák Forts (height 8,830 feet), 20 miles.—The road continues up the Toyanda valley and passes through precipitous hills rising some 3,000 feet above the bed of the stream, which has to be frequently crossed, both on this and the last march. At 12 miles pass the "Past Kurghan" or Lower Fort, garrisoned by a detachment from the larger forts at Chákmák further on. A few Kirghiz tents *en route*, but no other habitations. From Chákmák a road goes across the hills to the east to the Terekty Forts.

4. Balghún Báshi (height 10,540 feet), 10 miles.—The road continues up stream, and at about eight miles passes the Suok outpost at the junction of two streams from the Suok and Turgat passes. The former is two days' journey in a north-west direction by a very difficult road; two miles above the outpost is the camp, where plenty of firewood, though but little or no grass.

5. Turgat Bela (height 11,090 feet), 15 miles.—Road always up stream at first through precipitous hills, which open out somewhat as the camp is approached. Occasional Kirghiz tents; plenty of grass near camp; but fuel very scarce.

6. To Chadyrkul (Lake), 20 miles.—13 miles to the crest of the Turgat Pass, a gentle ascent right up to the foot of the pass, from which to the crest (12,760 feet) there is an ascent of about 400 feet in a distance of a mile. From the pass the road passes along a spur for about three miles, and then rapidly descends to the lake, which lies about 1,500 feet lower than the pass. Plenty of grass, but little or no fuel obtainable.

The road from Kashghar to Chadyrkul is good throughout, and could with very little labour be made available for light carts and field guns. In January a little snow lay by the roadside to the north of the pass, but none whatever on the south side.

The route just described is on the main caravan route between Kashghar and Almati (Fort Vernoye), for details of which maps can be consulted.

ROUTE VII.
KASHGHAR TO BELOWTI PASS, (CAPTAIN TROTTER) FEBRUARY 1874.
(On road to Ush Turfan.)

Kashghar (Yangi-Shahr) to—

1. Altyn Artysh (height 4,100 feet), 22 miles.—Over plain for a great part of the way; road good; pass Kashghar River by wooden bridge (in cold season), and subsequently

cross two smaller streams and canals, and traverse a low ridge before entering the Artysh valley, which contains numerous villages aggregating perhaps 2,000 houses.
2. Kalti Ailák (height 3,950 feet), 22 miles.—Good road over level plain.
3. Kyr Bulak (height 5,340 feet), 33 miles.—Good road passes over plain and then through a range of low hills up the Sogon stream, on which is a military outpost, then crosses a low pass and emerges into a large plain. Camping ground is occasionally used by Kirghiz.
4. Jai Tupa (height 4,910 feet), 20 miles.—An occasional camping ground of Kirghiz; water scarce; situated near the centre of an extensive forest of stunted poplar trees; good road passing over level plain; plenty of grass and fuel.
5. Ui Bulák (height 6,650 feet), 27 miles.—Road good but stony; crosses a low spur into the Ui Bulák valley, where plenty of fire-wood and a moderate amount of grass; water scarce, but plenty of snow.
6. Tigarek, 17 miles.—Road up stream and then over a spur from the main range, stony, but otherwise not difficult. Tigarek is in a large grassy plain (no water) surrounded by hills; is sometimes used by Kirghiz as a winter pasture ground, when snow is used as a substitute for water.
7. Belowti Pass (height 11,360 feet), 9 miles.—Road crosses some low spurs and then passes up a ravine; a steady ascent of four miles followed by a sharp pull of two miles up to the pass; no high peaks near the crest, but undulating grassy ridges. The road descends on the north side of the pass in the valley of the Kokshál river. The Belowti Pass was the furthest point reached by Captain Trotter, and from it the marches to Ush Turfan were said to be as follows:—
8. Ak-chi, 10 miles, on Kokshal River.
9. Kuyok Tokai, 22 miles, down river.
10. Safr Bai.
11. Karawal, 22 miles.
12. Ush Turfan, 16 miles.

Total distance, Kashghar to Uch Turfan, 242 miles; from Safr Bai (No. 10) a road is said to go to Karakul (near the old Issigh-Kul Fort) by four difficult marches, crossing the Bedul and the Zanku passes, and the head-waters of the Naryn River. From Karakul roads go to Kuldja and to Vernoye (Almati).

ROUTE VIII.

YANGI HISSAR TO KILA PANJAH, WAKHAN, BY THE LITTLE PAMIR (CAPTAIN BIDDULPH) MARCH AND APRIL 1874.

1. Ighizyar (height 5,600 feet), 19 miles.—Large village. Road nearly due south, through sand-hills and cultivation, crossing two small streams, over soda plain for 5 miles, cross stream by village, and over stony plain for 7 miles; practicable for wheeled traffic.
2. Aktala (height 7,345 feet), 17 miles.—Kirghiz camp, south-west four miles over plain to Aktala valley, then up valley 13 miles. At six miles pass through ruined Chinese fort closing the valley. Fuel, grass, and water abundant; road good.
3. Sasak Taka (height 9,455 feet), 13 miles. Out of main valley, into side valley to south, first few miles narrow and stony, then opens out and travelling improves. Wood and grass abundant. Kirghiz camp at Sasak Taka.
4. Kaskasu (height 10,960 feet), 14 miles.—Kirghiz camp up valley; travelling good; grass plentiful, but fuel scarce. Several Kirghiz camps in the valley.
5. Chehil Gumbaz (height 10,310 feet), 8½ miles.—Kirghiz camp; half mile from Kaskasu road turns up small valley to south, and at another mile is foot of Kaskasu Pass, first 200

yards steep, then for three miles winding through undulating grassy hills round head of valley to top of pass 13,000 feet, road good half mile along narrow ridge then steep zigzag descent of 1,000 feet into Charling valley to Chehil Gumbaz at junction of two valleys. Grass and water plentiful; fuel scarce.

6. Past Robat (height 9,370 feet), 9 miles.—Road up valley to west for 2½ miles to foot of Torat Pass; 1½ mile of ascent; not difficult for laden animals to top of pass, 13,400 feet; long steep descent into narrow valley; road stony and bad; into broad valley, to south to Past Robat; Kirghiz camp at junction of two valleys; grass, fuel, and water abundant.

7. Tárbáshi (height 11,515 feet), 8 miles.—Kirghiz four miles up valley to fork. The valley to the right leads to Tashkurghan by the Yambulak Pass, only used in summer. Up valley to left for two miles along narrow gorge, among rocks and boulders, the stream having to be crossed and recrossed more than a dozen times. Many hot springs in the defile, steep ascent of 400 feet into upper valley, when road again becomes good. This route can only be used when the stream is low in winter and early spring.

8. Shindi, 17 miles.—Up the valley for eight miles of gentle ascent to the Chichiklik plain, about 1½ mile in diameter; to south-west is the Kok Moinak Pass, used in spring and summer, by which Sirikol is reached in 1½ marches; to north is the route by Yambulak Pass before mentioned. Bending to south a long descent, steep and stony, brings one to Shindi, where are a few Sarikoli huts.

9. Tashkurghan (height 10,270 feet), 19 miles.—Down valley for four miles to Yárkand River. From here a road up valley to east leads over the Shindi Dawan to Tarbashi. Continues up Yárkand River to foot of Tashkurghan. Road good all the way. Grass and fuel plentiful.

10. Kanshábúr (height 12,980 feet), 17 miles.—Due west from fort into Shingan valley. The first three miles of narrow defile strewn with boulders, very difficult travelling, after which valley opens out and road gradually improves. Fuel and grass plentiful.

11. Aktásh (height 12,600 feet), 18 miles.—Up valley to right, and after a mile up fork to left to foot of Nezatash Pass 15,000 feet. Three miles of gentle ascent, last 300 yards to top steep. Descend into valley running north-west along this for eight miles, over low spur into broad Aktash valley running south. Grass and fuel plentiful.

12. Gház Kul, or lake of Little Pamir (height 13,200 feet), 46 miles.—Down Aktash valley to south into Little Pamir due west, travelling excellent the whole way. Grass and fuel plentiful everywhere. Camp by lake. At six miles from the lake is Kabr-i-Bozai, deserted Kirghiz huts, opposite which is road leading to Kunjúd by Tagdúng-bash Pamir, over Kujroi Pass.

13. Langar (height 12,530 feet), 25 miles.—Continue due west; at 10 miles Pamir narrows into rocky valley, and travelling becomes difficult; road winding along face of hill with many small ascents and descents. At Langar deserted village; fuel and grass plentiful. Opposite Langar is road leading to Kunjoot by Bykurra Pass, closed three months in the year. This is the road generally used between Wakhan and Kunjúa.

14. Sarhadd (height 11,150 feet), 24 miles.—Down main valley, travelling bad; road much encumbered with boulders, and there are two steep ascents and three steep descents, very trying to animals. The stream has to be crossed many times, and the road in consequence of melting snow becomes impassable after 1st May. From Sarhadd road leads to south to Yassin and Chitrál by Baroghil, Darkot, and Ishkaman Passes. Sarhadd is the frontier village of Wakhan.

15. Kila Panja, 55 miles.—Down valley to foot, road good for laden animals villages at intervals the whole way; grass and fuel plentiful. By the village of Yur, 18 miles from Sarhadd, is a summer road into Mastuj. At Vost, 38 miles from Sarhadd, is a road leading into Chitrál said to be only practicable to men on foot.

(140)

ROUTE IX.

KILA PANJAH (ROUTE VIII) TO ÁKTASH BY THE GREAT PAMIR (CAPTAIN TROTTER), APRIL 1874.

Kila Panjah (Wakhan) to—

1. **Langarkish village** (height 9,350 feet), 6 miles.—Road lies along the banks of the main Panjah River, and then up the northern branch; pass on right bank the villages of Zaug and Hissar. All supplies for the journey across the Great Pamir have to be taken from Langarkish, which is the highest village on the north branch of the Panjah river. The valley is bounded by lofty and precipitous mountains.
2. **Yumkhána or Jangalik** (height 11,440 feet), 18 miles.—The road follows the right bank of the river, above which it rises in many places to a height of 1,000 feet; cross the Ab-i-zer-i Zamin (River), four miles beyond which is the camp. Plenty of grass and fire-wood.
3. **Yol Mazar** (height 12,320 feet), 13 miles.—Road still along right bank of stream, at four miles cross the Ab-i-Matz (river) up which passes a summer road to Shighnan, two miles further is Boharak, the commencement of the Great Pamir. Plenty of grass and *boortsee*. Road good.
4. **Bilaor Bas** (height 13,120 feet).—March along right bank of river through a grassy plain bounded on both sides by undulating hills.
5. **Mazár Túpa** (height 13,760 feet), 20 miles.—Road up gentle ascent the whole way, and on the right bank of the stream.
6. **Sarikol** (head of the lake), (height 13,950 feet), 16½ miles.—Road up gentle grassy slope to Victoria Lake, passing along its northern edge. The lake is ten miles long and nowhere more than two miles in breadth. Camp at the east end of the lake; whole ground under snow, but very fine pasturage in summer. From Sarikol a road leads across to Langar, at the west end of the Little Pamir, crossing the Warram Pass.
7. **Shash Tupa** (height 13,760 feet), 19½ miles.—Cross a low water-shed a few miles from camp and then enter a valley, the stream down which flows into the Ak-su river; very gentle descent through broad open valley to camp. Roads traverse the Pámir here in all directions.
8. **Dahn-i-Isligh** (mouth of the Isligh River), height 13,220 feet, 18 miles.—Gentle descent through open valley, pass several broad open ravines. This camp may be considered the termination of the Great Pámir. Plenty of grass and fuel.
9. **Ak-tash** (height 12,600 feet), 37 miles.—Road follows the Isligh River until it joins the Ak-su, both of these streams partially frozen, but ice breaking up making journey somewhat difficult. The Isligh River passes through precipitous mountains; after entering the Ak-su valley turn south to Ak-tash, which is the same as station 11 of Route VIII.

ROUTE X.

TASHKURGHAN TO YARKAND, VIA CHARLING RIVER (CAPTAIN TROTTER, FROM KISHEN SING).

Tashkurghan (No. 9 of Route VIII) to—

3. **Chehil Gumbaz** (No. 5 of Route VIII), 56 miles.
4. **Tashkerim**, 19 miles.—Road passes down **Charling River**; Kirghiz encampments; wood and grass; pass on road Alumbitte Kurghan. From Tashkerim a foot-path leads across the hills to Kinkol camp.

5. Khaizak-vil, 14½ miles.—The road continues down Charling River. Pass on left bank at eight miles the small village of Bagh (30 houses), also the villages of Kiok-tash, Mirgul (25 houses), and Yoya (15 houses).
6. Arpalik, 21 miles.—Road leaves Charling River and passes up a tributary stream to small village of Yamunarik. Thence goes over two low passes, the Kara Diwan (at 11¼ miles) and the Kizil Diwan.
7. Kizil-tagh, 15½ miles.—Road good for three miles to Tangitar, where the river (Kizil) passes for five miles along a very narrow ravine, very difficult to traverse in the afternoon owing to floods caused by the melting of the snow on the hills above.
8. Yak-arik, 23½ miles.—Good road over the "Shaitan kum" or "Devil's sand."
9. Yárkand, 20 miles. Road passes over a well cultivated and thickly inhabited plain.

Total distance, Tashkurghan to Yárkand, 188 miles.

ROUTE XI.

Route from Kila Panjah (WAKHAN) to Kila Wámar (ROSHAN) along the river Panjah. Authority Captain Trotter (from Abdul Subhan.)

Number of stages.	Names of places.	Country or district.	Distance in miles.	REMARKS.
1	Kila Panjah to Khandot.	Wakhán	16	A village with about 30 houses and mud fort. Road stony, passes through village of Parg at 2½ miles, Pakui at 5½ miles, and ruins of Ishmúrgh at 9 miles. From Pakui to Khandát is a dense forest of stunted poplar trees.
2	Pigish	Ditto	6	A village of 30 houses. Road good, and along left bank of river; much cultivation. Supplies plentiful.
3	Shikharbi Pareshan	Ditto	20	A scattered village of 30 houses. At 13 miles is the large village of Argund. Road bad and stony and along left bank of river. Supplies plentiful.
4	Patúr	Ditto	17	A frontier village between Wakhan and Ishkashim, subject to Mír of Wakhan, consisting of 25 houses, villages passed on road are Verg at 7 miles, Sad Ishtrag at 10 miles, and Kázideh at 11½ miles. From Sad Ishtrag a road strikes off southward to Chitrál, the capital of Káshkaro. Four miles beyond Kázideh the river turns abruptly northwards, and is dangerous here for horses, as it passes over a narrow ledge of rock overhanging the river. Road stony. Supplies plentiful.
5	Yaghduru (Doyam) or 2nd.	Shikashim	17	A village of 15 houses. Valley in this march wider and river broader. At 6 miles is the large village of Ishkashim of 60 houses. A road joins here from Faizabád. At 8 miles village of Yaghduru (Aval) or first. Road good, and through rich cultivation. Supplies plentiful.
6	Barshár	Ghárán (Badakshán.)	9	A small village belonging to the Ghárán district situated on the right bank of river Panjah. River forded 3 miles above village of Sar-i-Shakh, left bank avoided being dangerous for horses. Road stony and bad. Supplies plentiful.
7	Nawábád	Ditto	14	A deserted village on the left bank, river recrossed at ford near deserted village of Kázideh at a mile and half from Barshár. Another road from Badakshan to Ghárán (viá Aghirda Pass) and to Shákh Darrah valley, crosses at the same ford. At 5 miles is the deserted village of Zieb, on the opposite bank of river is a ruby mine. No supplies here. Cultivation scanty. Grass and wood plentiful.

(142)

ROUTE XI.

Route from Kila Panjah (WAKHAN) to Kila Wamar (ROSHAN) along the river Panjah. Authority Captain Trotter (from Abdul Subhan)—concluded.

Number of stages.	Names of places.	Country or district.	Distance in miles.	REMARKS.
8	Darmárakht	Shighnán	11½	Camp on the left bank. Darmárakht is on the opposite bank from whence supplies are procured by means of a wooden bridge thrown across the river, which is about 150 yards wide here. From Nawabád at 3 miles is the large village of Shekh Beg in ruins, and further on the road runs through a tunnel called Kuguz Parín, or "hole in the rock." Road bad and stony. The Kuguz Parín in the boundary between Gbáran and Shighnán.
9	Viár	Ditto	14½	A scattered village of about 40 houses. At two miles from Darmarakht a large tributary of the Panjah river called Arakht is crossed by a strong wooden bridge. At 9½ miles the road ascends and traverses the Mithina and Tarseb passes. Road bad and stony. Supplies plentiful.
10	Kila Bar Panjah	Ditto	5½	A large town on the left bank, the capital of Shighnán. Adjacent to it stands a stone fort on the margin of the river. At Dasht-i-Khust, the river Suchán falls into the Panjah. At 3½ miles is the small village of Deh-i-Murghán. Road good. Supplies plentiful.
11	Sácharb	Ditto	9	A village of 20 houses on the right bank. Sácharb is reached by crossing the river either by ferry at Kila Bar Panjah, or by ford at the village of Dislár at 3 miles lower down. Yumj village is at 4½ miles from Sacharb. Road good. Supplies plentiful.
12	Kila Wámar	Roshan	22	A large town, the capital of Roshán, situated about 1½ miles above the junction of the Murgháhi river with the Panjah. Fort and town on the high bank of the Panjah. At 13 miles is the small village of Past Khúf. At 16 miles stands the Darband tower, built on a rock. This is the boundary between Shignán and Roshan.
		Total distance	161½	

ROUTE XII.

YÁRKAND TO AKSU.   AUTHORITY, CAPTAIN CHAPMAN.

BHAN SING.

FROM YÁRKAND TO AKSÚ AND ONWARDS.

1. Yárkand, *Torek Langar, 7 tash,** Ek Shamba and Char Shamba Bazaars *en route*; cultivation and gardens to within one mile of the halting ground.

* NOTE.—A tash is the ordinary unit of measurement of distances in Eastern Turkistan, and on many of the principal roads *tash-boards* have been erected similar to the wooden sign posts, still existing in some parts of England. They were put up between Khotan and Kashghar shortly after the accession of the present Ruler, but the Yarkand road the following measurements were made by Kishen Sing Pandit :—

	Number of paces.	Average number of paces per tash.
From 1st to 5th Tash Post	36,350	9,112
„ 5th to 8th „	27,880	92.93
„ 8th to 11th „	26,800	8,933
Mean value of each tash		9,113

or almost exactly 4½ English statute miles. Theoretically the tash is equal to 12,000 **paces of a riding camel**, and it is by means of this measure that the distances **are** said to have been laid **out between Yarkand** and Kashghar.—[H. T.]

Terek Lángár, a village of about 40 houses, with two musjids, in every house a room for the accommodation of travellers.

2. To *Lai Lik*, 7 *tash*, through desert and low jungle; at 4 tash a deserted Lángár of the time of the Chinese; at Lailik, 22 houses, the inhabitants support themselves by the entertainment of travellers; supplies, &c.

3. To *Menut*, 4 *tash*, through a jungle of high trees. The road within one tash of Lailik (on the Yárkand side) approaches the Yárkand river; it is touched three times by the road during this stage. At Menut 16 houses in all, accommodation for travellers; supplies, water, &c.

4. To *Alaigur*, 5 *tash*, through a jungle of high trees, the river is encountered twice *en route*. At Alaigur 23 houses, accommodation in each; supplies and water; the river is nowhere crossed, but the road follows its bank.

5. To *Aksák Marál*, 3 *tash*, through jungle as during previous stage, the road approaching the river once *en route*; 14 houses at the halting stage, accommodation in each, and supplies, &c.

6. To *Shamál*, 5 *tash*. Here is only an old rest-house, but about a mile to the east on the bank of the river is a cluster of some six houses, whence the traveller may get some supplies; the entire route through jungle. From this point the river runs wide of the road.

7. To *Marálbáshi*, 3 *tash*. High jungle encountered *en route*, but in patches, there being here and there strips of sand and bog, the only water being obtained from springs. A fort, and considerable place. *Vide* Captain Biddulph's report.

8. To *Charwágh*, 3 *tash*. The spurs of a range of hills stretching out from the Tianshan are to the north of the road which runs through jungle with cultivation here and there, the drainage from this point is into the *Kashghar River* from which canals are cut to Marálbáshi and onwards; there are about 40 houses in Charwágh, each having accommodation for travellers.

9. To *Tumshuk*, 4 *tash*. Half way a hill is to the north of the road under which the road immediately runs; on the top of this hill is a Mázar and also one at the base. Captain Biddulph gives this hill the name of Pir Shereh Kuddam Múrtaza Ali Tagh, and thinks the rock must be basaltic. Beyond this hill is a fort, and at the distance of about a tash is a ruined city at the base, and on the slope of a second hill (this is one of the buried cities) the houses are of earth and not of stone. One tash further to Tumshuk, through a low jungle, a place of 32 houses, accommodation for travellers. A canal from the Kashghar river is crossed at 2 miles from Tumshuk by a bridge; this is narrow and comparatively deep, being only some 10 yards across, it runs away east.

10. To *Chadyrkul*, 3½ *tash*, through a jungle of high trees; 15 houses.

11. To *Yaka Kuduk*, 4 *tash*, through a jungle of high trees; water from a well about 30 feet deep; there is a slight drainage from this point; southwards towards the Yárkand river about 12 houses in Yarkudut, where travellers are accommodated.

At this point the road divides into two, the shorter and more direct road going by—

12. *Yazdah*, 5 *tash*. High trees during half the march when these change to low jungle. No water *en route*, spring near Yazdah itself. About eight houses in Yazdah.

13. To *Chilán*, 3 *tash*. Low jungle and sandy desert; no water *en route*; 22 houses in Chilán; two large trees at this place which are conspicuous; two tanks at Chilán supplied by springs.

The longer one by—

12 *Snget*, 4 *tash*. A deserted Lángár, but no water; no one halts here; if a halt is intended, water must be carried.

13. *Chilán*, 6 *tash*. A low jungle, but no water on the surface; but it may readily be obtained by digging. This is the easterly of the two roads.

This road is closed after the winter season when the thaw sets in and occasionally when the springs swell and bring an extra amount of water.

14. To *Chol Kuduk*, 4 *tash*. Through desert without water. At Chol Kuduk water obtained from a well, but the water is brackish. There is a large serai here with a musjid. Here is a low range of hills on the north-west, close to which the road runs, and behind which is the bed of the Kashghar Daria.

15. To *Sai Arik Langar*, 4 *tash*. Through a desert, with sand and small stones. At Sarek Lángár there are two serais, and a post for the examination of passports; some 30 or 40 houses with cultivation, &c.; water by a canal from the Kashghar Daria.

16. To *Kumush* or *Kumbásh*, 3 *tash*. The Kashghar Daria is crossed at one mile from Sai Arik Lángár. After the crossing there is a group of hamlets known as Aykol, beyond this eastwards at about one and half tash is a considerable sheet of water; in the district, which takes its name of Aykol from this, are some 2,000 houses. Cultivation may be said to extend from Sai Arik Lángár as far as Aksú; there is a bazaar held at Kum. In Aykol are two serais and a considerable bazaar (Thursday); the country is cut up by canals from the Kashghar river. The *Kum district* stretches towards Ush Turfán and eastwards; it is said to contain 8,000 houses. Kum Bazaar, which is the head-quarters of this district, is off the road some 2½ miles. At the stage of Kumbásh there is merely a Lángár.

17. To *Aksú*, 4 *tash*. After leaving Kumbásh, about two tash, the Ush Turfán river is crossed; it runs in three principal channels, one of which is crossed by a ferry during the cold season; the Kashghar Daria was crossed in four separate channels at some distance from each other, and all bridged. After leaving the Ush Turfán river the road rises to a plateau along the skirts of which it passes. It drops suddenly upon Aksú. A small stream from the north passes to the west of Aksú at about one mile distance and falls into the Aksú Daria about three miles south of the town.

Total distance 73½ tash or 75½ tash from Yárkand to Aksú.

At Terek Lángár, the first march from Yárkand, the natives are Dulans, a tribe presumably of Kálmák origin, having a distinct dialect of Turki and many customs different from those in force elsewhere; they extend as far as *Chilán*, the 13th march; they remain distinct from the natives of the Aksú and Yárkand districts.

Kokshál is the name usually given, not only to the Ush Turfán river, but to all the streams in the Aksú district, on account of the rice grown in the fields which they fertilize.

Kokshál (rice producing).

Kok really means blue, all green things springing from the ground are called Kok.

From Aksú to Ush Turfán—

1. To Sayik, 4 tash, through cultivation at the base of the hills and in the valley
2. *Achtágh*, 6 tash.
3. *Ush Turfán*, 4 tash. Two serais in Ush Turfán, the last two places are in the Ush Turfán district, which is a separate command; it contains 8,000 houses, and is a highly productive district; flocks and cattle abound.

The water of Aksú is from springs, there is only one tank in the Yangi-shahr.

There is a very large sale of horses in Aksú; the Dadkhwah taxes the sale of horses, taking 12 puls on each transaction. On market day 600 loads of Indian-corn and wheat, 1 tanga per charak; 300 loads of rice, 2 tangas the charak.

There are 200 dyers in Aksú.

SERAIS IN AKSU.

1. Khotan Serai, 50 rooms.
2. Kashgaree Serai, 60 rooms.
3. Sheik Beg Serai.
4. Mullah Saduk Serai.
5. Dhung Serai.
6. Khona Serai.
7. Nar Kurgan Bai Serai.
8. Andijání Serai.
9. Yárkandee Serai.

There are three other serais within the walls.

Outside the walls.

1. The Custom House.
2. Charee Hakim Serai.
3. Kirghiz ditto.
4. Aíd Darogah Serai.
5. Mahomed Tokhta Bai.
6. Badshahi Serai.
7. Hají Serai.
8. Kush Najuk Serai.
9. Imam Khwaja Serai.
10. Shukutlik Serai.
11. Abdullah Beg Serai.
12. Hikmut Baki Serai.
13. Eesah Kor.
14. Arjak.
15. Abdullah Bai.
16. Shah Mahomed Niaz.
17. Lalú Sheik.
18. Yanús Bai.
19. Túdi Bai.
20. Músa Akhúnd.
21. Mahomed Tej Bai.
22. Abrahim.
23. Shamsh Akhúnd.
24. Toonganee Serai.

There are altogether 33 serais outside the walls.
Inside the walls there are 84 musjids, and in the Yangi-shahr of Aksú 4 musjids.
Inside the walls 800 shops; every house is a shop almost.
Outside the walls 500 shops; 35 Coppersmiths; 33 Butchers; 22 Ashkhanas; 19 Bakers.
Outside the walls; 45 Coppersmiths; 40 Bakers; 34 Ashpaz; 50 Shoemakers.
The greater part of the population are in the suburb outside the walls.
In the entire district of Aksú there are 30,000 houses.
The principal merchants resident are—

1. *Shumsh Tar Akhoond.*—This man has agents who travel to Turfan, Úrumtsi, and Ili; he is said to be worth 500 Yamboos.

2. *Ahmed Shah Bai.*—He trades with Almati, Kashghar, Turfan, Úrumtsi; property valued at 400 Yamboos.

3. *Jait Darogah.*—Trades with all the cities before mentioned and possesses property valued at 500 Yamboos.

4. *Kassim Bai, Andijáni.*—Property valued at 1,000 Yamboos: this is the principal trader.

The tanab in Aksú district is measured in the square of 12 Kulaj (the length covered by the arms at sketch), a tanab is calculated to take 2 charaks of grain. Five tanabs make a putmun.
The tax on crops is fixed by valuation for cotton.

ROUTE No. XIII.

FROM AKSÚ TO KUCHÁR. AUTHORITY, CAPTAIN CHAPMAN.

From Aksú to Kuchár. The tash on this road are marked on regular Tash posts.

1. To *Jamgu*, 4 **tash**, through cultivation and past frequent habitations; watered by small canals. At Jamgu two serais and a small bazaar; about 50 houses.

2. To *Kara-Yalghán*, 3 *tash*. **Kara** (black) Yalghán (tamarisk), a low shrub jungle with willows, &c., tamarisk; water from springs about half way, where are a few shepherds' huts.

(146)

3. To *Yagh-Arik*, 7 *tash*. *(Oil-canal)* Through desert and low hills; at 3 tash there is a small place of shelter for cattle known as a Dhung; at the 4th tash there is a similar shelter, water procurable at both these places, streams from springs; at the 6th tash is a newly-constructed Karawul and some few houses with cultivation. About two miles to the south-east of this Karawul is a copper mine. The road here passes through a spur of the main range which is, however, very low at this point, canals. About 50 houses in Yagh Arik, a tank, gardens, &c. Yagh Arik is in the district of *Bái*.

4. To *Bai*, 7 *tash*. For 1½ tash through highly cultivated district with gardens, houses, &c., to the bank of a river flowing south; the bed of the stream nearly half a mile across and very stony, the stream is rapid even in winter and is divided into three channels; the cultivation continues from the opposite bank all the way to Bai. This is a long stage and can be broken without difficulty at the hamlets *en route*. Bai is a walled town with three gates, and has its own Governor. There is a regular *urda*, four serais, musjids, &c., and three large tanks in the town; there are 62 principal shops inside the walls; there are two Madrassas and two schools. Bazaar is held on Friday after mid-day.

There is a garrison of 200 soldiers, 4 Yuzbashis, and 20 Panja Bashis.

There are six serais outside the walls of the town. It is estimated that there are 4,000 houses in the entire district of Bai.

Mahomedan population of the same type as at Aksú.

About 8 tash to the north of Bai are hot springs to which miraculous cures are attributed, the springs having been, it is said, called into existence by Hazrat Alli after a fight with infidels. There is a Ziarat at this place, and it is a place of pilgrimage; the road to it is a very difficult one.

5. To *Sairám*, 4 *tash*. The Bai district is left at about two miles from the walls; the entire road is through hamlets and cultivation, a considerable stream running through a shallow* bed immediately after leaving Bai. Sairám is larger than Bai, but there are no walls round it. The Hakim is under the orders of the Governor of Bai. There are 16 serais, 11 musjids, 4 tanks, and 75 principal shops, the population of the district is approximately the same as that of Bai. Bazaar is held on Thursday. Intermediate between Bai and Sairám and to the north about one stage, iron of a superior quality is obtained: this is only worked for local purposes.

* Shah-Yar River.

Grain is exceedingly cheap, and rice is grown, but in smaller quantity than in the Aksú district.

6. To *Toga Dhung*. A single stage house, where provisions can be obtained; water procured from a distance, 5 *tash*.

The road on leaving Sairám very soon passes strips of cultivated ground and through a tamarisk jungle, 2 tash to Kizzil. Kizzil lies in a sandy strip; a stream is here encountered flowing south; there are willow trees and a few houses grouped on either bank; the bed of the stream is 40 yards across; from Kizzil to Toga Dhung a stony desert; to the south there are small sand hills, and the road here takes a more northerly direction.

7. To *Kuchár*, 6 *tash*. About two miles from Toga Dhung across a low ridge on the top of which is a serai. This gives a better halting place than the last stage, but water is obtained at the serai with great difficulty and must be paid for, the road turns southwards immediately after crossing this low ridge. There is no cultivation to within about two miles of *Kuchár*, but about 2 tash from the ridge is a Karawul in a gorge where the rocks appear to have been subject to volcanic action and are of a very dark color on a high hill to the north-east. At this point is a ruined city, the people commonly call this "Takht-i-Touran," the outskirts of these ruins are actually on the road; the

(147)

hill is of bare rock and, as before stated, presumably volcanic, but the ruins are of earth of a deep yellow color quite unlike anything on the hill itself; there are besides a large number of caves, excavated for residence; from below a high wall is visible, which is said to be the wall of an old palace. The city is said to have existed previous to the first Chinese occupation; the current story is that the city was consumed by fire sent down from heaven owing to the refusal of its ruler to adopt the Mahomedan faith, the blackened appearance of the rocks having given rise to this tale.

From the Karawul to Kuchár proper is 3 *tash*. *Kuchár* is a walled city of a circular form with four gates two of which have been lately closed.

The garrison of Kuchar is as follows:—There are two Panjsads, 20 Yuzbashis, 50 Panja Bashis, and about 600 soldiers; there are two schools and three Madrassas. The present Dadkhwah is Mahomed Tokhta Beg.

There are 205 principal shops inside the walls, 100 of which are always open, the remainder being closed except on bazar days. Four serais inside the wall; the city wall is surrounded by a ditch, which is kept full of water; there are 140 shops outside the wall, 15 serais outside. The Túngani have a separate quarter; they have 45 shops and have 9 serais; corn is ground by mills in which horses are worked; these are kept by Túnganis; the suburbs of the city are large in proportion to the rest of the town, there being only some 400 houses inside the walls, and 1,300 houses outside. The population of the district is said to be considerable, there being, according to calculated accounts, 22,000 houses in the district.

Alum and salammoniac are brought from Kuchar, and Pushum of a superior quality; it is considered the best obtainable.

Rice is grown in small quantities, but this is produced in large quantities at Shah Yart, the south of Kuchar, some 8 tash distant.

About 16 tash to north of Kuchar a large idol is said to exist, which is cut out of the rock; it is reported to be from 40 to 50 feet in height, it has 10 heads and 20 hands, and it is carved with the tongue hanging outside the mouth; the mountain behind this idol is exceedingly difficult of ascent, rumour says that it is resorted to by game of all kinds, but that the animals, owing to the protection of the idol, cannot be killed by the huntsman. A mountain lake of considerable size is said to exist in this neighbourhood, the drainage of which falls into the Yulduz and makes its way to Karashahr. The idol referred to above is said to grow thin during the daytime, but to increase in size during the night.

Salammoniac is obtained in large quantities from the neighbourhood of a volcano, which is at a distance of eight tash from Kuchar; this sells in Kuchar at 3 tangas the jing. The people of Kuchar declare that a description of rat circulates freely in the flames of this volcano without being injured; it goes by the name of Salamander. *Surrundoo (alum)* is also obtained in this neighbourhood, and sells for a half tanga the jing. The farming of the salammoniac and alum is let out for 4 *kurus* yearly.

There are copper mines between *Yagh Arik and Bai*. There is no monopoly with reference to the mining for copper ore; there are regular miners who can be hired by any one who chooses to try for copper, the agreement with them being that they are to receive one-half of what is extracted.

The copper is found in a low range of hills, and at a depth of from 30 to 36 feet; there is a smelting furnace on the spot, which is under Government supervision; the charcoal and the wages of the smelters are paid for by the finders of the ore, and from the copper extracted one-seventh goes to the Government.

It is usually calculated that the ore yields from one-ninth to one-eighth of pure copper which sells in Bai for $3\frac{1}{2}$ tangas the jing.

(148)

Route XIV.

Route from Karghalik viâ KHOTAN to Tankse.

AUTHORITY CAPTAIN TROTTER FROM PUNDIT KISHEN SINGH.

Number of stage.	Names of stages.	Country or district.	Distance in miles.	REMARKS.
1	Karghalik to Yakin Langar.	Karghalik	13	A small village of four or five houses only, country well cultivated. At four miles is the village of Besharik, and at eight miles Lob village. Cart road all the way. Yakin is a halting-place for traders. Water, fuel, and supplies plentiful.
2	Chulák Langar	Gúma	20	A small village of 10 houses. At four miles is Khush Langar, and is the boundary between Karghalik and Guma. Country up to Khush Langar is cultivated, the rest of the journey is over a sandy desert, and no water except in a reservoir at Dabzokum brought daily from Chulak Langar. Supplies plentiful.
3	Gúma (height 4,340 feet).	Ditto	23	A small town and district with about 1,000 houses and a bazar of 300 shops. A Dadkwah or Governor and 200 sepoys are posted here. Two Langars or rest-houses are built on the road, viz., Silak Langar at 9½ miles, and Hajif Langar at 14 miles. The Kilian river is crossed near Guma. Road runs over a sandy plain the whole way.
4	Moji village (height 4,290 feet).	Ditto	24	A large village with a bazar. Road through a level cultivated country. At three miles the dry bed of a branch of the Kilian river, about 200 paces broad: is crossed. Súpi Khájam village is 9 miles, Cholo village of 50 houses 10 miles; Mukhila Langar at 11 miles; and the large village of Chuda at 19 miles. Road over a sandy plain. Fuel and pasture plentiful.
5	Piálma	Ditto	35½	A large village and bazar. At 2½ miles is Kosha Langar; at 10½ miles Kondla Langar; at 14 miles Jhanguia, a large place with a fort. The road from Sanju to Khotan joins at Jhanguia. The entire journey is over a sandy plain without habitation between Jhanguia and Pialma. Water, fuel, and pasture plentiful.
6	Jáwá or Záwá Kúrghán (height 4,430 feet).	Khotan	25	Road over sand hills all the way. Water scarce, to be had only at Ak Robat at 15 miles, from a deep pucka well; again at Imam Salar's tomb and at Jawa Kurghán, a large village and bazar. Supplies plentiful.
7	Khotan City (Ilchi Shahr) (height 4,490 feet).	Ditto	20	Road over a cultivated country thickly inhabited throughout. The Karakash river, about half a mile wide with several channels, is crossed at 14 miles. Khotan is a large town, where a Governor and several hundred sepoys are posted. Numerous canals from the Karakash river intersect a large area of country around Khotan. At a distance of 15 miles north-west is the large commercial town of Karakash.
8	Yurung Kash (height 4,370 feet).	Ditto	3½	A large place of 500 shops. At 2½ miles the river Yurung Kash, (the same size as the Karakash) in two channels is crossed The road for several weeks is flooded in hot weather. Jade and gold are found up the stream. Road good, and rich cultivation all round.
9	Dol Langar (height 4,420 feet).	Ditto	13	A large village of 150 houses. Excellent road, thickly inhabited, and rich cultivation all through the journey. At 10½ miles is Lob village and bazar of 50 shops.
10	Chíra (height 4,220 feet).	Ditto	35	A town on the banks of a small stream with a bazar of 150 shops. Road as far as Ak Langar. The first 6 miles over a sandy plain covered with jungle. Elman Bazar 10 miles; Beshtoghrak Langar at 15 miles; Aisma Langar at 26 miles; Yakin Langar at 30 miles: all these places have rest-houses for travellers, with water and supplies. No cultivation except at Chíra.

(149)

ROUTE XIV.

Route from Karghalik viâ **KHOTAN** *to Tankse.*—(Continued.)

Number of stages.	Names of stages.	Country or district.	Distance in miles.	REMARKS.
11	Karákia Langar	Khotan	25	A small village of 10 **houses**. Road over an open country. At 10½ miles is the **village** and bazar of Gulukma; at 16½ miles Domaká **village**; from thence the country is covered with high forest. Supplies plentiful.
12	Kiria Bazar (height 4,580 feet).	Ditto	27½	A large town and bazar of 600 shops; at 5 miles is Ya Langar; at 9½ miles Siasgol; at 14½ miles Yaka Langar; at 22 miles Phundra village of about 100 houses. From Yaka Langar to Kiria country thickly populated and extensive cultivation. Felt is manufactured at Kiria. A branch road goes from Kiria to Sorghák gold fields as follows:—*1st March*, Toghrák (height 5,760 feet), 15 miles, a village of 50 houses, road over sand hills. No habitation except at Oi Toghrak. Kiria river 500 paces wide (with several channels), crossed near Kiria. *2nd March*, 15 miles, a rest-house with scanty cultivation round it. Road open and over sand hills. *3rd March*, Sorghák (height 7,060 feet), 34 miles, a place famed for its gold fields: these fields are worked all round the year by men from Kiria, who with their wives and families sleep in temporary huts. One-fifth of the produce is paid as a tax to the ruler of Kashghar, who also purchases the remaining produce at a fixed rate.
13	Toghrak Langar	Ditto	23	A small village of 5 houses. Road through cultivation at 15 miles, the rest-house of Bughuz, to east of which, at 200 yards, **is** the Kiria canal here called Toghrak Ustang.
14	Polu village (height 8,430 feet).	Ditto	32	A village of 50 houses with scanty cultivation. Road runs along side the river over a plain for 8 miles, to where the river issues from a mountain gorge, up which the road passes to within 2 miles of Polu, when the river turns off to south-east. Road good.
15	Khiskde Camp	Ditto	17	Road, stony and bad, runs along the valley of the Khúrap or Polu river to Khiskde. A little fuel and grass. Gold dust is found in the stream here.
16	Ghubolik Camp (height 16,960 feet).	Ditto	25½	Camp near Ulugh Shahi Kul. A lake with sulphur mines in its neighbourhood. For 6 miles from Khiskde the road runs along the Polu stream through a narrow gorge between hills called Tangitar, then ascends the Ghubolik. At Diwan Pass, difficult for laden ponies. A gradual descent from thence for 14 miles to Ghubolik. Road bad at the pass. Grass, fuel, and water plentiful.
17	Aksu Camp	Ditto	19½	Camp on grassy plain between two small streams. At 12 miles a small pass crossed. Road good. Fuel and grass plentiful.
18	Arash Camp (height 16,020 feet).	Ditto	12	Camp on northern bank of the Kiria river. At 8 miles the Kizil Diwan pass is crossed. Road good, but stony at the pass. Grass and fuel plentiful.
19	Kiria Daria-i-bash Kul (height 16,880 feet).	Ditto	15½	Camp on small lake, the source of the Kiria river. Road stony and bad, slightly ascending to the lake. Grass scarce, and fuel plentiful.
20	Camp	Rudok	22	Camp near a small stream. Grass and wood plentiful. At 16½ miles a pass is crossed forming boundary between Kashghar and Thibet.
21	Nikong Chumik	Ditto	17½	Camp on an extensive plain, with grass and **fuel** at hand. A mile from camp a pass is crossed. At **10** miles road runs along the west bank of the Yeshil **Kul** lake (height 16,160 feet). Grass and wood plentiful. Water scarce. Road good **the** whole way.
22	Daknák Camp	Ditto	25	Camp on an extensive plain. Grass and **wood** plentiful. Road along the banks of **a dry** water-course.

(150)

ROUTE XIV.

Route from Karghalik viâ KHOTAN to Tankse.—(Concluded.)

Number of stages.	Names of stages.	Country or district.	Distance in miles.	REMARKS.
23	Tashliak Kul (height 16,620 feet).	Rudok	28½	Camp on the northern edge of a fresh water lake. Two small passes are crossed, one at 10 miles and the other at 25 miles. Road good. Grass and wood plentiful.
24	Chumik Lakmo (height 16,600 feet).	Ditto	27½	Camp at the base of low hills. At 9½ miles the road runs along the eastern edge of the Mangchaka or Mangtza lake. At 13 miles ascends a low range of hills. At 19 miles passes a small lake. Road good. Water from a neighbouring spring. Wood and grass plentiful.
25	Lugrang Camp	Ditto	19	Camp between a range of hills. A pass crossed at about a couple of miles from Chumik Lakmo, from thence the road to Lugrang along bed of a partially dry stream. Water scarce. Wood and grass plentiful.
26	Sumzi Ling* (height 15,570 feet).	Ditto	17	Camp on left bank of Rudok river. At 4 miles the Kiangla (pass) is crossed, from thence along the Rudok stream to Sumzi Ling. Road stony. Fuel and grass plentiful.
27	Angche Chiortan	Ditto	31	Camp on right bank of Naichu river. Road for 8 miles good, at 10 miles ascend a pass, from thence along the river to camp. Wood and grass plentiful.
28	Noh village	Ditto	10	A small village of 25 houses on the Naichu river. Sparse cultivation. Road good and along the stream. Rudok lies about one long day's journey (by a circuitous route) to the south.
39	Pal	Ditto	20	Camp on the upper or east end of the Pangong Lake called here Chomo Ngala Ring Cho. Road in a westerly direction and along the banks of the Lake but very stony. Water good. Wood and grass plentiful.
30	Dal	Ditto	21	Camp on the Chomo Ngala Ring lake. Road stony, along the edge of the lake. Water good. Fuel and grass plentiful.
31	Aot	Ditto	12	Camp on south side of Pangong. Road crosses the lake by a shallow ford near encampment. About 2 or 3 miles north-west is the ruined fort of Kharnak. Water fuel and grass plentiful.
32	Thakung	Ladakh	29	Camp on south side of lake near a mountain stream which falls into it. Scarcity of fresh water. Road stony and along banks of the lake. Wood and grass plentiful.
33	Shushul	Ditto	8½	A village of 30 or 40 houses, with sparse cultivation. Road good, and supplies plentiful.
34	Lung Barma	Ditto	31	Good camping ground in the Lungchu valley. At 4½ miles from Shushul cross Gongta-la-pass, from thence along river bank. Road stony. Fuel and grass plentiful.
35	Tankse (Station V of Route III) (height 12,900 feet).	Ditto	24	A village of 50 or 60 houses, with some cultivation. Road stony and along Lungchu stream. Fuel and grass plentiful.
		From Tankse to Leh, vide Route III.		
		Total distance	742	

* The Pandit's thermometers were broken here.

ROUTE No. XIVa.

YÁRKAND TO KHOTAN.

AUTHORITY CAPTAIN CHAPMAN (COMPILED FROM NOTES BY RAMCHAND).

FROM YÁRKAND TO KHOTAN, BY KARGHÁLIK.

From Karghálik to Egun, two tash, across a ravine and for four miles across desert, and then entering cultivated land which continues for two miles, after which there is desert close up to Egun, beyond Egun desert, at three miles a Langar (Gombaz) with tank and two old tombs; eight miles beyond this through a bare desert to a place where a tank (containing about 20 mussuks of water) is prepared and covered in. Water is brought to this daily (one donkey load) from a distance of ten miles, under the orders of the Hakim of Gúma. Beyond this 10 miles through desert to Chúlák (Langar), where there is a tank. This is the usual halting stage, and there is a post here for the examination of passports.

From Chúlák, 13 miles, to Serik Langar through desert. These Langars are all comfortably fitted up for travellers. Four miles beyond this is another Langar, where are trees and water; at this point the road divides, one going direct to Khotán and the other to the Gúma Bazaar; six miles to Gúma by taking the direct road, and not going to Gúma about four miles are saved, but all Rahdaris (passports) have to be shewn to the Hákim of Gúma.

Gúma is a considerable place; its district comprises that of Sánju. It extends from Egun to Piálmá in the Khotán direction, and southward as far as the Sánju pass. Gúma, for three miles through cultivated ground, then through desert for 12 miles to Mocha. Here is a comfortable rest-house prepared by a Mullah where travellers are entertained. A road diverges at this point to Sánju, which is distant 15 miles.

From Mocha (or Moji) for about 14 miles through desert to Zungoé or Jhanguiá; here is a small bazaar, and the place is surrounded by a wall built in the time of Habbibúlla; cultivation beyond this for some two miles, where there is a Langar, after which there is desert for 12 or 15 miles. Here there is a Langar, but no tank, only a well of extreme depth from which water is drawn. Five miles to Piálmá. Here there is a small bazaar. From Piálmá 15 miles to Ak-Robát. Here is a new rest-house prepared by the Amír's orders where travellers are entertained; there are two wells in the court-yard, which is 100 feet square: these wells are deeper than the one at the last Langar. Here there is a very high pole upon which a bell is hung, in order that during storms of sand travellers may be directed to the rest-house; during the night it is customary to place a light on the top of this pole for the same purpose. There is a regular establishment for the care of the serai. From Ak-Robát five miles to the Mazár of Imám Mahomed Shah. This stands in the middle of a desert; a large number of pigeons are kept by the Shaik custodian, for which a regular allowance of grain is made; the road is through a heavy sandy desert. There is a high pole at this point with a bell on it similar to the one at Ak-Robát. Through desert for five miles to Jawa this is a small village of 20 houses, also surrounded by a wall in the time of Habbibúlla; there is a post for the inspection of passes and for search for gold and jade carried out of the Khotán District without permission. This is the point where the Atalik halted before the capture of Khotan, and from whence he enticed Habbibúlla into his camp. To the east of this village is a considerable stream flowing from the Sánju Diwán, which is crossed by a wooden bridge built after the fashion of Kashmir bridges. This is about 20 yards across. On the other side is a regular rest-house for the Hakim of superior construction. From this point cultivation and habitations extend uninterruptedly to Khotan at a distance of 25 miles.

Ten miles from Jawa the Kárákásh is crossed, where the breadth of the bed of the stream is about 400 yards. On the bank of the Kárákásh there is also a rest-house built to accommodate travellers detained by the rising of the river.

Seven miles short of Khotan is Do-Shamba Bazaar: this is a small village.

Marches.	Stages.
1.	Posgám.
2.	Karghálik.
3.	Egun.
4.	Chúlák.
5.	Gúma.
6.	Mocha.
7.	Zungoé or Jhanguiá.
8.	Piálmá.
9.	Ak-Robát, a short stage owing to heavy sand.
10.	Beyond Jawa, to the banks of Kárákásh.
11.	Khotan (Ilchi).

A road starting between Piálmá and Ak-Robát makes up the Kárákásh valley to the Suget pass and the Kárákorum.

To the east of Khotan and flowing close to the Yangí-shahr, 500 yards outside the wall, is the Yúrúng Kásh River; the bed of this stream is 600 yards broad, and in the dry season it flows in two channels; the road is often closed in this direction. Niaz Beg attempted the construction of a bridge, which was carried away by the stream.

From Khotan up the valley of the Yúrúng Kásh to Ladák; this was the road taken by Jumma Khan; it is said to be very difficult.

From Khotan (Ilchi) by 6 marches in a southerly direction crossing the Yúrúng Kásh at (Ilchi)—

3 tash to Sumpula.		
3	„	Hasha.
3	„	Gunjutagh.
4	„	Num.
4	„	Imám Mazár.
5	„	Polú.

These six marches are through cultivated lands by small villages; no river encountered.

Fifteen marches from this point by a comparatively easy road to Changthang where the road between Leh and Lhassa is joined. Grass and wood during the entire route. Changthang is from 12 to 15 marches distance from Leh.

Water is procured by digging. This is a summer route; it was pursued by Nujjuf Shah, Envoy of the Maharaja of Kashmir, in 1864, with Nika, Mogul, who is now in Khotan.

The province of Khotan is divided into the following districts:—

Ilchi (Khotán proper).
Kárákásh (a Beg).
Keria (a Beg).
Chíra (a Beg).
Yúrúng Kásh united with Ilchi.
Nía united with Chíra.

The city of Khotan is of an irregular form, the circumference being approximately a mile.

The Fort and Urda of the Hakim are outside. The old Chinese wall round the town has fallen into ruin, but a wall now stands encircling the town and a large portion of the district at some considerable distance from the place itself: this is said to be some 20 miles in circuit. The gate through this on the Yárkand road is 1½ miles distant from the town.

Khotan is the great manufacturing city in the Amír's territory. The province yields very little cotton and very little grain, these being imported from Kashghar and from Gúma and Karghálik. Copper comes from Aksú and is worked into vessels, in great favor throughout the country. Rice is obtained from the same place.

Khotan is the great silk-producing province. Its gold mines and supply of jade are sources of wealth, the population, however, remain poor owing in a great measure to their indolence, work being taken up only as there is immediate necessity for the supply of daily wants. The immorality of the women of Khotan is proverbial, and the excess of women over men leads to much licentiousness. The inhabitants are chiefly artizans as distinguished from the cultivators of the other provinces of the Amír's kingdom. The resources of this province may be best arrived at by reviewing them separately.

Gold mines ... { Sorghák. Kappa. Chuggulaka. Charchand. Kárátagh.

There are said to be altogether 22 places in which this mineral is found, but the above are those which are regularly worked.

3,000 people are employed at Sorghák; the mine at this place is said to be 400 feet deep.

4,000 people are employed at Kappa; the mine is said to be 100 feet deep.

At the other places there are no more than 40 or 50 workers.

The Sorghák gold is obtained in small beads and is of a red color.

At Kappa, large nuggets are obtained, but the gold is of a light color and mixed with sand. Gold is also obtained in the Yúrúng Kásh sands after the flood of the hot season has passed. The only tools used are a pick and shovel; no sieve is in use, but the soil is dug out in blocks and disintegrated by the heat of the sun.

The sieve is used in extracting gold from the sand of the Yúrúng Kásh river. On this last there is no tax paid.

The working of the mines is thus conducted. The workers are the poor of the country who sell the gold they obtain to established buyers, who keep a supply of utensils of food, &c., to meet the requirements of the workers. From these gold purchasers one-fifth of the yield is at once confiscated as the property of the Amír, who retains the right of purchasing any further quantity he may require at 120 tangas per ser (the market value being 138 tangas the ser). The whole of the gold obtained is indeed supposed to be purchased for the Amír, but a large amount finds its way surreptitiously into the market. On the road between Keria and Khotán there is a regular searching house where men are stripped if they are supposed to have concealed gold about them, women are examined and are then made to jump over a ditch, in order that any gold they have concealed may fall out. No large guard is kept at the mines, but a small detachment of soldiers watch the proceedings of the buyers.

The officials, however, even to the Beg of Keria, who is in charge, are said to be open to bribes and to study their own advantage.

The punishment for secreting gold is very light. The probable yearly yield of gold in the Khotan District is said to approach 7,000 sers, of which 5,000 sers, reach the [Amír and about 2,000 are smuggled into the market.

The sale of gold is winked at, though disallowed. If a merchant is discovered to have obtained gold, no more than one-fifth will be confiscated, and the remainder is purchased at the fixed price.

Gold is readily bought up by merchants from India and Andiján.

A profit of one-eighth may be realized by conveying Khotan gold to either country.

Silver is also found in the province, but the yield was found insufficient to pay the working expenses and the mine opened has been abandoned.

(154)

Jade is obtained near the bed of the Yúrúng Kásh. There are two principal mines, one at a distance of 15 miles and the other at 25 miles from Ilchi. It is also procured from the bed of the river.

The tax on the working is one-fifth part paid into the treasury, and a tax of 1 in 40 from all traders who carry jade to other places; besides this all pieces that are of superior size and quality are bought up at a price fixed by the Dadkhwah of Khotan.

The old skilled carvers of jade have almost disappeared since the Chinese have been ejected. The mines and the working of the jade were closed until two years ago when Chinese traders began to reach Almáti. The Amír, however, allowed the market of Almáti to be flooded the first year and so much of the jade carried there from Khotan was inferior that it was not purchased, but returned to Khotan in this year.

The value of large pieces of this mineral may be judged by the following fact:—Quite lately some five men obtained a large block of a good description weighing some 40 jings; it was taken before the Dadkhwah, who purchased it as it was, in an uncut state, for 12 yamboos, the market price fixed upon it was however 60 yamboos; there was however no single merchant rich enough to purchase.

The existence of gold and jade is necessarily demoralising to the population; the number of workers in jade fluctuates, but the supply is in no wise exhausted.

Coal is said to be obtained in the Kuen Luen, but it has not been used since the Chinese were in authority; it was then brought from a considerable distance to Khotan.

Silk.—From the earliest time Khotan has been celebrated for its silk manufactures. *Sericulture* in Khotán is the same as already noted in Yangi Hissar, this is purely a domestic business: there is however a regular sale for cocoons in the market, the purchasers are regular traders who sell again to the reelers who purchase as they are in want of cocoons. There are poor people who dispose of the spun silk in the markets, which is chiefly bought by Andijáni merchants; there are however a great number of silk weavers (these color their own silks). Silk cloth made at Khotan is not exported, but spun raw silk goes in large quantities to Andiján. It is also found profitable to send the "waste" to the Almáti market, where it is purchased for Russian paper manufactories (it is a rumor that Russian notes are made from silk "waste").

Reeling does not go on during the winter season.

The white, black, and red and a fruitless mulberry are all known in Khotan, but the worms are fed only on the leaves from the fruitless tree and from that yielding a black fruit.

The produce of silk in its various stages, from the tending of the worm to the final operation, affords occupation to the bulk of the population in the Khotan province.

There are two kinds of silk, the white and the yellow, the latter being most esteemed: this is known as "Taiful," and is chiefly bought up for Andiján; the former is called "Kalawur," each of these are classed in two classes. As a rule the silk is reeled off on a single chirka, but lately an Andijáni has set up a wheel working 16 reels at one time.

Carpets.—Khotán carpets are celebrated for the excellence of their manufacture and for the variety of their patterns; they are made at three places in the Khotan province, more particularly Sumpula, Yúrúng Kásh (Char Shamba Bazaar), and at another village on the Keria road about three tash from the city (Se-Shamba Bazaar). Carpets are made of silk and of wool, gold thread is also sometimes worked into the silk carpets.

The wool used in the carpets is chiefly obtained from the hill districts through the Kirghiz; it is spun off and sold in the weekly bazaars. The dyeing is carried out by the carpet-makers.

The mordants used are—alum for dyes of yellow, brown, and red, and their various shades.

Grape juice for blues, and for mixed colors.

If green, the wool is first dyed yellow then put into an indigo solution.

If purple, it is first dyed red and then put into an indigo solution.

The dyes are indigo, madder, tookmuck (a seed), 'bukum.'

(155)

The price of labor is exceedingly cheap in the Khotan District, and the carpet makers are **hired as** required by those who **are** rich enough to purchase the materials and set up the frames.

There are two kinds **of frames, standard,** which are placed perpendicularly, and **long flat** frames near the ground ; **the latter are usually** required for very large **carpets,** but the **standard** frames allow of better work **being done.**

The size of the carpets ranges from the small saddle carpet on which one man works at a time to carpets 3½ yards wide, upon which 10 men are employed at one time. The pattern is given out **by head** of the party whom they term Aksakal. The patterns do not exist on paper, but are **passed on** from master **to** pupil and so remain from generation to generation. There are **some 200** masters who are known for their carpet work.

It is **to** be noticed that **in** comparison with other parts of the country sheep are very abundant **in** the Khotan province, and that the wool is Khotan lamb skins of white color, form the linings of hats and posteens.

Men employed in carpet making under the Government receive **20** phools daily each man, **and are** not supplied with food ; in ordinary houses, the daily **wages** is 10 phools and food for **the** day.

The copper vessels made in Khotan are superior to all others prepared in the Amir's **terri**tory ; they are worked in a variety of patterns. There are about 30 shops at Khotan **(Ilchi)** where these are made. The copper, as previously stated, is obtained from Aksú.

Vessels for tea and for water are those principally made, the iron vessels from Russia being preferred as cooking utensils.

Patterns of various kinds **are** cut upon the Khotan copper work in very neat fashion.

Iron.—Iron work, **stirrup irons, spoons,** knife handles, &c., made of iron are inlaid **with** copper wire, which is usually **of English** manufacture **and** is obtained from Hindoostan ; there are some 12 masters in this **work** at Khotan ; the pattern is cut out in the iron of the stirrup, spoon or whatever article it **is** intended to ornament, and the wire is run into the pattern and the whole heated **in the** fire.

Hides.—Cow **hides are** largely exported from Khotan to Yárkand with sheep skins and goat. **This** is due **rather to** the existence of a large number of cattle and sheep in the Khotan province than to superiority in the manner of preparation. Skins of animals obtained in the Kuen Luen are also exported for the lining of posteens.

Sandal-wood and tea (brick) are obtained from the buried cities. The sandal is worked into beads, and the tea is sold in the market. The buried cities proper are said to be at a distance of many marches to the east of Khotan. A discovery of buried ruins has, however, lately been made quite close to the city of Khotan (Ilchi) at a distance of about four miles to the north-west. A cultivator working in his field was watering his crop ; on the water suddenly disappearing **into** a hole and continuing **to** be absorbed, he **dug up the** place where the water disappeared and obtained a golden ornament said to **have been a cow** Lately excavations have been ordered by the Dadkhwah and **more gold has bee**n **found ;** the diggers are paid for any gold they may excavate at **110** tangas the ser. **In** the beginning of April 1874 a gold ornament of about eight sers weight was found by a man who had gone out in search of charcoal—this was in the shape of a small vase and had a chain attached to it. Rumour declared it to be neck ornament of the Great Afrasiab, and the finder was declared to have hit upon the spot where Afrasiab's treasure was buried ; **he was** paid for the ornament at the rate of 100 tangas the ser, and a party was at once **organized to** search the neighbourhood. At **present** no fresh discovery has been made, **and I cannot in** any way fix the locality, but it is **at no** great distance **from** Khotan itself.

	PRICES.						Tangas.	Phools.
Cotton cloth, *Kám,*	per than (	7 yards	× ½ yard)	...	...	...	1	30
„ *Tolma,*	„ (	7 „	„ „)				2	25
„ *Chakman*	„ (	22 „	× ½ „)				4	0
Kummerband (10 girras × 2½ yards)							1	0

40

MIXED CLOTHS OF COTTON AND SILK.

				Tangas.	Phools.
Gazina (10 yards × 9 girras) per than	...			5	0
„ (10 „ „ „) „	No. 2		...	4	0
Mushroo (7 „ × ½ yard) „	...		...	7	0
„ (7 „ „ „) „	...		...	5	0

This is largely exported and is in general use in the province; it formerly obtained nearly double its pressent price, but the introduction of a large quantity of red chintz (Gulánár) from Russia has swamped the market. Mushroo is both dyed and stamped.

SILKS.

				Tangas.	Phools.
Dariaye (7 yards × ½ yard) per strip	...		...	6	0
„ (7 „ „ „) „	No. 2		...	4	0
„ (7 „ „ „) „	„ 3		...	3	0
Silk Chakman (13 yards × ½ yard)	...		...	20	0
„ (13 „ „ „)	No. 2		...	17	0

This is chiefly sold for the making up of chogas, the coloring of the strips is invariably made in pairs; the size of the than is however arranged so as to make one choga.

This silk is largely used for chogas throughout the country, but is not carried across the frontier.

				Tangas.	Phools.
Shiaye (7 yards × ½ yard), Nos. 1 and 2	...	...	...	15	0
Dorooya (7 „ „ „) „ „		...	...	10	0

These descriptions are largely imported from Andiján, the manufactured articles of Khotan being coarser than those from Andiján.

Numdahs for spreading on floor—

		Tangas.	Phools.
Ranging from the prayer Numdah	...	2	25
To large Numdahs at	... ...	20	0

They are made largely at Yúrúng Kásh.

		Tangas.	Phools.
Numdahs for packing bales of merchandize of a dark color	...	1	10
Rope is made from the bark of the mulberry and also from hemp, which is, however, very little grown in this province, each rope		2	0
Rope is also made of wool, per rope	...	2	0

There is no large sale in the Khotan market for foreign goods, nor are there established merchants in Khotan who trade across the frontier; the result is that goods are not so easily disposed of as in the Yárkand market, and there is more difficulty in obtaining by barter articles required for a return consignment.

Shrines in the Province of Khotan to which pilgrimages are made are—

Imám Akbar, Mazar, in the Káráskásh valley.
„ Asgar „ „ „
„ Assim „ } Abu Bakr. } Yúrúng Kásh valley.
„ Kassim „
„ Ichran at Chira.
„ Nasrudin ...
„ Khwámudin ... } All at Mayartágh.
„ Zahurudin ...
„ Mayaudin ...
„ Azail ... Kerai.
„ Saydlik ... Nia.

Lungi Khanem, the gift of Imám Jafir Sádik, at Nia.

Imám Jáfir Sádik, in the desert beyond Nia, the principal place of pilgrimage from Khotán.

Imám Musa Kasim, at Khotán.

Trees known in the Khotan district are—

Saféda, poplar, six kinds	—Tarek Kara Tarek Kuppuk Tarek Hangi Tarek Malja Tarek Tagh Tarek	
	Suget.	
Willow, four kinds	Tetoo Suget Kara „ Tagh „ Sirigh „	Khotan is also celebrated for its melons
Jigda, three kinds	Jigda Khaga Jigda Kunkkisk Jigda	
Peaches, three kinds	Zard Alú Sis „ Ita „	
Plums, black and white	Yenista Khurmáni Ookcha	
Pears Quince. Pomgranate. Mulberries, black, white, and red berries.	Amrút	
Grapes of four kinds	Kismis or Kishmish. Munaka, and white Munaka.	

The raisins of Khotan are exported to Yárkand and Kashghar; sugar is also made from the grape and exported.

GEOGRAPHICAL APPENDIX.

SECTION G.—ROUTES.

PART II.—*Routes in Turkestan derived from verbal information supplied by natives.*

ROUTE XV.

KUCHAR TO KARASHAHR, AUTHORITY CAPTAIN TROTTER, COMPILED FROM VARIOUS SOURCES.

Kuchar to—
1. **Yakar, 4 tash.** A small village.
2. **Awát, 6 tash.** Small village.
3. **Bugar or Buigar or Bighol, 5 tash.** Cross a river flowing south. Town and district containing about 100 houses, snowy mountains visible towards the north, large numbers of camel, sheep, and horses in this country.
4. **Yangi-shahr, 6 tash.** Cross Karatal River, road passes through sandy soil.
5. **Achma Urtang,** 5 tash. Country sandy; small village; cold climate; snowy mountains visible both to north and south.
6. **Charchi, 5 tash.** Good pasture grounds, and plenty of fuel.
7. **Shákur or Iebertchou, 6 tash.** Large lake in vicinity, country marshy.
8. **Kurla or Koila or Kurungla, 4 tash.** Large town, Kalmak population. District contains about 5,000 houses; town is situate on left bank of a large river; climate mild; and abundance of grain; grapes and other fruit in great profusion.
9. **Yash Uigur, 4 tash.** A post stage; coal found near.
10. **Karashahr, 5 tash.** Formerly an enormous city, one of, if not, the largest in East Turkestan; three days to its north is the important town and district of Lukchin, now chiefly inhabited by Kalmaks who migrate to the hills in summer. Climate cold, and much snow falls here; wheat, barley, and Indian-corn grow. There is but little fruit. A great rendezvous for merchants.

ROUTE XVI.

KARASHAHR TO TURFAN, AUTHORITY CAPTAIN TROTTER, COMPILED FROM VARIOUS SOURCES.

1. **Tawalgha, 4 tash.** Road through cultivation, mountains visible on north of road.
2. **Tagharchi, 3 tash.**
3. **Ushak Tal, 3 tash.** A post house.
4. **Kárá Kizil, 7 tash.** Road passes through sandy desert.
5. **Kumush, 5 tash.** Road passes through hills.
6. **Ighar Bulák, 5 tash.** Cross mountain ridge *en route*.
7. **Subáshi, 3½ tash.**
8. **Takshun, 5 tash.** A large town. Cross a mountain ridge *en route*.
9. **Bugum, 4 tash.**

10. Turfán, 4 tash. A large city. Climate hot, and fruits and grain produced in abundance. Snowy mountains on north, but at a considerable distance. Iron, copper, and gold found in neighbourhood. Water is procured from wells, and irrigation is carried on by means of underground canals.

ROUTE XVII.

TURFÁN TO KÁMÓL OR KHÁMIL OR HÁMÍ (AUTHORITY DR. BELLEW,[†] FROM NATIVE INFORMATION).

1. Kará Khoja, 4 tash. Town of 500 houses. Musalmán families.
2. Yangi Khhin, 4 tash. 100 houses. Water from *Kárez* or *Khhin* streams. At 2 tash is the Mazár Abúl Futtáh. 300 houses and bazar. Musalmáns.
3. Lukchun, 4 tash. Town of 2,000 houses. A stream from Ghochan Tágh north of Pichán, flows through the town on to the desert. In flood seasons it reaches Lob Nor.
4. Pichán[*] 4 tash. Town of 500 houses; all Musalmáns. Stream from Ghochan Tágh flows through the town. Outside is a Chinese fort.
5. Chightan, 5 tash. 100 houses. Springs. Kashghar frontier.
6. Lotu Changza, 5 tash. Camp ground at a well on Gobi desert.
7. Kosh, 6 tash. Well. Gobi desert.
8. Kudúk, 5 tash. Well. Gobi desert. Cyclones, sandstorms, and whirlwinds common on this part of the desert, and sometimes shifting sands overwhelm the traveller. Diabolical sounds and spirit calls here mislead the unwary to destruction in the trackless waste.
9. Otar Kima, 5 tash. Custom House, and 20 houses. Springs.
10. Otun Oza, 4 tash. Small village, cook-shop and restaurant. Springs.
11. Lodung, 5 tash. 50 houses of Musalmáns. Springs.
12. Shothá, 3 tash. 15 houses of Musalmáns. Springs.
13. Jighdá, 4 tash. 40 houses of Musalmáns.
14. Taghochi, 4 tash. 100 houses of Musalmáns. Bazar and fort. A river from the Kazanchi Tágh on the south flows by the city to Lupchuk and Karátaba and Lob Nor.
15. Sumcágho, 5 tash. 300 houses. Bazar and fort. Musalmáns. *Kárez* conduits. At 3 tash is Abdul Alim Fort, 2 gates; 500 houses. *Kárez*.
16. Kamul, 5 tash. Commercial city; 2,500 houses. A Chinese Governor with a Musalmán *Wang* over the Muhammadans. The city has three gates, and populous suburbs.

ROUTE XVIIa.

TURFÁN TO ORÚMCHÍ OR URUMTSÍ. (DR. BELLEW[†] FROM NATIVE INFORMATION.)

1. Shamál Ortang, 5 tash. Four houses. Stream from hills.
2. Dabánchí, 5 tash. Town and fort. 350 houses, in a valley amongst hills.

---

[*] There is an alternative road to Pichán or Pidjan passing by Sangbin and Lemtsin. There is also an alternative road from Pidjan to Kamul, lying to the south of the road here described. The southern road passes through the towns of Khoing and Khartoube.—H.T.

[†] I have not the means of verifying many of the routes given by Dr. Bellew, and they are inserted as given by him.—H. T.

3. Kaburghá Ortang, 4 tash. Four houses in ruins. Hilly country.
4. Dacyáyúnus, 5 tash. Ten houses and an *ortang*. Ruins of ancient city.
5. Orúmchí, 4 tash. A strong city; 8,000 houses. Double walls and four gates. Population mostly Khitáy and Tungani with Musalmán traders. Suburbs populous and extensive. Kalmák camps in hill country around.

ROUTE XVIII.
Orúmchí to Manás (Dr. Bellew).

1. Gumátur, 5 tash. Town, 500 houses of Kará Khitáy or Chinese.
2. Sánjú Ortang or Síjú, 5 tash. Ten houses. Mountainous country.
3. Sánjú, 4 tash. City and fort. 600 houses. Residence of Dádd Khalífa.
4. Langar, 4 tash. Ten houses and an ortang.
5. Manás, 5 tash. City and fort. 800 houses; 3 gates.

ROUTE XIX.
Manás to Yuldúz (Dr. Bellew).

1. Shitáy, 4 tash. Fifty houses of Kará Khitáy and Túrgút Kalmák.
2. Kápotáy, 6 tash. 100 houses of ditto ditto.
3. Káydú, 4 tash. Town of 200 houses of ditto ditto on Káydú river.
4. Karású, 8 tash. 12,000 tents of Kará Khitáy and Kalmák of the Orúmchí District scattered about the streams all over the valley.
5. Purgáchí, 4 tash. 100 tents of the Karású camps.
6. Tomodá, 4 tash. 200 farms of Kará Khitáy of Yuldúz.
7. Tolí, 4 tash. 30 tents of Túrgút Kalmák. Salt mine in hills here.
8. Yuldúz, 5 tash. City of 1,000 houses. Capital of Kalmák Queen.

ROUTE XX.
Yuldúz to Ghúlja or Ila (Dr. Bellew).

1. Otáy, 4 tash. 100 tents of Túrgút Kalmák.
2. Tághí Yanza, 3 tash. 100 tents of Túrgút Kalmák. Wheat and barley grown here.
3. Sitáy, 4 tash. 60 tents of Chághir Kalmák of Yuldúz. Deer abound here.
4. Sintáy, 5 tash. Ten houses and an *ortang*. Ila or Ghúlja territory begins here.
5. Sarim Kol, 3 tash. The lake is two days' circuit and is fed from the Talakí hills, and has no outlet.
6. Tábahán, 1 tash. Chághir and Kará Kalmák camps on Talakí river
7. Tálji, 7 tash. Ditto ditto ditto.
8. Chongshahr, 8 tash. Commercial town. Russian Consul resides here.
9. Ghúlja or Ila, 6 tash. Capital city. Russian frontier town and Telegraph Office. Emporium of China trade.

ROUTE XXI.
KÚRLA TO LOB (DR. BELLEW).

1. Yár Kurul, 4 tash. Over sandy waste with reeds, poplars, and pools.
2. Konchí, 5 tash. On the Tárim river below junction of the united streams from Kurla and Kúchá. Country desert waste. River banks belted with reeds and thickets of poplar and tamarisk; full of wild pig, stags, wolves, lynxes, and tigers.
3. Chol, 4 tash. Camp on desert of salt and reeds and pools.
4. Kará Kochún, 5 tash. Across a desert waste to the bank of Tárim river. Reed huts of Musalmán Kirghiz and Kalmák on river bank. Here the Lob district begins and extends eastward to the lake along the river course in little settlements of reed huts each with its own boats.

ROUTE XXII.
KARÁSHAHR TO YULDÚZ VALLEY (DR. BELLEW).

1. Kará Modun, 6 tash. Ruins of a former Kalmák Khan's house.
2. Khapchigháy, 5 tash. Over a mountain pass; easy for horses and camels.
3. Bálghontáy, 5 tash. Waste country, cross low ridges and streams. Pine trees on the mountains.
4 & 5. Cross several hill ridges and camp on streams in the hollows at 5 tash each day. Vegetation very scanty. No fuel.
6. Dálan Dawán, 5 tash. Camp on snow at top of pass. No fuel nor forage.
7 & 8. Cross "Yatmish Dawán" = "Seventy Hills" by two stages of five tash each, and camp on snow. No fuel nor forage.
9. Yuldúz, 6 tash. Descend to Yuldúz valley. Meadows and streams, and Kalmák camps all over the valley.

The foregoing routes have been derived from Native traders and travellers, and are on the whole, I believe, tolerably correct, though varying in the different ideas as to distance and number of houses, and sometimes as to the nature of the road.

ROUTE XXIII.
FROM KHOTAN TO AKSÚ.
AUTHORITY CAPTAIN CHAPMAN, FROM NATIVE INFORMATION.

Khotan to—
1. Tarashi-gul. Through cultivation.
2. Lokul. Ditto.
3. Agroya. Desert.
4. Koshlush (or Katilich). This is the point where the Kárákásh and the Yurúngkásh Rivers unite.
5. Tagag. Desert.
6. Mazar-tágh. Sand hills.

7. Booksam (or *Bash Bonksem*).
8. Kolu.
9. Badlik Kotagh (or *Bedelik Kudok*).
10. Nurs-shakúro.
11. Balfuz-nakúm.
12. Khal.
13. Darialoe.
14. Máhtung. Here cultivation is encountered.
15. Karatal (*Kharatal*).
16. Besh-turkimirum (*Besh-arik*).
17. Aksú.

} Stages through desert

These are stages for donkeys, the chief trade being carried on with donkeys—copper, rice, iron, gold silk, and country cotton cloths going from Khotan. A trader with horses will accomplish the journey in 10 stages.

NOTE.—This route would appear to be reliable. Names in italics are found by me in Klaproth's Map.—H. T.

ROUTE XXIV.

FROM *Khotan* TO *Polu* (DIRECT). AUTHORITY CAPTAIN CHAPMAN, FROM NATIVE INFORMATION.

Khotan to—
1. Sampúla ... ... 3 tash.
2. Hásha ... ... 3 tash.
3. Ganju-tágh ... ... 3 tash. A large town.
4. Múra ... ... 4 tash.
5. Imám Mazar or Chehar Imám, 4 tash.
6. Polu ... ... 5 tash.

} These six marches are through cultivated lands with small villages. No rivers encountered.

NOTE.—This route agrees very well with another procured by me from a different source.—H. T.

ROUTE XXV.

KHOTAN TO CHARCHAND AND KURLA. AUTHORITY CAPTAIN TROTTER, COMPILED FROM VARIOUS SOURCES OF NATIVE INFORMATION.

Khotan to—
1. Dol 16½ Miles.
2. Chíra 35 "
3. Karákia 25 "
4. Kiria 27½ "
5. Ui Toghrak 15 "
6. Yessulghun.
7. Auras.
8. Naia. At a day's journey from **Naia in** a southerly direction lie the Sorghák gold fields. The river, from Sorghák flows by Naia and passes in a northerly direction to Mazár Imám Jafr Sadík, a favourite place of pilgrimage, two days' journey north of Naia. From Naia to Charchand lie two roads across **the desert,** the northern road passes the camps of—

} *Vide* Route XIV.

9. Baliklik.
10. Yer-tunguz.
11. Haidil-shah Kuduk.
12. Andhira.
13. Shiodang.

14. Kára Buran.
15. Yantagh Kuduk.
16. Kok-muran.
17. Yang-arik.
18. Charchand.

At all these camps wells have been dug. On the alternative southern route the camping grounds are as follows :—

    9. Subed (from here a road goes to Sorghák).
   10. Apálik.
   11. Shrine of Bibí Tujilik.
   12. Moljia.
   13. The Kápa gold fields.
   14. Tokpai.
   15. Hassan Gunj.
   16. Achian.
   17. Charchand.

The marches from Naia probably average between 20 and 25 miles in length.

Charchand is a place of some importance, and is said to be used as a penal settlement; a large river is said to flow through it coming from Thibet and ultimately finding its way to Lob. The geographical position of Charchand is not fixed with any degree of certainty but it is probably about equidistant from Keria (Route XIV.) and Kurla (Route XV.), to which latter place a road passes *viâ* Tartang and Chaktuk. Between Charchand and the Lob District are said to be oases where wandering tribes of Sokpos (Kalmaks) wander about with their flocks and herds. Near Charchand are the Khadlak gold fields, where 100 diggers are employed.

ROUTE XXVI.

KILA WÁMUR (ROSHAN) TO KILA KHUMB (DARWÁZ), AUTHORITY CAPTAIN TROTTER THROUGH ABDUL SUBHAN, FROM NATIVE INFORMATION.

Kila Wámur, chief town of Roshan.
1. Waznúd.
2. Amern.
3. Kila Chamarj.
4. Wadkhod.
5. Jarf.
6. Kila Khumb.

Road down Panjah or Amu river the whole way. Valley very narrow and precipitous, and not practicable for laden horses.

An alternative road goes in a northerly direction by which Kila Khumb may be reached in three days from Wamur.

ROUTE XXVII.

FROM BAR PANJAH (SHIGHNAN) TO KASHGHAR, AUTHORITY CAPTAIN TROTTER THROUGH ABDUL SUBHAN, FROM NATIVE INFORMATION.

From Bar Punjah—
1. Ghund village.
2. Ishtim or Wiar.
3. Charsim Fort.
4. Bugrúmal Pamir.* From here a road diverges to Khokand *viâ* Bartang.
5. Sasik-kul (2 lakes and Pamir)
6. Kara-su.
7. Murghabi.
8. Raug-kul.
9. Moji Chakr Arghin (Kirghiz).
10. Bulghár Pass (very high).
11. Tashbálig.
12. Káshghar.

ROUTE XXVIII.

FROM BUGRÚMAL PAMIR (NO. 4 OF ROUTE XXVII) TO KHOKAND.

1. Marjanai.
2. Sirich Fort (the capital of Bartang).
3. Kára Bulák (on Murghabi river).
4. Takhta Korum.
5. Altun Mazar, cross the Mazár Pass.
6. }
7. } Two marches in the Alai.
8.
9. Osh Kurghán by Draot (Deraout).
10. Marjilan.
11. Khokand.

NOTE.—These routes are very meagre, but have been used in conjunction with other sources of information in the compilation of my preliminary map. From Wamur there is a pathway up the Murghabi River to Sirich Fort, but so difficult that travellers nearly always go by the Ghund river in preference.—H. T.

---

* Probably the western prolongation of the Alichur Pamir.

ROUTE XXIX.

FROM YUR (SEE NO. 15 OF ROUTE VIII) TO CHITRÁL, AUTHORITY CAPTAIN BIDDULPH FROM NATIVE INFORMATION.

Yur to—
1. Suneen.
2. Over pass.*
3. Kusht.
4. Topkhana.
5. Gazan (inhabited).
6. Manzagram.
7. Mastuch.
8. Booni.
9. Risht.
10. Ragh.
11. Chitrál.

} These are marches for a man on foot.

ROUTE XXX.

TASHKÚRGHÁN, NO. 9 OF ROUTE VIII, OR SARÍGH-KÚL TO HANZA IN KANJÚD (DR. BELLEW).

1. Davdár, 4 tash. Across valley and amongst hills to camp ground. The first stage from "Táshkúrghán. No habitation.
2. Jilghar, 3 tash. Easy road amongst hills. Desert. No fuel or forage.
3. Ghajakbáy,† 4 tash. The same.
4. Rang or Zastol, 4 tash. Up a narrow gorge and over a glacier to
5. Rangal, 3 tash. Down a defile along a torrent. Road rough. Hills bare.
6. Talictáy, 4 tash. The same as last stage.
7. Lúpgal, 5 tash. Continue down the valley. Mountains high and bare.
8. Udmurkish, 4 tash. Desert country amongst hills.
9. Misgar.
10. Sás.
11. Khybar.
12. Passú.
13. Garnít.
14. Syábán.

} These are all the names of camp grounds. Each a day's journey from the other in vallies amongst hills. Streams from all sides, and scanty brushwood. Country very difficult and bare. Under snow for half the year.

15. Muhammadábád. First village from Táshkurghán. Fields and orchards on river bank.
16. Kanjúd, 3 tash. 1,000 houses and fort. Capital of Hanza on a large river. Fields and fruit trees in terraces on hill slopes.

ROUTE XXXI.

SARHADD, NO. 14 OF ROUTE VIII, WAKHÁN, TO KANJÚD (DR. BELLEW).

1. Sháwar. In a glen. Fuel, water, and grass.
2. Langar.‡ On border of Pámir Khurd. Grass, fuel, and water.
3. Khaldarchit. In a glen of the Pamir hills. Ditto. No trees.
4. Láptúk. A deep narrow defile in the mountains. Grass and water.
5. Irshál. Over a high mountain and a glacier down to
6. Astán. A long march down a defile along a river which flows all the way to Kanjúd.
7. Ispinj. A short march down course of the same river which is unfordable and only crossed on the ice in winter.
8. Reshit. Short march down the river.
9. Kirmín. Ditto.
10. Gírcha *or Goorki*. Twenty scattered houses and terraced fields.
11. Khybar. 6 houses, Ditto.
12. Passú *or Basoo*. 20 houses, Ditto.

---

* Closed for several months in the year.
† Probably Kila Ujadbai.—H. T.
‡ Station 13 of Route VIII.—H. T.

13. Sissúni or *Sasoni*. 10 houses, scattered houses and terraced fields. A very short stage to
14. Gholki. 30 houses,   Ditto.
15. Gulmík or *Gulmit*. 100 houses on right bank of river. Leave river here and cross Durband Kotal, not high nor difficult in two stages to
17. Kanjud. 1,000 houses and a fort. Capital of the country, on a river which flows to Gilgit.

These routes, XXX. and XXXI., probably meet about Gircha. The accounts given are inconsistent, but as very little is known of the Hanza country, every contribution to a knowledge of it is valuable.—H. T.

YÁRKAND TO SHAHIDULA *viâ* KILIK (CAPTAIN TROTTER).

1. Yarkand to   } Route I.
2. Karghálik   }
3. Beshterek. 40 or 50 houses; 4 tash.
4. Balerak Kurba. 200 houses, 2 tash.
5. Akchik. 4 or 5 houses, 2 tash.
6. Takmà or Chakmà Camp, 4 tash. Kirghiz camp. Plenty of cattle.
7. Tupa Diwan, 4 tash. Pass. Good road.
8. Azghan or Kilik. Plenty of wood and grass.
9. Kilik Diwan. Higher than Tupa Diwan.
10. Larcha Ya Tuba, 3 tash. Good road. Plenty of grass and wood.
11. Gor Jilga, 4 tash.
12. Mazár Khoja, 2 tash. Large stream.
13. Shahidúla. (Routes I. to III.)

This road is said to be shorter and better than any other road between Yárkand and Shahidúla; grass and wood are to be found at every stage. Shahidúla can be reached by a horseman in five days from Yárkand. The man who supplied this route has tried all the roads from Yárkand and reports the road *viâ* the Kilik Pass to be much the best for foot passengers.